Integrating and Extending BIRT

eclipse the eclipse series

SERIES EDITORS Erich Gamma ▪ Lee Nackman ▪ John Wiegand

Eclipse is a universal tool platform, an open extensible integrated development environment (IDE) for anything and nothing in particular. Eclipse represents one of the most exciting initiatives hatched from the world of application development in a long time, and it has the considerable support of the leading companies and organizations in the technology sector. Eclipse is gaining widespread acceptance in both the commercial and academic arenas.

The Eclipse Series from Addison-Wesley is the definitive series of books dedicated to the Eclipse platform. Books in the series promise to bring you the key technical information you need to analyze Eclipse, high-quality insight into this powerful technology, and the practical advice you need to build tools to support this evolutionary Open Source platform. Leading experts Erich Gamma, Lee Nackman, and John Wiegand are the series editors.

Titles in the Eclipse Series

John Arthorne and Chris Laffra
Official Eclipse 3.0 FAQs
0-321-26838-5

Frank Budinsky, David Steinberg, Ed Merks, Ray Ellersick, and Timothy J. Grose
Eclipse Modeling Framework
0-131-42542-0

David Carlson
Eclipse Distilled
0-321-28815-7

Eric Clayberg and Dan Rubel
Eclipse: Building Commercial-Quality Plug-Ins, Second Edition
0-321-42672-X

Adrian Colyer, Andy Clement, George Harley, and Matthew Webster
Eclipse AspectJ: Aspect-Oriented Programming with AspectJ and the Eclipse AspectJ Development Tools
0-321-24587-3

Erich Gamma and Kent Beck
Contributing to Eclipse: Principles, Patterns, and Plug-Ins
0-321-20575-8

Jeff McAffer and Jean-Michel Lemieux
Eclipse Rich Client Platform: Designing, Coding, and Packaging Java™ Applications
0-321-33461-2

Steve Northover and Mike Wilson
SWT: The Standard Widget Toolkit, Volume 1
0-321-25663-8

Diana Peh, Alethea Hannemann, Paul Reeves, and Nola Hague
BIRT: A Field Guide to Reporting
0-321-44259-8

Jason Weathersby, Don French, Tom Bondur, Jane Tatchell, and Iana Chatalbasheva
Integrating and Extending BIRT
0-321-44385-3

For more information on books in this series visit www.awprofessional.com/series/eclipse

Integrating and Extending BIRT

Jason Weathersby • Don French • Tom Bondur
Jane Tatchell • Iana Chatalbasheva

✦Addison-Wesley

Upper Saddle River, NJ • Boston • Indianapolis • San Francisco
New York • Toronto • Montreal • London • Munich • Paris • Madrid
Capetown • Sydney • Tokyo • Singapore • Mexico City

Many of the designations used by manufacturers and sellers to distinguish their products are claimed as trademarks. Where those designations appear in this book, and the publisher was aware of a trademark claim, the designations have been printed with initial capital letters or in all capitals.

The authors and publisher have taken care in the preparation of this book, but make no expressed or implied warranty of any kind and assume no responsibility for errors or omissions. No liability is assumed for incidental or consequential damages in connection with or arising out of the use of the information or programs contained herein.

The publisher offers excellent discounts on this book when ordered in quantity for bulk purchases or special sales, which may include electronic versions and/or custom covers and content particular to your business, training goals, marketing focus, and branding interests. For more information, please contact:

U.S. Corporate and Government Sales
(800) 382-3419
corpsales@pearsontechgroup.com

For sales outside the United States please contact:

International Sales
international@pearsoned.com

Visit us on the Web: www.awprofessional.com

 This Book Is Safari Enabled

The Safari® Enabled icon on the cover of your favorite technology book means the book is available through Safari Bookshelf. When you buy this book, you get free access to the online edition for 45 days.

Safari Bookshelf is an electronic reference library that lets you easily search thousands of technical books, find code samples, download chapters, and access technical information whenever and wherever you need it.

To gain 45-day Safari Enabled access to this book:

- Go to http://www.awprofessional.com/safarienabled
- Complete the brief registration form
- Enter the coupon code QWH2-PJ4H-5BCB-5GH4-3K8C

If you have difficulty registering on Safari Bookshelf or accessing the online edition, please e-mail customer-service@safaribooksonline.com.

Library of Congress Cataloging-in-Publication Data

Integrating and extending BIRT/ Jason Weathersby... [et al.].
   p. cm.
   Includes index.
   ISBN 0-321-44385-3 (pbk. : alk. paper)
   1. Computer software--Development.   2. Application software--Development.   3. Client/server computing.   I. Weathersby, Jason.
   QA76.76.D47I552 2006
   005.1—dc22

                                                                        2006014602

ISBN 0-321-44385-3

Text printed in the United States on recycled paper at R.R. Donnelley in Crawfordsville, Indiana.
First printing, October 2006

Foreword . . . . **xvii**

Preface . . . . **xix**
About this book xix
Who should read this book xx
Contents of this book xxi
Typographical conventions xxiv
Syntax conventions xxv

Acknowledgments . . . . **xxvii**

Part I   Installing and Deploying BIRT **1**

Chapter 1   Prerequisites for BIRT **3**
Requirements for the BIRT report designers 3
    About installing required software 5
    BIRT RCP Report Designer software requirements 5
    BIRT Report Designer Full Eclipse Install software requirements 5
    BIRT Report Designer software requirements 6
Prerequisites for other BIRT packages 7
    BIRT Chart Engine software requirements 7
    BIRT Demo Database software requirements 8
    BIRT Report Engine software requirements 9
    BIRT Samples software requirements 9
    BIRT Test Suite software requirements 9
About types of BIRT builds 10

Chapter 2   Installing a BIRT Report Designer **13**
Installing BIRT Report Designer 14
    Downloading and installing BIRT Report Designer .14
    Installing the auxiliary file for BIRT Report Designer 14
    Testing the BIRT Report Designer installation 15
Installing BIRT Report Designer Full Eclipse Install 15

Downloading and installing BIRT Report Designer Full Eclipse Install 15
Installing the auxiliary file for BIRT Report Designer 16
Installing BIRT RCP Report Designer 16
Downloading and installing BIRT RCP Report Designer 17
Installing the auxiliary file for BIRT Report Designer 17
Testing the BIRT RCP Report Designer installation 18
Troubleshooting installation problems 18
Avoiding cache conflicts after you install a BIRT report designer 18
Specifying which Java Virtual Machine to use when you start a BIRT report designer . . . 19
Installing a language pack 19

Chapter 3   Installing Other BIRT Packages 23
Installing BIRT Chart Engine 23
Installing BIRT Chart Engine from the Eclipse BIRT web site 24
Avoiding cache conflicts after installing 24
Installing BIRT Demo Database 25
Installing BIRT Demo Database from the Eclipse BIRT web site 25
Testing the BIRT Demo Database installation 25
Installing BIRT Report Engine 26
Installing BIRT Report Engine from the Eclipse BIRT web site 27
Testing the BIRT Report Engine installation 27
Installing BIRT Samples 28
Installing BIRT Test Suite 29

Chapter 4   Updating a BIRT Installation 31
Using the Eclipse Update Manager to update BIRT Report Designer installation 31
Updating BIRT RCP Report Designer installation 32

Chapter 5   Deploying a BIRT Report to an Application Server 33
About application servers 33
About deploying to Tomcat 33
About deploying to other application servers 34
Placing the BIRT report viewer on an application server 34
Installing the BIRT report viewer files 34
Installing the auxiliary file 35
Installing your JDBC drivers 35
Testing the BIRT report viewer installation 35
Using a different context root for the BIRT report viewer 36
Placing the viewer in a different location 36
Mapping the folders that the BIRT report viewer uses 36
Verifying that Apache Tomcat is running BIRT report viewer 39
Placing fonts on the application server 40
Viewing a report using a browser 40
Understanding the run and frameset servlets 41
Using the URL parameters for the run and frameset servlets 41
__report parameter 42
__document parameter 42

__format parameter 43
__locale parameter 43
__isnull parameter 43
__svg parameter 43
Report parameters 44

Part II Understanding the BIRT Framework 45

Chapter 6 Understanding the BIRT Architecture 47

Understanding the BIRT integration 47
About the BIRT applications 51
About BIRT Report Designer and BIRT RCP Report Designer .51
About the BIRT report viewer 51
About the BIRT engines 52
About the report design engine 52
About the report engine 52
About the generation engine 52
About the presentation engine 52
About the chart engine 53
About the data engine 53
About data engine components 53
About the ODA framework 53
About the types of BIRT report items 53
About standard report items 54
About custom report items 54
About chart report items 54
About the ROM 54
About the types of BIRT files 54
About report design files 55
About report document files 55
About report library files 55
About report template files 55
About custom Java applications 56
About custom report designers 56
About custom Java report generators 56
About extensions to BIRT 57

Chapter 7 Understanding the Report Object Model 59

About the ROM specification 59
ROM properties 60
ROM slots 61
ROM methods 61
ROM styles 62
About the ROM schema 62
About the rom.def file 63
About the primary ROM elements 66

About the report item elements 67
   About the report items 67
   Understanding the report item element properties 67
About the data elements 68

Part III   Scripting in a Report Design 71

Chapter 8   Using Scripting in a Report Design 73
Overview of BIRT scripting 73
   Choosing between Java and JavaScript 73
   Using both Java and JavaScript to write event handlers 74
Understanding the event handler execution sequence 74
   About event firing sequence dependency 74
      About the onCreate and onRender firing sequence dependencies 75
      About the ReportDesign firing sequence dependencies 75
   About the pageBreak event 75
   Analysis of the execution sequence phases 75
      Overview of the report execution process 76
      Preparation phase 76
      Report body processing phase 76
      Clean-up processing phase 78
      Row execution sequence 78
      Table and list method execution sequence 78
About a report item event handler 81
About data source and data set event handlers 82
   ODA data source events 82
   Scripted data source events 82
   ODA data set events 82
   Scripted data set events 82
About ReportDesign event handlers 82
Writing event handlers for charts 83
   Chart events 83
   Chart script context 85
   Chart instance object 86
      Chart instance getter methods 86
      Chart instance setter methods 87
   Writing a Java chart event handler 87
   Writing a JavaScript chart event handler 87
Getting a dynamic image from a Microsoft Access database 89

Chapter 9   Using JavaScript to Write an Event Handler 91
Using BIRT Report Designer to enter a JavaScript event handler 91
   Creating and using a global variable 92
   Understanding execution phases and processes 93
Using the reportContext object 94
   Passing a variable between processes 95
   Getting information from an HTTP request object 95

Using the this object 95
   Using the this object's methods 95
   Using the this object to set the property of a report item 96
Using the row object 99
Getting column information 99
Getting and altering the query string 100
Getting a parameter value 101
Changing the connection properties of a data source 101
Determining method execution sequence 102
   Providing the ReportDesign.initialize code 102
   Providing the code for the methods you want to track .103
   Providing the ReportDesign.afterFactory code 103
Tutorial 1: Writing an event handler in JavaScript 104
   Task 1: Open the report design 104
   Task 2: Create and initialize a counter in the Table.onCreate( ) method 104
   Task 3: Conditionally increment the counter in the Row.onCreate( ) method. 106
   Task 4: Display the result, using the ReportDesign.afterFactory( ) method. 107
Calling Java from JavaScript 108
   Understanding the Packages object 108
   Understanding the importPackage method 109
   Using a Java class 109
   Placing your Java classes where BIRT can find them 110
   Issues with using Java in JavaScript code 110

Chapter 10   Using Java to Write an Event Handler 111
Writing a Java event handler class 111
   Locating the JAR files that an event handler requires 112
   Extending an adapter class 112
Making the Java class visible to BIRT 116
Associating the Java event handler class with a report element 116
BIRT Java interface and class naming conventions 117
Writing a Java event handler 118
   Using event handler adapter classes 118
   Using event handler interfaces 118
   About the Java event handlers for report items 119
   Using Java event handlers for the DataSource element 120
   Using Java event handlers for the DataSet element 120
   Using Java event handlers for the ScriptedDataSource element 121
   Using Java event handlers for the ScriptedDataSet element 122
   Using Java event handlers for the ReportDesign 122
Understanding the BIRT interfaces 123
   About the element design interfaces 124
      About the methods for each report element 124
      About the IReportElement interface 124
   About the element instance interfaces 125
   Using the IReportContext interface 126
   Using the IColumnMetaData interface 128

Using the IDataSetInstance interface 128
Using the IDataSetRow interface 129
Using the IRowData interface 129

Chapter 11 Using a Scripted Data Source 131

Creating a scripted data source and scripted data set 131
Tutorial 2: Creating and scripting a scripted data source 133
  Task 1: Create a new report... 133
  Task 2: Create a scripted data source................................. 133
  Task 3: Create a scripted data set 134
  Task 4: Supply code for the open( ) and close( ) methods of the data source 135
  Task 5: Supply code for the open( ) method of the data set 135
  Task 6: Define output columns.. 135
  Task 7: Place the columns on the report layout 137
  Task 8: Supply code for the data set fetch( ) method................. 138
Using a Java object to access a data source 139
  Performing initialization in the data set open( ) method 139
  Getting a new row of data in the data set fetch( ) method 140
  Cleaning up in the data set close( ) method 140
  Deciding where to locate your Java class 140
  Deploying your Java class 141
Using input and output parameters with a scripted data set 141

Part IV Integrating BIRT Functionality into Applications. . 143

Chapter 12 Understanding the BIRT APIs 145

Package hierarchy diagrams 146
About the BIRT Report Engine API 147
  Creating the BIRT Report Engine 148
  Using the BIRT Report Engine API 148
    EngineConfig class 148
    ReportEngine class 148
    IReportRunnable interface 149
    IReportDocument interface 149
    IEngineTask interface 149
    IGetParameterDefinitionTask interface 149
    IDataExtractionTask interface 150
    IRunTask interface 150
    IRenderTask interface 150
    IRunAndRenderTask interface 150
  Report engine class hierarchy 151
  Report engine interface hierarchy 152
About the design engine API 153
  Using the BIRT design engine API 154
    DesignEngine class 154
    SessionHandle class 154
    ModuleHandle class 155

ReportDesignHandle class 155
LibraryHandle class 156
DesignElementHandle class 156
Individual element handle classes 156
Design engine class hierarchy 157
ReportElementHandle hierarchy 159
ReportItemHandle hierarchy 160
ElementDetailHandle hierarchy 161
StructureHandle hierarchy 162
About the BIRT Chart Engine API 163
Using the BIRT Chart Engine API 164
Chart engine class hierarchy 164
chart.aggregate hierarchy 165
chart.datafeed hierarchy 165
chart.device class hierarchy 166
chart.device interface hierarchy 166
chart.event class hierarchy 166
chart.exception class hierarchy 168
chart.factory class hierarchy 168
chart.log class hierarchy 169
chart.model class hierarchy 169
chart.model.attribute interface hierarchy 170
chart.model.attribute class hierarchy 172
chart.model.component interface hierarchy 173
chart.model.data interface hierarchy 174
chart.model.layout interface hierarchy 176
chart.model.type interface hierarchy 176
chart.render hierarchy 177
chart.script hierarchy 178
chart.util class hierarchy 179

Chapter 13 Programming with the BIRT Reporting APIs 181
Building a reporting application 182
About the environment for a reporting application 183
About plug-ins used by the report engine 183
About libraries used by the report engine 184
About required JDBC drivers 185
Modifying a report design with the API 185
Generating reports from an application 185
Setting up the report engine 186
Configuring the engine home 186
Configuring the report engine 187
Setting up a stand-alone or WAR file environment 188
Using the logging environment to debug an application 190
Opening a source for report generation 190
Understanding an IReportRunnable object 191
Understanding an IReportDocument object 191
Accessing a report parameter programmatically 192

Preparing to generate the report 199
    Setting the parameter values for running a report design 200
    Setting up the rendering options 200
    Setting up the rendering context 200
    Providing an external connection to run a report design 202
Generating the formatted output programmatically 203
Accessing the formatted report 203
About programming with a report design 204
About BIRT model API capabilities 205
Opening a report design programmatically for editing 206
    Configuring the design engine to access a design handle 206
    Using an IReportRunnable object to access a design handle 206
Using a report item in a report design 207
    Accessing a report item by name 207
    Accessing a report item by iterating through a slot 207
    Examining a report item programmatically 208
    Accessing the properties of a report item 208
    Modifying a report item in a report design programmatically 210
    Accessing and setting complex properties 211
    Adding a report item to a report design programmatically 213
Accessing a data source and data set with the API 214
    About data source classes 214
    About data set classes 215
    Using a data set programmatically 215
Saving a report design programmatically 217
Creating a report design programmatically 217

Chapter 14   Programming with the BIRT Charting APIs 219
About the environment for building a charting application 220
Verifying the development environment for charting applications 221
Using the charting API to modify an existing chart 222
    Getting a Chart object from the report design 222
    Modifying chart properties 222
        Modifying axes properties 223
        Modifying plot properties 223
        Modifying the legend properties 223
        Modifying the series properties 224
    Adding a series to a chart 224
    Adding a chart event handler to a charting application 224
        Adding a Java chart event handler to a charting application 224
        Adding a JavaScript chart event handler to a charting application 225
Using the charting APIs to create a new chart 225
    Creating the chart instance object 226
    Setting the properties of the chart instance object 227
        Setting the chart color and bounds 227
        Setting plot properties 227
        Setting legend properties 227
        Setting legend line properties 227

Setting axes properties 228
Creating a category series 228
Creating a y-series 228
Defining the y-series queries 229
Setting the y-series properties 229
Setting the properties of the x- and y-series 230
Adding a series definition to the Axis object 230
Adding series, queries, and categories to the series definitions 230
Creating sample data 231
Getting an element factory object 231
Getting an extended item handle object 231
Setting the chart.instance property on the report item 231
Getting a data set from the report design 232
Binding the chart to the data set 232
Adding the new chart to the report design 232
Saving the report design after adding the chart .232
Putting it all together 233
Using the BIRT charting API in a Java Swing application 239
Understanding the chart programming examples 246
DataCharts 246
GroupOnXSeries 246
GroupOnYAxis 246
AutoDataBinding 247
FormatCharts 247
InteractivityCharts 247
PDFChartGenerator 247
StyleProcessor 248
ScriptViewer 248
Viewer 248
ChartWizardLauncher 249
Report 250
Preference 250

Part V Working with the Extension Framework 251

Chapter 15 Building the BIRT Project 253
About building the BIRT project 253
Assuring that you have the correct software on your system 254
Configuring the Eclipse workspace to compile BIRT 254
Creating Eclipse projects 256
Specifying the repository locations 257
Checking out the BIRT source 259
Adding the extra JAR file 261
Building the web viewer 262

Chapter 16 Extending BIRT 267
Overview of the extension framework 267

Understanding the structure of a BIRT plug-in 268
    Understanding an extension point schema definition file 268
    Understanding a plug-in manifest file 271
    Understanding a plug-in run-time class 272
Working with the Eclipse PDE 275
    Understanding plug-in project properties 277
    Understanding the Eclipse PDE Workbench 277
Creating the structure of a plug-in extension 279
Creating the plug-in extension content 283
Building a plug-in extension 287
    Generating an Ant build script 290
    Testing a plug-in extension 291
Deploying the extension plug-in 291
    Installing feature updates and managing the Eclipse configuration 293
    Creating an update site project 294
Downloading the code for the extension examples 297

Chapter 17 Developing a Report Item Extension 299

Understanding a report item extension 299
Developing the sample report item extension 301
    Downloading BIRT source code from the CVS repository 302
    Creating a rotated label report item plug-in project 302
    Defining the dependencies for the rotated label report item extension 305
    Specifying the run-time package for the rotated label report item extension 307
    Declaring the report item extension points 307
    Creating the plug-in extension content 312
Understanding the rotated label report item extension 316
    Understanding RotatedLabelItemFactoryImpl 318
    Understanding RotatedLabelUI 319
    Understanding RotatedLabelPresentationImpl 319
    Understanding RotatedLabelReportItemImpl 320
    Understanding RotatedLabelPropertyEditUIImpl 320
    Understanding GraphicsUtil 321
Deploying and testing the rotated label report item plug-in 324
    Deploying a report item extension 324
    Launching the rotated label report item plug-in 324

Chapter 18 Developing a Report Rendering Extension 329

Understanding a report rendering extension 329
Developing the CSV report rendering extension 330
    Downloading BIRT source code from the CVS repository 330
    Creating a CSV report rendering plug-in project 331
    Defining the dependencies for the CSV report rendering extension 334
    Declaring the emitters extension point 335
Understanding the sample CSV report rendering extension 337
    Implementing the emitter interfaces 337
    Implementing the content interfaces 339

Understanding the CSV report rendering extension package 341
   Understanding CSVReportEmitter 341
   Understanding CSVTags 348
   Understanding CSVWriter 348
  Understanding the BIRT report engine API package 348
   Understanding RenderOptionBase 349
   Understanding CSVRenderOption 349
   Understanding EngineConstants 349
Testing the CSV report rendering plug-in 350
  Launching the CSV report rendering plug-in 353
  About ExecuteReport class 357
  About the report design XML code 359

Chapter 19 Developing an ODA Extension 365

Understanding an ODA extension 366
Developing the CSV ODA driver extensions 366
  About the CSV ODA plug-ins 367
  Downloading BIRT source code from the CVS repository 367
Implementing the CSV ODA driver plug-in 368
  Defining the dependencies for the CSV ODA driver extension 370
  Specifying the run-time settings for the CSV ODA driver extension 370
  Declaring the ODA data source extension point 371
Understanding the sample CSV ODA driver extension 379
  Implementing the DTP ODA interfaces 379
  Understanding the CSV ODA extension package 381
   Understanding CSVFileDriver 382
   Understanding CSVFileQuery 382
   Understanding ResultSet 385
   Understanding ResultSetMetaData 387
   Understanding DataSetMetaData 388
   Understanding Messages 388
   Understanding DataTypes 388
   Understanding CommonConstant 389
Developing the CSV ODA UI extension 390
  Creating the CSV ODA UI plug-in project 390
  Defining the dependencies for the CSV ODA UI extension 392
  Specifying the run-time settings for the CSV ODA UI extension 393
  Declaring the ODA data source UI extension point 393
Understanding the sample CSV ODA UI extension 403
  Implementing the ODA data source and data set wizards 404
  Understanding the org.eclipse.birt.report.data.oda.csv.ui.wizards package 405
   Understanding Constants 405
   Understanding CSVFilePropertyPage 406
   Understanding CSVFileSelectionPageHelper 406
   Understanding CSVFileSelectionWizardPage 408
   Understanding FileSelectionWizardPage 409
Testing the CSV ODA UI plug-in 414

Developing a Hibernate ODA extension 419
  Creating the Hibernate ODA driver plug-in project 420
  Understanding the sample Hibernate ODA driver extension 426
    Understanding HibernateDriver 428
    Understanding Connection 428
    Understanding DataSetMetaData 430
    Understanding Statement 431
    Understanding ResultSet 435
    Understanding HibernateUtil 436
  Building the Hibernate ODA driver plug-in 439
  Developing the Hibernate ODA UI extension 441
  Understanding the sample Hibernate ODA UI extension 448
    Understanding HibernatePageHelper 449
    Understanding HibernateDataSourceWizard 452
    Understanding HibernatePropertyPage 452
    Understanding HibernateHqlSelectionPage 452
  Building the Hibernate ODA UI plug-in 458
  Testing the Hibernate ODA UI plug-in 460

Glossary 465

Index 525

It is a common misconception that Eclipse projects are focused on simply providing great tools for developers. Actually, the expectations are far greater. Each Eclipse project is expected to provide both frameworks and extensible, exemplary tools. As anyone who has ever tried to write software with reuse and extensibility in mind knows, that is far more difficult than simply writing a tool.

"Exemplary" is one of those handy English words with two meanings. Both are intended in its use above. Eclipse projects are expected to provide tools that are exemplary in the sense that they provide an example of the use of the underlying frameworks. Eclipse tools are also intended to be exemplary in the sense that they are good and provide immediate utility to the developers who use them.

Since its inception, the BIRT project has worked hard to create both reusable frameworks and extensible tools. This book focuses primarily on how to extend BIRT and how to use BIRT in your own applications and products. As such, it illustrates BIRT's increasing maturity and value as an embedded reporting solution.

As Executive Director of the Eclipse Foundation, I'm pleased with the tremendous progress the BIRT team has made since the project's inception in September of 2004, and I'm equally pleased with the vibrant community that has already grown up around it. As you work with BIRT and the capabilities that are described in this book, I'd encourage you to communicate your successes back to the community, and perhaps consider contributing any interesting extensions you develop. The BIRT web site can be found here:

```
http://www.eclipse.org/birt
```

It includes pointers to the BIRT newsgroup, where you can communicate and share your results with other BIRT developers, and pointers to the Eclipse installation of Bugzilla, where you can contribute your extensions. If you like BIRT—and I am sure this book will help you learn to love it—please participate and contribute. After all, it is the strength of its community that is the true measure of any open source project's success.

Mike Milinkovich
Executive Director, Eclipse Foundation

About this book

BIRT is a powerful reporting platform that provides end-to-end reporting solutions, from creating and deploying reports to integrating report capabilities into other enterprise applications. Two companion books, *BIRT: A Field Guide to Reporting* and *Integrating and Extending BIRT*, cover the breadth and depth of BIRT's functionality.

This book informs report developers about how to write scripts that:

- Customize the report-generation process

- Incorporate complex business logic in their reports

This book also informs application developers about how to:

- Deploy reports

- Integrate reporting capabilities into other applications

- Extend BIRT functionality

By its very nature, reporting is not a stand-alone technology. It draws on data generated by applications and is frequently integrated tightly within those applications. In some applications, such as performance monitoring, reporting provides the most tangible expression of value. Therefore, a successful reporting platform must emphasize interoperability and extensibility, and, a successful implementation of that platform must always involve some measure of integration and extension.

As you read this book, you will see the significant investment that has been made in BIRT to provide support for interoperability and extensibility. In the area of interoperability, for instance, BIRT supports flexible deployment of its report engine and viewer to a wide variety of J2EE application server environments. Other provisions for interoperability in the BIRT platform include the ability to dynamically build or modify reports from within an application using the design engine application programming interface (API) and the ability to access native data objects using the scripted data source mechanism.

In the area of extensibility, BIRT provides hooks to build upon platform capabilities in the following areas:

- Report Items

  New controls may be added to the BIRT designer palette using the report item extension API.

- Complex Logic

  Event handlers written in JavaScript or Java may be included in the generation or presentation phase of report or chart execution to incorporate custom logic required by the application.

- Data Access

  The Open Data Access (ODA) extension provides the means to develop drivers for new, non-JDBC data sources as well as create graphical user interfaces for query specification.

- Rendering

  New report output formats or output for specialized devices can be developed using the report rendering extension API.

Who should read this book

This book is intended for people who have a programming background. These readers can be categorized as:

- Embedders and integrators

  These individuals work with the software to integrate it into their current application infrastructure.

- Extenders

  These individuals leverage APIs and other extension points to add capability or to establish new interoperability between currently disparate components or services.

To write scripts in report design, you need knowledge of JavaScript or Java. More advanced tasks, such as extending BIRT's functionality, require Java development experience and familiarity with the Eclipse platform.

Contents of this book

This book is divided into several parts. The following sections describe the contents of each of the parts.

Part I, Installing and Deploying BIRT

Part I introduces the currently available BIRT reporting packages, the prerequisites for installation, and the steps to install and update the packages. Part I includes the following chapters:

- *Chapter 1, Prerequisites for BIRT.* BIRT provides a number of separate packages as downloadable archive (.zip) files on the Eclipse web site. Some of the packages are stand-alone modules, others require an existing Eclipse environment, and still others provide additional functionality to report developers and application developers. This chapter describes the prerequisites for each of the available packages.

- *Chapter 2, Installing a BIRT Report Designer.* BIRT provides two report designers as separate packages, which are downloadable archive (.zip) files on the Eclipse web site. This chapter describes the steps required to install each of the available report designers.

- *Chapter 3, Installing Other BIRT Packages.* This chapter describes the steps required to install each of the available packages.

- *Chapter 4, Updating a BIRT Installation.* BIRT packages are Eclipse-based, so it is easy to update any of them from earlier releases to release 2.0 or later. This chapter describes how you can install the latest packages without interrupting your work.

- *Chapter 5, Deploying a BIRT Report to an Application Server.* This chapter introduces the distribution of reports through an application server such as Apache Tomcat, IBM WebSphere, or BEA WebLogic. The instructions in the chapter provide detailed guidance about deploying a BIRT report to Apache Tomcat version 5.5.7. From those instructions, a developer can infer how to deploy to other versions.

Part II, Understanding the BIRT Framework

Part II introduces the BIRT architecture and the Report Object Model (ROM) and provides background information that will help programmers design or modify reports programmatically, instead of using the graphical tools in BIRT Report Designer. Part II includes the following chapters:

- *Chapter 6, Understanding the BIRT Architecture.* This chapter provides an architectural overview of BIRT and its components, including the relationships among the BIRT components and BIRT's relationship to Eclipse and Eclipse frameworks. Architectural diagrams illustrate and clarify the relationships and workflow of the components. The chapter also provides brief overviews of all the major BIRT components.

- *Chapter 7, Understanding the Report Object Model.* This chapter provides an overview of the BIRT ROM. ROM is a specification for a set of XML elements that define both the visual and non-visual elements that comprise a report design. The ROM specification includes the properties and methods of those elements, and the relationships among the elements.

Part III, Scripting in a Report Design

Part III describes how a report developer can customize and enhance a BIRT report by writing event handler scripts in either Java or JavaScript. Part III includes the following chapters:

- *Chapter 8, Using Scripting in a Report Design.* This chapter introduces the writing of a BIRT event handler script in either Java or JavaScript, including the advantages and disadvantages of using one language over the other. BIRT event handlers are associated with data sets, data sources, and report items. BIRT fires specific events at specific times in the processing of a report. This chapter identifies the events that BIRT fires and describes the event firing sequence.

- *Chapter 9, Using JavaScript to Write an Event Handler.* This chapter discusses the coding environment and coding considerations for writing a BIRT event handler in JavaScript. This chapter describes several BIRT JavaScript objects that a developer can use to get and set properties that affect the final report. The BIRT JavaScript coding environment offers a pop-up list of properties and functions available in an event handler. A JavaScript event handler can also use Java classes. This chapter includes a tutorial that describes the process of creating a JavaScript event handler.

- *Chapter 10, Using Java to Write an Event Handler.* This chapter discusses how to write a BIRT event handler in Java. BIRT provides Java adapter classes that assist the developer in the creation of Java event handlers. The report developer uses the property editor of the BIRT Report Designer to associate a Java event handler class with the appropriate report element. This chapter contains a tutorial that steps through the Java event handler development and deployment process. This chapter also describes the event handler methods and their parameters.

- *Chapter 11, Using a Scripted Data Source.* BIRT supports getting data from any data source that can be processed with Java or JavaScript. To use a scripted data source in a BIRT report, the report developer implements an open and a close method for the data source and an open, a fetch, and a close method for the data set. A scripted data source can be an EJB, an XML stream, a Hibernate object, or any variety of custom sources of data. This chapter provides a tutorial about how to add a scripted data source to a report and how to write the event handlers for that data source.

Part IV, Integrating BIRT Functionality into Applications

Part IV describes the public APIs that are available to Java developers, except the extension APIs.

- *Chapter 12, Understanding the BIRT APIs.* This chapter introduces BIRT's public API, which are the classes and interfaces in three package hierarchies:

  - The report engine API, in the org.eclipse.birt.report.engine.api hierarchy, supports developers of custom report generators.

  - The design engine API, in the org.eclipse.birt.report.engine.api hierarchy, supports the development of custom report designs.

  - The chart engine API, in the org.eclipse.birt.chart hierarchy, is used to develop a custom chart generator.

- *Chapter 13, Programming with the BIRT Reporting APIs.* This chapter describes the fundamental requirements of a reporting application and lists the BIRT API classes and interfaces that are used to create a reporting application. This chapter describes the tasks that are required of a reporting application and provides an overview of how to build a reporting application. The org.eclipse.birt.report.engine.api package supports the process of generating a report from a report design. The org.eclipse.bert.report.model.api package supports creative new report designs and modifying existing report designs.

- *Chapter 14, Programming with the BIRT Charting APIs.* This chapter describes the requirements of a charting application, either in a stand-alone environment or as part of a reporting application. The org.eclipse.birt.chart hierarchy of packages provides the charting functionality in BIRT. By describing the fundamental tasks required of charting applications, this chapter introduces the API classes and interfaces that are used to create a chart. This chapter also describes the chart programming examples in the chart examples plug-in.

Part V, Working with the Extension Framework

Part V shows Java programmers how to add new functionality to the BIRT framework. By building on the Eclipse platform, BIRT provides an extension mechanism that is familiar to developers of Eclipse plug-ins. This part also provides information about how to build the BIRT project for developers who need access to the complete BIRT open source code base. Part V includes the following chapters:

- *Chapter 15, Building the BIRT Project.* This chapter explains how to download BIRT 2.0.1 source code and build the BIRT project for development. This chapter describes how to configure an Eclipse workspace, download BIRT and Data Tools Platform (DTP) source code from the Eclipse Concurrent Versions System (CVS) repository, and build the BIRT report and web viewers.

- *Chapter 16, Extending BIRT.* This chapter provides an overview of the BIRT extension framework and describes how to use the Eclipse Plug-in

Development Environment (PDE) and the BIRT extension points to create, build, and deploy a BIRT extension.

- *Chapter 17, Developing a Report Item Extension.* This chapter describes how to develop a report item extension. The rotated text extension example is a plug-in that renders the text of a report item as an image. The extension rotates the image in the report design to display the text at a specified angle. This chapter describes how to build the rotated text report item plug-in and add the report item to the BIRT Report Designer using the defined extension points.

- *Chapter 18, Developing a Report Rendering Extension.* This chapter describes how to develop a report rendering extension. The Comma-Separated Values (CSV) extension example is a plug-in that writes the table data in a report to a file in CSV format. This chapter describes how to extend the emitter interfaces using the defined extension points to build and deploy a customized report rendering plug-in that runs in the BIRT Report Engine environment.

- *Chapter 19, Developing an ODA Extension.* This chapter describes how to develop several types of DTP ODA extensions. The CSV ODA driver example is a plug-in that reads data from a CSV file. The Hibernate ODA driver example uses Hibernate Query Language (HQL) to provide a SQL-transparent extension that makes the ODA extension portable to all relational databases. This chapter shows how to develop an ODA extension to the BIRT Report Designer 2.0.1 user interface that allows a report designer to select an extended ODA driver. This chapter also describes how to implement an extension to an ODA JDBC driver to use a supplied connection.

The *Glossary* contains a glossary of terms that are useful to understanding all parts of the book.

Typographical conventions

Table P-1 describes the typographical conventions that are used in this book.

Table P-1   Typographical conventions

Item	Convention	Example
Code examples	Courier font	`StringName = "M. Barajas";`
File names	Initial capital letter, except where file names are case-sensitive	SimpleReport.rptdesign

Table P-1   Typographical conventions *(continued)*

Item	Convention	Example
Key combination	A + sign between keys means to press both keys at the same time	Ctrl+Shift
Menu items	Capitalized, no bold	File
Submenu items	Separated from the main menu item with a small arrow	File→New
User input	Courier font	2006
User input in Java code	Courier italics	chkjava.exe *cab_name*.cab

Syntax conventions

Table P-2 describes the symbols that are used to present syntax.

Table P-2   Syntax conventions

Symbol	Description	Example
[ ]	Optional item	int count [= <value>];
	Array subscript	matrix[ ]
< >	Argument that you must supply	<expression to format>
	Delimiter in XML	<xsd:sequence>
{ }	Groups two or more mutually exclusive options or arguments when used with a pipe	{TEXT_ALIGN_LEFT | TEXT_ALIGN_RIGHT}
	Defines array contents	{0, 1, 2, 3}

	Delimiter of code block	if (itemHandle == null)
		{
		  // create a new handle
		}

|	Separates mutually exclusive options or arguments in a group	[public | protected | private] <data type> <variable name>;
	Java bitwise OR operator	int newflags = flags |4

Acknowledgments

John Arthorne and Chris Laffra observed, "It takes a village to write a book on Eclipse." In the case of the BIRT books, it has taken a virtual village in four countries to create these two books. Our contributors, reviewers, Addison-Wesley editorial, marketing, and production staff, printers, and proofreaders are working in Austin, Boston, Closter, Indianapolis, Inman, Los Angeles, Paris, San Francisco, San Jose, Shanghai, South San Francisco, Upper Saddle River, and Windsor.

We want to thank Greg Doench, our acquisitions editor, who asked us to write a book about BIRT and has been holding his breath ever since to see if we could possibly make the schedule that we set for ourselves. Of course, we want to acknowledge the staff at Addison-Wesley who are working to support our schedule. In particular, we would like to acknowledge John Fuller, Mary Kate Murray, Julie Nahil, Sandra Schroeder, and Beth Wickenhiser. We also want to thank Mike Milinkovich at the Eclipse Foundation and Mark Coggins at Actuate Corporation for providing the forewords for the books.

We particularly want to acknowledge the many, many managers, designers, and programmers too numerous to name who have worked diligently to produce BIRT, giving us a reason for these two books. You know who you are and know how much we value your efforts. The following technical staff members at Actuate Corporation have been of particular assistance to the authors: Linda Chan, Wenbin He, Petter Ivmark, Rima Kanguri, Nina Li, Wenfeng Li, Yu Li, Jianqiang Luo, David Michonneau, Kai Shen, Aniruddha Shevade, Pierre Tessier, Krishna Venkatraman, Mingxia Wu, Gary Xue, Jun Zhai, and Lin Zhu. In addition, we want to acknowledge the support and significant contribution that was provided by Paul Rogers.

Creating this book would not have been possible without the constant support of the members of the Developer Communications team at Actuate Corporation. Many of them and their families sacrificed long personal hours to take on additional tasks so that members of the team of authors could create this material. In particular, we wish to express our appreciation to Tigger Newman, who provided the technical review of this book, and to Terry Ryan, who pulled together the terminology in the glossary that accompanies each of the books. In addition, Mary Adler, Frances Buran, Chris Dufour, Bruce Gardner, Melia

Kenny, Cheryl Koyano, Madalina Lungulescu, Liesbeth Matthieu, Audrey Meinertzhagen, and Lois Olson all contributed to the success of the books.

Installing and Deploying BIRT

1

Prerequisites for BIRT

BIRT provides a number of separate packages as downloadable archive (.zip) files on the BIRT downloads page. Some of the packages are stand-alone modules, others require an existing Eclipse environment, and still others provide additional functionality to report developers and application developers. This chapter describes the requirements for each of the available packages:

- BIRT Chart Engine
- BIRT Demo Database
- BIRT Report Designer
- BIRT Report Designer Full Eclipse Install for Linux
- BIRT Report Designer Full Eclipse Install for Windows
- BIRT Report Engine
- BIRT Rich Client Platform (RCP) Report Designer
- BIRT Samples
- BIRT SDK
- BIRT Test Suite

Requirements for the BIRT report designers

There are two designer applications that you can use to create BIRT reports:

- BIRT RCP Report Designer

BIRT Report Designer is a stand-alone module for report designers who do not have programming experience. BIRT RCP Report Designer is a stand-alone component that only requires a Java JDK. BIRT RCP Report Designer appears on the BIRT download page as RCP Report Designer.

- BIRT Report Designer

  BIRT Report Designer requires Eclipse, a Java JDK, and several other components. BIRT Report Designer is useful for report designers who may want to modify the underlying Java or JavaScript code that BIRT uses to create a report.

  You can install BIRT Report Designer in either of the following two ways:

  - Download and install an all-in-one archive file, which contains Eclipse, BIRT Report Designer, Graphics Editor Framework (GEF), and Eclipse Modeling Framework (EMF).

    The all-in-one archive file contains all the components necessary to run BIRT Report Designer except the Java SDK and itext-1.3.jar. The all-in-one archive file appears on the BIRT download page as BIRT Report Designer Full Eclipse Install.

  - Independently download and install all the components that are required to run BIRT Report Designer.

    To independently install the BIRT Report Designer component, you must first download and install Eclipse. After installing Eclipse, you must also download and install GEF and EMF. You must install itext-1.3.jar only after installing BIRT. The BIRT Report Designer archive file appears on the BIRT download page as Report Designer.

- BIRT Report Designer and SDK

  BIRT Report Designer and SDK is identical to BIRT Report Designer except that it also includes the Java source code for the plug-ins. The requirements for BIRT Report Designer and SDK are identical to the requirements for BIRT Report Designer.

This section describes the prerequisites for each designer package and lists the recommended versions for each component. Table 1-1 provides more information about supported configurations.

Table 1-1   Supported configurations

Component	Required version
Eclipse	3.2
GEF	3.2
EMF	2.2
JDK	1.4.2 or 1.5

About installing required software

Because BIRT is a Java-based platform, installing a required component typically involves only unpacking an archive. Most BIRT components are packed in archives that have an Eclipse directory at the top level. As a result, you follow the same unpacking procedure for most modules. A common installation mistake that new BIRT users make is unpacking archives in the wrong directory. Before you unpack an archive, examine its structure to confirm that you are unpacking it to the correct directory.

The BIRT web site provides the most current information about BIRT installation. To get additional tips, access the BIRT newsgroup, or see an installation demo, visit the following URL:

```
http://download.eclipse.org/birt/downloads/
```

BIRT RCP Report Designer software requirements

BIRT RCP Report Designer requires the following software:

- J2SE 1.4.2 or later

  If you do not have J2SE 1.4.2 or later already installed, choose the latest release, and install it in an appropriate location on your system. The latest JDK download is available at the following URL:

  ```
  http://java.sun.com/products/
  ```

  The JDK is available as a self-extracting executable file for Windows operating systems and as an archive file for UNIX and Linux platforms.

- iText

  iText is a library that BIRT uses to generate PDF files. Download itext-1.3.jar from the following URL:

  ```
  http://prdownloads.sourceforge.net/itext/itext-1.3.jar
  ```

  Copy itext-1.3.jar into $RCP_BIRT/plugins/com.lowagie.itext_1.3.0/lib.

BIRT Report Designer Full Eclipse Install software requirements

BIRT Report Designer Full Eclipse Install Release 2.1 requires the following software:

- Java JDK J2SE 1.4.2 or later

  If you do not have JDK 1.4.2 or later already installed, install the latest JDK release in an appropriate location on your system. The latest JDK download is available at the following URL:

  ```
  http://java.sun.com/products/
  ```

The JDK is available as a self-extracting executable file for Windows operating systems and as an archive file for UNIX and Linux platforms.

- iText

iText is a library that BIRT uses to generate PDF files. Download itext-1.3.jar from the following URL:

```
http://prdownloads.sourceforge.net/itext/itext-1.3.jar
```

You copy iText to a directory that is created upon installing BIRT. You must therefore install iText after you install BIRT. Copy itext-1.3.jar into $ECLIPSE/plugins/com.lowagie.itext_1.3.0/lib.

BIRT Report Designer software requirements

BIRT Report Designer requires the following software:

- Java J2SE 1.4.2 JDK or later

If you do not have Java already installed, choose the latest release, and install it in an appropriate location on your system. The latest JDK download is available at the following URL:

```
http://java.sun.com/products/
```

The J2SE JDK is available as a self-extracting executable file for Windows operating systems and as an archive file for UNIX and Linux platforms.

Release 2.1 requires J2SE 1.4.2 JDK or later and does not support earlier versions.

- Eclipse Platform

BIRT Report Designer Release 2.1 is only compatible with Eclipse 3.2. BIRT Report Designer does not support earlier versions of Eclipse.

You can download and install Eclipse SDK 3.2 from the following URL:

```
http://www.eclipse.org/downloads
```

The Eclipse SDK is an archive file that you must extract to your hard drive. The installation of Eclipse is complete once you extract the archive. Eclipse does not have a setup or install program.

The result of the Eclipse archive extraction is a folder named eclipse. You must specify to the archive extraction program where on your hard drive you want the eclipse folder to reside. You may extract the Eclipse archive to any location you prefer. A typical location for Eclipse is the root directory of the C drive. If you specify the root directory of the C drive, the result of installing Eclipse is the following folder:

```
c:/eclipse
```

- Graphics Editor Framework

  GEF is an Eclipse plug-in that BIRT Report Designer's user interface requires.

  Download GEF 3.2 Runtime from the following URL:

  ```
  http://download.eclipse.org/tools/gef/downloads
  ```

  GEF is available as a ZIP archive file. Extract GEF to the directory that contains Eclipse.

  Eclipse 3.2 requires GEF 3.2 and does not support earlier versions.

- Eclipse Modeling Framework

  EMF is a collection of Eclipse plug-ins that BIRT charts use. EMF download includes the required Service Data Objects (SDO) component. Download EMF and SDO 2.2 Runtime from the following URL:

  ```
  http://download.eclipse.org/tools/emf/scripts/downloads.php
  ```

  EMF is available as a ZIP archive file. Extract EMF to the directory that contains Eclipse.

  Eclipse 3.2 requires EMF 2.2 and does not support earlier versions.

- iText

  iText is a library that BIRT uses to generate PDF files. Download itext-1.3.jar from the following URL:

  ```
  http://prdownloads.sourceforge.net/itext/itext-1.3.jar
  ```

  You copy iText to a directory that is created upon installing BIRT. You must therefore install iText after you install BIRT. Copy itext-1.3.jar into $ECLIPSE/plugins/com.lowagie.itext_1.3.0/lib.

Table 1-1 lists the required configurations for developing report designs using BIRT Report Designer 2.1. You cannot use any other versions of any of the listed components.

Prerequisites for other BIRT packages

BIRT provides a number of supporting packages for the BIRT Report Designers. This section describes the prerequisites for each of these packages.

BIRT Chart Engine software requirements

This section describes the software required to use BIRT Chart Engine.

BIRT Chart Engine requires the following software:

- Java J2SE 1.4.2 JDK or later

If you do not have JDK 1.4.2 or later already installed, choose the latest release, and install it in an appropriate location on your system. The latest JDK download is available at the following URL:

```
http://java.sun.com/products
```

The JDK is available as a self-extracting executable file for Windows operating systems and as an archive file for UNIX and Linux platforms.

- Eclipse Platform

  BIRT Report Designer Release 2.1 is compatible with Eclipse 3.2. BIRT Report Designer does not support any earlier version of Eclipse.

  You can download and install Eclipse SDK 3.2 from the following URL:

  ```
  http://www.eclipse.org/downloads
  ```

- Graphics Editor Framework

  GEF is an Eclipse plug-in that BIRT Report Designer's user interface requires.

  Download GEF 3.2 Runtime from the following URL:

  ```
  http://download.eclipse.org/tools/gef/downloads
  ```

  GEF is available as a ZIP archive file. Extract GEF to the directory that contains Eclipse.

- Eclipse Modeling Framework

  EMF is a collection of Eclipse plug-ins that BIRT charts use. EMF download includes the required SDO component. Download EMF and SDO 2.2 Runtime from the following URL:

  ```
  http://download.eclipse.org/tools/emf/scripts/downloads.php
  ```

  EMF is available as a ZIP archive file. Extract EMF to the directory that contains Eclipse.

  Eclipse 3.1 requires EMF 2.1 and does not support EMF 2.2 or later.

BIRT Demo Database software requirements

Both BIRT Report Designer and BIRT RCP Report Designer ship with a demo database called Classic Models that uses Apache Derby. You do not need to download any other files to use this database. The database is built in to the designer builds.

BIRT Demo Database requires one of the following database platforms:

- Apache Derby version 5.1 or higher
- MySQL Connector/J version 3.x or MySQL client version 4.x

You can download this sample database from the following URL:

```
http://www.eclipse.org/birt/phoenix/db/
```

BIRT Report Engine software requirements

This section describes the software required to use BIRT Report Engine.

BIRT Report Engine requires Java J2SE 1.4.2 JDK or Java J2SE 5.0 JDK.

If you do not have J2SE 5.0 already installed, choose the latest release and install it. The latest J2SE download is available at the following URL:

```
http://java.sun.com/j2se/1.5.0/download.jsp
```

J2SE 5.0 JDK is available as a self-extracting executable file for Windows operating systems and as an archive file for UNIX and Linux platforms. Extract the contents of this file into an appropriate location on your system.

Note that Sun renamed the Java 1.5 version to 5.0 and thus documentation on Sun's site may at times appear to refer to two different versions. Versions 5.0 and 1.5 are the same version.

BIRT Samples software requirements

BIRT Samples requires either BIRT Report Designer or BIRT Report Engine. The version of the BIRT Samples files should match the version of the BIRT package you use. Use BIRT Samples 2.1 with BIRT Report Designer 2.1.

You can get BIRT Samples from the following URL:

```
http://www.eclipse.org/birt/phoenix/examples/
```

BIRT Test Suite software requirements

This section describes the software required to use BIRT Test Suite.

BIRT Test Suite requires the following software:

- Java J2SE 1.4.2 JDK or Java J2SE 5.0 JDK

  If you do not have J2SE 5.0 already installed, choose the latest release and install it. The latest J2SE download is available at the following URL:

  ```
  http://java.sun.com/j2se/1.5.0/download.jsp
  ```

  J2SE 5.0 JDK is available as a self-extracting executable file for Windows operating systems and as an archive file for UNIX and Linux platforms. Extract the contents of this file into an appropriate location on your system.

  Note that Sun renamed the Java 1.5 version to 5.0 and thus documentation on Sun's site may at times appear to refer to two different versions. 5.0 and 1.5 are essentially synonymous.

- Eclipse Platform

BIRT Report Designer Release 2.1 is compatible with Eclipse 3.2. BIRT Report Designer does not support earlier versions of Eclipse.

You can download and install Eclipse SDK 3.2 from the following URL:

```
http://www.eclipse.org/downloads/
```

- Graphics Editor Framework

GEF is an Eclipse plug-in that BIRT Report Designer's user interface requires.

Download GEF 3.2 Runtime from the following URL:

```
http://download.eclipse.org/tools/gef/downloads/
```

GEF is available as a ZIP archive file. Extract GEF to the directory that contains Eclipse.

- Eclipse Modeling Framework

EMF is a collection of Eclipse plug-ins that BIRT charts use. EMF download includes the required SDO component. Download EMF and SDO 2.2 Runtime from the following URL:

```
http://download.eclipse.org/tools/emf/scripts/downloads.php
```

EMF is available as a ZIP archive file. Extract EMF to the directory that contains Eclipse.

Eclipse 3.2 requires EMF 2.2.

- JUnit Regression Testing Framework

BIRT Test Suite requires JUnit 4.1. JUnit is available as a ZIP archive file. Download the archive from the following URL:

```
http://www.junit.org
```

- BIRT Report Designer source code

In your Eclipse Workbench, use CVS to download the BIRT Report Designer source code into your workspace.

About types of BIRT builds

The Eclipse BIRT download site makes available several types of builds for BIRT. The following list describes the types of builds that are available:

- Release build

A release build is of production quality and passes the complete test suite for all components and features. Use the release build to develop applications.

- Milestone build

A milestone build provides access to newly completed features. The build is stable, but it is not of production quality. Use this type of build to preview new features and develop future reporting applications that depend on those features.

- Stable build

  A stable build passes a reduced test suite. New features are in an intermediate stage of development in this type of build. Use a stable build to preview new features and provide feedback to the development team.

- Nightly build

  BIRT is built every night. As an open source project, these builds are available to anyone. These builds are part of an ongoing development process and are unlikely to be useful to report developers in general; however, if a certain feature that you require does not work, you can file a bug report. When the bug has been fixed, and the fix has been included in the build, you can download BIRT and confirm that the fix solves the problem that you reported.

2

Installing a BIRT Report Designer

BIRT provides two report designers, BIRT Report Designer and BIRT RCP Report Designer. Both designers are reporting systems that integrate with your J2EE-based web application to enable report developers to produce compelling reports in both web and PDF formats. BIRT Report Designer is for report developers who want to use programming or scripting in their report designs. BIRT RCP Report Designer does not support the use of programming or scripting in Java.

Each designer is packaged as an archive (.zip) file and can be downloaded from the Eclipse web site.

The available packages are:

- BIRT Report Designer

  If you already have installed an Eclipse environment, you can download and install BIRT Report Designer.

- BIRT RCP Report Designer

  If you have installed a Java environment, you can download and install BIRT RCP Report Designer. This designer is easier to use but does not support programming or scripting in Java.

- BIRT Report Designer Full Eclipse Install

  If you have an installed Java environment, and you want to be able to program or use JavaScript in your report design, you can download and install BIRT Report Designer Full Eclipse Install. This package contains BIRT Report Designer and all the Eclipse components that you need in one ZIP file.

Installing BIRT Report Designer

BIRT Report Designer integrates into an existing Eclipse platform on your computer by providing the report design perspective. BIRT Report Designer also includes the Software Development Kit (SDK) and the components provided in the BIRT Chart Engine, BIRT Demo Database, BIRT Report Engine, and BIRT Samples packages.

You install BIRT Report Designer by downloading an archive (.zip) file from the Eclipse web site and extracting it in your existing Eclipse environment. The following examples use BIRT Release 2.1.

Downloading and installing BIRT Report Designer

Complete the following procedure to download and install BIRT Report Designer on a Windows or UNIX system.

How to install BIRT Report Designer

1 Using your browser, navigate to the following URL:

```
http://download.eclipse.org/birt/downloads/
```

2 From Download, choose the following build:

```
Release build 2_1_0
```

The BIRT Release Build: 2_1_0 page appears.

3 Choose the Report Designer ZIP file:

```
birt-report-framework-2_1_0.zip
```

The Eclipse downloads page appears. This page shows all the sites that provide this download file.

4 Choose the download site that is closest to your location.

birt-report-framework-2_1_0.zip downloads to your system.

5 Extract the archive file to the folder that contains your Eclipse directory.

Be certain to extract the archive into the directory that contains the eclipse folder and not into the eclipse folder. For example, if your eclipse folder is located at C:\eclipse, extract the archive into C:\.

6 Download and install the auxiliary file that is necessary for PDF creation, as described in the following section.

Installing the auxiliary file for BIRT Report Designer

BIRT Report Designer also requires iText, an open source Java-PDF library that BIRT uses to generate PDF versions of reports. You must install iText after you install BIRT Report Designer.

1 Download itext-1.3.jar from the following URL:

```
http://prdownloads.sourceforge.net/itext/itext-1.3.jar
```

2 Copy itext-1.3.jar to the following location in your Eclipse installation:

```
/plugins/com.lowagie.itext_1.3.0/lib
```

Testing the BIRT Report Designer installation

To test your BIRT Report Designer installation, start Eclipse, then start BIRT Report Designer. BIRT Report Designer is a perspective within Eclipse.

How to test the BIRT Report Designer installation

1 Start Eclipse.

2 From the Eclipse window menu, choose Open Perspective→Report Design. If Report Design does not appear in the Open Perspective window, choose Other. A list of perspectives appears. Choose Report Design.

Eclipse displays the BIRT Report Designer perspective.

If the test fails, see "Avoiding cache conflicts after you install a BIRT report designer," later in this chapter.

Installing BIRT Report Designer Full Eclipse Install

If you are new to Eclipse and BIRT, you can download and install this package to start developing and designing BIRT reports immediately. This package includes BIRT Report Designer, an Eclipse environment, and other required components.

In BIRT Release 2.1, the BIRT Report Designer Full Eclipse Install package contains:

- Eclipse Platform 3.2
- Graphics Editor Framework 3.2
- Eclipse Modeling Framework 2.2
- BIRT Report Designer 2.1

You install BIRT Report Designer Full Eclipse Install by downloading and extracting an archive (.zip) file. The following examples use BIRT Release 2.1.

Downloading and installing BIRT Report Designer Full Eclipse Install

Complete the following procedure to download and install BIRT Report Designer and the other necessary components on a Windows or UNIX system.

How to install BIRT Report Designer Full Eclipse Install

1 Using your browser, navigate to the following URL:

   ```
   http://download.eclipse.org/birt/downloads/
   ```

2 Select the following build:

   ```
   Release build 2_1_0
   ```

   The BIRT Release Build: 2_1_0 page appears.

3 Choose the Report Designer Full Eclipse Install ZIP file:

   ```
   birt-report-designer-all-in-one-2_1_0.zip
   ```

   The Eclipse downloads page appears. This page shows all the sites that provide this download file.

4 Choose the download site that is closest to your location.

   birt-report-designer-all-in-one-2_1_0.zip downloads to your system.

5 Extract the archive file.

6 Download and install the auxiliary file that is necessary for PDF creation, as described in the following section.

Installing the auxiliary file for BIRT Report Designer

BIRT Report Designer also requires iText, an open source Java-PDF library that BIRT uses to generate PDF versions of reports. You must install iText after you install BIRT Report Designer.

1 Download itext-1.3.jar from the following URL:

   ```
   http://prdownloads.sourceforge.net/itext/itext-1.3.jar
   ```

2 Copy itext-1.3.jar to the following location in your Eclipse installation:

   ```
   /plugins/com.lowagie.itext_1.3.0/lib
   ```

To test your installation, see "Testing the BIRT Report Designer installation," earlier in this chapter.

Installing BIRT RCP Report Designer

BIRT RCP Report Designer is a stand-alone report design application that enables report developers to produce compelling reports in both web and PDF formats. This application uses the Eclipse Rich Client Platform (RCP) to provide a report design environment that is less complex than the full Eclipse platform and SDK. If you need the project-based environment that the full Eclipse platform provides, install BIRT Report Designer instead. BIRT RCP Report Designer only runs on Windows.

To integrate reports that you create in BIRT RCP Report Designer into your J2EE-based web application, you also must install BIRT Report Engine. BIRT RCP Report Designer includes the components that are provided in the BIRT Demo Database package.

You install BIRT RCP Report Designer by downloading and extracting an archive (.zip) file. The following examples use Release 2.1.

Downloading and installing BIRT RCP Report Designer

Complete the following procedure to download and install BIRT RCP Report Designer on a Windows system.

How to install BIRT RCP Report Designer

1 Using your browser, navigate to the following URL:

```
http://download.eclipse.org/birt/downloads/
```

2 Select the following build:

```
Release build 2_1_0
```

The BIRT Release Build: 2_1_0 page appears.

3 Choose the BIRT RCP Report Designer ZIP file:

```
birt-rcp-report-designer-2_1_0.zip
```

The Eclipse downloads page appears. This page shows all the sites that provide this download file.

4 Choose the download site that is closest to your location.

birt-rcp-report-designer-2_1_0.zip downloads to your system.

5 Extract the archive to a suitable directory. You can either create a directory or choose an existing directory. The root directory of the archive is birt-rcp-report-designer-2_1_0.

6 Download and extract the auxiliary files that are necessary for report viewing and PDF creation, as described in the following section.

Installing the auxiliary file for BIRT Report Designer

BIRT Report Designer also requires iText, an open source Java-PDF library that BIRT uses to generate PDF versions of reports. You must install iText after you install BIRT Report Designer.

1 Download itext-1.3.jar from the following URL:

```
http://prdownloads.sourceforge.net/itext/itext-1.3.jar
```

2 Copy itext-1.3.jar to the following location in your Eclipse installation:

```
/plugins/com.lowagie.itext_1.3.0/lib
```

Testing the BIRT RCP Report Designer installation

To test the installation, start BIRT RCP Report Designer.

How to test the BIRT RCP Report Designer installation

1 Navigate to the birt-rcp-report-designer-2_1_0 subdirectory.

2 To run BIRT RCP Report Designer, double-click BIRT.exe. BIRT RCP Report Designer appears.

Troubleshooting installation problems

Installing a BIRT report designer is a straightforward task. If you extract the archive file to the appropriate location and the required supporting files are also available in the expected location, your BIRT report designer will work. Because of this fact, one of the first steps in troubleshooting an installation problem is confirming that you extracted all files to the correct location. In particular, verify that the /eclipse/plugins directory contains jar files whose names begin with org.eclipse.birt, org.eclipse.emf, and org.eclipse.gef. Beyond this step, there are a few things that you can do to resolve installation problems. The following sections describe ways of troubleshooting and resolving two common installation errors.

Avoiding cache conflicts after you install a BIRT report designer

Eclipse caches information about plug-ins for faster start-up. After you install or upgrade BIRT Report Designer, using a cached copy of some pages can lead to errors or missing functionality. BIRT RCP Report Designer can also have this problem. Symptoms of this problem include:

- The Report Design perspective does not appear in Eclipse.

- You receive the message "An error occurred" when you open a report or use the report design perspective.

- JDBC drivers that you installed do not appear in the driver manager.

The solution is to remove the cached information. The recommended practice is to start either Eclipse or BIRT from the command line with the -clean option.

To start Eclipse, use the following command:

```
eclipse -clean
```

To start BIRT RCP Report Designer, use the following command:

```
birt -clean
```

Specifying which Java Virtual Machine to use when you start a BIRT report designer

You can specify which Java Virtual Machine (JVM) to use when you start a BIRT report designer. This specification is important, particularly for users on UNIX, when path and permission problems prevent the report designer from locating an appropriate JVM to use. A quick way to overcome such problems is by specifying explicitly which JVM to use when you start the BIRT report designer.

In both Windows and UNIX systems, you can either start a BIRT report designer from the command line or create a command file or shell script that calls the appropriate executable file with the JVM path. The example in this section uses BIRT Report Designer on a Windows system.

How to specify which JVM to use when you start a BIRT report designer

On the command line, type a command similar to:

```
eclipse.exe -classpath <$JAVA_HOME>/j2sdk1.4.2_05/bin/java.exe
```

Installing a language pack

All BIRT user interface components and messages are internationalized through the use of properties files. BIRT uses English as the default language, but other languages are supported by installing a language pack that contains the necessary properties files. There are 24 BIRT language packs, four each for the following six BIRT products:

- BIRT Report Designer Full Eclipse Install
- BIRT Report Designer
- BIRT RCP Report Designer
- BIRT Report Engine
- BIRT Chart Engine
- BIRT Framework SDK

Each of the four language packs contains support for a specific set of languages. The names of the language packs are identical for each product, although the archive file names differ. The following list describes the four language packs and the languages that they support:

- NLpack1

The NLpack1 language pack supports German, Spanish, French, Italian, Japanese, Korean, Brazilian Portuguese, traditional Chinese, and simplified Chinese.

■ NLpack2

The NLpack2 language pack supports Czech, Hungarian, Polish, and Russian.

■ NLpack2a

The NLpack2a language pack supports Danish, Dutch, Finnish, Greek, Norwegian, Portuguese, Swedish, and Turkish.

■ NLpackBidi

The NLpackBidi language pack supports Arabic and Hebrew. Hebrew is only for Eclipse runtime, GEF runtime, and EMF runtime.

The following instructions explain how to download and install a language pack.

How to download and install a language pack

To download and install a language pack, perform the following steps:

1 Point your browser to the BIRT download page at:

    http://download.eclipse.org/birt/downloads/

2 In the Download section of the BIRT download page, choose Release Build 2_1_0.

3 In the Build Documentation section of the BIRT Release Build page, choose Language Packs.

4 Download the language pack for the product and language that meets your needs.

5 Extract the language pack archive file into the directory above the Eclipse directory.

6 Start Eclipse and choose Window➤Preferences➤Report Design➤Preview.

7 Select the language of choice from the drop-down list in Choose your locale.

8 Restart Eclipse.

If Windows is not running under the locale you need for BIRT, start Eclipse using the -nl <locale> command line option, where <locale> is a standard Java locale code, such as es_ES for Spanish as spoken in Spain. Sun Microsystems provides a list of locale codes at the following URL:

    http://java.sun.com/j2se/1.5.0/docs/guide/intl/locale.doc.html

Eclipse remembers the locale you specify on the command line. On subsequent launches of Eclipse, the locale is set to the most recent locale setting. To revert to a previous locale, launch Eclipse using the -nl command line option for the locale to which you want to revert.

3

Installing Other BIRT Packages

Beyond the BIRT Report Designer packages, BIRT provides a number of other separate packages as downloadable archive (.zip) files on the Eclipse web site. Some of the packages are stand-alone modules, others require an existing Eclipse or BIRT environment, and still others provide additional functionality to report developers and application developers. This chapter describes the steps required to install each of the available packages, shown in the following list:

- BIRT Chart Engine

- BIRT Demo Database

- BIRT Report Engine

- BIRT Samples

- BIRT Test Suite

BIRT supports several languages for displaying user interface components and messages. Support for languages other than English requires installing a language pack. This chapter describes the steps required to install a language pack.

Installing BIRT Chart Engine

BIRT Chart Engine supports adding charting capabilities to a Java application. An application can use BIRT Chart Engine without using the BIRT reporting functionality or BIRT Report Engine. BIRT Chart Engine integrates into an existing Eclipse platform on a Microsoft Windows, UNIX, or Linux platform.

You can also install BIRT Chart Engine onto an existing J2EE application server. To use BIRT Chart Engine, you use its public API, org.eclipse.birt.chart.

BIRT Report Designer includes all the components of BIRT Chart Engine. Thus, if you are using a BIRT Report Designer, you do not need to install BIRT Chart Engine separately.

The birt-charts-2.1.zip download file includes documentation and examples on how to use BIRT Chart Engine. To view this documentation, see the following location after extracting the archive:

```
eclipse/plugins/org.eclipse.birt.doc_2.1/Samples/
    org.eclipse.birt.chart.examples/readme.html
```

Installing BIRT Chart Engine from the Eclipse BIRT web site

To install BIRT Chart Engine, you extract an archive (.zip) file. Complete the steps in the following section to download and install BIRT Chart Engine on a Microsoft Windows, UNIX, or Linux platform.

How to install BIRT Chart Engine

1 Using your browser, navigate to the following URL:

```
http://download.eclipse.org/birt/downloads/
```

2 Select the following build:

```
Release build 2.1
```

The BIRT Release Build: 2.1 page appears.

3 Choose the Chart Engine archive (.zip) file:

```
birt-charts-2.1.zip
```

The Eclipse downloads page appears. This page shows all the sites that provide this BIRT Chart Engine download file.

4 Choose your closest download site.

birt-charts-2.1.zip downloads to your system.

5 Extract the archive file to the folder that contains your Eclipse directory.

Avoiding cache conflicts after installing

Eclipse caches information about plug-ins for faster start-up. After you install or upgrade BIRT Chart Engine, using a cached copy of some pages can lead to errors or missing functionality.

The solution is to remove the cached information. The recommended practice is to start Eclipse from the command line with the -clean option:

```
eclipse -clean
```

Installing BIRT Demo Database

The BIRT Demo Database package provides the Classic Models database that this book uses for example procedures. The database is provided in the following formats:

- Apache Derby
- Microsoft Access
- MySQL

BIRT Report Designer and BIRT RCP Report Designer include this database in Apache Derby format, as the Classic Models Inc. sample database data source. Install BIRT Demo Database if you want to use the native drivers to access this data source.

Installing BIRT Demo Database from the Eclipse BIRT web site

To install BIRT Demo Database, you extract an archive (.zip) file. Complete the steps in the following section to download and install BIRT Demo Database on a Microsoft Windows, UNIX, or Linux platform.

How to install BIRT Demo Database

1 Using your browser, navigate to the following URL:

    http://www.eclipse.org/birt/phoenix/db/

2 In the Install instructions, select sample database.

3 In the dialog box for the ZIP file download that appears, select Open.

    The name of the ZIP file is birt-database-2_0_1.zip.

4 Extract the archive file to a location of your choice.

    Extracting creates a directory, ClassicModels, that contains the BIRT Demo Database in Apache Derby, Microsoft Access, and MySQL formats.

Testing the BIRT Demo Database installation

To test the BIRT Demo Database, first connect to the database with the native database client tool or a Java application. Next, connect to the database from BIRT Report Designer or BIRT RCP Report Designer.

How to access BIRT Demo Database

Perform one of the following sets of tasks, based on your preferred database:

- Apache Derby database

    Connect to the database located in the derby subdirectory of ClassicModels.

- Microsoft Access database

  Perform one of the following tasks:

  - Use Microsoft Access to connect to the database located in the msaccess subdirectory of ClassicModels.

  - Use ODBC to access the database.

    1 Create an ODBC data source on the database located in the msaccess subdirectory of ClassicModels.

    2 Use a JDBC:ODBC bridge driver to access the ODBC data source.

- MySQL

  1 Navigate to the mysql subdirectory of ClassicModels.

  2 Create a database to use or edit create_classicmodels.sql to uncomment the lines that create and select the classicmodels database.

  3 Use the mysql command line interface to run create_classicmodels.sql.

  4 Review load_classicmodels.sql to determine if the script can be used on your platform without editing. Use the mysql command line interface to run load_classicmodels.sql.

How to access BIRT Demo Database from a BIRT Report Designer

Now, connect to the database using BIRT Report Designer or BIRT RCP Report Designer.

1 To access the Classic Models database in Apache Derby or MySQL format, first add the driver Java archive (.jar) files to your BIRT Report Designer or BIRT RCP Report Designer installation.

2 In any report design, create a data source on the database. In the same report design, create a data set on the data source.

Installing BIRT Report Engine

BIRT Report Engine supports adding reporting capabilities to a Java application. BIRT Report Engine integrates into an existing Eclipse platform on a Microsoft Windows, UNIX, or Linux platform. You can also install report engine components onto an existing J2EE application server. To support quick deployment of reporting functionality to an application server, BIRT Report Engine includes a web archive (.war) file.

Installing BIRT Report Engine from the Eclipse BIRT web site

To install BIRT Report Engine, you extract an archive (.zip) file. Complete the steps in the following section to download and install BIRT Report Engine on a Microsoft Windows, UNIX, or Linux platform. For more information about setting up the BIRT Report Engine, see Chapter 5, "Deploying a BIRT Report to an Application Server."

How to install BIRT Report Engine

1 Using your browser, navigate to the following URL:

```
http://download.eclipse.org/birt/downloads
```

2 Select the following build:

```
Release build 2.1
```

The BIRT Release Build: 2.1 page appears.

3 Choose the Report Engine archive (.zip) file:

```
birt-runtime-2.1.zip
```

The Eclipse downloads page appears. This page shows all the sites that provide this BIRT Report Engine download file.

4 Choose your closest download site.

birt-runtime-2.1.zip downloads to your system.

5 Extract the archive file to a suitable directory.

6 Create a system variable, BIRT_HOME.

Set the value of BIRT_HOME to the BIRT Report Engine installation directory. For example:

```
C:\birt-runtime-2.1
```

Testing the BIRT Report Engine installation

To test the installation, run the BIRT Report Engine command line example.

How to test the BIRT Report Engine installation

1 From the command line, navigate to the directory where you installed BIRT Report Engine.

2 Navigate to the Command Line Example subdirectory.

3 To run the genReport script, use the following syntax:

■ On a Windows platform

```
genReport [-e <target encoding>] [-f {HTML|FO|PDF}]
    [-F <full path of report parameter file>]
```

```
                    [-l <locale>] [-o <full path of output file>]
                    [-p <report parameter name=value>]
                    <full path of report design file>
```

- On a UNIX or Linux platform

```
        genReport.sh [-e <target encoding>] [-f {HTML|FO|PDF}]
                    [-F <full path of report parameter file>]
                    [-l <locale>] [-o <full path of output file>]
                    [-p <report parameter name=value>]
                    <full path of report design file>
```

Enclose the value for a command line parameter in quotes. A report parameter value specified by the -p command line argument overrides the value in a report parameter file. For example, the following Windows platform command uses the value, Hello, for the parameter, sample, to generate an HTML file from the report design, test.rptdesign:

```
        genReport -p "sample=Hello"
            "C:\birt-runtime-2_0_1\Web Viewer Example\test.rptdesign"
```

genReport generates the required output file.

4 Open the output file.

Installing BIRT Samples

BIRT Samples provides examples of a BIRT report item extension and of charting applications. The report item extension integrates into BIRT Report Designer and BIRT Report Engine.

To install BIRT Samples, you extract an archive (.zip) file. Complete the steps in the following section to download and install BIRT Samples on a Windows, UNIX, or Linux platform.

How to install BIRT Samples

1 Using your browser, navigate to the following URL:

```
        http://download.eclipse.org/birt/downloads
```

2 Select the following build:

```
        Release build 2.1
```

The BIRT Release Build: 2.1 page appears.

3 Choose the Samples archive (.zip) file:

```
        birt-samples-plugins-2.1.zip
```

The Eclipse downloads page appears. This page shows all the sites that provide this BIRT Samples download file.

4 Choose your closest download site.

birt-samples-plugins-2.1.zip downloads to your system. Extract the archive file to the folder that contains your Eclipse directory.

Installing BIRT Test Suite

BIRT Test Suite provides the test suite used by BIRT developers. Install this package if you are a contributor to the BIRT project or if you want to customize the BIRT packages to your own needs.

To install BIRT Test Suite, you extract an archive (.zip) file. Complete the steps in the following section to download and install BIRT Test Suite on a Windows, UNIX, or Linux platform.

How to install BIRT Test Suite

1 Using your browser, navigate to the following URL:

```
http://download.eclipse.org/birt/downloads/
```

2 Select the following build:

```
Release build 2.1
```

The BIRT Release Build: 2.1 page appears.

3 Choose the Test Suites archive (.zip) file:

```
birt-tests-suite-2.1.zip
```

The Eclipse downloads page appears. This page shows all the sites that provide this BIRT Test Suite download file.

4 Choose your closest download site. birt-tests-suite-2.1.zip downloads to your system.

5 Extract the archive file to the folder that contains your Eclipse directory.

6 Set up the BIRT Test Suite plug-ins so that they have access to the JUnit libraries. For information about using the JUnit tests, see BIRT API Test Reference.doc, which can be found in the following location in the BIRT Test Suite package:

```
eclipse\plugins\org.eclipse.birt.tests.data
```

4

Updating a BIRT Installation

As BIRT Report Designer is a Java-based application, updating an installation typically requires replacing the relevant files. Eclipse supports the update process for BIRT Report Designer by providing the Update Manager. BIRT RCP Report Designer is a stand-alone product, so you must replace the existing version with a newer version.

This chapter describes important considerations and the steps you should follow to update the following packages:

- BIRT Report Designer
- BIRT RCP Report Designer

Using the Eclipse Update Manager to update BIRT Report Designer installation

Use the Update Manager to find and install newer major releases of BIRT Report Designer. To install a milestone release or other prerelease version, use the manual update instructions.

How to update BIRT Report Designer installation using the Update Manager

1 In Eclipse, choose Help→Software Updates→Find and Install. Feature Updates appears.

2 Select Search for updates of currently installed features, and choose Finish. The Update Manager may display a list of update sites. Choose one to

continue. Search Results appears and displays any updates that are available.

3 Select a feature to update, then choose Next. Feature License appears.

4 To accept the license and continue installing the update, choose Next. Installation appears.

5 Choose Finish to download and install the selected updates.

Updating BIRT RCP Report Designer installation

Unlike BIRT Report Designer, BIRT RCP Report Designer is a stand-alone application. To update this application, you delete the entire application and reinstall a newer version. If you created your workspace in the birt-rcp-report-designer-<version> directory structure, you should back up your workspace or the reports that you want to keep before you delete BIRT RCP Report Designer. After you install a newer version of the application, you can copy your workspace folder back to the application's directory structure.

As a best practice, do not keep your workspace in the birt-rcp-report-designer-<version> directory structure. Keeping your workspace in a different location enables you to update your installation more easily in the future.

How to update BIRT RCP Report Designer

1 Back up the workspace directory if it is in the birt-rcp-report-designer-<version> directory structure.

2 Delete the birt-rcp-report-designer-<version> directory.

3 Download and install BIRT RCP Report Designer as described earlier in this book.

4 Restore the workspace directory, if necessary.

5 Restart BIRT RCP Report Designer with the -clean option:

```
birt -clean
```

Deploying a BIRT Report to an Application Server

One way to view a BIRT report on the web is to deploy the BIRT report viewer to an application server, such as Apache Tomcat, IBM WebSphere, JBOSS, or BEA WebLogic.

You deploy the BIRT report viewer by copying files from the BIRT Report Engine, which you must install separately from the BIRT Report Designer. The BIRT Report Engine includes the BIRT report viewer as a web archive (.war) file and as a set of files and folders.

This chapter provides information about deploying the BIRT report viewer using either of these sources.

About application servers

The instructions in this chapter specifically address deploying a BIRT report to Apache Tomcat version 5.5.7. While the information in this chapter is specific to this version of Tomcat, a BIRT report can also be deployed to other versions of Tomcat and to other application servers.

About deploying to Tomcat

There are only minor differences between the requirements for deploying to Tomcat version 5.5.7 and deploying to earlier versions of Apache Tomcat. Apache Tomcat 5.5.7 runs Java 5 by default, which is also the recommended version to use for BIRT 2.1. If you use an earlier version of Java, you need to install a compatibility package and configure Apache Tomcat to use the Java 1.4

run-time environment. For information about configuring Apache Tomcat to use Java run-time 1.4, see the Apache Tomcat help pages. You can download Apache Tomcat from jakarta.apache.org/tomcat.

About deploying to other application servers

Most application servers require a WAR file that contains everything that the application requires, including a web.xml file describing the application and various deployment preferences. A WAR file appropriate for Tomcat is included with BIRT. In most cases, the WAR file will not require modification. In some cases, however, developers who have experience with other application servers can modify the web.xml file to reflect the requirements of their environments. For more information about setting the web.xml parameters, see the section on mapping the report viewer folders, later in this chapter.

If you are deploying to JBoss, you might need to copy axis.jar and axis-ant.jar from WEB-INF/lib to the following directory:

```
jboss/server/default/lib
```

This step might not be necessary for some versions of JBoss, but if you are experiencing difficulty with a JBoss deployment, copying these files might be the solution to your problem.

Placing the BIRT report viewer on an application server

You must place the BIRT report viewer in a location where Apache Tomcat can access it. The most common location is in the $TOMCAT_INSTALL/webapps directory. By placing the BIRT report viewer in $TOMCAT_INSTALL/webapps, Apache Tomcat automatically recognizes and starts the BIRT report viewer the next time you restart Apache Tomcat.

You must also install an auxiliary file, as explained later in this chapter.

Installing the BIRT report viewer files

The following instructions assume that you have installed the BIRT Report Engine from the BIRT web site, that your web application directory is $TOMCAT_INSTALL/webapps, and that your BIRT run-time install directory is $BIRT_RUNTIME.

To install the BIRT report viewer from the BIRT Report Engine WAR file, first place the BIRT report viewer WAR file on Apache Tomcat by copying birt.war to $TOMCAT_INSTALL/webapps, as illustrated in the following DOS command:

```
copy $BIRT_RUNTIME/birt.war $TOMCAT_INSTALL/webapps
```

Then, restart Apache Tomcat.

How to install the BIRT report viewer from the BIRT Report Engine viewer folder

1 Navigate to $TOMCAT_INSTALL/webapps.

2 Create a subdirectory named birt.

3 To place the BIRT Report Engine on Apache Tomcat, copy the web viewer example directory and all its subdirectories to:

```
$TOMCAT_INSTALL/webapps
```

as illustrated in the following DOS command:

```
xcopy /E "$BIRT_RUNTIME/WebViewerExample"
    $TOMCAT_INSTALL/webapps/birt
```

4 Restart Apache Tomcat.

Installing the auxiliary file

There is one auxiliary file that you must install on Apache Tomcat. The file is itext_1.3.jar and you must place it in the following directory:

```
$TOMCAT_INSTALL/birt/WebViewerExample/WEB-INF/platform/
    plugins/com.lowagie.itext/lib
```

You can download itext_1.3.jar from:

```
http://prdownloads.sourceforge.net/itext/itext-1.3.jar
```

Installing your JDBC drivers

Add the JAR files for your JDBC drivers to the following directory:

```
$TOMCAT_INSTALL/birt/WEB-INF/platform/plugins/
    org.eclipse.birt.report.data.oda.jdbc/drivers
```

Testing the BIRT report viewer installation

To test the installation of the BIRT report viewer, type the following URL in a web browser address:

```
http://server_name/birt
```

where *server_name* is the name of the application server.

There is a JavaServer Page (JSP) called index.jsp in both the WAR file and in the /birt directory. There is also a simple BIRT report design file, test.rptdesign, in both the WAR file and the /birt directory. If the BIRT report viewer is installed correctly, Tomcat uses index.jsp to process the report design file and generate the report described by the design file.

Using a different context root for the BIRT report viewer

By default, the context root of the URL for a web application is the path to the application directory or the WAR file. The default application directory for the BIRT report viewer is /birt, so the default URL to access a BIRT report from Apache Tomcat is:

```
http://localhost:8080/birt/run?__report=myReport.rptdesign
```

To change the BIRT context root, change the name of the /birt directory or the WAR file in $TOMCAT_INSTALL/webapps. After making this change, you must restart Apache Tomcat. Whatever name you choose, specify that name in the URL to access your BIRT report. For example, if you choose reportViewer, the URL to access a BIRT report becomes:

```
http://localhost:8080/reportViewer/
    run?__report=myReport.rptdesign
```

The URL examples shown in this section access the report design with a relative path. You must set the BIRT_VIEWER_WORKING_FOLDER variable to access the report design with relative paths.

Placing the viewer in a different location

If you choose to place the BIRT report viewer in a location other than $TOMCAT_INSTALL/webapps, you must add a context mapping entry to the server.xml file in $TOMCAT_INSTALL/conf.

To add a context mapping entry, add the following lines to server.xml just above the </host> tag near the end of the file:

```
<Context path="/birt"
    docBase="BIRT_Path"/>
```

where BIRT_Path is the absolute path to the directory containing the BIRT report viewer.

Save your changes to server.xml and restart Apache Tomcat to make your changes active.

Mapping the folders that the BIRT report viewer uses

To determine the locations for report designs, images in reports, and log files, the BIRT report viewer uses context parameters defined in the web.xml file. Table 5-1 describes the context parameters for mapping folders. The default values of some of the context parameters described in the table depend on whether the application is deployed as a WAR file or a folder structure. When an application is deployed as a WAR file, the application is referred to as a WAR deployment. When an application is deployed as a folder structure, the application is referred to as a non-WAR deployment.

Table 5-1   BIRT context parameters

Parameter	Description	Default value
BIRT_VIEWER _IMAGE_DIR	Required for WAR deployment. Optional for non-WAR deployment. Absolute path to a writable directory for creating images and chart representations for a report.	No default value for WAR deployment <context root> /report/images for non-WAR deployment
BIRT_VIEWER _LOG_DIR	Optional. Absolute path to a writable directory for BIRT Report Engine log messages. For WAR deployment, BIRT Report Engine logs messages only when this parameter has a value.	No default value for WAR deployment <context root>/logs for non-WAR deployment
BIRT_VIEWER _WORKING _FOLDER	Optional. Absolute path to a writable directory for report designs and temporary files. Specifying report designs by relative path is possible only when this parameter has a value.	No default value for either WAR deployment or non-WAR deployment
BIRT_VIEWER _SCRIPTLIB _DIR	Optional. Absolute path to a directory containing Java event handler JAR files.	No default value for WAR deployment <context root> /scriptlib for non-WAR deployment
BIRT_VIEWER _LOG_LEVEL	Defines the level of error logging, using the standard Java logging level identifiers. Allowable values are ALL, CONFIG, FINE, FINER, FINEST, INFO, OFF, SEVERE, WARNING. For more information about the logging levels, see the Javadoc for java.util.logging.Level.	OFF for both WAR deployment and non-WAR deployment

How to set the location for report designs

You can avoid including the full path to the report design in the URL if you define BIRT_VIEWER_WORKING_FOLDER in the BIRT report viewer application's web.xml file.

1 Navigate to $TOMCAT_INSTALL/webapps.

2 Open web.xml in a code editor.

To open web.xml in an editor, perform one of the following steps, based on your deployment configuration:

- If you use a WAR file to deploy the BIRT report viewer, extract web-inf/web.xml from birt.war into a temporary location.

- If you use a folder to deploy the BIRT report viewer, navigate to birt/WEB-INF.

3 Locate the following element:

```
<context-param>
    <param-name>BIRT_VIEWER_WORKING_FOLDER</param-name>
    <param-value />
</context-param>
```

4 Change the param-value element, so that it includes the absolute path to the folder for the report designs:

```
<context-param>
    <param-name>BIRT_VIEWER_WORKING_FOLDER</param-name>
    <param-value>Report_Folder</param-value>
</context-param>
```

where *Report_Folder* is the absolute path to the folder for the report designs.

5 If you prefer not to use the default directory for event handler JAR files, define the desired path by creating or modifying the following context parameter:

```
<context-param>
    <param-name>BIRT_VIEWER_SCRIPTLIB_DIR</param-name>
    <param-value>Event_Handlers</param-value>
</context-param>
```

where *Event_Handlers* is the absolute path to the folder containing the event handler JAR files.

6 Save web.xml and close the editor.

7 If you use a WAR file to deploy the BIRT report viewer, replace web-inf/web.xml in birt.war with the name of the file you just modified.

8 Copy your report designs into the folder you specified in the param-value element for BIRT_VIEWER_WORKING_FOLDER.

9 If your report uses Java event handler classes, copy the JAR files containing the event handler classes into <BIRT_VIEWER_SCRIPTLIB_DIR>.

10 Restart Apache Tomcat.

Verifying that Apache Tomcat is running BIRT report viewer

To verify that Apache Tomcat is running BIRT report viewer, run the Tomcat manager. To run the Tomcat manager, you need a manager's account. If you have not already set up a Tomcat manager account, you can do so by adding the following two lines to $TOMCAT_INSTALL/conf/tomcat-users.xml:

```
<role rolename="manager"/>
<user username="admin" password="tomcat" roles="manager"/>
```

Once you have a manager's account open the Tomcat account manager by opening the Tomcat main page, which for a typical Apache Tomcat installation is http://localhost:8080, shown in Figure 5-1.

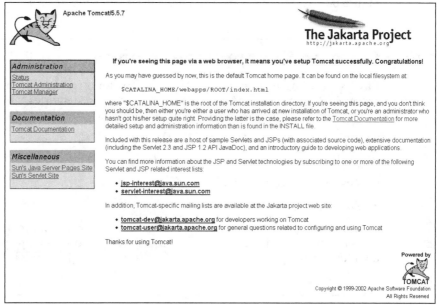

Figure 5-1   Apache Tomcat home page

On the Tomcat main page, choose Tomcat Manager. In the manager login window, supply the username and password from the manager account entry in tomcat-users.xml file. The Running status for the Eclipse BIRT report viewer is true, as shown in Figure 5-2.

| Tomcat Web Application Manager | | | | | | The Tomcat Serv |

Tomcat Web Application Manager

| Message: | OK | | | | | | |

Manager

| List Applications | HTML Manager Help | Manager Help | Server Status |

Applications

Path	Display Name	Running	Sessions	Commands			
/	Welcome to Tomcat	true	0	Start	Stop	Reload	Undeploy
/admin	Tomcat Administration Application	true	0	Start	Stop	Reload	Undeploy
/balancer	Tomcat Simple Load Balancer Example App	true	0	Start	Stop	Reload	Undeploy
/birt-viewer	Eclipse BIRT Report Viewer	true	0	Start	Stop	Reload	Undeploy

Figure 5-2   Running status for the Eclipse BIRT report viewer

Placing fonts on the application server

BIRT Report Engine requires certain TrueType fonts in order to display a PDF report. BIRT searches for fonts in the common font directories for Windows and Linux. The list of directories that BIRT searches is quite long but includes:

- /windows/fonts for drives A through G

- /WINNT/fonts for drives A through G

- /usr/share/fonts/default/TrueType

- /usr/share/fonts/truetype

If your PDF reports appear to be missing content, you can place the appropriate fonts in any of the directories in the preceding list. You also can specify your own font search path by creating the environment variable BIRT_FONT_PATH.

Viewing a report using a browser

Once you deploy the BIRT report viewer to your J2EE container, you can access your BIRT reports using a web browser. To view a BIRT report using a browser, you navigate to a URL having one of the following two formats:

```
http://localhost:8080/birt/run?parameter_list
http://localhost:8080/birt/frameset?parameter_list
```

where *parameter_list* is a list of URL parameters.

For more information about the URL parameters that you can use, see the section about URL parameters, later in this chapter.

Understanding the run and frameset servlets

When you use the run servlet, it displays the report as a stand-alone web page or a PDF file. If the report requires parameters, you must specify them in the URL.

When you use the frameset servlet, the browser displays a page with a toolbar with four buttons to do the following tasks:

- Print the report.

- Display a table of contents.

- Display a parameters dialog.

- Display a dialog for exporting data.

Using the URL parameters for the run and frameset servlets

The parameter list for the run and frameset servlets must contain the __report parameter. The other parameters are optional.

Table 5-2 lists the URL parameters for accessing BIRT reports.

Table 5-2   URL parameters for accessing BIRT reports

Parameter	Values	Required?	Default value
__report	Path to report design file	The URL must contain either a __report parameter or a __document parameter.	No default
__document	Path to document file	The URL must contain either a __report parameter or a __document parameter.	No default
__format	html or pdf	Optional	html
__locale	Locale code	Optional	JVM locale
__isnull	Any user-defined report parameter values	Optional	Not applicable
__svg	true or false	No	false
Other report parameters	User-defined	As specified in the report design	As specified in the report design

__report parameter

The __report parameter specifies the name and location of the report design file for the report you want to display. If the URL contains a __report parameter, a new report document file is generated from the report design file specified by this parameter. The URL must contain either a __report parameter or a __document parameter, but not both.

The path can be either absolute or relative. If you specify an absolute path, the servlet uses that absolute path. If the path is relative, the location depends on whether the working folder parameter, BIRT_VIEWER_WORKING_FOLDER, is defined in the web.xml file. If the working folder parameter is defined in web.xml, the base for the relative path is the path that the working folder parameter specifies. If your application is deployed as a folder structure instead of a WAR file and the working folder parameter is not defined in web.xml, then the base for the relative path defaults to $TOMCAT_INSTALL/webapps/birt. If your application is deployed using a WAR file, BIRT_VIEWER_WORKING_FOLDER must specify a value.

The following three examples of a __report parameter illustrate the possibilities:

- The path to the report is an absolute path and the parameter is:

  ```
  __report=C:\myReport.rptdesign
  ```

  The report path is:

  ```
  C:\myReport.rptdesign
  ```

  The path in this example is absolute, so the value of BIRT_VIEWER_WORKING_FOLDER is not relevant.

- The path to the report is relative, BIRT_VIEWER_WORKING_FOLDER is not defined in web.xml, and the parameter is:

  ```
  __report=Report\myReport.rptdesign
  ```

  The path to this report is:

  ```
  $TOMCAT_INSTALL1\webapps\birt\Report\myReport.rptdesign
  ```

- The path to the report is relative, BIRT_VIEWER_WORKING_FOLDER is defined as C:\Reports, and the parameter is:

  ```
  __report=myReport.rptdesign
  ```

  The path to this report is:

  ```
  C:\Reports\myReport.rptdesign
  ```

__document parameter

The __document parameter specifies the name and location of the report document file for the report you want to display. If the __document parameter is present, the report viewer displays the report encapsulated in the specified file. The URL must contain either a __report parameter or a __document parameter, but not both. The rules for specifying the name and location of the report document file are the same as the rules for specifying a report design file, as explained in the previous section.

__format parameter

Use the __format parameter to specify whether the report should display as an HTML page or as a PDF document.

__locale parameter

Use the __locale parameter to specify a Java locale, such as en for English or ch-zh for Chinese. The choice of locale affects the language in which certain report items appear in the report. The report items that have internationalization capability are those whose ROM elements contain a resource property.

__isnull parameter

Use the __isnull parameter to specify that one of the other optional parameters is null. The following rules govern the setting of parameter values:

- If you include __isnull=*parameterName* in the URL and this parameter does not appear elsewhere in the URL, then *parameterName* takes the value null, which, in this context, means unknown.

- If you include __isnull=*parameterName* in the URL but this parameter is also set to a value in the URL, then *parameterName* takes the value of a blank string.

- If you do not include __isnull=*parameterName* in the URL and this parameter is set to a value in the URL, then *parameterName* takes the value assigned in the URL.

- If you do not include __isnull=*parameterName* in the URL and this parameter does not appear elsewhere in the URL, then *parameterName* is assigned its default value.

__svg parameter

Use the __svg parameter to enable Scalable Vector Graphics (SVG) support in the report engine when the browser does not contain SVG support. SVG support is only relevant for charts and the __svg parameter is only relevant for the run servlet, not the frameset servlet. A parameter value of true enables SVG support.

Report parameters

Report parameters are parameters that the report developer creates when designing the report. BIRT Report Designer includes report parameters in the report design file.

Understanding the BIRT Framework

6

Understanding the BIRT Architecture

BIRT consists of many components that relate to one another in various ways. This chapter provides an overview of the BIRT architecture, the BIRT components, the Eclipse components upon which BIRT relies, and the relationships that tie them all together.

Understanding the BIRT integration

BIRT is an Eclipse project, which means that it is tightly integrated with Eclipse frameworks and platforms. Like all Eclipse projects, BIRT is implemented as a set of Eclipse plug-ins. The BIRT plug-ins provide the functionality for all BIRT components, including BIRT applications, the engines that drive the applications, and supporting application programming interfaces (APIs). The BIRT plug-ins also provide the interface mechanism for communicating with several Eclipse frameworks and platforms.

The relationships between BIRT and the Eclipse components are best viewed as a stack, where each tier in the stack depends upon, uses, and integrates with the tier below it. Figure 6-1 illustrates this stack of dependent tiers.

Figure 6-2 illustrates the various BIRT components and how they relate to one another. In this diagram, a component in a solid box is a standard BIRT component. A component in a dashed box is a custom component that a Java developer can provide. Some custom components are extensions of BIRT and other custom components are applications that use the BIRT APIs. A component in a dotted box is a standard BIRT component that the containing component uses. For example, because BIRT Report Designer uses the design engine, the design engine appears in a dotted box within the box for BIRT Report Designer.

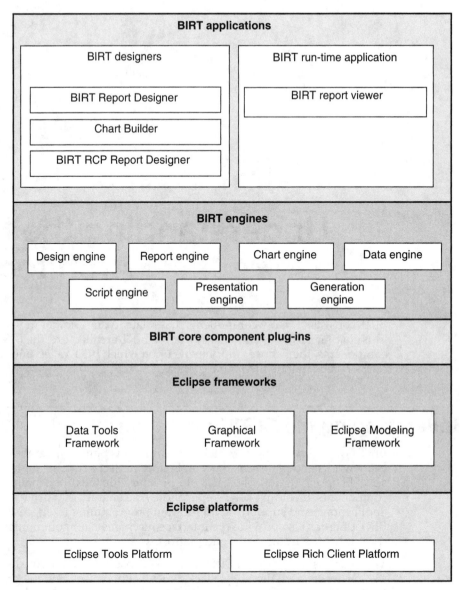

Figure 6-1   BIRT components as plug-ins to the Eclipse platform

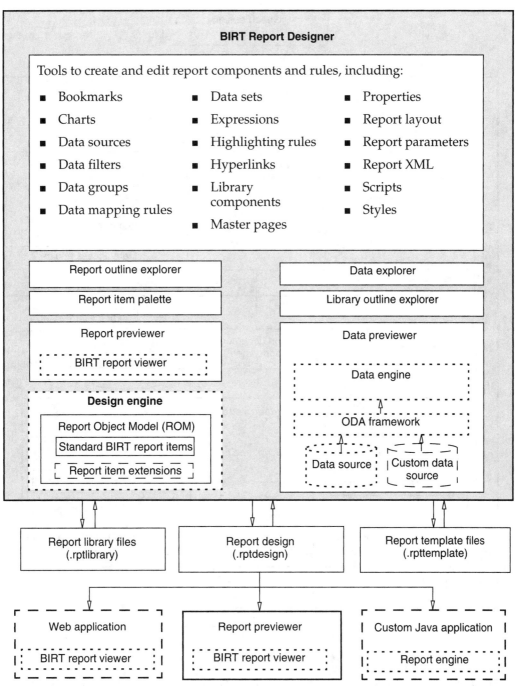

Figure 6-2 Relationships of standard BIRT components and custom components *(continued)*

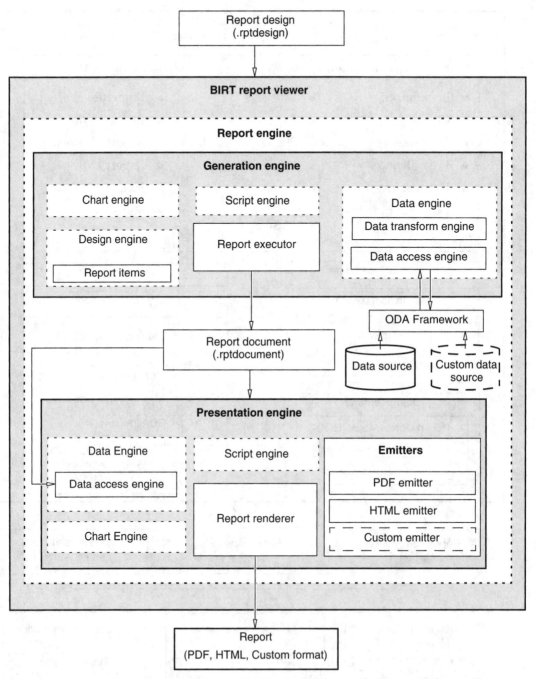

Figure 6-2   Relationships of standard BIRT components and custom components

About the BIRT applications

There are three BIRT applications: BIRT Report Designer, BIRT RCP Report Designer, and the BIRT report viewer. BIRT Report Designer and BIRT RCP Report Designer are very similar. BIRT Report Designer runs as an Eclipse plug-in and lets you build reports within the Eclipse workbench. BIRT RCP Report Designer has a simplified report design interface based on Eclipse RCP.

About BIRT Report Designer and BIRT RCP Report Designer

BIRT Report Designer is a graphical report design tool. BIRT Report Designer uses the report design engine to generate a report design file based on the ROM. ROM supports the standard set of BIRT report items and custom report items.

BIRT RCP Report Designer has a simplified report design interface based on Eclipse RCP. The primary functional differences between the BIRT RCP Report Designer and BIRT Report Designer are:

- BIRT RCP Report Designer can only have one design open at a time.

- BIRT RCP Report Designer has no integrated debugger.

- BIRT RCP Report Designer does not support Java event handlers.

Other than these differences, the functionality of the two report designers is identical and all further mentions of BIRT Report Designer in this chapter apply equally to BIRT RCP Report Designer.

BIRT Report Designer also supports the reuse of a report design by saving it as a template. You can also save individual report components in a component library, which is accessible to other report designs.

About the BIRT report viewer

The BIRT report viewer is a web application servlet that prepares and delivers a BIRT report. The BIRT report viewer uses the generation engine and the report design to create a report document. The report viewer then uses the report document and the presentation engine to generate the desired report.

The report previewer that is a part of the BIRT Report Designer uses the BIRT report viewer to preview a report. A web application can also use the BIRT report viewer, after you deploy the BIRT report viewer to an application server.

You can deploy the BIRT report viewer to the J2EE container of your choice, such as Apache Tomcat, IBM WebSphere, or BEA WebLogic.

About the BIRT engines

BIRT contains several engines. An engine is a set of Java APIs that provide functionality in a specific domain. For example, the data engine contains the APIs for managing data and the chart engine contains APIs to generate a chart.

About the report design engine

The report design engine contains the APIs for validating and generating a report design file. The report design engine is used by BIRT Report Designer and by any custom Java application that generates a BIRT report design. The generation engine also uses the report design engine when building the report document. The design engine contains APIs to validate the elements and structure of the design file against the ROM specification.

About the report engine

The report engine consists of two parts, the generation engine and the presentation engine. The BIRT report viewer and custom Java applications use the report engine to process a report design and generate a report in the format specified in the design.

About the generation engine

The generation engine consists of APIs for reading and interpreting a report design. The generation engine uses the data engine to retrieve and transform data from the data sources identified in the report design. The output of the generation engine is a report document, which is an intermediate document in the production of a report.

About the presentation engine

The presentation engine processes the report document created by the generation engine and produces the report in the format specified in the design.

Like the generation engine, the presentation engine uses the data engine. During the presentation stage, however, the data engine retrieves data from the report document rather than from a data source.

The presentation engine uses whichever report emitter it requires to generate a report in the format specified in the design. BIRT has two standard emitters, HTML and PDF. BIRT also supports custom emitters for formats other than HTML or PDF.

Chart report items and custom report items extend the presentation engine to provide display capability for those items.

About the chart engine

The chart engine contains APIs for generating charts and associating them with data from a data source. The use of the chart engine is not restricted to a BIRT application. Any Java application can use the chart engine APIs to create and display a chart. The BIRT report viewer interprets the chart design information in the report design and uses the chart engine to generate the chart.

About the data engine

The data engine contains the APIs to retrieve and transform data. When used by the generation engine, the data engine retrieves data directly from the data source. When used by the presentation engine, the data engine retrieves data from the report document.

About data engine components

The data engine consists of two primary components, the data access component and the data transform component. The data access component communicates with the ODA framework to retrieve data. The data transform component of the data engine performs such operations as sorting, grouping, aggregating, and filtering the data returned from the data access component.

About the ODA framework

The ODA framework manages ODA and native drivers, loads drivers, opens connections, and manages data requests. The ODA framework uses the Eclipse Data Tools Platform project to manage connections.

The ODA framework contains extension points through which you can add a custom ODA driver. The data engine extension provides the connection method and the driver for the data source. A custom ODA driver is necessary if you have a data source that BIRT does not support. When you create a custom ODA driver you may need to extend not only the data engine but also BIRT Report Designer. A BIRT Report Designer extension is necessary if the data source requires a GUI component to specify the data set.

About the types of BIRT report items

A report item is a visual component of a report, such as a label or a list or a chart. There are three categories of report items in BIRT: standard report items, custom report items, and the chart report item.

About standard report items

A report item is a visual component of a report. A report item can be as simple as a label or as complex as a 3D chart. Every report item has an icon on BIRT Report Designer Palette.

About custom report items

You can create new report items and you can extend an existing report item. An example of a simple extension to a report item is adding a property, such as color. An example of a new report item extension is the rotated text report item, which is a reference implementation of a report item extension.

Creating a new report item and extending an existing report item both involve extending BIRT through the Eclipse plug-in mechanism. Some custom items require an extension to a single component, while other custom items require extensions to multiple components. Depending on the report item, one or more of the following components may require an extension to support the new item:

- BIRT Report Designer
- The report design engine
- The report engine

About chart report items

A chart report item is a standard BIRT component, but it is implemented as a BIRT extension. The user interface for creating a chart report item is a chart builder that steps the report developer through the process of designing the chart and associating it with the appropriate database columns.

About the ROM

ROM is the model upon which BIRT is based. ROM is a specification for the structure, syntax, and semantics of the report design. The ROM specification appears in a series of documents on the BIRT web site at:

```
http://www.eclipse.org/birt/ref
```

The formal expression of ROM is through an XML schema and a semantic definition file.

About the types of BIRT files

BIRT Report Designer uses four types of files: report design files, report document files, report library files, and report template files. The following sections provide a brief overview of each of these file types.

About report design files

A report design file is an XML file that contains the report design, the complete description of a BIRT report. The report design describes every aspect of a report, including its structure, format, data sources, data sets, and JavaScript event handler code. BIRT Report Designer creates the report design file and BIRT report engine processes it. The file extension of a report design file is .rptdesign.

About report document files

A report document file is a binary file that encapsulates the report design, incorporates the data, and contains additional information, such as data rows, pagination information, and table of contents information. The file extension of a report document file is .rptdocument.

About report library files

A report library file is an XML file that contains reusable and shareable BIRT report components. A report developer uses the library outline explorer in BIRT Report Designer to manage access to and additions to the library.

A BIRT report library can contain such items as:

- Embedded images
- Styles
- Visual report items
- Code
- Data sources
- Data sets

The file extension of a report library file is .rptlibrary.

About report template files

A report template is an XML file that contains a reusable design. A report developer can use the template as a basis for developing a new report. A report developer uses a report template to maintain a consistent style across a set of report designs and for streamlining the report design process. A report template can specify many different elements of a report, including:

- One or more data sources
- One or more data sets
- Part or all of the layout of a report design, including grids, tables, lists, and other report items

- Grouping, filtering, and data binding definitions
- Cheat sheets
- Styles
- Library components
- Master page

A template is a flexible tool for report development. For example, one template can specify almost every aspect of a report design, while another can specify just a table format. A report template can be personalized after the report developer uses it to create the report design. Report templates are useful for maintaining a consistent style across a set of report designs and for streamlining the report design process.

The file extension of a report template file is .rpttemplate.

About custom Java applications

Java developers can use the BIRT APIs to create a custom report designer or a custom report viewer.

About custom report designers

A custom report designer is a Java application that a Java developer creates to generate a well-formed report design file based on specific requirements. A custom report designer does not necessarily include a user interface. A typical example of a custom report designer is a Java application that dynamically determines the content, structure, or data source for a report, based on business logic. A custom report designer uses the same design engine API as BIRT Report Designer.

About custom Java report generators

A custom Java report generator performs the same function as the BIRT report generator, except that it is typically integrated into either a web application or a stand-alone Java application. Like the BIRT report viewer web application, a custom Java report generator uses the API of the report engine to read a report design file and generate a report. A custom Java report generator can use business logic to manage security issues, control content, and determine the output format.

About extensions to BIRT

Through its public APIs and the BIRT extension framework, BIRT enables a Java developer to expand the capabilities of BIRT. A list of possible custom extensions includes:

- A custom report item

  A custom report item is a report item extension. This report item can be an extension, an existing BIRT report item, or a new report item.

- A custom ODA data source driver

  A custom ODA data source driver is a custom ODA extension that connects to a data source type other than those that BIRT directly supports.

- A custom report emitter

  A custom report emitter generates a report in a format other than HTML or PDF.

Understanding the Report Object Model

This chapter provides an overview of the BIRT ROM and the primary elements that comprise the model. ROM defines the rules for constructing a valid report design file in much the same way that HTML defines the rules for constructing a valid web page. ROM, therefore, is the model for the BIRT report design file in the same way that HTML is the model for the web page. For information about every component of ROM, see the online help entry at Help→Help Contents→BIRT Developer Guide→Reference→Report Object Model (ROM) Definitions Reference.

About the ROM specification

The ROM specification defines a set of XML elements for describing both the visual and non-visual components of a report. Visual elements include items that appear in a report, such as a table, list, or label. Non-visual elements include such things as report parameters, data sources, and data sets.

The XML file that BIRT Report Designer generates to describe a report consists entirely of ROM elements. The ROM specification defines the elements, their properties, and an element's relationship to other elements. ROM elements describe:

- The report page layout

- The placement, size, style, and structure of report items

- The data source and query with which to populate a report

ROM properties

ROM elements can have properties and every property has a type. Property types are similar to variable types in programming or data types in database terminology. Like variables and data types, ROM property types can be simple or complex. Simple types include string, number, dimension, color, and so forth. Complex types include structure and list. A complex type contains more than one component. For example, a text type contains both the text and a resource key used for internationalizing the text.

The components of a ROM property are:

- Property values

  Most elements have simple properties that are defined by a name-value pair. There are several property types, described later in this section.

- User-defined property definitions

  The userProperties array provides a way for users to define custom properties. Each item in the array is a UserProperty object.

- Executable expressions

  The methods array is an associative array of method names. The method name is the key into the array. The return value is a string that contains the method text.

The property types defined in ROM include:

- property

  This property type is the simplest and most common property type. A property definition of this type has the following syntax:

  ```
  <property name="propName">value</property>
  ```

- property-list

  This property type defines a set of properties, such as custom colors. A property definition of the property-list type has the following syntax:

  ```
  <property-list name="propName">
  [ <structure> ... </structure> ] *
  </property-list>
  ```

- xml-property

  This property type defines custom XML. A property definition of the xml-property type has the following syntax:

  ```
  <xml-property name="propName">value</xml-property>
  ```

- expression

  The value for this property type is an expression. A property definition of the expression type has the following syntax:

  ```
  <expression name="propName">value</expression>
  ```

- ex-property

  This property type is useful for defining properties that do not have well-formed property names. A property definition of the ex-property type has the following syntax:

  ```
  <ex-property>
     <name>propName</name>
     <value>value</value>
  </ex-property>
  ```

- structure

  This property is a collection of two or more properties. A property definition of the structure type has the following syntax:

  ```
  <structure name="propName">
     <property name="member1">value1</property>
     <property name="member2">value2</property>
  </structure>
  ```

ROM slots

A ROM slot is a collection of identically typed elements. For example, a report element has a slot of style elements that comprise all the styles available to the report.

ROM methods

A ROM element can have one or more methods, called event handlers. BIRT fires many different events during the course of executing a report. When BIRT fires an event, the appropriate event handler is executed to handle the event. By default, event handlers are empty methods that do nothing. By supplying code for an event handler, a report developer can customize and extend the functionality of BIRT. Supplying code for an event handler is called scripting. An event handler can be scripted in either JavaScript or Java.

Report items have four events: onPrepare, onCreate, onPageBreak, and onRender. Each of these events fires during different phases of report creation. The onPrepare event fires in the preparation phase. The onCreate event fires during the generation phase. The onRender and onPageBreak events fire during the presentation phase.

Report items are not the only ROM elements to have event handler methods. BIRT online help contains a complete reference for all the ROM elements and their properties and methods.

ROM styles

The ROM style system is based on cascading style sheets (CSS), where a style set in a container cascades to its contents. The Report element contains all other elements, so the style property of the Report element defines the default style for the entire report. An element within the report can override the default style. A report developer can either choose a style from a defined set of styles or create a new style. Typical style attributes include color, text size, alignment, background image, and so forth. For more information about the styles, see the ROM reference in the BIRT online help.

About the ROM schema

The ROM specification is encapsulated in a schema written in the language of XML Schema. XML Schema provides a standard way of defining the structure, content, and semantics of an XML file. XML Schema is similar to Document Type Definition (DTD).

The ROM schema, therefore, contains the formal expression of the content, structure, and semantics of the ROM report design. The ROM schema is located at:

```
http://www.eclipse.org/birt/2005/design
```

A statement similar to the following statement appears at the top of every report design file:

```
<report xmlns="http://www.eclipse.org/birt/2005/design"
    version="3.2.2" id="1">
```

This statement identifies the schema upon which BIRT bases the report design. If the design contains elements extraneous to or in violation of the rules set forth in the schema, it is not a valid design.

Opening a report design file with a schema-aware tool such as XMLSpy provides a means of verifying the report design against the schema. Using a schema-aware tool also can help a developer of a custom report designer to verify the output of the custom report designer.

The ROM schema defines syntax that allows extensions to BIRT without making changes to the actual schema. For example, an extended item uses the following tag:

```
<extended-item name="extension">
```

The ROM schema defines properties using the following syntax:

```
<property name="propertyName">value</property>
```

The ROM schema describes a syntax for representing properties. The ROM schema does not define any actual properties. ROM element properties are defined in another file, rom.def.

About the rom.def file

The rom.def file contains metadata defining the specific ROM elements, their properties, their slots, and their methods. You can find rom.def in:

```
$INSTALL_DIR\eclipse\plugins
    \org.eclipse.birt.report.model_2.1.0.jar
```

The rom.def file is an internal file that the design engine uses to present a property sheet for a ROM element. The property sheet for an element contains the element's properties and their types, the element's methods, and valid choice selections for each of the element's properties.

The rom.def file specifies the following kinds of metadata:

- Choice

  A choice definition specifies all the allowable values that an attribute can have. Most choice definitions relate to style attributes. The following example from rom.def defines all the allowable font families available to a fontFamily style specification.

  ```
  <ChoiceType name="fontFamily">
    <Choice displayNameID="Choices.fontFamily.serif"
      name="serif" />
    <Choice displayNameID="Choices.fontFamily.sans-serif"
      name="sans-serif" />
    <Choice displayNameID="Choices.fontFamily.cursive"
      name="cursive" />
    <Choice displayNameID="Choices.fontFamily.fantasy"
      name="fantasy" />
    <Choice displayNameID="Choices.fontFamily.monospace"
      name="monospace" />
  </ChoiceType>
  ```

- Class

  A class definition defines a Java class that a report designer application can access using the BIRT model API. There are class descriptions for data types, such as String, Date, and Array. There are also class descriptions for the functional classes such as Total, Finance, and DateTimeSpan. Finally, there are class definitions for the report object definitions, such as Report, DataSet, DataSource, ReportDefn, and ColumnDefn. A class definition consists of definitions of the class attributes, methods, and localization identifiers. The following example from rom.def defines the Report class.

  ```
  <Class displayNameID="Class.Report" name="Report"
    toolTipID="Class.Report.toolTip">
    <Member dataType="ReportDefn"
      displayNameID="Class.Report.design" name="design"
      toolTipID="Class.Report.design.toolTip" />
    <Member dataType="Object[]"
  ```

```
        displayNameID="Class.Report.params" name="params"
        toolTipID="Class.Report.params.toolTip" />
      <Member dataType="Object[]"
        displayNameID="Class.Report.config" name="config"
        toolTipID="Class.Report.config.toolTip" />
    </Class>
```

The preceding class definition does not have methods. The following
example illustrates a class method definition.

```
<Method displayNameID="Class.Total.sum" isStatic="true"
    name="sum" returnType="number"
    toolTipID="Class.Total.sum.toolTip">
    <Argument name="expr" tagID="Class.Total.sum.expr"
        type="number" />
    <Argument name="filter" tagID="Class.Total.sum.filter"
        type="String" />
    <Argument name="group" tagID="Class.Total.sum.group"
        type="String" />
</Method>
```

- Element

    An element definition consists of the element's name, display name,
    methods, and properties, as well as the element from which it inherits. The
    rom.def file contains an element definition for every ROM element. The
    following example from the rom.def file illustrates an element definition.

```
<Element canExtend="true"
    displayNameID="Element.OdaDataSource"
    extends="DataSource"
    isAbstract="false" isNameRequired="true"
    javaClass="org.eclipse.birt.report.model.elements
        .OdaDataSource" name="OdaDataSource" since="1.0"
    xmlName="oda-data-source">
    <Property
        displayNameID="Element.OdaDataSource.extensionID"
        isIntrinsic="true" name="extensionID" since="1.0"
        type="string" />
    <Property detailType="ExtendedProperty"
        displayNameID=
        "Element.OdaDataSource.privateDriverProperties"
        isList="true" name="privateDriverProperties"
        since="1.0"
        type="structure" />
    <PropertyVisibility name="extensionID"
        visibility="hide" />
    <PropertyVisibility name="privateDriverProperties"
        visibility="hide" />
</Element>
```

The preceding element definition does not contain any methods. The
following example illustrates an element method definition.

```
<Method context="factory"
    displayNameID="Element.ScriptDataSource.open"
    name="open" since="1.0"
    toolTipID="Element.ScriptDataSource.open.toolTip">
    <Argument name="reportContext"
        tagID="Element.ScriptDataSet.open.reportContext"
        type="org.eclipse.birt.report.engine.api.script
            .IReportContext" />
    <Argument name="object"
        tagID="Element.ScriptDataSet.open.object"
        type="Object" />
</Method>
```

- Structure

    A structure is a complex data type that usually consists of two or more
    members. A few structures that are candidates for future expansion have
    only a single member. The following example from the rom.def file
    illustrates the definition of a structure.

```
<Structure displayNameID="Structure.DateTimeFormatValue"
    name="DateTimeFormatValue" since="1.0">
    <Member detailType="dateTimeFormat"
        displayNameID="Structure.DateTimeFormatValue.category"
        isIntrinsic="true" name="category" since="1.0"
        type="choice" />
    <Member
        displayNameID="Structure.DateTimeFormatValue.pattern"
        isIntrinsic="true" name="pattern" since="1.0"
        type="string" />
</Structure>
```

- Style

    A style definition contains the least information of any type of metadata
    described in rom.def. A style definition defines the name of the style, its
    display name, and a reference value. The following example illustrates a
    style definition.

```
<Style displayNameID="Style.Report" name="report"
    reference="Overall default" />
```

- Validator

    A validator definition specifies a Java class with which to do validation. Two
    of the validator classes are for validating values and all the rest are semantic

validators. The following example from rom.def shows how to specify a validator.

```
<SemanticValidator
  class="org.eclipse.birt.report.model.api.validators
    .DataSetResultSetValidator"
  modules="design, library"
  name="DataSetResultSetValidator" />
```

About the primary ROM elements

The primary ROM elements consist of abstract elements from which other elements derive and concrete elements that provide the overall report definition. The following elements are the primary components that form the basis for understanding ROM:

- DesignElement

  The DesignElement element is an internal, abstract element used to implement basic features of ROM elements. DesignElement represents anything that has properties.

- Listing

  The Listing element is the abstract base element for lists and tables. Both elements support a data set, filtering, sorting, methods, and so forth.

- MasterPage

  The MasterPage element is an abstract base element that defines the basic properties of a page.

- ReportDesign

  The ReportDesign element contains information about a report design, defining properties that describe the design as a whole. Report design properties do not inherit because a design cannot extend another design.

- ReportElement

  The ReportElement element is an abstract report element that represents anything that can be named and customized. Most of the major components in ROM derive from ReportElement, including the elements visible in the user interface, such as data sets, styles, master pages, report items, and so forth.

- ReportItem

  The ReportItem element is the base element for the visual elements. A report item includes a style. The style provides visual characteristics for anything that prints in a report: a section or report item.

About the report item elements

There are many types of visual report components. Every type of visual report component has a corresponding ROM element that derives from the ReportItem element. Visual report components are called report items.

About the report items

There are top-level and low-level report items. The top-level items are items that can contain other items. Examples of top-level items include:

- List

  A list contains a set of arbitrary content based upon data retrieved from a data set. A list is appropriate when some report items require a sophisticated layout and then repeat that layout for each row in a query.

- Table

  A table contains a tabular layout of data retrieved from a data set.

- Text

  Text contains a block of text with centered headings, paragraphs, and so forth.

- Grid

  A grid contains a set of report items arranged into a grid with a fixed set of columns and a variable number of rows. Each cell in the grid can contain a single item or a container of items.

Lower level layout items have properties that describe them in various ways, but they are not structural and do not contain other items. For example, the Image element is not a container of other elements.

Understanding the report item element properties

The elements that derive from ReportItem are called the report item elements. Every report item has an entry in the palette, the visual BIRT Report Designer component that the report developer uses to build a report layout.

Each visual component has its own set of properties in addition to the properties it inherits from ReportItem. The types of inherited report item properties include:

- Method

  Defines executable code.

- Property

  Includes such things as names and dimensions.

- Slot

  Contains Type elements that define its contents, as shown in the following element definition.

  ```
  <Slot name="reportItems"
     displayNameID="Element.FreeForm.slot.reportItems"
     multipleCardinality="true">
         <Type name="Label" />
         <Type name="Data" />
         <Type name="Text" />
  </Slot>
  ```

- StyleProperty

  Defines style-related characteristics, such as color and font size.

About the data elements

There are several elements in the ROM specification that apply to data rather than visual report items. These data elements describe data sources, data sets, and rows of data. The following elements are data elements:

- DataSource

  The DataSource element represents a connection to an external data system, such as an RDBMS, text file, or XML file.

- ScriptedDataSource

  The ScriptedDataSource element represents a connection to an external data system that is not an ODA data source. The developer must provide scripts for opening and closing a scripted data source. ScriptedDataSource inherits from DataSource.

- DataSet

  The DataSet element represents a tabular result set retrieved from a data source. A DataSet element defines a query, filters, parameters, and result set columns.

- JointDataSet

  The JointDataSet element represents a data set that results from a join of several data sets.

- ScriptedDataSet

  The ScriptedDataSet element represents a data set that is associated with a scripted data source. The developer must provide scripts for opening, closing, and fetching a row from a scripted data source. ScriptedDataSet inherits from DataSet.

- Row

  The Row element represents an integral set of column values that are a part of a result set.

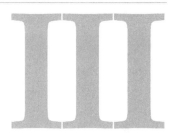

Scripting in a Report Design

8

Using Scripting in a Report Design

BIRT provides a powerful scripting capability with which a report developer can provide custom code to control various aspects of report generation.

Overview of BIRT scripting

When developing a BIRT report using the Eclipse workbench, you can write custom event handlers in either Java or JavaScript. When developing a BIRT report using the Eclipse RCP, you can write only JavaScript event handlers. Whether you use Java or JavaScript, the set of event handlers that you can write is the same.

Choosing between Java and JavaScript

Both Java and JavaScript have advantages and disadvantages when writing an event handler. For a developer who is familiar with only one of the two languages, the advantage of using the familiar language is obvious but for all others, the decision depends on the report requirements.

The advantages of using JavaScript to write an event handler include:

■ Ease of adding a simple script for a particular event handler

Adding a JavaScript event handler to a report is less complicated than adding a Java event handler. When writing a JavaScript event handler, there is no need to create a Java environment in Eclipse or to learn the Eclipse Java development process. You are not required to specify a package, implement an interface, or know the parameters of the event handler you write.

To add a JavaScript event handler, you type the code for the event handler on the Script tab after selecting the name of the event handler from a drop-down list.

- Simpler language constructs, looser typing, and less strict language rules

  JavaScript is less demanding to code than Java due to simpler language constructs, looser typing, and less strict language rules.

The advantages of using Java to write an event handler include:

- Availability of the Eclipse Java development environment

  The Eclipse Java development environment is very powerful, and includes such features as autocompletion, context sensitive help, keyboard shortcuts, parameter hints, and much more.

- Ease of finding and viewing event handlers

  All the Java event handlers for a report exist in readily viewable Java files. By contrast, the JavaScript event handlers are embedded in the design and you can view only one handler at a time.

- Access to an integrated debugger

  The integrated debugger only supports Java event handlers, not JavaScript event handlers.

Using both Java and JavaScript to write event handlers

You are not limited to writing all event handlers in one language. You can write some in Java and others in JavaScript. If you have both a Java and a JavaScript event handler for the same event, BIRT uses the JavaScript handler.

Understanding the event handler execution sequence

This section explains the order of execution of the BIRT event handlers.

About event firing sequence dependency

The event firing sequence for ReportItem and ReportDesign events depends on whether the report is run in the BIRT Report Designer previewer or elsewhere, such as in the Web Viewer. When a report runs outside the previewer, the generation phase always completes before the presentation phase begins. When a report runs in the previewer, the generation and presentation phases are not distinctly separated. The onCreate event is a generation-time event and the onRender is a presentation-time event.

About the onCreate and onRender firing sequence dependencies

When a report runs in the BIRT Report Designer previewer, all ReportItem onRender events fire immediately after their corresponding onCreate events. When a report runs outside the previewer, all onCreate events fire as a part of the generation process, while the onRender events fire as a part of the presentation process.

About the ReportDesign firing sequence dependencies

When a report runs in the previewer, the ReportDesign initialize event fires only once, and is always the first event fired. When a report runs outside the previewer, the initialize event is fired twice, once at the beginning of the generation phase and once at the beginning of the presentation phase.

The ReportDesign beforeRender and afterRender events also fire at different times, depending on whether the report runs in the previewer. When a report runs in the previewer, beforeRender fires once near the start of the report, just after beforeFactory fires. The ReportDesign afterRender event fires once, near the completion of the report, just before the afterFactory event fires.

When the report runs outside the previewer, the ReportDesign beforeRender event fires once, immediately after the firing of the initialize event in the presentation phase. When the report runs outside the previewer, the ReportDesign afterRender event is the last event fired.

About the pageBreak event

Table and Text objects have event handlers for handling page break events. The pageBreak event is fired in the presentation phase whenever a page break occurs.

Analysis of the execution sequence phases

The following diagrams present a more detailed view of the event handler execution sequence. The diagrams reflect the processing sequence when a report is run inside the previewer. When the presentation phase is separate from the generation phase, as it is when a report is run outside the previewer, an additional rendering sequence occurs. The rendering sequence is identical to the generation sequence with the following exceptions:

- There are no onPrepare events.

- There are no onCreate events.

- There are no data source or data set events because data is retrieved from the report document rather than the database.

- There are no beforeFactory and afterFactory events.

Overview of the report execution process

Figure 8-1 shows an overview of the report execution process. Each box in the diagram refers to another diagram that appears later in the chapter.

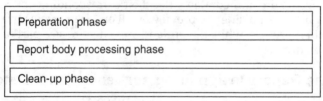

Figure 8-1   Method execution phases

Preparation phase

The preparation phase includes initialization and master page creation, followed by opening the data source. The preparation phase is identical for all reports. Figure 8-2 illustrates the method execution sequence for the preparation phase.

Figure 8-2   Preparation phase

In Figure 8-2, the master page processing sequence depends on the structure of the report. A master page typically consists of one or more header and footer grids with rows, their cells, and the cell contents. The execution sequence for a master page parallels that for creating an ungrouped table, except that the master page contains no detail rows.

Report body processing phase

BIRT processes a report body by processing all the report items that are not contained in other report items. BIRT processes the items, going from left to right and proceeding a row at a time toward the bottom right. A report item that is not contained in another report item is called a top-level report item. Every report has at least one top-level report item, usually a grid, a list, or a table. If a report has more than one top-level report item, BIRT processes the top-level items in order, from left to right and top to bottom.

For each top-level item, BIRT processes all the second-level items before proceeding to the next top-level item. A second-level report item is a report item that is contained within a top-level item. For example, a table contained in a grid is a second-level report item.

There can be any number of levels of report items. To see the level of a particular report item, examine the structure of the report design in Outline, as shown in Figure 8-3.

BIRT processes all items at all levels in an iterative fashion, following the same process at each level as it does for the top-level items.

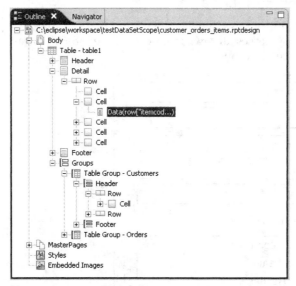

Figure 8-3   The Outline window, showing the level of a report item

Figure 8-4 illustrates the general report body processing phase.

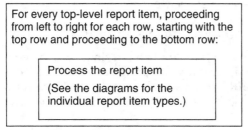

Figure 8-4   **Report body processing phase**

Clean-up processing phase

The clean-up phase consists of two methods that execute upon closing the data source, followed by a final method that executes after the generation phase. Figure 8-5 illustrates the method execution sequence for the clean-up phase.

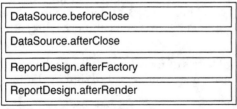

Figure 8-5   Clean-up phase

Row execution sequence

There are three kinds of rows: header, detail, and footer. Tables, lists, and groups have rows. BIRT processes all rows identically. Figure 8-6 illustrates the method execution sequence for a row.

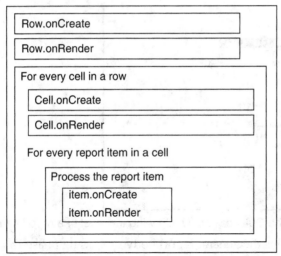

Figure 8-6   Row execution sequence

Table and list method execution sequence

A list is the same as a table, except it only has a single cell in every row. BIRT processes tables and lists identically except that for a list, BIRT does not iterate through multiple cells. BIRT processes tables in three phases, the setup phase, the detail processing phase, and the wrap-up processing phase, as shown in Figure 8-7.

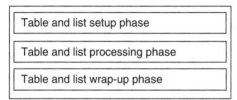

Figure 8-7   Table and list execution sequence

The following sections describe each of the three table and list execution sequence sections.

Table and list setup phase

The pre-table processing phase is the same for all tables, both grouped and ungrouped.

Figure 8-8 illustrates the method execution sequence for the pre-table processing phase.

```
┌─────────────────────────────────────────────────────────┐
│  DataSet.beforeOpen                                        │
│                                                           │
│  DataSet.afterOpen                                         │
│                                                           │
│  For every row in the data set                            │
│      ┌───────────────────────────────────┐               │
│      │  DataSet.onFetch                   │               │
│      └───────────────────────────────────┘               │
│                                                           │
│  Table.onCreate                                           │
│                                                           │
│  Table.onRender                                           │
│                                                           │
│  Process the header row or rows                           │
│  (See the row execution sequence diagram.)                │
└─────────────────────────────────────────────────────────┘
```

Figure 8-8   Table and list setup execution sequence

Table and list processing phase

The sequence for the table and list processing phase depends on whether the table or list is grouped. The diagram for an ungrouped table or list is shown in "Ungrouped table or list detail execution sequence," later in this chapter. The diagram for a grouped table or list is shown in "Grouped table or list execution sequence," later in this chapter.

Table and list wrap-up phase

The post-table processing phase is the same for all tables, both grouped and ungrouped. Figure 8-9 illustrates the method execution sequence for the post-table processing phase.

```
Process the footer row or rows
(See the row execution sequence diagram.)
```

Figure 8-9   Table and list wrap-up execution sequence

Ungrouped table or list detail execution sequence

A table or list with no grouping has a different sequence than one with grouping.

Figure 8-10 illustrates the execution sequence for a table or list without grouping.

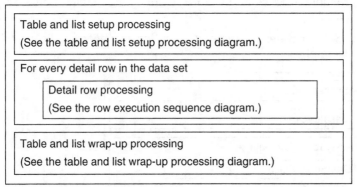

Figure 8-10   Ungrouped table or list detail execution sequence

Grouped table or list execution sequence

One of the differences between the processing sequence for a table or list with grouping and a table or list without grouping is that for a table with grouping, BIRT creates one ListingGroup item per group.

The ListingGroup element has three methods, onCreate, onRow, and onFinish, all of which are called one or more times when processing a grouped table or list. A ListingGroup is very similar to a table because it has one or more header rows, one or more detail rows, and one or more footer rows. BIRT processes grouping rows in the same way that it processes a table row.

Figure 8-11 illustrates the method execution sequence for a table that has groups.

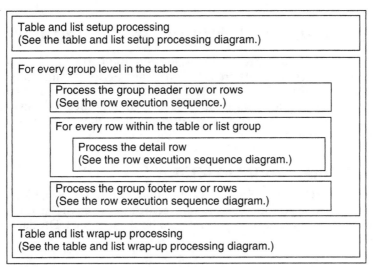

Figure 8-11   Grouped table execution sequence

If you need to verify the execution sequence of event handlers for a specific report, you can add logging code to your event handlers. For information about adding logging code, see the section on determining method execution sequence in the chapter on using JavaScript.

About a report item event handler

You can write event handlers for all report item elements, such as Label and List. Table 8-1 describes the report item event handler methods.

Table 8-1   Report item event handler methods

Method	Description
onPrepare( )	The onPrepare event fires at the beginning of the generation phase, before data binding or expression evaluation occurs. This event is useful for changing the design prior to data binding or expression evaluation.
onCreate( )	The onCreate event fires at the time the element is created in the generation phase, after it is bound to data. This event is useful for operations that depend on the data content of the element.
onRender( )	The onRender event fires in the presentation phase. This event is useful for operations that depend on the type or format of the output document.

About data source and data set event handlers

There are two kinds of data source elements and two kinds of data set elements. The data source elements are DataSource and ScriptedDataSource. The data set elements are DataSet and ScriptedDataSet. ScriptedDataSource and ScriptedDataSet elements are for non-ODA data sources. The events that BIRT fires for the ODA data sources are different from the events that it fires for non-ODA data sources.

ODA data source events

You use the ODA DataSource events, afterClose, afterOpen, beforeClose, and beforeOpen, to perform operations that are not directly related to managing the data source. There is no requirement to implement the ODA data source event handler methods.

Scripted data source events

You use the ScriptedDataSource events, open and close, to perform the actions of opening and closing the data source. You must implement the ScriptedDataSource event handlers.

ODA data set events

As with the ODA data source events, you are not required to provide event handlers for the ODA data set events. The ODA data set events include afterClose, afterOpen, beforeClose, beforeOpen, and onFetch.

Scripted data set events

You must handle the open, close, and fetch events of a ScriptedDataSet element. You use these events to open the data set, close the data set, and to fetch a data set row. In addition to the three ScriptedDataSet events for which you must provide handlers, there is one optional event, the describe event. You use the describe event handler to define dynamically generated columns.

About ReportDesign event handlers

There are several events associated with the ReportDesign element. There are five ReportDesign element events that fire during the report generation process. These five events are not associated with a specific report item, data source, or data set. The ReportDesign events are initialize, beforeFactory, afterFactory, beforeRender, and afterRender.

The initialize event fires before any other event and the initialize event handler is therefore the most logical place to include initialization code.

The beforeFactory event fires before the generation phase. The afterFactory events fire after the generation phase. The beforeRender event fires before the presentation phase.

The afterRender events fire after the presentation phase. There are no specific guidelines for what kind of code to include in these event handlers. They are available for whatever purpose you have for them.

Writing event handlers for charts

While a chart is a report item, it is a much more complex report item than any other. The set of events for a chart is much greater than for any other report item. As with all report items, chart scripting is supported in both Java and JavaScript.

Chart events

All chart Java event handlers receive a chart script context object, IChartScriptContext. The chart script context object has methods to get the chart instance, the locale, and the external context. Some chart event handler methods have arguments of the type Chart, Series, Block, MarkerRange, ISeriesRenderer, GeneratedChartState, DataSet, and IDataSetProcessor.

The chart has a different set of events for which you can write event handlers than the other report items. Table 8-2 lists the chart event handler methods and describes when they are called.

Table 8-2   Chart event handler methods

Method	Called
afterDataSetFilled(Series series, DataSet dataSet, IChartScriptContext icsc)	After populating the series data set
afterDrawAxisLabel(Axis axis, Label label, IChartScriptContext icsc)	After rendering each label on a given axis
afterDrawAxisTitle(Axis axis, Label label, IChartScriptContext icsc)	After rendering the title of an axis
afterDrawBlock(Block block, IChartScriptContext icsc)	After drawing each block
afterDrawDataPoint(DataPointHints dph, Fill fill, IChartScriptContext icsc)	After drawing each data point graphical representation or marker
afterDrawDataPointLabel(DataPointHints dph, Label label, IChartScriptContext icsc)	After rendering the label for each data point

(continues)

Table 8-2   Chart event handler methods *(continued)*

Method	Called
afterDrawFittingCurve(CurveFitting cf, IChartScriptContext icsc)	After rendering curve fitting
afterDrawLegendEntry(Label label, IChartScriptContext icsc)	After drawing each entry in the legend
afterDrawMarkerLine(Axis axis, MarkerLine mLine, IChartScriptContext icsc)	After drawing each marker line in an axis
afterDrawMarkerRange(Axis axis, MarkerRange mRange, IChartScriptContext icsc)	After drawing each marker range in an axis
afterDrawSeries(Series series, ISeriesRenderer isr, IChartScriptContext icsc)	After rendering the series
afterDrawSeriesTitle(Series series, Label label, IChartScriptContext icsc)	After rendering the title of a series
afterGeneration(GeneratedChartState gcs, IChartScriptContext icsc)	After generation of a chart model to GeneratedChartState
afterRendering(GeneratedChartState gcs, IChartScriptContext icsc)	After the chart is rendered
beforeDataSetFilled(Series series, IDataSetProcessor idsp, IChartScriptContext icsc)	Before populating the series data set using the DataSetProcessor
beforeDrawAxisLabel(Axis axis, Label label, IChartScriptContext icsc)	Before rendering each label on a given axis
beforeDrawAxisTitle(Axis axis, Label label, IChartScriptContext icsc)	Before rendering the title of an axis
beforeDrawBlock(Block block, IChartScriptContext icsc)	Before drawing each block
beforeDrawDataPoint(DataPointHints dph, Fill fill, IChartScriptContext icsc)	Before drawing each datapoint graphical representation or marker
beforeDrawDataPointLabel(DataPointHints dph, Label label, IChartScriptContext icsc)	Before rendering the label for each datapoint
beforeDrawFittingCurve(CurveFitting cf, IChartScriptContext icsc)	Before rendering curve fitting
beforeDrawLegendEntry(Label label, IChartScriptContext icsc)	Before drawing each entry in the legend
beforeDrawMarkerLine(Axis axis, MarkerLine mLine, IChartScriptContext icsc)	Before drawing each marker line in an axis
beforeDrawMarkerRange(Axis axis, MarkerRange mRange, IChartScriptContext icsc)	Before drawing each marker range in an axis

Table 8-2   Chart event handler methods *(continued)*

Method	Called
beforeDrawSeries(Series series, ISeriesRenderer isr, IChartScriptContext icsc)	Before rendering the series
beforeDrawSeriesTitle(Series series, Label label, IChartScriptContext icsc)	Before rendering the title of a series
beforeGeneration(Chart cm, IChartScriptContext icsc)	Before generation of a chart model to GeneratedChartState
beforeRendering(GeneratedChartState gcs, IChartScriptContext icsc)	Before the chart is rendered

Chart script context

All chart event handler methods for both Java and JavaScript receive a chart script context argument in the form of a ChartScriptContext object. The chart script context object provides access to the chart instance object, the Locale and ULocale objects, a logging object, and an external context object. You can also use the ChartScriptContext object to set the external context, the chart instance, and the ULocale.

Table 8-3 lists the methods of the chart script context object and their functions.

Table 8-3   Chart script context event handler methods

Method	Function
getChartInstance( )	Returns the chart instance object.
getExternalContext( )	Returns the IExternalContext object that provides access to a scriptable external object. External scriptable objects are defined in the user application.
getLocale( )	Returns the Locale object for the locale currently in use.
getLogger( )	Returns the Logger object, which can be used for logging messages and errors.
getULocale( )	Returns the ULocale object for the locale currently in use.
setChartInstance(Chart)	Sets the chart instance.
setExternalContext(IEXternalContext)	Sets the external context.
setLogger(ILogger)	Sets the logger.
setULocale(ULocale)	Sets the ULocale.

Chart instance object

As explained in the previous section, you get a chart instance object from the chart script context object. The chart instance object contains methods that provide chart modification functionality. Use the chart instance object to get properties, change properties, and test properties.

Chart instance getter methods

The chart instance getter methods allow you to get various properties of a chart.

Table 8-4 lists the chart instance getter methods and the property values they return.

Table 8-4   Chart instance getter methods

Method	Gets
getBlock( )	The value of the Block containment reference
getDescription( )	The value of the Description containment reference
getDimension( )	The value of the Dimension attribute
getExtendedProperties( )	The value of the Extended Properties containment reference list
getGridColumnCount( )	The value of the Grid Column Count attribute
getInteractivity( )	The value of the Interactivity containment reference
getLegend( )	The Legend block
getPlot( )	The Plot block
getSampleData( )	The value of the Sample Data containment reference
getScript( )	The value of the Script attribute
getSeriesForLegend( )	An array of series whose captions or markers are rendered in the Legend
getSeriesThickness( )	The value of the Series Thickness attribute
getStyles( )	The value of the Styles containment reference list
getSubType( )	The value of the Sub Type attribute
getTitle( )	The Title block for the chart
getType( )	The value of the Type attribute
getUnits( )	The value of the Units attribute
getVersion( )	The value of the Version attribute

Chart instance setter methods

The chart instance setter methods allow you to set various properties of a chart. Table 8-5 lists the chart instance setter methods and the values they set.

Table 8-5   Chart instance setter methods

Method	Sets
setBlock(Block value)	The value of the Block containment reference
setDescription(Text value)	The value of the Description containment reference
setDimension(Chart Dimension value)	The value of the Dimension attribute
setGridColumnCount(int value)	The value of the GridColumnCount attribute
setInteractivity(Interactivity value)	The value of the Interactivity containment reference
setSampleData( )	The value of the Sample Data containment reference
setScript( )	The value of the Script attribute
setSeriesThickness( )	The value of the Series Thickness attribute
setSubType( )	The value of the Sub Type attribute
setType( )	The value of the Type attribute
setUnits( )	The value of the Units attribute
setVersion( )	The value of the Version attribute

Writing a Java chart event handler

Writing a Java chart event handler is not different from writing a Java event handler for any other kind of report item. For more information about writing Java event handlers, see Chapter 10, "Using Java to Write an Event Handler."

Writing a JavaScript chart event handler

The process of writing a JavaScript chart event handler differs from the process of writing an event handler for other report items. The primary difference is that the Script tab does not contain a selectable list of chart events. For chart events, you must include every event handler script for the chart in one place.

The Script tab of the BIRT Report Designer for a chart contains a set of function stubs to assist you in writing a chart event handler. The set of stubs is a subset of the chart events, consisting only of the before events, such as beforeDataSetFilled( ). Figure 8-12 shows the Script tab as it appears before any event handlers have been typed.

```
/**
 * Called before populating the series dataset using the DataSetProcessor.
 *
 * @param series
 *           Series
 * @param dataSetProcessor
 *           DataSetProcessor
 * @param context
 *           IChartScriptContext
 */
//function beforeDataSetFilled( series, dataSetProcessor, context ){}

/**
 * Called before generation of chart model to GeneratedChartState.
 *
 * @param chart
 *           Chart Model
 * @param context
 *           IChartScriptContext
 */
```

Figure 8-12   Script tab

The before events are the most common events to script. If you need to write an after event handler, such as afterDataSetFilled( ), you can find the signature of the event handler earlier in this chapter or by viewing the interface IChartEventHandler in the Chart Engine API Reference in the BIRT online help.

To write handler code for one of the before chart events, uncomment the appropriate function statement in the Script tab and type the code between the parentheses, as shown in Figure 8-13.

```
/**
 * Called before populating the series dataset using the DataSetProcessor.
 *
 * @param series
 *           Series
 * @param dataSetProcessor
 *           DataSetProcessor
 * @param context
 *           IChartScriptContext
 */
//function beforeDataSetFilled( series, dataSetProcessor, context ){
function beforeDataSetFilled( series, dataSetProcessor, context ){
    logger.logFromScript("Logging before data set filled");
}
```

Figure 8-13   Chart event handler code with a standard function declaration

If you want to write an event handler that does not have a stub in the Script tab, you must type the function declaration yourself. When typing a new function declaration, follow the format of the function declarations in the stubs.

Figure 8-14 shows the entry of an afterDrawElement( ) script.

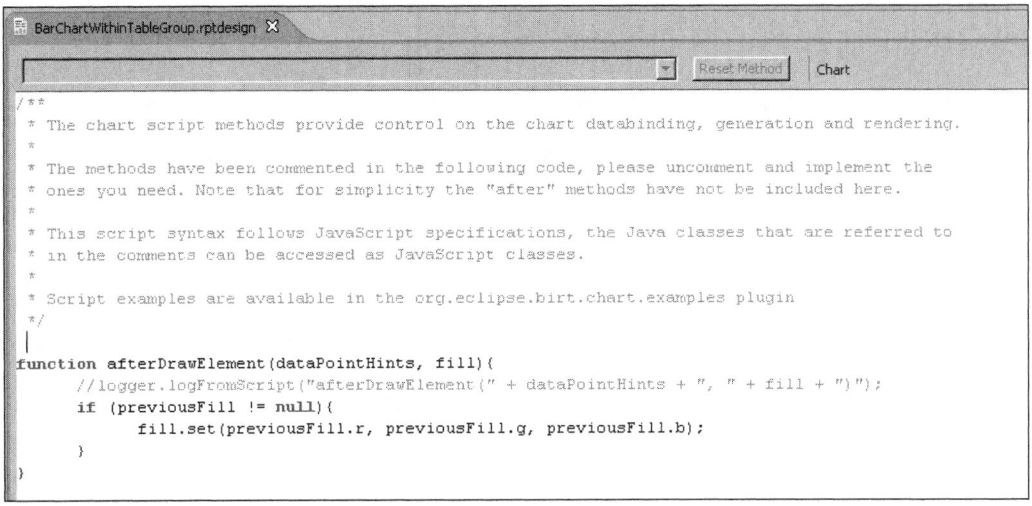

Figure 8-14   Chart event handler code with a custom function declaration

Getting a dynamic image from a Microsoft Access database

Microsoft Access stores an image as an array of image bytes preceded by 78 bytes of header information. BIRT does not use the header information. To get a dynamic image from an Access database, you must copy the image data from the database field into a Java array of type byte. You perform this copy operation in the dynamic image expression.

The following script is an example of how to copy the image data from the Access image field into a byte array that BIRT can use:

```
var picBytes = row["Picture"];
var offset = 78;
var lengthOfImage = picBytes.length - offset;
var imgBytes =
   java.lang.reflect.Array.newInstance(java.lang.Byte.TYPE,
   lengthOfImage);
java.lang.System.arraycopy(picBytes, offset, imgBytes, 0,
   lengthOfImage);
imgBytes;
```

Figure 8-19: ...

Figure 8-20: ...

Getting a dynamic image from a Microsoft Access Database

9

Using JavaScript to Write an Event Handler

BIRT scripting is based on the Mozilla Rhino implementation of JavaScript, also called ECMAScript. Rhino implements ECMAScript version 1.5 as described in the ECMA standard ECMA-262 version 3. The complete specification for Rhino is located at:

```
http://www.ecma-international.org/publications/standards/
    Ecma-262.htm.
```

Using BIRT Report Designer to enter a JavaScript event handler

You can use BIRT Report Designer to enter a JavaScript event handler and associate it with a specific event for a specific element.

How to use BIRT Report Designer to enter a JavaScript event handler

1 In Outline, select the report element, data source, or data set for which you want to write an event handler.

2 Choose the Script tab.

3 Choose an event handler from the drop-down list of methods.

4 Enter the event handler code in the script editor.

Figure 9-1 demonstrates entering a line of code in the onPrepare( ) method of a Table element.

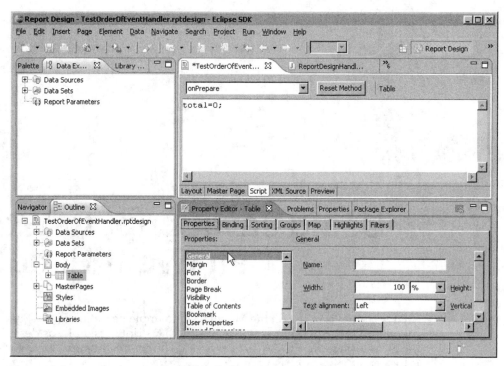

Figure 9-1   Code entry for the onPrepare( ) method

Creating and using a global variable

JavaScript has global variables and local variables. A local variable can only be accessed in the scope of the method in which it is created. You use the var identifier to create a local variable in JavaScript, as shown in the following line of code:

```
var localCounter = 0;
```

To create a global variable, you omit the var identifier, as shown in the following line of code:

```
globalCounter = 0;
```

When you create a global variable in JavaScript, that variable is visible to all other JavaScript code that executes in the same process. For example, you can use a global variable to count the detail rows in a table by first creating a global variable in the onCreate( ) method of the table, as shown in the following line of code:

```
rowCount=0;
```

Since rowCount is global, the onCreate( ) method of the detail row can access and increment it, as shown in the following line of code:

```
rowCount++;
```

Understanding execution phases and processes

As explained in the scripting overview chapter, there are three BIRT execution phases: the preparation phase, the generation phase, and the presentation phase. However, there can be either one or two execution processes. When a report is run in the BIRT Report Designer previewer, there is only one execution process. There are two execution processes when the report is run in the interactive viewer or when the report is deployed to an application server. The first process, called the factory process, contains the preparation phase and the generation phase. The second execution process, called the render process, contains only the presentation phase. The render process can occur at a much later time than the factory process and possibly on a different machine.

Because variables are only visible in the process in which they were created, it is important to know which event handlers run in which process. It is also important to be aware that code that works when the report is run in the previewer might not work at run time if there is a render process dependency on a variable created in the factory process.

The event handlers that run in the factory process, in the order executed, include:

- ReportDesign.initialize( )
- onPrepare( ) methods for every report item
- ReportDesign.beforeFactory( )
- DataSource.beforeOpen( )
- DataSource.afterOpen( )
- DataSet.beforeOpen( )
- DataSet.afterOpen( )
- DataSet.onFetch( )
- onCreate( ) methods for every report item
- DataSet.beforeClose( )
- DataSet.afterClose( )
- DataSource.beforeClose( )
- DataSource.afterClose( )
- ReportDesign.afterFactory( )

The event handlers that run in the render process, in the order executed, include:

- ReportDesign.initialize( )
- ReportDesign.beforeRender( )
- onRender( ) methods for every report item
- ReportDesign.beforeFactory( )
- ReportDesign.afterRender( )

It is worth noting that ReportDesign.initialize( ) runs in both processes.

Using the reportContext object

Almost every event handler has access to an object called the reportContext object. The four exceptions are the open( ) and close( ) event handlers for ScriptedDataSource and ScriptedDataSet. Table 9-1 lists commonly used reportContext object methods.

Table 9-1   reportContext object methods

Method	Task
deleteGlobalVariable( )	Deletes a global variable created using setGlobalVariable( )
deletePersistentGlobalVariable( )	Deletes a persistent global variable created using setPersistentGlobalVariable( )
getAppContext( )	Returns the application context
getConfigVariableValue( )	Returns the value of a config variable
getGlobalVariable( )	Returns a global variable created using setGlobalVariable( )
getHttpServletRequest( )	Returns the HTTP servlet request object
getLocale( )	Returns the current locale
getMessage( )	Returns a localized message from the localization resource file
getOutputFormat( )	Returns the format in which the report is emitted, either html or pdf
getParameterValue( )	Returns a parameter value
getPersistentGlobalVariable( )	Returns a persistent global variable created using setPersistentGlobalVariable( )
setGlobalVariable( )	Creates a global variable that can be accessed with getGlobalVariable( )

Table 9-1	reportContext object methods *(continued)*
Method	Task
setParameterValue( )	Sets the value of a named parameter
setPersistentGlobalVariable( )	Creates a persistent global variable that can be accessed using getPersistentGlobalVariable( )

Passing a variable between processes

Although a global JavaScript variable cannot be passed between processes, there is a way to pass a variable from the factory process to the render process. The setPersistentGlobalVariable( ) method of the report context object creates a variable that can be accessed using the getPersistentGlobalVariable( ) method. The only restriction on the variable is that it must be a serializable Java object.

Getting information from an HTTP request object

The HTTP servlet request object contains various methods to retrieve information about the request to run the report. One useful method of the HTTP request object gets the query string that follows the path in the request URL. The query string contains all the parameters of the request. By parsing the query string, your code can extract the parameters in the request URL to conditionally determine the report output. This feature can be used to pass in a user ID, for example, or to set or override a report parameter.

The following code gets the query string:

```
importPackage( Packages.javax.servlet.http );
httpServletReq = reportContext.getHttpServletRequest( );
formatStr=httpServletReq.getQueryString( );
```

Using the this object

Every JavaScript event handler is associated with a particular ROM element, such as a report item, a data source, a data set, or the report itself. Most report elements have properties that an event handler can access and, in some cases, change. Many report elements also have functions that you can call. A JavaScript event handler can access these properties and functions through a special object called the this object.

Using the this object's methods

The this object represents the element for which the event handler handles events. To use the this object, type the word, this, followed by a period in the script window for the event handler you are writing. At the time you type the period, a window pops up containing a scrollable list of all the properties and functions of the element, as shown in Figure 9-2.

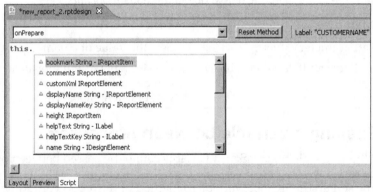

Figure 9-2   Using the this object to display a list of functions and properties

If the pop-up window disappears at any time, delete the period and re-enter it. Scroll down using the arrow keys or the scroll bar controls and press Enter or double-click when the property or function you want is highlighted.

Using the pop-up window to select a method or property can also be used for other objects. A procedure later in this chapter steps you through setting the background color of a label to yellow.

Using the this object to set the property of a report item

The following procedure assumes that you have a BIRT report that contains a label. The procedure sets the label's background color to yellow. The general process explained in this procedure is not specific to the label report item, however. You modify all report item event handlers in the same general way.

How to set a property of a report item using JavaScript

1   Select the label whose color you want to change by navigating the Outline view and selecting the appropriate report item, as shown in Figure 9-3.

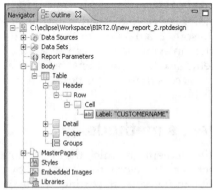

Figure 9-3   Selecting a report item to modify

2 Select onPrepare from the drop-down list in the Script window, as shown in Figure 9-4.

Figure 9-4   Selecting onPrepare( )

3 Enter the word this, followed by a period in the onPrepare script window, as shown in Figure 9-5.

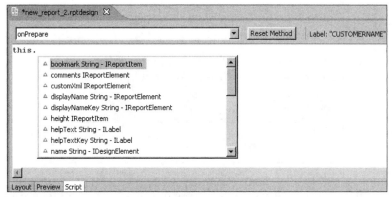

Figure 9-5   Using the this object

4 Select the getStyle( ) method from the scrollable list of properties and functions.

The onPrepare script window appears as shown in Figure 9-6.

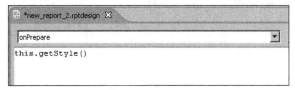

Figure 9-6   The onPrepare script window

5 Move the cursor to the end of the line in the onPrepare script window and type a period.

The scrollable list of properties and functions of the Style element appears, as shown in Figure 9-7.

Figure 9-7   Properties and functions of the Style element

6 Select backgroundColor from the list of Style properties and functions.

7 Complete the line of JavaScript in the onPrepare script window by appending ="yellow", as shown in Figure 9-8.

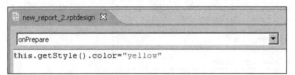

Figure 9-8   Changing the color of an element

8 Choose the Preview tab to see the effect of the onPrepare event handler script.

The label appears in the report with a yellow background, as shown in Figure 9-9.

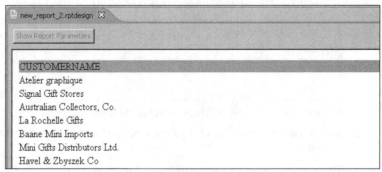

Figure 9-9   Preview of the color change

Using the row object

The row object provides access to the columns of the current row from within the DataSet.onFetch( ) method. You can retrieve the value of any column, using the column name in a statement similar to the following examples:

```
col1Value = row["custNum"];
col1Value = row.custNum;
```

You can only index the column position with the column name if the name is a valid JavaScript name with no spaces or special characters. Alternatively, you can use the column alias if the alias is a valid JavaScript name.

You can also get a column value by numerically indexing the column position, as shown in the following statement:

```
col1Value = row[1];
```

When you index the column position numerically, the number inside the brackets is the position of the column, beginning with 1. You can retrieve the row number with row[0].

Although you use array syntax to access the row object in JavaScript, this object is not a JavaScript array. For this reason, you cannot use JavaScript array properties, such as length, with the row object.

Getting column information

The DataSet object has a method called getColumnMetaData( ), which returns an IColumnMetaData object. The IColumnMetaData class has methods that provide information about the columns in a data set, as shown in Table 9-2.

Table 9-2   Methods of the IColumnMetaData class

Method	Returns
getColumnAlias( )	The alias of the specified column.
getColumnCount( )	The number of columns in a row of the result set.
getColumnLabel( )	The column label.
getColumnName( )	The column name at the specified index.

(continues)

Table 9-2   Methods of the IColumnMetaData class *(continued)*

Method	Returns
getColumnNativeTypeName( )	One of the following data types: ■ BOOLEAN ■ DATETIME ■ DECIMAL ■ FLOAT ■ INTEGER ■ STRING The data type is null if the column is a computed field or if the type is not known.
getColumnType( )	The data type of the column at the specified index.
getColumnTypeName()	The data type name of the column at the specified index.
isComputedColumn( )	True or false, depending on whether the column is a computed field or not.

You get the IColumnMetaData object from the dataSet object, as shown in the following statement:

```
columnMetaData = this.getColumnMetaData( );
```

You can use the count of columns to iterate through all the columns in the data set, as shown in the following example:

```
colCount = columnMetaData.getColumnCount( );
for ( i = 0; i < colCount; i++ )
{
   pw.println( "Column val for col position " + i + " = " +
      row[i] );
   pw.println( "Column name for col position " + i + " = " +
      columnDefinitions[i].name );
}
```

Getting and altering the query string

You get the text of the query in any DataSet event handler as shown in the following example:

```
query = this.queryText;
```

You can modify a query in the DataSet beforeOpen( ) event handler by setting the value of the queryText string. To change the query, set the queryText string to a valid SQL query, as shown in the following example:

```
queryText = "select * from CLASSICMODELS.CUSTOMERS WHERE
    CLASSICMODELS.CUSTOMERS.CUSTOMERNUMBER BETWEEN 470 AND 490";
```

One advantage of dynamically altering the query is that you can use business logic to determine the proper query. This approach can be more flexible than using parameters.

Getting a parameter value

A script can get the value of a report parameter by passing the name of the parameter to the getParameterValue( ) method of the reportContext object. The following statement gets the value of the UserID parameter:

```
userID = reportContext.getParameterValue( "UserID" );
```

Changing the connection properties of a data source

You can change the run-time connection properties of a data source by accessing the extensionProperties array of the DataSource object. The ODA extension defines the list of connection properties that can be set at run time. Table 9-3 describes the JDBC data source properties that affect the connection at run time.

Table 9-3   JDBC data source run-time connection properties

Property	Description
odaUser	The login user name
odaPassword	The login password
odaURL	The URL that identifies the data source
odaDriverClass	The driver class for accessing the data source

To change these properties, add code similar to the following statements in the DataSource.beforeOpen method:

```
extensionProperties.odaUser = "JoeUser";
extensionProperties.odaPassword = "openSesame";
extensionProperties.odaURL = "jdbc:my_data_source:xxx";
extensionProperties.odaDriverClass =
    "com.companyb.jdbc.Driver";
```

Determining method execution sequence

You can determine the sequence of method execution by writing code that generates a file containing a line for every method that you want to track.

To create an output file containing a sequence of method execution, include initialization code in the ReportDesign.initialize method and finalization code in the ReportDesign.afterFactory method. In each method that you want to track, add code to write a line of text to the output file. It is easier to write the code in JavaScript than Java, but it is possible to write analogous code in Java.

The following sections show you how to use JavaScript to determine method execution sequence.

Providing the ReportDesign.initialize code

The following code in the ReportDesign.initialize method creates a file on your hard drive and adds one line to the file.

```
importPackage( Packages.java.io );
fos = new java.io.FileOutputStream( "c:\\logFile.txt" );
printWriter = new java.io.PrintWriter( fos );
printWriter.println( "ReportDesign.initialize" );
```

The preceding code does the following tasks:

- Imports the Java package, java.io

- Creates a file output stream for the file you want to create

- Creates a PrintWriter object that every method can use to track method execution sequence

How to provide code for the ReportDesign.initialize method

You provide code for the ReportDesign.initialize method by performing the following steps:

1 Choose the Script tab.

2 Choose the Outline view.

3 In Outline, select the top line, as shown in Figure 9-10.

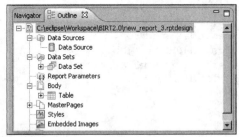

Figure 9-10   Selecting the report design

4 In Script, select the Initialize( ) method.

5 Type the code into the script editor.

The BIRT report designer appears, as shown in Figure 9-11.

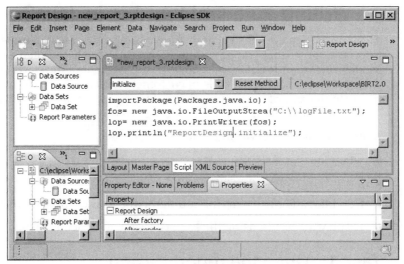

Figure 9-11   Providing ReportDesign.initialize code

Providing the code for the methods you want to track

For every method that you want to track, provide a single statement generating a line of output to your log file, as shown in the following statement:

```
printWriter.println( "Table.onRow" );
```

To provide code for a report item method you want to track, first select the appropriate object from Outline and select the appropriate method from the method selection list. Then use the same steps for entering code into a method, as described in the preceding section.

To provide code for a data set or the data source method, select the appropriate data source or data set from Data Explorer before selecting the method you want to track.

Providing the ReportDesign.afterFactory code

The following statement in the ReportDesign.afterFactory method closes the file.

```
printWriter.close( );
```

Using this method flushes all the buffers and ensures that all method output appears in the file.

To provide the ReportDesign.afterFactory code, select the top line of the outline and select the afterFactory method on the code page.

Tutorial 1: Writing an event handler in JavaScript

This tutorial provides instructions for writing a set of event handlers. The tutorial assumes that you have a basic report design based on the Classic Models, Inc. sample database. The only requirement of the starting report design is that it contains a table of customers with a column for the customer name. In this tutorial you count the customers whose names contain the string "Mini" and display the result in a pop-up window.

In this tutorial, you perform the following tasks:

- Open the report design.

- Create and initialize a counter in the Table.onCreate( ) method.

- Conditionally increment the counter in the Row.onCreate( ) method.

- Display the result, using the ReportDesign.afterFactory( ) method.

Task 1: Open the report design

Open a report design that uses the Classic Car sample database and displays a table of customer names.

1 If necessary, open Navigator by choosing Window➤Show View➤Navigator.

2 Double-click the appropriate report design. The file opens in the layout editor, as shown in Figure 9-12.

<CENTER><B><span...			
"Number of custo...			
Credit Limit	**Customer**	**Phone**	**Contact**
for(i=50000; i <...			
Detail Row	row ["CUSTOMERNAM...	row["PHONE"]	row["CONTACTFIRS...
"Customers: " + ...			
Footer Row			

Figure 9-12   Report design in the layout editor

Task 2: Create and initialize a counter in the Table.onCreate( ) method

In order to count the number of customers whose names contain the string "Mini," you must first declare a global counter and set its value to zero. The Table.onCreate( ) method is the most appropriate place to do this task because

Table.onCreate( ) executes before any rows are retrieved. You conditionally increment this counter in the Row.onCreate( ) method.

1 In Layout, select the table by placing the cursor near the bottom-left corner of the table. The table icon appears, as shown in Figure 9-13.

Figure 9-13 Table icon in the layout editor

2 Choose the Script tab. The script window appears, as shown in Figure 9-14.

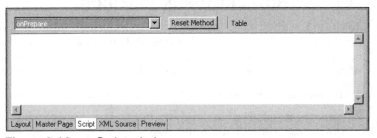

Figure 9-14 Script window

3 Type the following line of code in the script window for the onCreate( ) method:

```
countOfMinis = 0;
```

4 To run the report and verify that the code did not create any errors, choose Preview.

5 Scroll to the bottom of the report, where JavaScript error messages appear. If there are no errors, the report appears, as shown in Figure 9-15.

If you see an error message, you may have typed a statement incorrectly. If so, go back to the script window, select the method you just modified, correct the error, and choose Preview again.

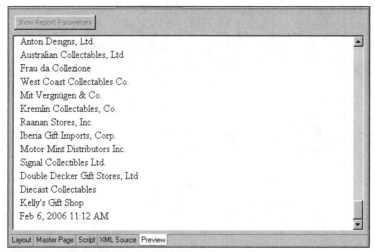

Figure 9-15   Report preview

Task 3: Conditionally increment the counter in the Row.onCreate( ) method

To count the number of customers with the string "Mini" in their names, you must examine each customer's name and add one to the counter for every occurrence. A logical place to do this task is in the Row.onCreate( ) method, which is executed upon every retrieval of a row of data from the data source.

1   In Layout, select the row and then choose Script.

2   Pull down the list of methods at the top of the script window and select onCreate, as shown in Figure 9-16.

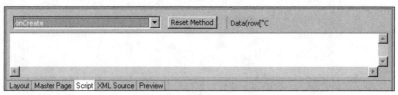

Figure 9-16   onCreate( ) in the Script window

3   Enter the following line of JavaScript code in the script window:

```
row1=this.getRowData( );
```

Notice that when you enter the period after this, a pop-up appears containing all the available methods and properties, including getRowData. This line of code gets an instance of IRowData. You use the method, getExpressionValue( ), on IRowData to get the contents of a column of the row.

4 Type the following line of JavaScript below the line you just entered:

```
CustName=row1.getExpressionValue( "row[CUSTOMERNAME]" );
```

This line of code returns the contents of the table column that comes from the CUSTOMERNAME column in the data set.

5 Type the following line of code to conditionally increment the counter you created in Task 2: "Create and initialize a counter in the Table.onCreate( ) method."

```
if( CustName.indexOf( "Mini" ) != -1 ) countOfMinis += 1;
```

You can use the JavaScript palette to insert each of the following elements in the preceding line:

- indexOf( )

  Select Native (JavaScript) Objects➤String Functions➤indexOf( )

- !=

  Select Operators➤Comparison➤!=

- +=

  Select Operators➤Assignment➤+=

6 Choose Preview to run the report again to verify that the code you entered did not create any errors.

Task 4: Display the result, using the ReportDesign.afterFactory( ) method

To display the count of customers with the string "Mini" in their names, you insert code in a method that runs after the processing of all the rows in the table. One logical place for this code is in the ReportDesign.afterFactory( ) method.

1 In Outline, select the report design, as shown in Figure 9-17.

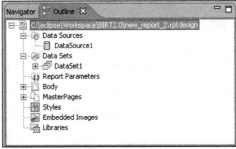

Figure 9-17   Selecting the report design in Outline

2 Select the afterFactory( ) method from the script window drop-down list.

3 Type the following code into the afterFactory( ) method:

```
importPackage( Packages.javax.swing );
frame = new JFrame( "Count of Minis = " + countOfMinis );
frame.setBounds( 310, 220, 300, 20 );
frame.show( );
```

4 Select Preview to see the results. If there were no errors in the code, you see a report similar to the one in Figure 9-18.

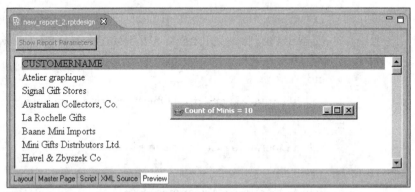

Figure 9-18   Result of changing the afterFactory( ) method

If you do not see the Count of Minis window, look for it behind the Eclipse window. If the Count of Minis window does not appear, the most likely reason is a scripting error caused by an error in one of your code entries.

If you suspect that a scripting error has occurred, scroll to the bottom of the report, where all scripting error messages appear. In most situations, there is a brief error message next to a plus sign (+). The plus sign indicates that there is a more detailed error message that is only visible after you expand the brief error message. To expand the brief error message, choose the plus sign. Scroll down to see the more detailed error message.

Calling Java from JavaScript

Rhino provides excellent integration with Java classes, allowing BIRT scripts to work seamlessly with business logic written in Java. Wrapping Java in JavaScript allows the developer to write powerful scripts quickly by leveraging both internal and external libraries of existing Java code. You can use static methods, non-static methods, and static constants of a Java class.

Understanding the Packages object

The Packages object is the JavaScript gateway to the Java classes. It is a top-level Rhino object that contains properties for every top-level Java package, such as java and com. Packages also contains a property for every package that it finds in its classpath. You use Packages to access a Java class for which Packages has a property by preceding the class name with Packages, as shown in the following statement:

```
var nc = new Packages.javax.swing.JFrame( "MyFrame" );
```

You can also use Packages to reference a Java class that is not a part of a package, as shown in the following statement:

```
var nc = new Packages.NumberConversion( );
```

For BIRT to find your custom Java class or package, you must place it in the BIRT classpath, as discussed later in this chapter.

Understanding the importPackage method

You can avoid writing a fully qualified reference to a Java class by using the top-level Rhino method importPackage( ). The importPackage( ) method functions like a Java import statement. Use the importPackage( ) method to specify one or more Java packages that contain the Java classes that you need to access, as shown in the following example:

```
importPackage( Packages.java.io, Packages.javax.swing );
```

You must prepend Packages to the name of each package. After the first time BIRT executes a method containing the importPackage( ) method, the specified packages are available to all succeeding scripts. For this reason, you should include the importPackage( ) method in the ReportDesign.initialize method, which is always the first method that BIRT executes.

Java imports java.lang.* implicitly. Rhino, on the other hand, does not import java.lang.* implicitly because JavaScript has several top-level objects with the same names as some classes defined in the java.lang package. These classes include Boolean, Math, Number, Object, and String. Importing java.lang causes a name collision with the JavaScript objects of the same name. For this reason, you should avoid using importPackage( ) to import java.lang.

Using a Java class

To use a Java class in a BIRT script, you set a JavaScript object equal to the Java object. You then call the Java class methods on the JavaScript object. The following example creates a Java Swing frame and sets the JavaScript object named frame to the Java JFrame object. Then the code calls the setBounds( ) and show( ) methods directly on the JavaScript object.

```
importPackage( Packages.javax.swing );
frame = new JFrame( "My Frame" );
frame.setBounds( 300, 300, 300, 20 );
frame.show( );
```

The effect of this code example is to display a Java window on your desktop containing the title, My Frame.

Placing your Java classes where BIRT can find them

For the BIRT report viewer to find your Java classes, the classes must be in a folder under:

```
$ECLIPSE_INSTALL\plugins org.eclipse.birt.report
   .viewer_*\birt\WEB-INF\classes
```

You can put a JAR file and individual classes at this location. If your Java class is a part of a package, you must create a hierarchy of folders under the classes folder that represents the package hierarchy. For example, if your Java class is in the com.acme.businessLogic package, your class must be in:

```
$ECLIPSE_INSTALL\plugins\org.eclipse.birt.report
   .viewer_*\birt\WEB-INF\classes\com\acme\businessLogic
```

When you deploy your report to an application server, you must also deploy your Java classes.

Issues with using Java in JavaScript code

There are many nuances of writing Java code, such as how to handle overloaded methods, how to use interfaces, and so forth. Refer to the Rhino page on scripting Java at http://www.mozilla.org/rhino/ScriptingJava.html for more information about these topics.

10

Using Java to Write an Event Handler

Creating a Java event handler is slightly more complex than creating a JavaScript event handler because you cannot simply enter Java code directly in the BIRT report designer. To create a Java event handler class, you must compile the source for the Java class and make certain that the class is visible to BIRT. Creating a Java event handler for BIRT is simplified, however, by the fact that Eclipse is a robust Java development environment and supports integrating a Java project with a BIRT project.

This chapter discusses the following topics:

- Writing the event handler class
- Making the event handler class visible to BIRT
- Associating the event handler class with a report item
- Understanding the classes and interfaces associated with Java event handlers

Writing a Java event handler class

When you provide one or more Java event handlers for a scriptable BIRT element, you must create one class that contains all the Java event handlers for that element. Creating a class that contains event handler methods for more than one element is not advisable.

BIRT provides a set of Java interfaces and Java adapter classes to simplify the process of writing a Java event handler class. There is one interface and one adapter class for every scriptable BIRT element. An element's event handler interface defines all the event handler methods for that element. A handler class must implement every method defined in the interface, even if some of the methods are empty.

Locating the JAR files that an event handler requires

There are two JAR files that contain all the classes and interfaces that an event handler requires. One of the JAR files is a part of BIRT Report Designer and SDK and the other one is a part of BIRT Report Engine.

The JAR file that you use for developing a Java event handler is org.eclipse.birt.report.engine_*Version*.jar, which is located in the Eclipse plugins directory for BIRT Report Designer and SDK.

The JAR file that you use when you deploy your report is scriptapi.jar, which is located in the \WebViewerExample\WEB-INF\lib directory of BIRT Report Engine. All JAR files in the \WebViewerExample\WEB-INF\lib directory are in a deployed report's classpath, so there is no need to do anything special to make scriptapi.jar accessible at run time.

Extending an adapter class

An element's adapter class implements the element's interface and provides empty stubs for every method. To use the adapter class, extend the adapter class and override the methods for which you are providing handler code. Eclipse recommends extending an adapter class rather than implementing an interface directly.

BIRT naming conventions for the event handler interfaces and adapter classes are discussed later in this chapter.

How to create an event handler class and add it to the Java project

This section describes the process for using the Eclipse Java development environment to create an event handler class for a scriptable BIRT element.

1 Add org.eclipse.birt.report.engine_*Version*.jar to your Java project, as outlined in the following steps:

    1 Select your Java project and choose File➤Properties➤Java Build Path➤Libraries. Java Build Path appears, as shown in Figure 10-1.

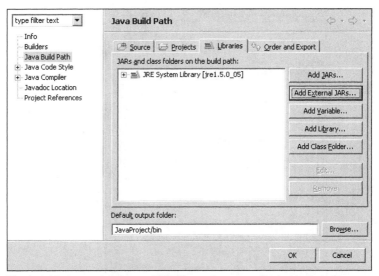

Figure 10-1 Adding a JAR file to the compiler's classpath

2 Choose Add External JARs. JAR Selection appears.

3 Navigate to Eclipse /plugins directory. In a default Eclipse installation, this directory is in the following location:

```
C:\eclipse\plugins
```

4 Select org.eclipse.birt.report.engine_*Version*.jar. Choose Add. Java Build Path appears.

5 Choose OK.

2 Select your Java project and choose File➔New➔Other. Select a wizard appears.

3 Expand Java and select Class, as shown in Figure 10-2.

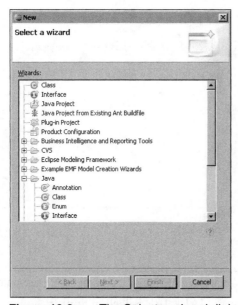

Figure 10-2   The Select a wizard dialog

Choose Next. Java Class appears, as shown in Figure 10-3.

Figure 10-3   Java Class

4 Navigate to the folder where you want the Java source file to reside by choosing the Browse button beside Source Folder.

5 If your new Java class is a part of a package, type the fully qualified package name in Package.

6 In Name, type a name for your class.

7 In Modifiers, choose Public.

8 Choose the Browse button beside Superclass. Superclass Selection appears, as shown in Figure 10-4.

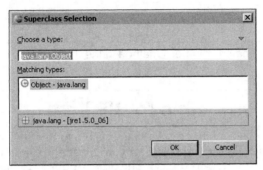

Figure 10-4   Superclass Selection

9 In Choose a type, type the name of the adapter class for the ROM element. For example, enter Label EventAdapter for the Label element. Choose OK. New Java Class reappears.

10 Select Generate comments. Choose Finish. A Java editor view appears, similar to the one shown in Figure 10-5.

```
MyLabelClass.java
    import org.eclipse.birt.report.engine.api.script.eventadapter.LabelEventAdapter;
    /**

    /**
     * @author dfrench
     *
     */
    public class MyLabelClass extends LabelEventAdapter {

    }
```

Figure 10-5   The Java editor

11 Add the event handler method for your new event handler class. Figure 10-6 shows the addition of an onPrepare( ) method that sets the background color of the label to red.

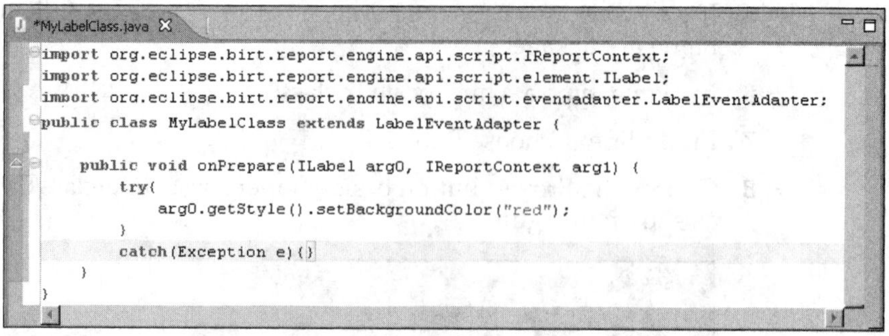

```
*MyLabelClass.java  ☒

import org.eclipse.birt.report.engine.api.script.IReportContext;
import org.eclipse.birt.report.engine.api.script.element.ILabel;
import org.eclipse.birt.report.engine.api.script.eventadapter.LabelEventAdapter;
public class MyLabelClass extends LabelEventAdapter {

    public void onPrepare(ILabel arg0, IReportContext arg1) {
        try{
            arg0.getStyle().setBackgroundColor("red");
        }
        catch(Exception e){}
    }
}
```

Figure 10-6   The onPrepare( ) method in the Java editor

Making the Java class visible to BIRT

One way to make a Java event handler class visible to the BIRT report designer is to create a Java development project for compiling the class in the same workspace as your BIRT report project. The other option is to place the class in a directory or JAR file that is specified in the BIRT classpath. When you deploy the report to an application server, however, you must copy the Java class to the appropriate location on the server. For more information about deploying Java classes to an application server, see the chapter about deploying BIRT to an application server.

Associating the Java event handler class with a report element

After you create the Java event handler class and code the appropriate handler methods, you must associate the class with the appropriate report element.

How to associate a Java class with a report element

The example in this procedure makes the following assumptions:

- The report design includes a scriptable report item, such as a label.

- A Java class containing event handler methods for the scriptable report item is visible to BIRT.

1 In Outline, select the report element for which an event handler class is visible to BIRT, as shown in Figure 10-7.

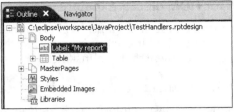

Figure 10-7   Selecting a report element

2   In Property Editor for the selected report element, select Event Handler and
enter the fully qualified name of your event handler class, as shown in
Figure 10-8.

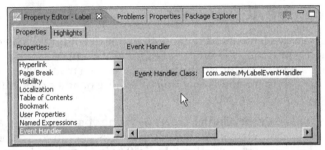

Figure 10-8   The event handler class name

BIRT Java interface and class naming conventions

When working with BIRT Java event handlers, you encounter event handler
interfaces, adapter classes, element instance interfaces, and element design
interfaces. All BIRT event handler classes and interfaces are named using
consistent naming conventions.

Naming convention for event handler interfaces

All BIRT ROM element interface names begin with the letter I, which is followed
by the name of the ROM element and then EventHandler. For example, the
interface for the Label element is ILabelEventHandler.

Naming convention for event handler adapter classes

All BIRT ROM element adapter class names begin with the name of the element,
followed by EventAdapter. For example, the name of the adapter class for a
Label element is LabelEventAdapter.

Naming convention for ROM element instance interfaces

All BIRT ROM element instance interface names begin with the letter I, followed by the name of the element and then Instance. For example, the ROM element instance interface for a Label element is ILabelInstance.

Naming convention for ROM element design interfaces

All BIRT ROM element instance design interface names begin with the letter I, followed by the name of the element. For example, the design interface for a Label element is ILabel.

Writing a Java event handler

Most scriptable elements have more than one event for which you can write a handler. If you write an event handler for any event of an element, the event handler class must include methods for all the events for that element. You can leave empty those methods that do not require handler code but the empty methods must appear in the class.

You can give an event handler class any name you choose. You associate the class with a report element in BIRT Report Designer in the Properties view, as explained earlier in this chapter. Your Java event handler class can either extend an adapter class or implement an event handler interface. Adapter classes and handler interfaces are explained in the next sections.

Using event handler adapter classes

BIRT provides event handler adapter classes for every scriptable report element. An event handler adapter class contains empty methods for every event handler method for the element. If your class extends an adapter class, you need to override only the methods for the events for which you want to provide handler code.

One advantage of using an adapter class instead of implementing an interface is that your class will compile even if methods are added to the interface in a future release. If the signature of an event handler method changes in a future release, however, you must change your implementation of that method to reflect the signature change. The class will compile even if you do not change the method with the changed signature, but the method with the wrong signature will never be called.

Using event handler interfaces

BIRT provides event handler interfaces for every scriptable report element. If your event handler class extends an adapter class, the adapter class implements the correct interface. If your class does not extend an adapter class, then your class must implement the appropriate interface for the report element you are scripting.

There are some advantages of specifying an interface instead of extending an adapter class. Eclipse generates stubs for every method the interface specifies. The stubs show the method arguments, so you can see the argument types of the methods you must implement. If your class extends an adapter class, there are no generated stubs for you to examine. You also have more freedom in the design of your class structure if you avoid using an adapter class. For example, you might want two or more event handler classes to extend a single base class. Because Java does not support multiple inheritance, the event handler class cannot extend both the adapter class and the base class. However, if the event handler class implements an interface instead of extending an adapter class, there is nothing to prevent the event handler class from extending the base class.

The disadvantage of using an interface over an adapter class is that if additional methods are added to an interface in a future release, a class that implements the interface fails to compile.

About the Java event handlers for report items

You can write an event handler for any or all the events that BIRT fires for a report item. Table 10-1 describes the events BIRT fires for each report item.

Table 10-1   Report item event handler methods

Method	Description
onPrepare( )	The onPrepare( ) method for every report element contains the following two arguments: ■ The element design interface ■ The report context interface
onCreate( )	The arguments to the onCreate( ) method depend on the particular element. Every onCreate( ) method contains at least the following two arguments: ■ The element instance interface ■ The report context interface
onPageBreak( )	The onPageBreak( ) method for every report element contains the following two arguments: ■ The element instance interface ■ The report context interface
onRender( )	The onRender( ) method for every report element contains the following two arguments: ■ The element instance interface ■ The report context interface

Using Java event handlers for the DataSource element

The DataSource event handler interface has four methods that you can implement to respond to events. A Java class to handle these events must implement the IDataSourceEventHandler interface or extend the DataSourceAdapter class.

All the event methods receive an IReportContext object. All the methods except the afterClose( ) method also receive an IDataSetInstance object. The onFetch( ) method also receives an IDataSetRow object. These interfaces are discussed later in this chapter. Table 10-2 lists the four methods that you can implement for a DataSource element.

Table 10-2   DataSource event handler methods

Method	Description
beforeOpen(IDataSourceInstance dataSource, IReportContext reportContext)	The beforeOpen event fires immediately before opening the data source. This handler is often used to change the connection properties, such as user name and password.
afterOpen(IDataSourceInstance dataSource, IReportContext reportContext)	The afterOpen event fires immediately after opening the data source.
beforeClose(IDataSourceInstance dataSource, IReportContext reportContext)	The beforeClose event fires immediately before closing the data source.
afterClose(IReportContext reportContext)	The afterClose event fires immediately after closing the data source.

Using Java event handlers for the DataSet element

BIRT fires five events for the DataSet element. A Java class to handle these events must implement the IDataSetEventHandler interface or extend the DataSetAdapter class. All DataSet event handler methods receive an IReportContext object. Additionally, all DataSet event handler methods except the afterClose( ) method receive an IDataSetInstance object. The onFetch( ) method receives a third object, an IDataSetRow object. These interfaces are described later in this chapter. Table 10-3 lists the five methods that you can implement for a DataSet element.

Table 10-3   DataSet event handler methods

Method	Description
beforeOpen(IDataSetInstance dataSet, IReportContext reportContext)	The beforeOpen event fires immediately before opening the data set. This event handler is often used to change the query text for a data set.
afterOpen(IDataSetInstance dataSet, IReportContext reportContext)	The afterOpen event fires immediately after opening the data set.
onFetch(IDataSetInstance dataSet, IDataSetRow row, IReportContext reportContext)	The onFetch event fires upon fetching each row from the data source.
beforeClose(IDataSetInstance dataSet, IReportContext reportContext)	The beforeClose event fires immediately before closing the data set.
afterClose(IReportContext reportContext)	The afterClose event fires immediately after closing the data set.

Using Java event handlers for the ScriptedDataSource element

The ScriptedDataSource interface extends the IDataSourceEventHandler interface, which has four methods. The ScriptedDataSource interface adds two new methods to the four of the IDataSourceEventHandler interface. A Java class that provides the ScriptedDataSource event handlers must implement IScriptedDataSourceEventHandler interface or extend the ScriptedDataSourceAdapter class. A Java class that provides the ScriptedDataSource event handlers must implement the two methods of the IScriptedDataSourceEventHandler interface plus the four methods of the IDataSourceEventHandler interface, which it extends.

Both of the two event handler methods of IScriptedDataSourceEventHandler receive an IDataSourceInstance object. Table 10-4 lists the two additional methods that you must implement for a ScriptedDataSource element.

Table 10-4   ScriptedDataSource event handler methods

Method	Description
open(IDataSourceInstance dataSource)	Use this method to open the data source.
close(IDataSourceInstance dataSource)	Use this method to close the data source and perform cleanup tasks.

Using Java event handlers for the ScriptedDataSet element

The ScriptedDataSet interface extends the IDataSetEventHandler interface, which has four methods. The ScriptedDataSet interface adds four new methods to the four of the IDataSourceEventHandler interface. Of the four new methods, three must be fully implemented and the fourth may be empty. A Java class that provides the ScriptedDataSet event handlers must implement IScriptedDataSetEventHandler interface or extend the ScriptedDataSetAdapter class. A Java class that provides the ScriptedDataSet event handlers must implement the four methods of the IScriptedDataSetEventHandler interface plus the four methods of the IDataSourceEventHandler interface, which it extends.

Table 10-5 lists the four additional methods that you must implement for a ScriptedDataSet element.

Table 10-5   ScriptedDataSet event handler methods

Method	Description
open(IDataSetInstance dataSet)	Called when the data set is opened. Use this method to initialize variables and to prepare for fetching rows.
fetch(IDataSetInstance dataSet, IUpdatableDataSetRow dataSetRow)	Called at row processing time. Use this method to fetch data with which to populate the row object. This method must return true if the fetch is successful and false if it is not.
close(IDataSetInstance dataSet)	Called upon completion of processing a data set. Use this method to perform cleanup operations.
describe(IDataSetInstance dataSet, IScriptedDataSetMetaData metaData metaData)	Use this method to define the column names and types of the data set.

Using Java event handlers for the ReportDesign

BIRT fires several events that the ReportDesign element handles. A Java class to handle these events must implement the IReportEventHandler interface or extend the ReportEventAdapter class. All of the event handler methods receive an IReportContext object. The beforeFactory( ) method also receives an

IReportDesign object. Table 10-6 lists the methods that you can implement for a ReportDesign element in the order in which they fire.

Table 10-6   ReportDesign event handler methods

Method	Description
initialize(IReportContext reportContext)	The initialize event is fired twice, once before the generation phase begins and once before the render phase begins.
beforeFactory(IReportDesign report, IReportContext reportContext)	The beforeFactory event is fired before the generation phase begins.
afterFactory(IReportContext reportContext)	The afterFactory event is fired after the generation phase ends.
beforeRender(IReportContext reportContext)	The beforeRender event is fired before the presentation phase begins.
afterRender(IReportContext reportContext)	The afterRender event is fired after the presentation phase ends.

Understanding the BIRT interfaces

A developer of Java event handlers needs to be familiar with several Java interfaces. Most of the handler method parameters and return values are Java interfaces rather than classes.

The most important Java interfaces for developing Java event handlers are:

- The element design interfaces
- The IReportElement interface
- The element instance interfaces
- The report context interfaces
- The IColumnMetaData interface
- The IDataSetInstance interface
- The IDataSourceInstance interface
- The IDataSetRow interface
- The IRowData interface

About the element design interfaces

Every element has a unique element design interface. The element design is a Java interface that specifies methods for accessing and setting specific features of the element's design. Every element design interface inherits methods from IReportElement.

About the methods for each report element

Besides the methods defined in IReportElement, each report element has methods that are only relevant for that report element. For example, ICell, the design interface for a Cell object, includes the following methods in addition to those defined in IReportElement:

- getColumn( )
- getColumnSpan( )
- getDrop( )
- getHeight( )
- getRowSpan( )
- getWidth( )
- setColumn(int column)
- setColumnSpan(int span)
- setDrop(java.lang.String drop)
- setRowSpan(int span)

In contrast, the methods for ITextItem, the design interface for a TextItem element, includes these additional methods:

- getContent( )
- getContentKey( )
- getContentType( )
- getDisplayContent( )
- setContent(java.lang.String value)
- setContentKey(java.lang.String resourceKey)
- setContentType(java.lang.String contentType)

For a complete list of all the design interfaces, see the BIRT Javadoc. To access the Javadoc, choose BIRT Developer Guide➤Reference in the online help.

About the IReportElement interface

The IReportElement interface is the base interface for all the report element interfaces. IReportElement has the following methods:

- getComments( )
- getCustomXml( )
- getDisplayName( )
- getDisplayNameKey( )
- getName( )
- getNamedExpression(java.lang.String name)
- getParent( )
- getQualifiedName( )
- getStyle( )
- getUserProperty(java.lang.String name)
- setComments(java.lang.String theComments)
- setCustomXml(java.lang.String customXml)
- setDisplayName(java.lang.String displayName)
- setDisplayNameKey(java.lang.String displayNameKey)
- setName(java.lang.String name)
- setNamedExpression(java.lang.String name, java.lang.String exp)
- setUserProperty(java.lang.String name, java.lang.Object value)

For more information about the methods defined in the IReportElement interface, including the arguments and return values of all its methods, see the BIRT Javadoc in the BIRT online help.

About the element instance interfaces

The element instance interfaces are available at run time, but not at design time. They contain the run-time instance of the element. The element instance interface is passed to both onCreate( ), the generation phase event handler, and to onRender( ), the presentation phase event handler.

Through instance interfaces, you have access to a different set of properties than you do at design time. There is no superinterface from which all element instance interfaces inherit. Like the element design interface, the set of methods in the instance interfaces varies from element to element.

For example, ICellInstance, the Cell instance interface, contains the following methods:

- getColSpan( )
- getColumn( )
- getRowSpan( )

- setColSpan(int colSpan)
- setRowSpan(int rowSpan)

By comparison, IRowInstance, the Row instance interface, contains these methods:

- getBookmarkValue( )
- getHeight( )
- getStyle( )
- setBookmark( )
- setHeight( )

For a complete list of all instance interfaces, see the BIRT Javadoc in the BIRT online help.

Using the IReportContext interface

An object of type IReportContext is passed to all event handlers except those for ScriptedDataSource and ScriptedDataSet objects. The IReportContext interface includes the methods shown in Table 10-7.

Table 10-7   IReportContext interface methods

Method	Task
deleteGlobalVariable(java.lang.String name)	Removes a global variable created using the setGlobalVariable( ) method.
deletePersistentGlobalVariable(java.lang .String name)	Removes a persistent global variable created using the setPersistentGlobalVariable( ) method.
getAppContext( )	Retrieves the application context object as a java.util.Map object. The report application can use the application context object to pass any information that is application-specific. One example of information passed through an application context object is the HTTPSession object.
getGlobalVariable(java.lang.String name)	Returns the object saved with the setGlobalVariable( ) method. The string argument is the key with which the object was saved.
getHttpServletRequest( )	Returns the HttpServletRequest object associated with the URL requesting the report. The HttpServletRequest object provides access to the request URL and any parameters that are appended to the request.

Table 10-7   IReportContext interface methods *(continued)*

Method	Task
getLocale( )	Returns the locale associated with the report execution or rendering task. This locale might be different from the local machine's system or user locale.
getMessage(java.lang.String key)	Returns a message from the default properties file.
getMessage(java.lang.String key, java.util.Locale locale, java.lang.Object[] params)	Returns a message from the properties file for a specified locale, using a parameters array.
getMessage(java.lang.String key, java.lang.Object[] params)	Returns a message from the default properties file, using a parameters array.
getOutputFormat( )	Returns a string containing either html or pdf, depending on which format was specified in the __format parameter of the request URL.
getParameterValue(java.lang.String name)	Returns the value of the parameter named in the name argument. The value returned is a java.lang.Object.
getPersistentGlobalVariable(java.lang .String name)	Returns the serializable object saved with the setPersistentGlobalVariable( ) method. The string argument is the key with which the serializable object was saved.
setGlobalVariable(java.lang.String name, java.lang.Object obj)	Saves an object that can be retrieved in the same execution phase as it is saved. The setGlobalVariable( ) method takes a string argument and an Object argument. You use the string argument as a key with which to later retrieve the saved object.
setParameterValue(java.lang.String name, java.lang.Object value)	Sets the value of a named parameter with the value contained in the value parameter.
setPersistentGlobalVariable(java.lang .String name, java.io.Serializable obj)	Saves an object that can be retrieved in a different execution phase than it is saved. The setPersistentGlobalVariable( ) method takes a string argument and a serializable object argument. You use the string argument as a key with which to later retrieve the serializable object. The object is serializable because it must be persisted between phases to support executing the two phases at different times and possibly on different machines. The serializable object is saved in the report document.

Using the IColumnMetaData interface

The IColumnMetaData interface provides information about the columns of the data set. Table 10-8 lists the methods in the IColumnMetaData interface class.

Table 10-8   IColumnMetaData interface methods

Method	Returns
getColumnAlias(int index)	The alias assigned to the column at the position indicated by the index argument
getColumnCount( )	The count of columns in the data set
getColumnLabel(int index)	The label assigned to the column at the position indicated by the index argument
getColumnName(int index)	A string containing the name of the column at the position indicated by the index argument
getColumnNativeTypeName (int index)	The name of the type of data in the column at the position indicated by the index argument
getColumnType(int index)	The data type of the column at the position indicated by the index argument
getColumnTypeName (int index)	The name of the type of data in the column at the position indicated by the index argument
isComputedColumn (int index)	True or false, depending on whether the column at the position indicated by the index argument is a computed field

Using the IDataSetInstance interface

The IDataSetInstance interface provides access to many aspects of the data set and associated elements. An IDataSetInstance object is passed to every DataSet event handler method.

Table 10-9 describes the methods in the interface IDataSetInstance.

Table 10-9   IDataSetInstance interface methods

Method	Returns
getAllExtensionProperties( )	The data set extension properties in the form of a java.util.Map object. The map object maps data extension names to their values.
getColumnMetaData( )	An IColumnMetaData object that provides the data set's metadata.
getDataSource( )	A DataSource object with which the data set is associated.

Table 10-9   IDataSetInstance interface methods *(continued)*

Method	Returns
getExtensionID( )	The unique ID that identifies the type of the data set, assigned by the extension that implements this data set.
getExtensionProperty(java.lang .String name)	The value of a data set extension property.
getName( )	The name of this data set.
getQueryText( )	The query text of the data set.
setExtensionProperty(java.lang .String name, java.lang.String value)	The value of an extension property.
setQueryText(java.lang.String queryText)	The query text of the data set.

Using the IDataSetRow interface

An object of the IDataSetRow type is passed to the DataSet.onfetch( ) event handler method. Table 10-10 lists the methods in the IDataSetRow interface. Note that there are two getColumnValue( ) methods. The two methods differ only in the argument that specifies the column containing the value. They both return a java.lang.Object object, which you must cast to the appropriate type for the column.

Table 10-10   IDataSetRow interface methods

Method	Returns
getColumnValue(int index)	The column data by index. This index is 1-based.
getColumnValue(java.lang.String name)	The column data by column name.
getDataSet( )	An IDataSetInstance object representing the data set that contains this row.

Using the IRowData interface

An object of the IRowData type is returned from the getRowData( ) method of IReportElementInstance, which every report element instance interface extends.

IRowData provides access to the bound values that appear in the table. The IRowData interface has two getExpressionValue( ) methods. Both methods return the display value for a specific column in the table. The two methods differ in the argument you pass to specify the column that you require. Table 10-11 lists the methods in the IRowData interface.

Table 10-11   IRowData interface methods

Method	Returns
getColumnCount( )	Return the count of the bounding expressions.
getColumnName(int index)	Return the name of the bounding expression by id.
getColumnValue(int index)	Return the value of the bounding expression by id. This index is 1-based.
getColumnValue(String name)	Return the value of the bounding expression by name.

Using a Scripted Data Source

BIRT supports accessing a data source using JavaScript code. A data source that you access using JavaScript is called a scripted data source. With a scripted data source, you can access objects other than a SQL, XML, or text file data source. Because the JavaScript code for accessing and managing a scripted data source can wrap Java objects, a scripted data source can be an EJB, an XML stream, a Hibernate object, or any other Java object that retrieves data.

A scripted data source must return data in tabular format so that BIRT can perform sorting, aggregation, and grouping.

Creating a scripted data source and scripted data set

Creating a scripted data source and creating a non-scripted data source are similar. The differences between creating a scripted data source and a non-scripted data source are:

- The report developer must select Scripted Data Source from the list of data source types when creating a scripted data source.

- The report developer can provide code for two event handler methods, open( ) and close( ), that are only available for a scripted data source.

Every scripted data source must have at least one scripted data set. The differences between creating a scripted data set and a non-scripted data set are:

- The report developer must associate the scripted data set with a scripted data source.

- The report developer must provide code for the scripted data set fetch( ) event handler method.

- The report developer uses a different dialog for identifying the columns of a scripted data set than for a non-scripted data set.

When you use BIRT Report Designer to create a scripted data source, you must perform the following tasks:

- Create a scripted data source.

  Right-click on Data Sources in the data explorer and select Scripted Data Source in the list of data source types.

- Create a scripted data set.

  Right-click on Data Sets in the data explorer and select a scripted data source from the list of available data sources.

- Define output columns.

  Define the names and types of output columns, using the scripted data set editor.

- Supply code for the data source open( ) and close( ) methods.

  There are two scripted data source event handler methods, open( ) and close( ). It is not mandatory that you implement either method, but most applications require the use of the open( ) method.

  Use the open( ) method to initialize a data source. Typically, you create a Java object for accessing the data source in the open( ) method.

  Use the close( ) method to clean up any loose ends, including setting object references to null to ensure that the objects are deleted during garbage collection.

- Supply code for the data set methods.

  There are three scripted data set event handler methods, open( ), fetch( ), and close( ). It is mandatory that you implement only the fetch( ) method.

  Use the open( ) method to initialize variables and to prepare the data source for fetching data.

  Use the fetch( ) method to get a row of data from the data source and to populate the columns of the row object. The fetch( ) method must return either true or false. A true value tells BIRT that there is another row to process. A false return value signifies that there are no more rows to process.

  Use the close( ) method to perform cleanup operations.

- Place the columns on the report layout.

  Place a data set column on a report layout the same way you place a column for a non-scripted data set.

The following tutorial guides you through the procedure required to perform each task in this process.

Tutorial 2: Creating and scripting a scripted data source

This tutorial provides instructions for creating and scripting a simulated scripted data source. Although this tutorial does not use an actual data source, you learn the process for scripting a real data source.

In this tutorial, you perform the following tasks:

- Create a new report.
- Create a scripted data source.
- Create a scripted data set.
- Supply code for the open( ) and close( ) methods of the data source.
- Supply code for the data set open( ) method.
- Define output columns.
- Place the columns on the report layout.
- Supply code for the data set fetch( ) method.

Task 1: Create a new report

In this task you create a new report in BIRT Report Designer and name it ScriptedDataSrc.rptdesign.

1 Choose File➤New➤Report.

2 In File Name in New Report, type:

```
ScriptedDataSrc.rptdesign
```

3 In Enter or Select the Parent Folder, accept the default folder. Choose Next.

4 In Report Templates, select My First Report. Choose Finish. The BIRT report design screen appears. If a Cheat Sheet tab appears, close it.

Task 2: Create a scripted data source

In this task you create the new data source.

1 In Data Explorer, right-click Data Sources and choose New Data Source. Select a Data Source type appears.

2 In New Data Source, select Scripted Data Source.

3 In Data Source Name, type:

```
ScriptedDataSource
```

4 Choose Finish.

Data Explorer and the code window for ScriptedDataSource appear, as shown in Figure 11-1.

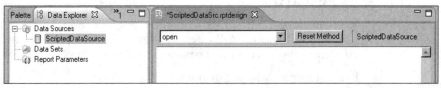

Figure 11-1   Data Explorer and ScriptedDataSource code window

Task 3: Create a scripted data set

In this task, you create the new data set.

1 In Data Explorer, right-click Data Sets. Choose New Data Set. New Data Set appears, as shown in Figure 11-2.

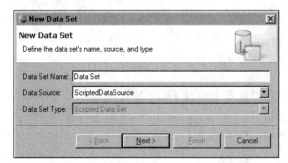

Figure 11-2   New data set for a scripted data source

2 In Data Set Name, type:

```
ScriptedDataSet
```

3 Choose Finish.

4 In Data Explorer, select ScriptedDataSet. The script window for the data set appears, as shown in Figure 11-3.

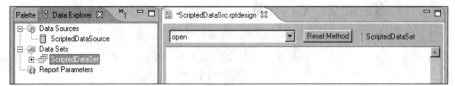

Figure 11-3   Code window for ScriptedDataSet

Task 4: Supply code for the open( ) and close( ) methods of the data source

In the open( ) method, you open the data source. In the close( ) method, you do cleanup tasks. In this tutorial, there is no actual data source but typically you need to place some code in these methods. The open( ) method is the default selected method upon creating a data set.

1 If necessary, select open from the pull-down list of methods.

2 Type the following code into the code window for the open( ) method:

```
dummyObject = new Object( );
```

The preceding code is a placeholder for the purpose of this simplified example. In a typical application, you use this method to initialize a Java object that provides access to the data for the report.

3 Select close from the pull-down list of methods.

4 Type the following code into the code window:

```
dummyObject = null;
```

Task 5: Supply code for the open( ) method of the data set

When you create the data set, the open( ) method is selected by default. Use the open( ) method of the data set to do initialization, such as defining a counter and setting it to zero.

1 Select open from the pull-down list of methods.

2 Type the following code into the code window:

```
recordCount = 0;
```

Task 6: Define output columns

To create the output columns for a scripted data set, you must edit the data set. The columns you create in the data set editor are the columns that the data set fetch( ) method generates.

1 In Data Explorer, double-click ScriptedDataSet. Edit Data Set—ScriptedDataSet appears, as shown in Figure 11-4.

Figure 11-4   Edit Data Set for a scripted data source

2 Select Output Columns. Output Columns appears.

3 In the Name column of the first row, type:

```
col1
```

4 Select the Type column of the first row. Select Integer from the drop-down list. Output Columns contains the definition of one output column, as shown in Figure 11-5.

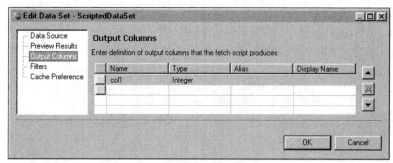

Figure 11-5   Column name and type in Output Columns

5 In the Name column of the second row, type:

```
col2
```

6 In the Type column of the second row, select String.

7 In the Name column of the third row, type:

```
col3
```

In the Type column of the third row, select Float. Output Columns contains the definition of three output columns, as shown in Figure 11-6. Choose OK.

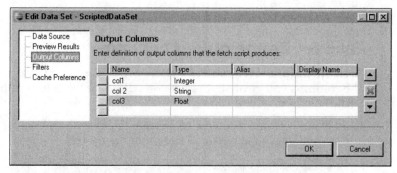

Figure 11-6   Column definitions

Task 7: Place the columns on the report layout

You place columns for a scripted data set in the same way as for a non-scripted data set.

1 On ScriptedDataSrc.rptdesign, select Layout.

2 Drag Table from Palette onto the layout.

3 Accept the default table size of three columns and one detail row.

4 In Data Explorer, expand ScriptedDataSet. The three columns you created appear in Data Explorer, as shown in Figure 11-7.

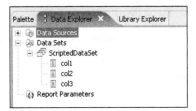

Figure 11-7   New columns in ScriptedDataSet

5 Add the columns to the report detail row:

1 Drag col1 from Data Explorer to the first column of the report detail row.

2 Drag col2 from Data Explorer to the second column of the report detail row.

3 Drag col3 from Data Explorer to the third column of the report detail row.

Figure 11-8 shows the three columns of the data set in the layout editor.

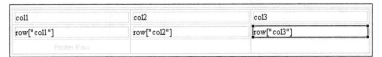

Figure 11-8   New columns in the report design

6 Choose Preview.

The preview of the report appears, as shown in Figure 11-9.

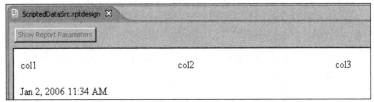

Figure 11-9   Report preview, showing the new columns

Task 8: Supply code for the data set fetch( ) method

Use the fetch( ) method to process row data. The fetch( ) method must return either true or false. Fetch( ) returns true to indicate that there is a row to process. Fetch( ) returns false to indicate that there are no more rows to process. The fetch( ) method also calculates the values of computed fields.

The report only has column headings at this point. To include data, you must add code to the fetch( ) method.

1 Choose the Layout tab.

2 Right-click ScriptedDataSet in Data Explorer. Choose Edit Script.

3 Select fetch in the drop-down list of methods.

4 Select fetch from the pull-down list of methods in the data set code window.

5 Type the following code into the code window. This code limits the number of rows that appear in the report to 19.

```
if(recordCount < 20) {
    recordCount++;
    row.col1 = recordCount;
    row["col2"] = "Count = " + recordCount;
    row[3] = recordCount * 0.5;
    return true;
}
else return false;
```

The three formats in the preceding script illustrate the different ways you can specify a column of a row. The code appears as shown in Figure 11-10.

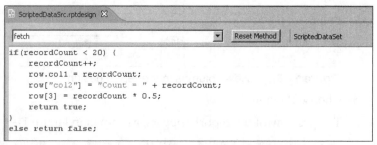

Figure 11-10   Code that generates column output

6 Choose Preview.

The report now contains 20 rows and 3 columns of data, as shown in Figure 11-11.

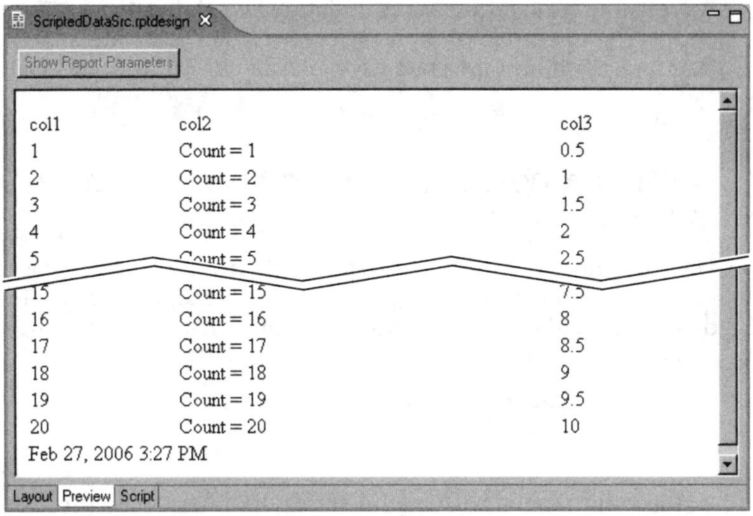

Figure 11-11 Report preview

Using a Java object to access a data source

A common use of a scripted data set is to access a Java object that accesses or generates the data for a report. This section shows how to access a Java class from within the JavaScript code for a scripted data set.

Performing initialization in the data set open( ) method

Use the data set open( ) method to perform initialization tasks. A typical initialization task is to get an instance of the Java object that provides the data for the report.

When referring to a Java object, first import its package into the JavaScript environment. For example, the following code imports the package com.yourCompany.yourApplication:

```
importPackage(Packages.com.yourCompany.yourApplication);
```

This statement is like the import statement in Java and allows you to omit the package name when referencing a class. This statement is normally the first line of code in the open( ) method. You typically follow the importPackage statement with code to create an instance of the Java object, as shown in the following example:

```
var myList = MyListFactory.getList();
```

A typical way of getting rows of data from a Java object is to use an iterator object. The open( ) method is the proper place to create an iterator object. For example, the following statement gets an iterator from myList:

```
var iterator = myList.getIterator();
```

Getting a new row of data in the data set fetch( ) method

Once you have a way to get rows of data from your Java object, use the fetch( ) method to call the Java method that returns the rows. The fetch( ) method determines if there are any more rows of data and returns false if there are none, as shown in the following code:

```
if(iterator.hasNext() == false ){
   return false;
}
```

At this point, the fetch( ) method can populate a row with data that it gets from the iterator, as shown in the following code:

```
var node = iterator.next( );
row[1] = node.getFirstCol( );
row[2] = node.getSecondCol( );
row[3] = node.getThirdCol( );
```

Then, you must return true to signal BIRT there is a valid row of data to process:

```
return true;
```

Cleaning up in the data set close( ) method

You can perform any cleanup in the close( ) method. This method is a good place to set to null any objects that you created. For example, the following code sets three object references to null:

```
myList = null;
iterator = null;
node = null;
```

Deciding where to locate your Java class

If a scripted data source uses a custom Java class, that class must reside in a location where BIRT can find it. BIRT can find the Java class if its location meets any of the following requirements:

- The Java class is in the classpath of the Java Runtime Environment (JRE) under which Eclipse runs.

  Consider using this option if your Java class is in this location for other reasons.

- The Java class is in <ECLIPSE_INSTALL>\plugins\
  org.eclipse.birt.report.viewer\birt\WEB-INF\lib.

  Consider using this option if your Java class is built and tested and ready to
  deploy.

- The Java class is a part of an Eclipse Java project that is in the same
  workspace as the BIRT report project.

  Consider using this option if you are developing your Java class
  simultaneously with developing your BIRT report.

Deploying your Java class

Before you deploy your BIRT report to an application server, you must place
your Java class in a JAR file. You must then deploy that JAR file to the proper
location on the application server so that the BIRT report viewer can find it at
run time. For more information about where to deploy Java classes on an
application server, see the chapter about deploying BIRT to an application
server.

Using input and output parameters with a scripted
data set

The scritped data set JavaScript event handler methods have two arrays you can
use to access parameters, inputParams and outputParams. The inputParams
array contains one string for every parameter whose direction is defined as
input. The outputParams array contains one string for every parameter whose
direction is defined as output.

For example, assume that you have a scripted data set with an input and an
output parameter, as shown in Figure 11-12:

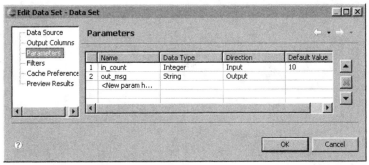

Figure 11-12 A scripted data set, with input and output parameters

You can get and set the values of the out_msg and in_count parameters by using the inputParams and outputParams arrays as in the following example:

```
outputParams["out_msg"] = "Total rows: " +
    inputParams["in_count"];
```

You can access a parameter in the array either by the name of the parameter or by a 1-based index value. The inputParams and outputParams arrays are not accessible to Java event handlers.

Integrating BIRT Functionality into Applications

Understanding the BIRT APIs

BIRT consists of hundreds of Java classes and interfaces, but most of them are only of interest to contributors to the BIRT open source project. Developers of applications only require access to the classes and interfaces that are in the public API. The public API consists of the classes and interfaces in the following package hierarchies:

- Report engine API

    The org.eclipse.birt.report.engine.api package hierarchy contains the API that a developer of a custom report generator uses. This API provides the most commonly used functionality for a reporting application. The key class in the report engine API is ReportEngine. This class provides access to creating a report from a report design or a report document.

- Design engine API

    The org.eclipse.birt.report.model.api package hierarchy is by far the larger of the two reporting APIs. This API provides access to the content and structure of a report design, a template, or a library. A reporting application can use this API to change the structure of a design. The design engine API is also the API that a developer of a custom report designer uses.

- Chart engine API

    The org.eclipse.birt.chart package hierarchy contains the API that a developer of a custom chart generator uses. A reporting application can also use this API to modify charts in a report design.

- Extension APIs

BIRT also provides a set of extension APIs for creating custom report items, custom data sources and data sets, custom rendering formats, and custom charts. Chapters later in this book describe how to use these extensions.

For information on class and interface methods, see the API Javadoc, which you can access from the BIRT Report Designer or Eclipse Workbench main menu at Help➤Help Contents➤BIRT Developer Guide.

Package hierarchy diagrams

This chapter contains hierarchical diagrams for packages. These diagrams show the hierarchy of the classes in the package and interfaces local to the package or implemented by classes in the package. Classes and interfaces preceded by a package name are not local to the package. The hierarchical diagrams indicate different attributes and relationships in the classes and interfaces by means of the graphics shown in Table 12-1.

Table 12-1 Conventions for the hierarchy diagrams

■ Abstract class	
■ Class that has one or more subclasses	
■ Class with no subclasses	
■ Final class	
■ Interface	
■ Solid lines indicate a superclass-subclass relationship	
■ Broken lines indicate an implementation relationship	
■ An asterisk indicates too many subclasses to list	

About the BIRT Report Engine API

The BIRT Report Engine provides report generation and rendering services in several different environments, including the following environments:

- Stand-alone engine

  A Java developer uses a stand-alone engine to render an existing BIRT report from a report design (.rptdesign) file. In this environment, the Java developer creates a command line application that writes a complete report to disk, either in HTML or PDF format.

- BIRT report viewer

  BIRT Report Designer uses the BIRT report viewer to view a report as paginated HTML. The BIRT report viewer is a web application that runs in the Tomcat Application Server, which is embedded in Eclipse. This viewer contains an embedded report engine.

- Custom report designer with an embedded engine

  A custom desktop reporting application integrates the BIRT Report Engine for the purpose of previewing the report.

- Web application that embeds the engine

  A web application similar to the BIRT report viewer can use the BIRT report engine to generate a web-based report.

The BIRT Report Engine is designed for easy customization to support the diverse environments in which it can be used. The BIRT Report Engine also supports seamless extension. The core engine runs and renders reports, leaving environment-dependent processing such as URL construction, image storage, and design file caching to the application that hosts the engine.

The BIRT Report Engine API consists of a set of interfaces and implementation classes. The BIRT Report Engine API supports integrating the run-time part of BIRT into your application. The API provides a set of task classes that support the following operations:

- Discover the set of parameters defined for a report.

- Get the default values for parameters.

- Run a report design to produce an unformatted report document.

- Run a report design or report document to produce an HTML or PDF formatted report.

- Extract data from a report document.

Creating the BIRT Report Engine

Each application, whether it is stand-alone or web-based, only needs to create one ReportEngine instance. Since the BIRT Report Engine is thread-safe, the single-instance recommendation is not a restriction.

Create the BIRT Report Engine with a constructor that takes an EngineConfig object as an argument. The configuration object can be null, in which case a default engine configuration is used. At termination, the application should call shutdown( ) to unload extensions and delete temporary files.

Using the BIRT Report Engine API

The following are the primary steps in using the BIRT Report Engine API:

- Create an instance of EngineConfig to set options for the report engine.
- Create an instance of the ReportEngine class.
- Open a report design using one of the openReportDesign( ) methods of ReportEngine or open a report document using the openReportDocument( ) method.
- Obtain information about report parameters using IGetParameterDefinitionTask.
- Run and render a report using IRunAndRenderTask or IRunTask followed by IRenderTask.
- Call shutdown( ) on your engine instance.

There are a few primary classes and interfaces that provide the core functionality of the BIRT Report Engine. The following sections provide an overview of these classes. For full details, see the Javadoc.

EngineConfig class

The EngineConfig class wraps configuration settings for a report engine. Use the EngineConfig object to set global options for the report engine, including:

- Specifying the location of engine plug-ins and Java archive (.jar) files
- Specifying the location of data drivers
- Adding application-wide scriptable objects
- Managing logging

ReportEngine class

The ReportEngine class represents the BIRT report engine. You create the ReportEngine class with a constructor that takes an EngineConfig object. If the configuration object is null, the environment must provide a BIRT_HOME variable that specifies the directory that contains the engine plug-ins and JAR files.

You use a ReportEngine object to perform the following tasks:

- Get the configuration object.

- Open a report design or a report document.

- Create an engine task to get parameter definitions and set parameter values.

- Create an engine task to access the data from a data set.

- Get supported report formats and MIME types.

- Create an engine task to run a report or render a report to an output format.

- Create an engine task to extract data from a report document.

- Clean up and shut down the engine.

IReportRunnable interface

To work with the report design with the engine, you must load the design using one of the openReportDesign( ) methods in the ReportEngine class. These methods return an IReportRunnable instance that represents the engine's view of the report design.

You use an IReportRunnable object to perform the following tasks:

- Get any parameter data.

- Get properties such as the report title and report author.

- Get any images embedded within the report design.

- Run the report.

IReportDocument interface

To work with a report document with the engine, you must load the document using the ReportEngine.openReportDocument( ) method. This method returns an IReportDocument instance.

You use an IReportDocument object to render a report to HTML or PDF with an IRenderTask object. You can use the table of contents markers in the IReportDocument to determine which pages to render.

IEngineTask interface

The IEngineTask interface provides the framework for the tasks that the report engine performs. The IEngineTask interface manages the scripting context and report locales. The other task interfaces extend IEngineTask.

IGetParameterDefinitionTask interface

The IGetParameterDefinitionTask interface extends IEngineTask to provide access to information about parameters. The engine factory method to create an

IGetParameterDefinitionTask object takes an IReportRunnable argument. Parameter definitions provide access to:

- Information that BIRT Report Designer specified at design time
- Static or dynamic selection lists
- User-supplied values
- The grouping structure of the parameters
- Custom XML
- User-defined properties

IDataExtractionTask interface

The IDataExtractionTask interface extends IEngineTask to provide access to the data stored in an IReportDocument object. You can use an IDataExtractionTask object to examine the metadata for a set of data rows. Using the metadata, you can select a set of columns to extract, sort, or filter. This interface can extract the data from:

- The whole report document
- A single report item
- A single instance of a report item

IRunTask interface

The IRunTask interface provides the methods to run a report design. This task saves the result as a report document (.rptdocument) file to disk.

An IRunTask object takes parameter values as a HashMap. Call the validateParameters( ) method to validate the parameter values before you run the report.

IRenderTask interface

The IRenderTask interface provides the methods to render a report document to PDF or to paginated or unpaginated HTML. This task can save the report to disk or to a stream.

You can set options that are specific to each of the HTML and PDF formats. Set these options through the HTMLRenderOption and PDFRenderOption classes. Pass the appropriate render option object for your report to the IRenderTask object before rendering the report.

IRunAndRenderTask interface

The IRunAndRenderTask interface provides the methods to render a report as unpaginated HTML. This task can save the report to disk or to a stream.

An IRunAndRenderTask object takes parameter values as a HashMap. Call the validateParameters( ) method to validate the parameter values before you run the report.

You can set options that are specific to HTML format. Set these options through the HTMLRenderOption class. Pass the render option object for your report to the IRunAndRenderTask object before running the report.

Report engine class hierarchy

The class hierarchy in Figure 12-1 illustrates the organization of the classes within the report engine package. The names of the classes in the diagram do not include the package name, which is org.eclipse.birt.report.engine.api.

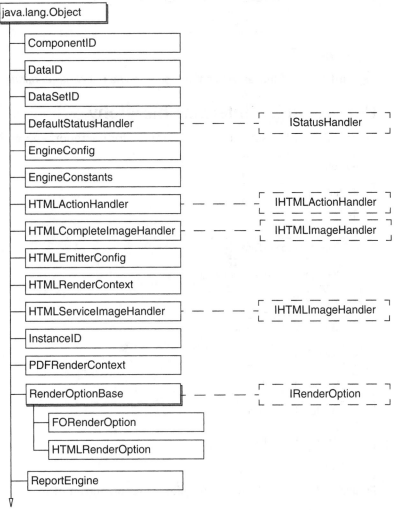

Figure 12-1   Classes within the report engine package *(continues)*

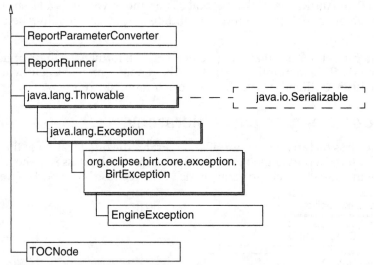

Figure 12-1   Classes within the report engine package *(continued)*

Report engine interface hierarchy

Figure 12-2 contains the interface hierarchy for the report engine API.

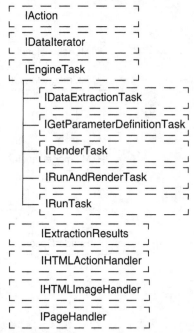

Figure 12-2   Interface hierarchy for the report engine API

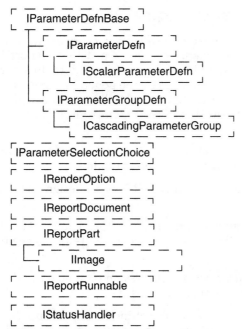

Figure 12-2 Interface hierarchy for the report engine API *(continued)*

About the design engine API

The design engine API is also known as the report model API. The design engine API is the API that a tool writer uses to build a design tool. The design engine API contains classes and methods to create, access, and validate a report design.

The org.eclipse.birt.report.model.api package contains the interfaces and classes that the tool writer uses to access the design model objects. Through the design engine API, you can do the following tasks:

- Read and write design files.

- Maintain the command history for undo and redo.

- Provide a rich semantic representation of the report design.

- Provide metadata about the ROM.

- Perform property value validation.

- Notify the application when the model changes.

Using the BIRT design engine API

The purpose of the BIRT design engine API is to modify or create a report design file that the BIRT report engine can use to generate a report. BIRT Report Designer, for example, uses the BIRT design engine API for this purpose. A custom report design tool, written for the same general purpose as BIRT Report Designer, can also use the BIRT design engine API to generate a design file. The design engine API also supports libraries and templates in the same way as report designs.

The BIRT design engine API does not include a user interface. A custom report design tool must provide its own user interface code.

With the design engine, you can create a BIRT report design by performing the following tasks:

- With a static DesignEngine method, instantiating a SessionHandle object to load the property definitions of the report elements and to begin a user session
- With the SessionHandle object, setting session parameters and creating an instance of the ReportDesignHandle class
- With the ReportDesignHandle object, setting the report-specific properties, adding elements to the report design, and providing access to the report elements
- Saving the report design file

The following sections describe the primary classes of the BIRT design engine API.

DesignEngine class

The DesignEngine class is the gateway to creating the other objects you need to build a report design tool. Use the static methods of the DesignEngine class to:

- Load the metadata system.

  The initialize( ) method takes an argument containing the path to a file containing report element metadata. The metadata system describes the BIRT ROM elements and their properties and relationships. The metadata file that BIRT Report Designer uses is called rom.def. If you use this file, you do not need to call initialize( ).

- Create a SessionHandle object.

  Use the newSession( ) method to perform this task. The SessionHandle provides a gateway to the ReportDesign object.

SessionHandle class

The SessionHandle class represents the user session. A SessionHandle object provides access to the set of open designs. A session has a set of default values for style properties and a default unit of measure. The session also has methods to create and open report designs, templates, and libraries. The methods to create or open a report design return a ReportDesignHandle object.

ModuleHandle class

ModuleHandle provides access to the common structure and functionality of report designs, templates, and libraries. It is the parent class of the ReportDesignHandle and LibraryHandle classes. ModuleHandle provides access to the generic properties, such as author and comments. You also use ModuleHandle for many tasks on the file, including:

- Saving the module to a file
- Accessing the command stack for undo and redo
- Navigating to the various parts of the module
- Accessing the command stack
- Getting configuration variables

The ModuleHandle also has methods to get handles to the individual report items and all the other elements in a report design, template, or library. These elements and supporting components include:

- Report items. These elements are visual report elements such as tables, grids, images, and text elements.
- Code modules. These modules are global scripts that apply to the file as a whole.
- Parameters.
- Data sources and data sets.
- Color Palette. This component is a set of custom color names.
- CSS files that the module uses.
- Theme. The theme is a group of styles that the module uses for formatting report elements.
- Master page. This element defines the layout of pages in paginated report output.
- Libraries. Any module can use one or more libraries to provide predefined elements.
- Resources. External files provide lists of messages in localized forms.
- Embedded images.

ReportDesignHandle class

ReportDesignHandle provides access to the report design-specific properties such as the scripts that execute when generating or rendering a report. This class also provides access to properties that templates use, such as the cheat sheet, display name, and icon file.

ReportDesignHandle inherits most of its behavior and functionality from ModuleHandle. You also use ReportDesignHandle to get handles to the individual report items and for many report design-specific tasks, including:

- Navigating to the various parts of the design

- Setting the initialization script that runs when the report executes

The ReportDesignHandle also has methods to gain access to the following report components:

- Styles, the list of user-defined styles for formatting report elements

- Base directory, used to find the location of file system resources that have relative paths

- Body, a list of the report sections and report items in the design

- Scratch Pad, a temporary place to move report items while restructuring a report

LibraryHandle class

LibraryHandle provides access to the library-specific properties, as shown in the following list. LibraryHandle inherits most of its behavior and functionality from ModuleHandle.

- Imported CSS styles

  Styles imported from CSS files

- Themes

  Groups of styles for formatting report elements

DesignElementHandle class

The DesignElementHandle class is the base class for report elements. The DesignElementHandle class provides generic services for all elements, including such things as:

- Adding a report item to a slot

- Registering a change event listener

- Getting and setting properties, names, and styles

- Dropping an element from the design

Individual element handle classes

The individual element handle classes derive from ReportDesignHandle. Each report element has its own handle class. To work with operations unique to a given report element, you cast the ReportDesignHandle to the appropriate subclass for the element. For example, the CellHandle class has methods such as getColumn( ), while the DataSourceHandle class has methods such as setBeforeOpen( ).

Design engine class hierarchy

Figure 12-3 illustrates the hierarchy of the classes within the design engine package. The hierarchy diagram omits package prefixes on class names for the classes and interfaces in the package org.eclipse.birt.report.model.api.

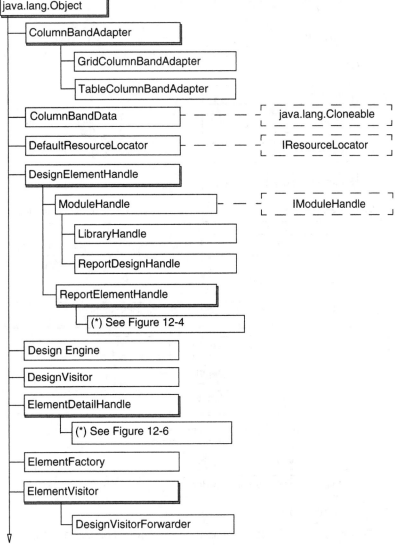

Figure 12-3   Classes within the report model package *(continues)*

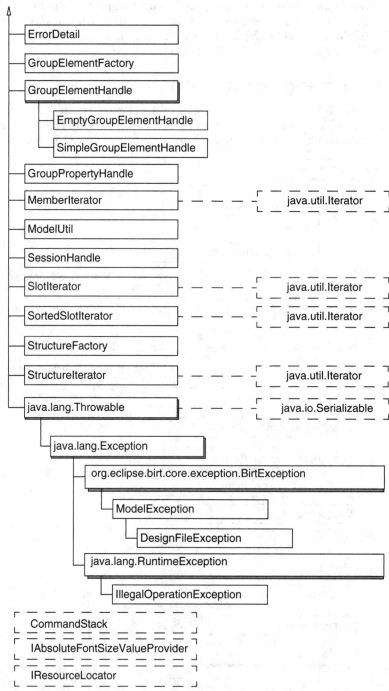

Figure 12-3   Classes within the report model package *(continued)*

ReportElementHandle hierarchy

Figure 12-4 contains the class hierarchy for ReportElementHandle and the classes that derive from it.

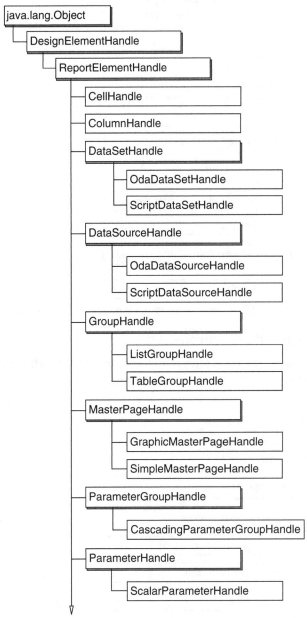

Figure 12-4   ReportElementHandle class hierarchy *(continues)*

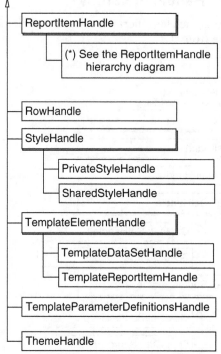

Figure 12-4 ReportElementHandle class hierarchy *(continued)*

ReportItemHandle hierarchy

Figure 12-5 contains the class hierarchy for ReportItemHandle and the classes that derive from it.

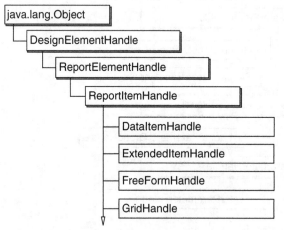

Figure 12-5 ReportItemHandle class hierarchy

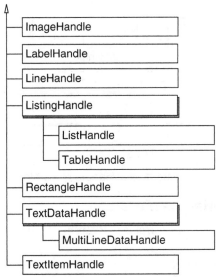

Figure 12-5   ReportItemHandle class hierarchy *(continued)*

ElementDetailHandle hierarchy

Figure 12-6 contains the class hierarchy for ElementDetailHandle and the classes that derive from it.

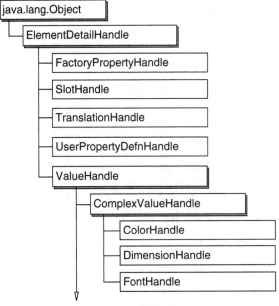

Figure 12-6   ElementDetailHandle class hierarchy *(continues)*

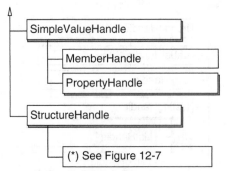

Figure 12-6   ElementDetailHandle class hierarchy *(continued)*

StructureHandle hierarchy

Figure 12-7 contains the class hierarchy for StructureHandle and the classes that derive from it.

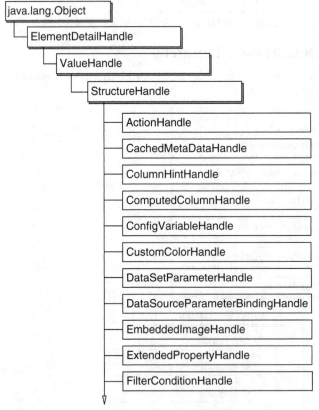

Figure 12-7   StructureHandle class hierarchy

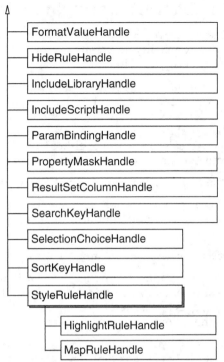

FormatValueHandle

HideRuleHandle

IncludeLibraryHandle

IncludeScriptHandle

ParamBindingHandle

PropertyMaskHandle

ResultSetColumnHandle

SearchKeyHandle

SelectionChoiceHandle

SortKeyHandle

StyleRuleHandle

HighlightRuleHandle

MapRuleHandle

Figure 12-7   StructureHandle class hierarchy *(continued)*

About the BIRT Chart Engine API

The Chart Engine API is based upon the EMF as a structured data model. The Chart Engine API includes many packages in the org.eclipse.birt.chart hierarchy.

Use the classes and interfaces in the chart engine API to modify chart objects within a BIRT reporting application or in a stand-alone charting application.

The model.* packages contain the core chart model interfaces and enumeration classes generated using EMF. The model.*.impl packages contain the core chart model implementation classes generated using EMF. All other packages are dependencies and indirect references from the core model.

There is a one-to-one correspondence between the classes in the impl packages and the interfaces in corresponding model packages. The classes in the impl packages implement the methods in the interfaces of the corresponding model classes. The impl classes also contain factory methods that you use to create an instance of a class.

Using the BIRT Chart Engine API

Although there are over 500 classes and interfaces in the BIRT Chart Engine API, most of functionality for creating or modifying a chart is concentrated in a small subset of classes and interfaces.

The primary interface in the BIRT Chart Engine API is the Chart interface. An object of the Chart type is called the chart instance object. The Chart interface has two subinterfaces, ChartWithAxes and ChartWithoutAxes. DialChart is a third interface that inherits from ChartWithoutAxes. You create a chart instance object with the create( ) method of either ChartWithAxesImpl, ChartWithoutAxesImpl, or DialChartImp, as in the following statement:

```
ChartWithAxes myChart = ChartWithAxesImpl.create( );
```

You set the basic properties of a chart, such as its title and dimensionality with setter methods of the Chart interface, such as:

```
myChart.setTitle( "Monthly Sales" );
myChart.setDimension( ChartDimension.THREE_DIMENSIONAL );
```

You set the more complex properties of a chart, like the characteristics of the chart's axes and series by getting an instance of the object you want to modify and then setting its properties. For example, to set the caption of a chart's x-axis, you can use the following code:

```
Axis xAxis = myChart.getPrimaryBaseAxes( )[0];
xAxis.getTitle( ).getCaption( ).setValue( "Months" );
```

Although charts are often identified by type, such as a pie chart or a line chart, a chart with multiple series of differing types cannot be classified as one type. A series, on the other hand, has a specific type. With the BIRT Chart Engine API, you can create a specific type of series by using the create( ) method of one of the SeriesImpl subclasses. For example, the following code creates a bar series:

```
BarSeries barSeries1 = ( BarSeries ) BarSeriesImpl.create( );
```

For more information about using the BIRT Chart Engine API, see the chapter about programming with the BIRT Chart Engine APIs.

Chart engine class hierarchy

The diagrams that follow contain hierarchies for the following chart engine packages:

- org.eclipse.birt.chart.aggregate
- org.eclipse.birt.chart.datafeed
- org.eclipse.birt.chart.device
- org.eclipse.birt.chart.event
- org.eclipse.birt.chart.exception

- org.eclipse.birt.chart.factory
- org.eclipse.birt.chart.log
- org.eclipse.birt.chart.model
- org.eclipse.birt.chart.model.attribute
- org.eclipse.birt.chart.model.component
- org.eclipse.birt.chart.model.data
- org.eclipse.birt.chart.model.layout
- org.eclipse.birt.chart.model.type
- org.eclipse.birt.chart.render
- org.eclipse.birt.chart.script
- org.eclipse.birt.chart.util

The hierarchy diagrams for the org.eclipse.birt.chart.model.*.impl packages are not included because they are simply implementations of the interfaces in the corresponding org.eclipse.birt.chart.model.* packages. The model packages, with two exceptions, contain only interfaces.

The first exception is org.eclipse.birt.chart.model, which has one class, ScriptHandler. The second exception is org.eclipse.birt.chart.model.attribute, which has a set of enumeration classes, one for each attribute. Each of the enumeration classes only contains a list of legal values for its attribute.

chart.aggregate hierarchy

Figure 12-8 contains the class hierarchy for org.eclipse.birt.chart.aggregate.

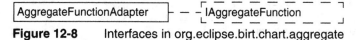

Figure 12-8   Interfaces in org.eclipse.birt.chart.aggregate

chart.datafeed hierarchy

Figure 12-9 contains the class hierarchy for org.eclipse.birt.chart.datafeed.

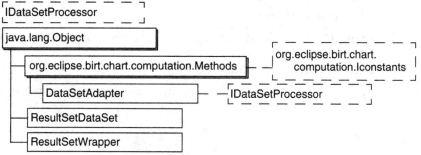

Figure 12-9   Interfaces in org.eclipse.birt.chart.datafeed

chart.device class hierarchy

Figure 12-10 contains the class hierarchy for org.eclipse.birt.chart.device.

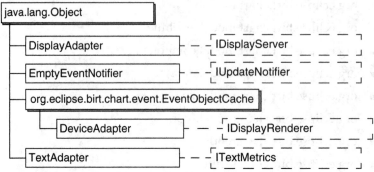

Figure 12-10   Classes in org.eclipse.birt.chart.device package

chart.device interface hierarchy

Figure 12-11 contains the interface hierarchy for org.eclipse.birt.chart.device.

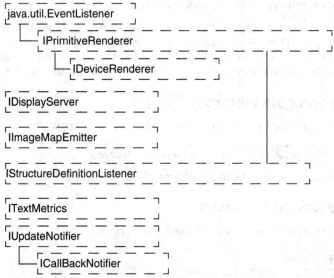

Figure 12-11   Interfaces in org.eclipse.birt.chart.device package

chart.event class hierarchy

Figure 12-12 contains the class hierarchy for org.eclipse.birt.chart.event.

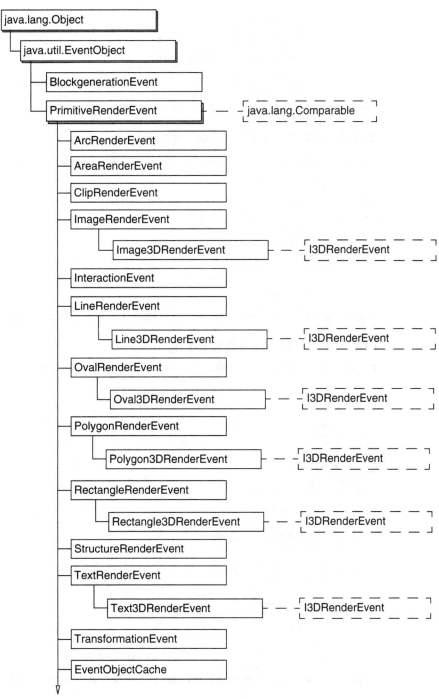

Figure 12-12 Classes in org.eclipse.birt.chart.event package *(continues)*

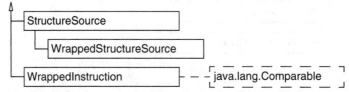

Figure 12-12   Classes in org.eclipse.birt.chart.event package *(continued)*

chart.exception class hierarchy

Figure 12-13 contains the class hierarchy for org.eclipse.birt.chart.exception.

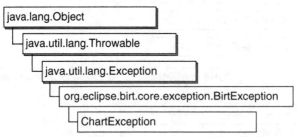

Figure 12-13   Classes in org.eclipse.birt.chart.exception package

chart.factory class hierarchy

Figure 12-14 contains the class hierarchy for org.eclipse.birt.chart.factory.

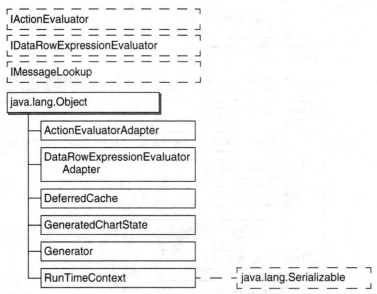

Figure 12-14   Classes and interfaces in org.eclipse.birt.chart.factory package

chart.log class hierarchy

Figure 12-15 contains the class hierarchy for org.eclipse.birt.chart.log.

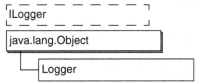

Figure 12-15   Classes in org.eclipse.birt.chart. log package

chart.model class hierarchy

Figure 12-16 contains the class hierarchy for org.eclipse.birt.chart.model.

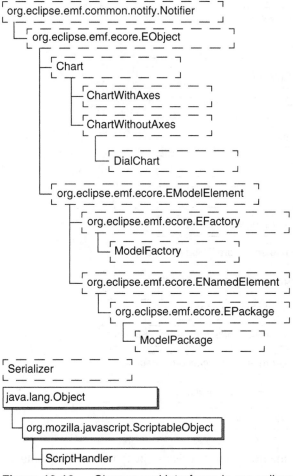

Figure 12-16   Classes and interfaces in org.eclipse.birt.chart.model package

chart.model.attribute interface hierarchy

Figure 12-17 contains the interface hierarchy for
org.eclipse.birt.chart.model.attribute.

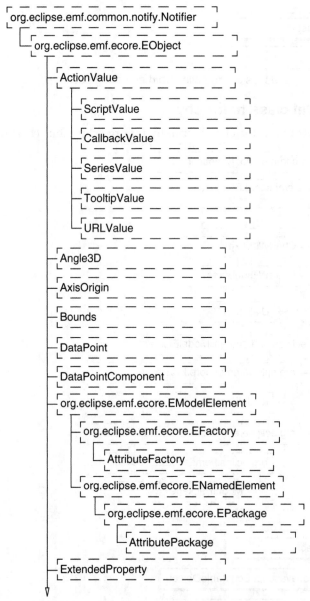

Figure 12-17   Interfaces in org.eclipse.birt.chart.model.attribute package

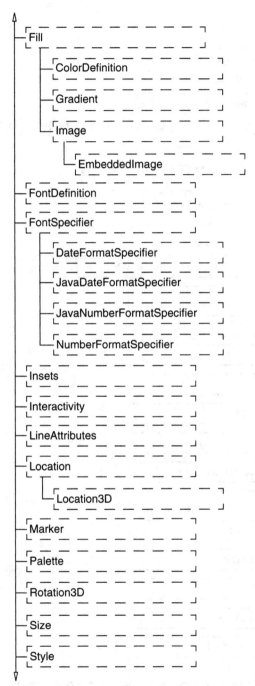

Figure 12-17   Interfaces in org.eclipse.birt.chart.model.attribute package
(continues)

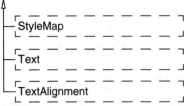

Figure 12-17 Interfaces in org.eclipse.birt.chart.model.attribute package
(continued)

chart.model.attribute class hierarchy

Figure 12-18 contains the class hierarchy for
org.eclipse.birt.chart.model.attribute.

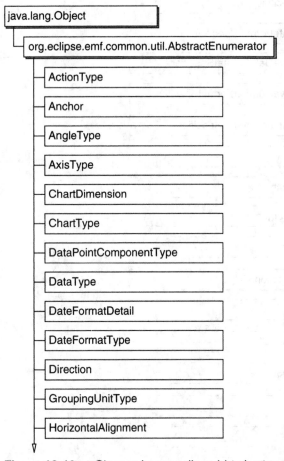

Figure 12-18 Classes in org.eclipse.birt.chart.model.attribute package

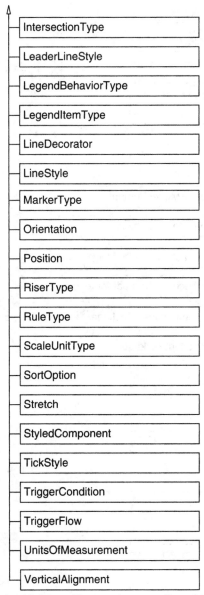

IntersectionType

LeaderLineStyle

LegendBehaviorType

LegendItemType

LineDecorator

LineStyle

MarkerType

Orientation

Position

RiserType

RuleType

ScaleUnitType

SortOption

Stretch

StyledComponent

TickStyle

TriggerCondition

TriggerFlow

UnitsOfMeasurement

VerticalAlignment

Figure 12-18   Classes in org.eclipse.birt.chart.model.attribute package
(continued)

chart.model.component interface hierarchy

Figure 12-19 contains the interface hierarchy for
org.eclipse.birt.chart.model.component.

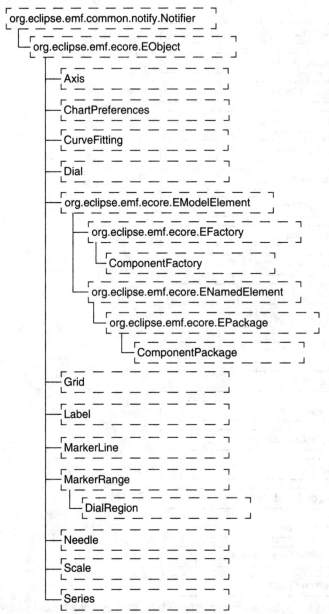

Figure 12-19   Interfaces in org.eclipse.birt.chart.model.component package

chart.model.data interface hierarchy

Figure 12-20 contains the interface hierarchy for
org.eclipse.birt.chart.model.data.

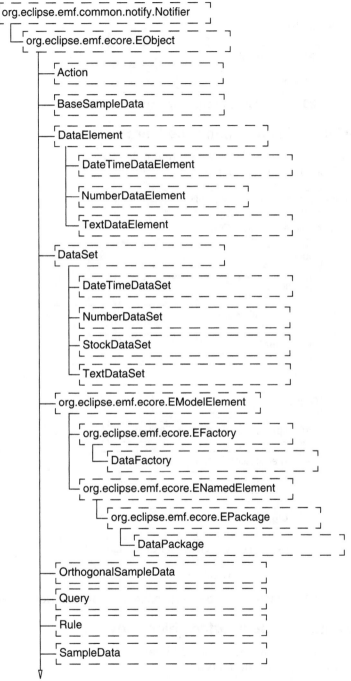

Figure 12-20 Interfaces in org.eclipse.birt.chart.model.data package *(continues)*

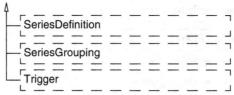

SeriesDefinition

SeriesGrouping

Trigger

Figure 12-20   Interfaces in org.eclipse.birt.chart.model.data package *(continued)*

chart.model.layout interface hierarchy

Figure 12-21 contains the interface hierarchy for
org.eclipse.birt.chart.model.layout.

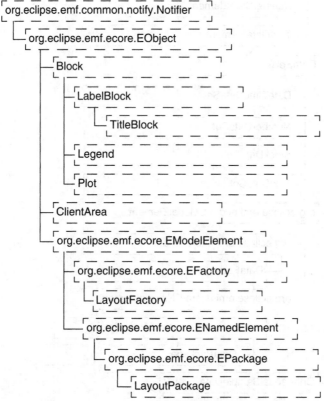

org.eclipse.emf.common.notify.Notifier

org.eclipse.emf.ecore.EObject

Block

LabelBlock

TitleBlock

Legend

Plot

ClientArea

org.eclipse.emf.ecore.EModelElement

org.eclipse.emf.ecore.EFactory

LayoutFactory

org.eclipse.emf.ecore.ENamedElement

org.eclipse.emf.ecore.EPackage

LayoutPackage

Figure 12-21   Interfaces in org.eclipse.birt.chart.model.layout package

chart.model.type interface hierarchy

Figure 12-22 contains the interface hierarchy for
org.eclipse.birt.chart.model.type.

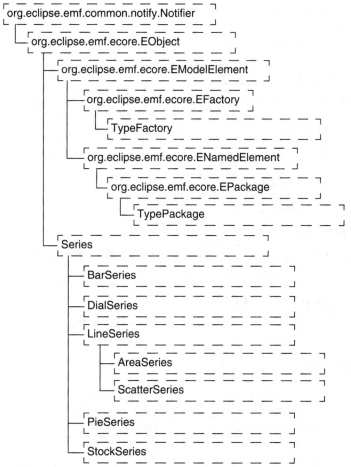

Figure 12-22 Interfaces in org.eclipse.birt.chart.model.type package

chart.render hierarchy

Figure 12-23 contains the class and interface hierarchy for org.eclipse.birt.chart.render.

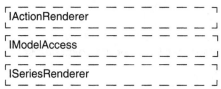

Figure 12-23 Classes and interfaces in org.eclipse.birt.chart.render package *(continues)*

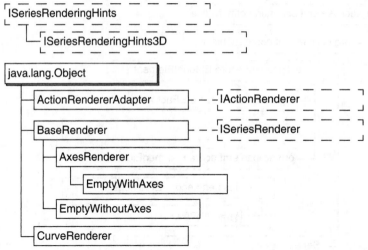

Figure 12-23 Classes and interfaces in org.eclipse.birt.chart.render package *(continued)*

chart.script hierarchy

Figure 12-24 contains the class and interface hierarchy for org.eclipse.birt.chart.script.

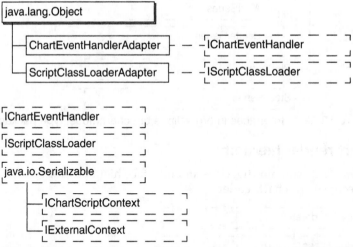

Figure 12-24 Classes and interfaces in org.eclipse.birt.chart.script package

chart.util class hierarchy

Figure 12-25 contains the class hierarchy for org.eclipse.birt.chart.util.

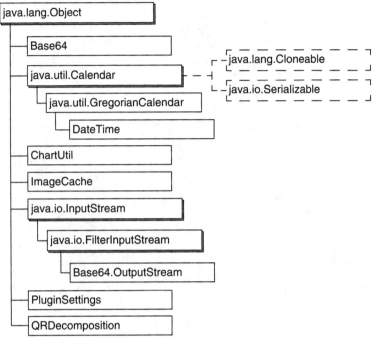

Figure 12-25　Classes in org.eclipse.birt.chart.util package

13

Programming with the BIRT Reporting APIs

A reporting application uses the BIRT report engine API to generate reports from report design (.rptdesign) files. Typically, the application produces the report as a formatted file or stream, in HTML or PDF format. Alternatively, the application can create a report document (.rptdocument) file that contains the report content in binary form, then renders the report to HTML or PDF later.

This chapter describes the fundamental requirements of a reporting application and describes the BIRT API classes and interfaces that you use in the application. This chapter also provides detailed information about the tasks to perform.

The BIRT APIs in the org.eclipse.birt.report.engine.api package support the process of generating a report from a report design. This package provides the ReportEngine class and supporting interfaces and classes.

Optionally, the reporting application can use the BIRT design engine API to access the structure of report designs, templates, and libraries. With this API, the application can create and modify report designs before generating a report. This API supports creating and modifying the report items and other elements within designs.

The org.eclipse.birt.report.model.api package and its subpackages provide access to all the items that comprise a report design.

For complete information about all the methods and fields of the classes and interfaces in these packages, see the online Javadoc. To view the Javadoc, open BIRT Report Designer and choose Help→Help Contents→BIRT Programmer Reference→Reference→API Reference. Choose Report Engine API Reference for the report engine API and Report Object Model API Reference for the design engine API. The Javadoc also shows supporting packages in the public API.

Building a reporting application

An application that generates a report must carry out at least the required tasks described in the following sections. Further tasks, such as supplying user-entered values for parameters, are optional.

Creating and configuring a report engine

Instantiate a ReportEngine object. Set the engine home directory and handler configuration for the desired output format. The engine home directory defines the location of required plug-ins and libraries.

A single report engine object can generate multiple reports from multiple report designs.

Opening a report design or report document

Use one of the openReportDesign( ) methods of the ReportEngine class to open a report design from a String file name or an input stream. These methods return an IReportRunnable object.

Use the openReportDocument( ) method of the ReportEngine class to open a report document (.rptdocument) file from a String file name. This method returns an IReportDocument object.

Ensuring access to the data source

Ensure that the report engine can locate the classes that connect to the data source and supply data to the data set. The report engine can either create a connection to the data source or use a Connection object that the application provides.

Preparing to create a report in the supported output formats

Use an IRenderOption object to set the output format, the output file name or stream, the locale, and format-specific settings. The HTMLRenderOption class supports the HTML output format. For PDF output, use RenderOptionBase.

Generating a report in one of the supported output formats

Use an IRunAndRenderTask object to create the report from the IReportRunnable object. Use an IRenderTask object to create the report from an IReportDocument object.

Alternatively, use a URL to access the report viewer servlet, such as when deploying a BIRT report to an application server, as described earlier in this book. The report viewer can generate a report from either a design file or a document file.

Shutting down the engine

Shut down the report engine if the application does not need to generate more reports.

Optional tasks

The tasks in the following list are optional for a reporting application. Typically, the application performs one or more of these tasks.

- Gather values for parameters.

  If the application uses a report design that has parameters, use the default values for the parameters or set different values.

- Create a report document file.

  A report document file contains the report in a binary storage form. If the application uses a report design, use an IRunTask object to create the report document as an IReportDocument object.

- Export data from a report document.

  Use an IDataExtractionTask object to extract data values from any item or set of items in the report document. Export the data values to a file or another application, or perform further processing on the data.

About the environment for a reporting application

You must ensure that the deployed application can access all the classes required for BIRT, your external data sources, and any other classes you need. The key requirement for BIRT is the location of the engine home. The engine home is the directory that contains the BIRT plug-ins and libraries needed to generate a report from a report design.

If you use the BIRT source code, you must ensure that the version that your application uses matches the version of the plug-ins and libraries in the BIRT engine home directory. If these versions are not the same, your reporting application is likely to fail.

The BIRT Report Engine package provides the complete environment for the reporting application. Earlier chapters in this book provide information about prerequisites and installing this package. The subdirectory, ReportEngine, of BIRT Report Engine contains all the plug-ins and libraries that the report engine uses. This directory contains a complete engine home that a reporting application requires.

About plug-ins used by the report engine

The engine home directory has a subdirectory, plugins, that contains the org.eclipse.birt and other plug-ins that a reporting application can use. Depending on the requirements of your reporting application and the items in your report designs, you can omit plug-ins that provide functionality that the application and designs do not use.

About libraries used by the report engine

The lib subdirectory of the engine home directory contains the JAR files described in Table 13-1. This location within the report engine ensures that the class loader of the application server in which you deploy the report engine can locate the libraries. To support generation of reports in PDF format, the library itext-1.3.jar must exist in the lib subdirectory of the report.engine.emitter.pdf plug-in.

Depending on the requirements of your reporting application and the items in your report designs, you can omit libraries that provide functionality that the application and designs do not use.

Table 13-1   Libraries in the engine home lib directory

Library	Description
chartengineapi.jar	From the chart.engine plug-in. Contains chart model and factory classes. Supports generation of charts in a report.
com.ibm.icu_3.4.4.1.jar	From IBM. Provides International Components for Unicode to support text in multiple locales.
commons-cli-1.0.jar	Used by the ReportRunner application in the report.engine plug-in. From the Apache Jakarta project. Provides command-line parsing. Reporting applications in a web environment do not require this library.
commons-codec-1.3.jar	Used by the report.engine plug-in. From the Apache Jakarta project. Provides encoding and decoding functionality.
coreapi.jar	From the core plug-in. Contains framework and utility classes.
dataadapterapi.jar	From the report.data.adapter plug-in.
dteapi.jar	From the data plug-in. Provides access to data sources. Transforms data that the data set provides.
engineapi.jar	From the report.engine plug-in. Required for generating a report from a report design.
flute.jar	Used by the report.model plug-in. From the W3 Consortium. Provides access to CSS functionality.
js.jar	From the core plug-in. Provides scripting functionality.

Table 13-1   Libraries in the engine home lib directory *(continued)*

Library	Description
modelapi.jar	From the report.model plug-in. Describes the report design.
org.eclipse.emf.common _2.2.0.v\<version>.jar	From the Eclipse EMF plug-in. Required for charts.
org.eclipse.emf.ecore.xmi _2.2.0.v\<version>.jar	From the Eclipse EMF plug-in. Required for charts.
org.eclipse.emf.ecore _2.2.0.v\<version>.jar	From the Eclipse EMF plug-in. Required for charts.
sac.jar	Used by the report.model plug-in. From the W3 Consortium. Required for CSS functionality.
scriptapi.jar	From the report.engine plug-in. Required for Java-based scripting.

About required JDBC drivers

The engine home plugins/org.eclipse.birt.report.data.oda.jdbc_\<version> subdirectory contains a subdirectory, drivers. Place the driver classes or Java archive (.jar) files that you require to access JDBC data sources in this location.

Modifying a report design with the API

A reporting application can also modify a report design before generating the report. The application uses classes in org.eclipse.birt.model.api to change the structure of a report design. Sections later in this chapter provide more information about the types of change you can make to a report design and how to use these classes.

To provide further customization of a report, during the generation of the output, a report design can use Java script classes or embedded JavaScript code to handle events. The reporting application can use the model API classes to include new scripts. Earlier chapters in this book provide more information about the functionality of scripting.

Generating reports from an application

To build a stand-alone reporting application, code the tasks listed earlier in this chapter. The following sections describe these tasks in greater detail. The application does not require the BIRT Report Designer user interface to generate a report.

The key tasks are to ensure that the report engine has access to an engine home, set any parameter values, set up the tasks to generate the report, and run the report.

The org.eclipse.birt.report.engine.api package contains the classes and interfaces that an application uses to generate reports. The main classes and interfaces are ReportEngine, EngineConfig, IReportRunnable, IRenderOption and its descendants, and IEngineTask and its descendants.

Setting up the report engine

A report engine is an instantiation of the ReportEngine class. This object is the key component in any reporting application. It provides access to runnable report designs, parameters, the structure of a report design, and the task for generating a report from a report design. You set the report engine's properties with an EngineConfig object. The following sections describe the various configuration options.

After setting all the required properties, instantiate the report engine with new ReportEngine( ). The constructor takes an EngineConfig object as its argument.

Configuring the engine home

The engine home is the key property that the report engine requires. The report engine cannot parse the report design nor run the report without a defined engine home.

For a stand-alone application, the engine home is an absolute path to a file system location. For an application running from a web archive (.war) file on an application server, the engine home is a relative path in the WAR file.

To set the engine home location, you use one of the following techniques:

- For a stand-alone application, call the EngineConfig.setEngineHome( ) method with an argument that is the path to your engine home directory, for example:

```
config.setEngineHome
    ("C:/Program Files/birt-runtime-2_1_0/ReportEngine" );
```

- In your application's environment, set the BIRT_HOME environment variable and set your CLASSPATH variable to access the required libraries. For example, in a Windows batch file that launches a stand-alone application, include commands similar to the following before running your application:

```
set BIRT_HOME=
    "C:\Program Files\birt-runtime-2_1_0\ReportEngine"
SET CLASSPATH=%BIRT_HOME%\<required library 1>;
    %BIRT_HOME%\<required library 2 and so on>;
    %CLASSPATH%
```

- For a web application that has a location in the file system, use the servlet context to find the real path of the engine home, for example:

```
config.setEngineHome
    (servletContext.getRealPath( "/WEB-INF" ) );
```

- For a web application that runs from a WAR file, use a relative path from the WAR file root, for example:

```
config.setEngineHome( "" );
```

- In Eclipse, set BIRT_HOME in the VM arguments in the Run dialog. For example, in VM arguments, type text similar to the following:

```
-DBIRT_HOME=
    "C:\Program Files\birt-runtime-2_1_0\ReportEngine"
```

Configuring the report engine

Optionally, you can also set other configuration properties using methods on an EngineConfig object. Table 13-2 describes these properties and how to set them with EngineConfig methods. The EngineConfig class also provides getter methods to access these properties. Sections later in this chapter provide examples of setting engine configuration properties and how an application uses them.

Table 13-2   EngineConfig properties

Property type	Setting the property
HTML emitter configuration	For custom handling of images or actions for HTML output. Create a new HTMLEmitterConfig object and set up the handlers. Then call setEmitterConfiguration( ).
Logging	To set the logging file location and level, call setLogConfig( ).
Platform context	To indicate whether the application and engine home are in a stand-alone environment or packaged as a web archive (.war) file, create an implementation of the IPlatformContext interface. Then call setEngineContext( ).
Resource files	To set the location where the reporting application can access resource files such as libraries and properties files that contain localized strings, call setResourcePath( ).
Scripting configuration	To provide external values to scripting methods, call setConfigurationVariable( ). To provide additional Java resources to scripting methods, call addScriptableJavaObject( ).
Status handling	To provide a custom status handler, create an implementation of the IStatusHandler interface. Then call setStatusHandler( ).
Temporary file location	To set up a custom location for temporary files, call setTempDir( ).

Setting up a stand-alone or WAR file environment

Two engine configuration properties depend on whether the environment in which the application runs is stand-alone or in a web archive (.war) file in an application server. These properties are the platform context and the HTML emitter configuration. The platform context provides the report engine with the mechanism to access files. The HTML emitter configuration provides the functionality to process images and handle hyperlinking and bookmark actions.

Setting up the platform context

For the platform context, the BIRT framework provides two implementations of the org.eclipse.birt.core.framework.IPlatformContext interface. These implementations provide all the required functionality for the platform context. For a stand-alone application, the context provides direct file system access to files. For an application running on an application server, the context uses the J2EE ServletContext class for file access. In the case of an application that runs from a WAR file, the platform context uses the resource-based access provided by the ServletContext class.

By default, BIRT uses a PlatformFileContext object, which provides the platform context for a stand-alone application. This context is also suitable for a web application that uses file system deployment on the application server.

For an application that runs from a WAR file on an application server, you must instantiate a PlatformServletContext object. The constructor for this class takes two arguments, a ServletContext object and a URL that is the path to the application. Use the PlatformServletContext object as the argument to the EngineConfig object's setEngineContext( ) method. For example, the code in Listing 13-1 sets up a platform context for a reporting application that uses MarketApp as its context root.

Setting up the HTML emitter

When you generate a report in HTML format, BIRT's HTML emitter creates image files for image elements and chart elements. The emitter also handles hyperlink, bookmark, and drill-through actions.

To set up an image handler, instantiate an implementation of the IHTMLImageHandler interface. For a stand-alone application, create an HTMLCompleteImageHandler object. Typically, the functionality that this class provides is sufficient, so your application does not need to extend it. For an application that runs from a WAR file on an application server, instantiate an HTMLServerImageHandler object. Typically for the application server environment, you need to extend from the base class that BIRT provides.

To set up an action handler, instantiate an implementation of the IHTMLActionHandler interface. This object handles the hyperlink, bookmark, and drill-through actions that the IAction interface defines.

To set up the HTML emitter, instantiate an HTMLEmitterConfig object. To configure the image handler, call the HTMLEmitterConfig.setImageHandler( )

method. To configure the action handler, call the HTMLEmitterConfig
.setActionHandler( ) method. Call the EngineConfig.setEmitterConfiguration( )
method to complete the emitter configuration. This method takes two
arguments, the output format type, which is RenderOptionBase
.OUTPUT_FORMAT_HTML, and an HTMLEmitterConfig object. For a
reference implementation of an emitter configuration for HTML format, see the
org.eclipse.birt.report.viewer plug-in.

Listing 13-1   Setting up the platform context for WAR file deployment

```
// Instantiate an engine configuration object.
EngineConfig config = new EngineConfig( );
// Set the relative path of the engine home in the WAR file.
config.setEngineHome( "" );
// Create the platform context as a hard-coded string.
// Alternatively, use HTTPServletRequest methods to retrieve
// the context dynamically.
// In this code, servletContext is a ServletContext object.
IPlatformContext context = new PlatformServletContext
    ( servletContext, "http://localhost:8080/MarketApp" );
// Set the engine context in the configuration object.
config.setEngineContext( context );
```

How to set up a report engine

Listing 13-2 shows an example of setting up a report engine as a stand-alone
application on a Windows system. The application uses the engine home
located in the BIRT run-time directory. The report output format is HTML. The
application configures the HTML emitter, then creates the engine with
completed EngineConfig object.

Listing 13-2   Setting up the report engine

```
// Create an EngineConfig object.
EngineConfig config = new EngineConfig( );
// Set up the path to your engine home directory.
config.setEngineHome
    ( "C:/Program Files/birt-runtime-2_1_0/ReportEngine" );
// Explicitly set up the stand-alone application
IPlatformContext context = new PlatformFileContext( );
config.setEngineContext( context );
// Set up writing images or charts embedded in HTML output.
HTMLCompleteImageHandler imageHandler =
   new HTMLCompleteImageHandler( );
HTMLEmitterConfig hc = new HTMLEmitterConfig( );
hc.setImageHandler( imageHandler );
config.setEmitterConfiguration
    ( RenderOptionBase.OUTPUT_FORMAT_HTML, hc );
// Create the engine.
ReportEngine engine = new ReportEngine( config );
```

Using the logging environment to debug an application

BIRT Report Engine uses the java.util.logging classes, Logger and Level, to log information about the processing that the engine performs. When you run an application in the Eclipse workbench, by default, the messages appear in the console. When you run an application external to Eclipse, the default location of the log messages depends on your environment. The default logging threshold is Level.INFO. Typically, you change this level in your application to reduce the number of internal logging messages.

To set up the logging environment to write the engine's log messages to a file on disk, use the EngineConfig.setLogConfig( ) method. This method takes two arguments, the directory in which to create the log file and the lowest level at which to log information. BIRT Report Engine creates a log file with a name whose format is ReportEngine_YYYY_MM_DD_hh_mm_ss.log. Set the logging level to a high threshold so that the engine logs a reduced number of messages.

Typically, you want to see information at INFO level when you first develop a block of code. To modify the amount of information that the engine logs, use the ReportEngine.changeLogLevel( ) method. This method takes a single argument, which is a Level constant. When the code is stable, you no longer need to see all the engine's INFO messages. At that point, you can delete or comment out the call to changeLogLevel( ).

How to use BIRT logging

The following example shows how to use logging in an application. You set up the logging environment, then modify it later in your application.

1 Set up the logging configuration on the report engine object.

```
// Create an EngineConfig object.
EngineConfig config = new EngineConfig( );
//Set up the location and level of the logging output.
config.setLogConfig( "C:/Temp", Level.ERROR );
// Set up any other required configuration settings here.
// Create the report engine.
ReportEngine engine = new ReportEngine( config );
```

2 In any newly written code, increase the amount of logging.

```
engine.changeLogLevel( Level.INFO );
```

Opening a source for report generation

BIRT Report Engine can generate a report from either a report design or a report document. The engine can also generate a report document from a report design.

To open a report design, you call one of the openReportDesign( ) methods on ReportEngine. These methods instantiate an IReportRunnable object, using a String that specifies the path to a report design or an input stream.

To open a report document, you call the ReportEngine.openReportDocument( ) method. This method instantiates an IReportDocument object, using a String that specifies the path to a report document. You must handle the EngineException that these methods throw.

Understanding an IReportRunnable object

The IReportRunnable object provides direct access to basic properties of the report design. The names of report design properties are static String fields, such as IReportRunnable.AUTHOR. To access a report design property, use the getProperty( ) method with a String argument that contains one of these fields.

To access and set the values of parameters, you use methods on a parameter definition task object, described later in this chapter. To generate a report from a design, open the report design as shown in the following example, then perform the tasks shown later in this chapter.

How to access a report design

Listing 13-3 shows how to open a report design and find a property value. If the engine cannot open the specified report design, the code shuts down the engine. The variable, engine, is a ReportEngine object.

Listing 13-3   Accessing a report design

```
String designName = "./SimpleReport.rptdesign";
IReportRunnable runnable = null;
try {
   runnable = engine.openReportDesign( designName );
}
catch ( EngineException e )
{
   System.err.println
      ( "Design " + designName + " not found!" );
   engine.shutdown( );
   System.exit( -1 );
}
// Get the value of a simple property.
String author = ( String ) runnable.getProperty
   ( IReportRunnable.AUTHOR );
```

Understanding an IReportDocument object

The IReportDocument object provides access to the data in a report and the report's structure. IReportDocument provides methods to retrieve table of contents entries, bookmarks, and page information.

To access table of contents entries, use the findTOC( ) method. This method takes a TOCNode argument and returns a TOCNode object. To find the root table of contents entry, use an argument of null. To find the subentries of a table of contents entry, use the getChildren( ) method. This method returns a List of

TOCNode objects. From a TOCNode object, you can retrieve the display value of the entry and a Bookmark object.

In turn, you can use the Bookmark object as an argument to the getPageNumber( ) method, which returns the number of the page to which the bookmark links. With this information, you can specify particular pages to render to a formatted report.

How to access a report document

Listing 13-4 shows how to open a report document and navigate its table of contents to find a page. If the engine cannot open the specified report design, the code shuts down the engine. The variable, engine, is a ReportEngine object.

Listing 13-4   Accessing a report document

```
String dName = "./SimpleReport.rptdocument";
IReportDocument doc = null;
try { doc = engine.openReportDocument( dName );
} catch ( EngineException e ) {
  System.err.println( "Document " + dName + " not found!" );
  engine.shutdown( );
  System.exit( -1 );
}
// Get the root of the table of contents.
TOCNode td = doc.findTOC( null );
java.util.List children = td.getChildren( );
long pNumber;
// Loop through the top level table of contents entries.
if ( children != null && children.size( ) > 0 ) {
  for ( int i = 0; i < children.size( ); i++ ) {
    // Find the required table of contents entry.
    TOCNode child = ( TOCNode ) children.get( i );
    if ( child.getDisplayString( ).equals( "103" ) ) {
      // Get the number of the page that contains the data.
      pNumber = doc.getPageNumber( child.getBookmark( ) );
      System.out.println( "Page to print is " + pNumber );
    }
  }
}
```

Accessing a report parameter programmatically

A report parameter is a report element that provides input to a report design before the application generates the report. A report document does not use report parameters for generating a report. If your report source is a report document or the default values for all report parameters for a report design are always valid, you do not need to perform the tasks in this section.

Report parameters have attributes that a reporting application can access. The most commonly used attributes are name and value. The report engine uses the report design logic and the report parameter values to perform tasks such as filtering a data set or displaying an external value in the report.

After the reporting application sets the values for the report parameters, it must pass these values to the task that generates the report, as shown later in this chapter. To access report parameters and their default values and to set user-supplied values to a parameter, the reporting application uses the BIRT report engine API classes and interfaces shown in Table 13-3.

Table 13-3   Classes that support report parameters

Class or interface	Description
ReportEngine	Call the createGetParameterDefinitionTask( ) method to access parameters. This method returns an IGetParameterDefinitionTask object.
IGetParameterDefinition Task	The interface to access a single report parameter or a collection of all the report parameters in a report design. This interface also provides access to valid values for parameters that use restricted sets of values, such as cascading parameters.
IParameterDefnBase	The base interface for report parameter elements. Scalar parameters implement the derived interface, IScalarParameterDefn. Parameter groups implement the derived interface IParameterGroupDefn. To get information about parameter attributes, use objects of these types.
IParameterGroupDefn	The base interface for report parameter groups. Cascading parameter groups implement the derived interface ICascadingParameterGroup.
IParameterSelectionChoice	The interface for valid values for a report parameter that uses a restricted set of values, such as a cascading parameter.
ReportParameter Converter	The class that converts a String value provided by a user interface into a locale-independent format.

The following sections describe how to access report parameters by name or with generic code. You use generic code if the application must be able to run any report design, for example, if you access report designs from a list that depends on user input. If the application runs only a fixed set of known report designs, you can access the report parameters by name.

Creating a parameter definition task object for the report design

A single IGetParameterDefinitionTask object provides access to all parameters in a report design. Create only one of these objects for each report design, by using the ReportEngine.createGetParameterDefinitionTask( ) method.

Testing whether a report design has report parameters

To test if a report design has report parameters, call the getParameterDefns( ) method on IGetParameterDefinitionTask. This method returns a Collection. To test whether the Collection has elements call the Collection.isEmpty( ) method. If the application runs only known report designs, you do not need to perform this task.

Getting the report parameters in a report design

To access a single report parameter with a known name, use the IGetParameterDefinitionTask.getParameterDefn( ) method. This method returns an object of type IParameterDefnBase. Alternatively, use the IGetParameterDefinitionTask.getParameterDefns( ) method to return a Collection of IParameterDefnBase objects. The application can then use an Iterator to access each report parameter from this Collection in turn.

The getParameterDefns( ) method takes a Boolean argument. When the argument is false, the method returns an ungrouped set of report parameters. When the argument is true, the method returns parameter groups, as defined in the report design. To create a user interface that replicates the parameter group structure, use a value of true.

To check whether a report parameter is a group, the application must call IParameterDefnBase.getParameterType( ). This method returns IParameterDefnBase.PARAMETER_GROUP when the parameter is a group or IParameterDefnBase.CASCADING_PARAMETER_GROUP when the parameter is a cascading parameter group.

To access the group's report parameters, use the IParameterGroupDefn .getContents( ) method. This method returns an ArrayList object that contains objects of type IScalarParameterDefn.

Getting the default value of each report parameter

This task is optional. To get the default value of a single known report parameter, use IGetParameterDefinitionTask.getDefaultValue( ). This method returns an Object. To determine the effective class of the Object, use IScalarParameterDefn.getDataType( ). This method returns an int value, which is one of the static fields in IScalarParameterDefn.

To get the default value of all parameters in the report design, use IGetParameterDefinitionTask.getDefaultValues( ). This method returns a HashMap object, which maps the report parameter names and their default values.

Getting valid values for parameters using a restricted set of values

Some report parameters accept only values from a restricted list. In some cases, this list is a static list of values, such as RED, BLUE, or GREEN. In other cases, the list is dynamic and a query to a database provides the valid values. For example, a query can return the set of sales regions in a sales tracking database.

To determine the list of valid values, call the IGetParameterDefinitionTask .getSelectionList( ) method. This method returns a Collection of IParameterSelectionChoice objects. IParameterSelectionChoice has two methods. getLabel( ) returns the display text and getValue( ) returns the value. If the Collection is null, the report parameter can take any value.

Getting the attributes of each report parameter

This task is optional. To get the attributes of a report parameter, use the IScalarParameterDefn methods. The application can use the attributes to generate a customized user interface. For example, to get the data type of a report parameter, use the getDataType( ) method.

Collecting an updated value for each report parameter

To provide new values for the report parameters, provide application logic such as a user interface or code to retrieve values from a database. To set the value of the parameter, call IGetParameterDefinitionTask.setParameterValue( ).

If you provide a user interface that returns String values to your application for date and number parameters, you must convert the String into a locale-independent format before setting the value. To perform this task, first call ReportParameterConverter.parse( ) to set the value to a locale-independent format. Next, call IGetParameterDefinitionTask.setParameterValue( ).

After setting the report parameter values, call the IGetParameterDefinitionTask .getParameterValues( ) method. This method returns a HashMap object that contains values that calls to IGetParameterDefinitionTask.setParameterValue( ) set. You can later use this HashMap object to set the report parameter values for report generation, as described later in this chapter.

How to set the value of a known report parameter

The code sample in Listing 13-5 shows how to set the value of a report parameter that has a known name. The sample creates a HashMap object that contains the parameter values to use later to run the report. The variable, engine, is a ReportEngine object. The variable, runnable, is an object of type IReportRunnable.

This sample does not show details of code for retrieving the parameter value from a user interface or a database. The code to perform these tasks depends on your application's requirements.

Listing 13-5   Setting the value of a single parameter

```
// Create a parameter definition task.
IGetParameterDefinitionTask task =
   engine.createGetParameterDefinitionTask( runnable );
// Instantiate a scalar parameter.
IScalarParameterDefn param = (IScalarParameterDefn)
   task.getParameterDefn( "customerID" );
// Get the default value of the parameter.
// The code assumes that the data type of the parameter,
// customerID, is Double.
int customerID =
    ((Double) task.getDefaultValue( param )).intValue( );

// Get a value for the parameter. This example does not
// provide the code for this task. This example assumes that
// this step creates a correctly typed object, inputValue.

// Set the value of the parameter.
task.setParameterValue( "customerID", inputValue );
// Get the values set by the application for all parameters.
HashMap parameterValues = task.getParameterValues( );
```

How to use the Collection of report parameters

The code sample in Listing 13-6 shows how to use the Collection of report parameters. The sample uses the ReportParameterConverter class to convert the String values that the user interface supplies into the correct format for the parameter. The sample creates a HashMap object that contains the parameter values to use later to run the report. The variable, engine, is a ReportEngine object. The variable, runnable, is an object of type IReportRunnable.

This sample does not show details of code for retrieving the parameter values from a user interface or a database. The code to perform these tasks depends on your application's requirements.

Getting the values for cascading parameters

A cascading parameter group uses a query to retrieve values from a database. The parameter definition task filters the values for each parameter in the group, based on the values of preceding parameters in the group. For example, consider a cascading parameter group that uses the following query.

```
SELECT
   PRODUCTS.PRODUCTLINE,
   PRODUCTS.PRODUCTNAME,
   PRODUCTS.PRODUCTCODE
FROM CLASSICMODELS.PRODUCTS
```

Listing 13-6   Setting the values of multiple parameters

```
// Create a parameter definition task.
IGetParameterDefinitionTask task =
   engine.createGetParameterDefinitionTask( runnable );
// Create a collection of the parameters in the report design.
// This example does not use the parameter grouping.
Collection params = task.getParameterDefns( false );
// Get the default values of the parameters.
HashMap parameterValues = task.getDefaultValues( );

// Get values for the parameters. This example does not
// provide the code for this task. Later code in this example
// assumes that this step creates a HashMap object,
// inputValues. The keys in the HashMap are the parameter
// names and the values are those that the user provided.

// Iterate through the report parameters, setting the values
// to use for generating the report. Ensure that the values
// are in standard locale-independent format.
Iterator iterOuter = params.iterator( );
while ( iterOuter.hasNext( ) )
{
   IParameterDefnBase param =
      (IParameterDefnBase) iterOuter.next( );
   String pname = param.getName( );
   String value = (String) inputValues.get( pname );
   if ( value != null )
   {
      ReportParameterConverter cfgConverter = new
         ReportParameterConverter( "", Locale.getDefault() );
      Object obj =
         cfgConverter.parse( value, param.getDataType( ) );
      parameterValues.put( pname, obj );
   }
}
```

The group contains two parameters, ProductLine on PRODUCTS
.PRODUCTLINE and ProductCode on PRODUCTS.PRODUCTCODE. The
display text for ProductCode is PRODUCTS.PRODUCTNAME. Figure 13-1
shows the appearance of the requester that prompts for values for these
parameters when you preview the report in BIRT Report Designer.

To use the report engine API to get the values for cascading parameters,
perform the tasks in the following list. Figure 13-1 shows an example of
performing these tasks.

■ To prepare the data values for the cascading parameters, call the method,
  IGetParameterDefinitionTask.evaluateQuery( ). This method takes the String
  name of the parameter group as a parameter.

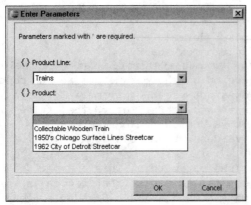

Figure 13-1 Cascading report parameters

- To populate the list of values for the first report parameter in the group, call the IGetParameterDefinitionTask.getSelectionListForCascadingGroup( ) method. This method takes two parameters, the String name of the parameter group and an array of Object. For the first parameter, this array is empty. The method returns a Collection of IParameterSelectionChoice objects.

- To populate the list of values for further report parameter in the group, call getSelectionListForCascadingGroup( ) again. In this case, the Object[] array contains the values for the preceding report parameters in the group. In the example shown in Figure 13-1, the Object[] array is:

```
new Object[] {"Trains" }
```

How to use cascading parameters

The code sample in Listing 13-7 first shows how to run the query for cascading parameters. Next, the sample accesses the set of valid values for each parameter in the cascading parameter group in turn. The variable, task, is an object of type IGetParameterDefinitionTask.

Listing 13-7 Getting the valid values for cascading parameters

```
// Create a grouped collection of the design's parameters.
Collection params = task.getParameterDefns( true );
// Iterate through the parameters to find the cascading group.
Iterator iter = params.iterator( );
while ( iter.hasNext( ) ) {
   IParameterDefnBase param = (IParameterDefnBase)
   iter.next();
   if ( param.getParameterType() ==
      IParameterDefnBase.CASCADING_PARAMETER_GROUP ) {
      ICascadingParameterGroup group =
         (ICascadingParameterGroup) param;
      Iterator i2 = group.getContents( ).iterator( );
```

```
        // Run the query for the cascading parameters.
        task.evaluateQuery( group.getName() );
        Object[] userValues =
           new Object[group.getContents( ).size( )];
        // Get the report parameters in the cascading group.
        int i = 0;
        while ( i2.hasNext( ) ) {
           IScalarParameterDefn member =
              (IScalarParameterDefn) i2.next( );
           // Get the values for the parameter.
           Object[] setValues = new Object[i];
           if ( i > 0 )
              System.arraycopy( userValues, 0, setValues, 0, i );
           Collection c =
              task.getSelectionListForCascadingGroup
                 ( group.getName(), setValues );
           // Iterate through the values for the parameter.
           Iterator i3 = c.iterator();
           while ( i3.hasNext( ) ) {
              IParameterSelectionChoice s =
                 ( IParameterSelectionChoice ) i3.next( );
              String choiceValue = s.getValue( );
              String choiceLabel = s.getLabel( );
           }
   // Get the value for the parameter from the list of choices.
   // This example does not provide the code for this task.
           userValues[i] = inputChoiceValue;
           i++;
        }
     }
```

Preparing to generate the report

BIRT provides two output formats for reports, HTML and PDF. You can also
provide custom output formats by creating a new renderer from the rendering
extension points, as discussed later in this book.

Three task classes support generating a report from a source. Sections earlier in
this chapter described how to open the two types of source, a report design and
a report document. The tasks that you use to generate a report from the source
are:

- IRunAndRenderTask. An object of this type creates a report in unpaginated
  HTML format by running a report design directly. To instantiate this object,
  call the ReportEngine method, createRunAndRenderTask( ).

- IRunTask. An object of this type creates a report document (.rptdocument)
  file from a report design. To instantiate this object, call the ReportEngine
  method, createRunTask( ). After creating the report document, you create the
  report with an IRenderTask object.

- IRenderTask. An object of this type creates a complete report or a set of pages from a report by formatting the contents of a report document. To instantiate this object, call the ReportEngine method, createRenderTask( ).

Each type of task object can act on multiple sources. When the application no longer needs the task object, call the task's close( ) method.

Setting the parameter values for running a report design

To set the values for parameters for generating a report, use methods on an IRunAndRenderTask or an IRunTask object. These tasks run a report design to generate output. IRenderTask does not support changing the parameters for a report because its source is a report document. The IRunTask object that created the report document already specified the parameter values.

Call setParameterValues( ) to set the values for all the parameters. This method takes a HashMap as an argument. To create a suitable HashMap, perform the tasks described in "Accessing a report parameter programmatically," earlier in this chapter.

To set the value for a single parameter when generating a report, call the setParameterValue( ) method. When the task generates the report or the report document, it uses the default values for any parameters that were not set by either of these methods.

Setting up the rendering options

Before generating a report to either HTML or PDF, the application must set options that determine features of the output. The options must specify either an output file name or a stream. Other configuration options, such as setting whether to create embeddable HTML, are optional. BIRT supports two types of HTML output, HTML and embeddable HTML. Embeddable HTML is suitable for including inside another web page. This format contains no header information nor the <html> tag.

The application uses a rendering options object to set the output options on an IRunAndRenderTask or an IRenderTask object. The format-specific rendering options classes implement IRenderOption and extend RenderOptionBase. The rendering options class supporting the HTML format is HTMLRenderOption. There are no format-specific options for PDF output. To set options for PDF output, use the RenderOptionBase class.

Setting up the rendering context

Before generating a report, the application must provide context settings to the rendering task. Use the setAppContext( ) method on an IRenderTask or an IRunAndRenderTask object. This method performs no function on an IRunTask object because this task does not render to an output format.

To set up the context for HTML rendering, use an HTMLRenderContext object. To set up the context for PDF rendering, use a PDFRenderContext object. To apply a context setting, use setter methods on the rendering context object. These classes also have getter methods that retrieve context settings.

Both HTML and PDF rendering contexts support a base URL for an action handler and a list of the image formats that the output format accepts, as shown in the following list. The output format of the report defines which other context settings are available.

- Action handler base URL. If you use a custom action handler, set its base URL with the setBaseURL( ) method.

- Supported image formats for extended report items such as charts or custom extended items. The final rendering environment for the report, such as the browser for a report in HTML format, affects this context value. To set the supported formats, use setSupportedImageFormats( ) with a String that contains a list of the supported image formats as its argument. The image formats are standard types, such as BMP, GIF, JPG, and SVG. Semicolons (;) separate the items in the list. The method getSupportedImageFormats( ) returns a String of the same format.

After creating the rendering context object, call the task's setContext( ) method. This method takes a HashMap object as an argument. The key to the hash-map entry is one of the constants APPCONTEXT_HTML_RENDER_CONTEXT or APPCONTEXT_PDF_RENDER_CONTEXT in the EngineConstants class. The value of the entry is the rendering context object. Listing 13-8 includes code that sets the rendering context for HTML.

Setting up the HTML rendering context

Before generating an HTML report that uses images on disk or creates images or charts in a report, the application must provide additional context settings. The HTMLRenderContext class provides the following settings:

- Image base directory. If your report designs use relative paths to access static images, set the path to their location with the HTMLRenderContext .setBaseImageURL( ) method.

- Image output directory. Many reports include images, either as static images or dynamically created images, such as charts. HTML reports place all images in a defined location. To set this location, call the HTMLRenderContext.setImageDirectory( ) method. If you do not set the base location, the report engine cannot place images in your report.

Setting up the PDF rendering context

Before generating a PDF report that uses fonts from non-standard locations or needs to embed fonts in a report, the application must provide additional context settings. The PDFRenderContext class provides the following settings:

- Font directory. If your deployment platform uses fonts from a custom location, set the path to their location with the setFontDirectory( ) method.

This method takes a String argument, which is a list of directories separated by semicolon characters.

- Embedding fonts. If you need to embed custom fonts in the PDF document, call PDFRenderContext.setEmbededFont( ) with an argument of true.

How to configure properties for a report in HTML format

The code sample in Listing 13-8 shows the use of rendering options on an IRunAndRenderTask object to set report parameter values, the output format of the report, and the output file name. The variable, engine, is a ReportEngine object. The variable, runnable, is an object of type IReportRunnable. The variable, name, is the name of the report design.

Listing 13-8   Configuring properties on an IRunAndRenderTask object

```
// Create a run and render task object.
IRunAndRenderTask task =
   engine.createRunAndRenderTask( runnable );
// Set values for all parameters in a HashMap, parameterValues
task.setParameterValues( parameterValues );
// Validate parameter values.
boolean parametersAreGood = task.validateParameters( );
// Set the name of an output file.
HTMLRenderOption options = new HTMLRenderOption( );
String output = name.replaceFirst( ".rptdesign", ".html" );
options.setOutputFileName( output );
// Apply the rendering options to the task.
task.setRenderOption( options );
// Instantiate an HTML rendering context object and
// set the name of the directory for images.
HTMLRenderContext renderContext = new HTMLRenderContext();
renderContext.setImageDirectory("image");
// Apply the rendering context to the task.
HashMap appContext = new HashMap( );
appContext.put
   ( EngineConstants.APPCONTEXT_HTML_RENDER_CONTEXT,
   renderContext );
task.setAppContext( appContext );
```

Providing an external connection to run a report design

In many application server environments, web applications have access to a pool of Connection objects. In order to use an external connection from such a pool for the data source in a report design, you must pass information to the data driver plug-in that the report design uses. You pass the information in the rendering context HashMap object. For example, the code in Listing 13-9 sets up the connection to a custom driver, mydatapluginname. The variable task is an IRunAndRenderTask object or an IRunTask object.

The standard data drivers in BIRT do not support using an external connection. You must extend the drivers to perform this task. Later chapters in this book explain this process.

Listing 13-9 Setting up an external Connection object

```
HashMap contextMap = new HashMap( );
HTMLRenderContext renderContext = new HTMLRenderContext();
contextMap.put
   ( EngineConstants.APPCONTEXT_HTML_RENDER_CONTEXT,
   renderContext );
// Get a connection from the pool
Connection myConnection = getConnectionFromPool( );
contextMap.put( "org.eclipse.birt.mydatapluginname",
   myConnection );
task.setContext( contextMap );
```

Generating the formatted output programmatically

To generate a report, the application must call the run( ) method on an IRunAndRenderTask or an IRunTask object. The application must handle the EngineException that run( ) can throw.

After generating the report, the application can reuse the report engine to generate further reports. If your application only generates a single report, shut down the engine after performing the report generation.

How to generate a report

The code sample in Listing 13-10 generates a report, then shuts down the report engine. The variable, engine, is a ReportEngine object. The variable, task, is an IRunAndRenderTask or an IRunTask object. The variable, name, is the name of the report design. The variable, output, is the name of the output file.

Listing 13-10 Generating a report from a report design or a report document

```
try {
   task.run( );
   System.out.println( "Created Report " + output + "." );
}
catch ( EngineException e1 ) {
   System.err.println( "Report " + name + " run failed." );
   System.err.println( e1.toString( ) );
}
engine.shutdown( );
```

Accessing the formatted report

When you generate a report document as a file on disk, you can access the report in the same way as any other file. For example, you open HTML documents in a web browser and PDF documents using Adobe Reader. If you send the report to a stream, the stream must be able to process the information.

About programming with a report design

A reporting application typically generates a report from a report design. In this type of reporting application, you typically develop a report design and include the design along with your application at deployment time. Any changes to the generated report depend on the values of report parameters and the data from the data set. To access the report design, the application uses an IReportRunnable object.

Sometimes business logic requires changes to the report design before generating the report. You can make some changes through using parameters and scripting. Other changes can only occur through modification of the report design itself.

A reporting application can make changes to the report design and the ROM elements that make up the design. To access the structure of the report design, the application obtains a ReportDesignHandle object from the design engine. To access the design engine, an application must first instantiate a report engine, as in any other reporting application.

The ReportDesignHandle object provides access to all properties of the report design and to the elements that the report design contains. The model API provides handle classes to access all ROM elements. For example, a GridHandle object provides access to a grid element in the report design. All ROM element handles, including the report design handle, inherit from DesignElementHandle. Report items inherit from ReportElementHandle and ReportItemHandle.

After making changes to a report design or its elements, the application can write the result to a stream or a file. The report engine can then open an IReportRunnable object on the resulting design and generate a report.

An application typically accesses the items in a report design to perform one of the following tasks:

- Modify an existing report design programmatically to change the contents and appearance of the report output.

  An application can modify page characteristics, grids, tables, and other report items in the design, the data source, and the data set that extracts data from a data source.

- Build a report design and generate report output entirely in an application without using BIRT Report Designer.

A reporting application can access and modify the structures in a template or a library file in the same way as the structures in a report design. The techniques described in the rest of this chapter are applicable to these files as well as to report designs.

A template has identical functionality to a report design. For this reason, the ReportDesignHandle class provides access to a template. The LibraryHandle class provides access to a library. Both these classes derive from the ModuleHandle class, which provides the fields and methods for the common functionality, such as accessing elements in the file.

The package that contains the classes and interfaces to work with the items in a report design, library, or template is org.eclipse.birt.report.model.api.

About BIRT model API capabilities

A report developer can write an application that creates and modifies a report design programmatically. The BIRT model API has the same capabilities as BIRT Report Designer. For example, the following list shows some of the ways in which you can use the BIRT model API to manipulate a report design programmatically:

- Modifying a report item in a report design:
  - Format a report item, changing the font, font color, fill color, format, alignment, or size.
  - Modify the expression or other property of a report item.
  - Change the data set bound to a table or list.
- Adding a report item to a report design:
  - Add a simple report item such as a data item, label, or image.
  - Set the value to display in the new report item, such as the expression of a data item or the text in a label item.
  - Create a complex item such as a grid, table, or list.
  - Add other items into a grid, table, or list.
- Changing the structure of a report design:
  - Add or delete a group or column in a table or list.
  - Add a report parameter.
- Modifying non-visual elements in a report design:
  - Specify a data source for a data set.
  - Set a design property such as a report title, author, wallpaper, or comment.
  - Set a page property, such as height, width, or margins.

Opening a report design programmatically for editing

To access a report design and its contents, the application must instantiate a report engine, then use a ReportDesignHandle object. You instantiate a ReportDesignHandle by calling a method on another class, such as the model class, SessionHandle, or the report engine interface, IReportRunnable.

The SessionHandle object manages the state of all open report designs. Use a SessionHandle to open, close, and create report designs, and to set global properties, such as the locale and the units of measure for report elements. The SessionHandle can open a report design from a file or a stream. Create the session handle only once. BIRT supports only a single SessionHandle for a user of a reporting application.

Configuring the design engine to access a design handle

The DesignEngine class provides access to all the functionality of the Report Object Model (ROM) in the same way that the ReportEngine class provides access to report generation functionality. To create a DesignEngine object, you first create a DesignConfig object to contain configuration settings for the design engine. The DesignConfig object sets up custom access to resources and custom configuration variables for scripting. Instantiate a DesignEngine object with the DesignConfig object as an argument to the constructor.

Create the SessionHandle object by calling the method, newSessionHandle( ) on the DesignHandle object. To open the report design, call the method, openDesign( ), on the SessionHandle object. This method takes the name of the report design as an argument and instantiates a ReportDesignHandle object.

Using an IReportRunnable object to access a design handle

You can also open a report design from an IReportRunnable object by using the getDesignHandle( ) method. The ReportDesignHandle object provides access to the design opened by the report engine. Changes to the report design do not affect the IReportRunnable object. To generate a report from the changed report design, you must reopen the design as an IReportRunnable object.

How to open a report design for editing

The code sample in Listing 13-11 creates a DesignEngine object, which it uses to create a SessionHandle object. The code then uses the SessionHandle object to open a report design.

Listing 13-11   Opening a report design for editing

```
// Create a design engine configuration object.
DesignConfig dConfig = new DesignConfig( );
DesignEngine dEngine = new DesignEngine( dConfig );
// Create a session handle, using the system locale.
SessionHandle session = dEngine.newSessionHandle( null );
// Create a handle for an existing report design.
```

```
String name = "./SimpleReport.rptdesign";
ReportDesignHandle design = null;
try {
   design = session.openDesign( name );
} catch (Exception e) {
   System.err.println
      ( "Report " + name + " not opened!\nReason is " +
      e.toString( ) );
   return null;
}
```

Using a report item in a report design

A report item is a visual element in the report design. Typically, a report developer adds a report item to the design in BIRT Report Designer by dragging an item from the palette to the layout editor. Sometimes you need to change the properties of certain report items in the design before running the report. An application uses methods on the ReportDesignHandle class to access a report item either by name or from a list of items in a slot in a container report item.

A slot is a logical component of a report item. For example, a table element has five slots: Header, Detail, Footer, Groups, and Columns. In turn, each of these slots can have further slots. Each slot has zero or more members of the appropriate report item type. For example, the Header, Detail, and Footer slots all contain elements of type RowHandle. RowHandle has a Cell slot that contains all the cells in the row. For a visual representation of the slots in an individual report item, see the Outline view in BIRT Report Designer.

Accessing a report item by name

To make a report item accessible by name, the item must have a name. A report developer can set the name in BIRT Report Designer or programmatically by using the item's setName( ) method. To find a report item by name, use the findElement( ) method. This method returns a DesignElementHandle object. All report items derive from this class.

Accessing a report item by iterating through a slot

To access a report item through the report design's structure, the application first gets the slot handle of the report body by calling the getBody( ) method. This slot handle holds the top-level report items in the report design. For example, consider a simple report structure that has three top-level items: a grid containing header information, a table containing data, and a label that displays a report footer. Figure 13-2 shows its outline view in BIRT Report Designer.

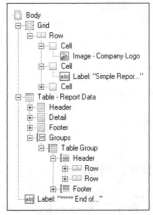

Figure 13-2   Slots in a report design

To access the top-level items in this report design, you iterate over the contents of the body slot handle. These contents all derive from DesignElementHandle. To access the iterator for a slot handle, call SlotHandle.iterator( ). Each call to Iterator.getNext( ) returns a report item. Alternatively, to access a report item at a known slot index, call SlotHandle.get( ). The slot index number is zero-based. The ReportDesignHandle class also provides finder methods, which can access an item or other report element by name.

Examining a report item programmatically

To examine a report item, check the class of the report item, cast the object to its actual class, then call methods appropriate to that class. For example, the class of a label element handle is LabelHandle. To get the text that the label displays, call LabelHandle.getText( ).

Some report items, such as a label or a text element, are simple items. Other items, such as a grid or a table element, are structured items. You can access properties for the whole of a structured item in the same way as for a simple item.

You can also iterate over the contents of the structured item. For example, use this technique to determine the contents of a cell in a table. To access the contents of a structured item, you call a method to retrieve the slot handle for rows or columns. For example, to access the RowHandle objects that make up a table element's footer, call TableHandle.getFooter( ). Table and list elements also have a slot for groups. Like the body slot handle, the slot handles for the contents of structured report items can contain zero, one, or multiple elements.

Accessing the properties of a report item

To provide information about report items, each class has getter methods specific to the report item type. For example, an image element handle, ImageHandle, has the getURI( ) method. This method returns the URI of an image referenced by URL or file path. The DesignElementHandle class and other ancestor classes in the hierarchy also provide generic getter methods, such as getName( ).

Some properties of a report item are simple properties, with types that are Java types or type wrapper classes. An example of this type of property is the name property, which is a String object. Some of these properties, like name, have arbitrary values.

Other simple properties have restricted values from a set of BIRT String constants. The interface, DesignChoiceConstants in the org.eclipse.birt.report.model.api.elements package, defines these constants. For example, the image source property of an image element can have only one of the values, IMAGE_REF_TYPE_EMBED, IMAGE_REF_TYPE_EXPR, IMAGE_REF_TYPE_FILE, IMAGE_REF_TYPE_NONE, or IMAGE_REF_TYPE_URL.

Other properties are complex properties and the getter method returns a handle object. For example, the DesignElementHandle.getStyle( ) method returns a StyleHandle object and ReportItemHandle.getWidth( ) returns a DimensionHandle object.

The handle classes provide access to complex properties of a report item, as described later in this chapter. These classes provide getter methods for related properties. For example, StyleHandle classes provide access to font and background color.

How to access a report item by name

The code sample in Listing 13-12 finds an image item by name, checks its type, then examines its URI. The variable, design, is a ReportDesignHandle object.

Listing 13-12   Finding a report item with a given name

```
DesignElementHandle logoImage =
   design.findElement( "Company Logo" );
// Check for the existence of the report item.
if ( logoImage == null) {
   return null;
}
// Check that the report item has the expected class.
if ( !( logoImage instanceof ImageHandle ) ) {
   return null;
}
// Retrieve the URI of the image.
String imageURI = ( (ImageHandle ) logoImage ).getURI( );
return imageURI;
```

How to use the report structure to access a report item

The code sample in Listing 13-13 finds an image item in a grid, checks its type, then examines its URI. Use this technique for generic code to navigate a report design structure or if you need to find an item that does not have a name. The variable, design, is a ReportDesignHandle object.

Modifying a report item in a report design programmatically

To set the simple properties of report items, each class has setter methods specific to the report item type. For example, an image element handle, ImageHandle, has the setURI( ) method. This method sets the URI of an image referenced by URL or file path. The DesignElementHandle class and other ancestor classes in the hierarchy also provide generic setter methods, such as setName( ). Setter methods throw exceptions, such as NameException, SemanticException, and StyleException.

To set attributes of a complex property, such as a style, you must call methods on a handle object, as described later in this chapter. These classes provide setter methods for related properties. For example, StyleHandle classes provide access to style properties, such as font and background color.

Listing 13-13 Navigating the report structure to access a report item

```
// Instantiate a slot handle and iterator for the body slot.
SlotHandle shBody = design.getBody();
Iterator slotIterator = shBody.iterator()
// To retrieve top-level report items, iterate over the body.
while (slotIterator.hasNext()) {
   Object shContents = slotIterator.next();
   // To get the contents of the top-level report items,
   // instantiate slot handles.
   if (shContents instanceof GridHandle) {
      GridHandle grid = ( GridHandle ) shContents;
      SlotHandle grRows = grid.getRows( );
      Iterator rowIterator = grRows.iterator( );
      while (rowIterator.hasNext()) {
         // Get RowHandle objects.
         Object rowSlotContents = rowIterator.next();
         // To find the image element, iterate over the grid.
         SlotHandle cellSlot =
            ( ( RowHandle ) rowSlotContents ).getCells( );
         Iterator cellIterator = cellSlot.iterator( );
         while ( cellIterator.hasNext( ) ) {
            // Get a CellHandle object.
            Object cellSlotContents = cellIterator.next( );
            SlotHandle cellContentSlot =
               ((CellHandle) cellSlotContents).getContent( );
            Iterator cellContentIterator =
               cellContentSlot.iterator( );
            while (cellContentIterator.hasNext( )) {
               // Get a DesignElementHandle object.
               Object cellContents =
                  cellContentIterator.next( );
```

```
            // Check that the element is an image.
            if (cellContents instanceof ImageHandle) {
                String imageSource = ( ( ImageHandle )
                    cellContents ).getSource( );
                // Check that the image has a URI.
                if ((imageSource.equals( IMAGE_REF_TYPE_URL ))
                || (imageSource.equals(IMAGE_REF_TYPE_FILE))){
                    // Retrieve the URI of the image.
                    String imageURI = ( ( ImageHandle )
                        cellContents ).getURI( );
                }
            }
        }
    }
}
```

Changes that you make to items in the report design do not affect the design file until you save the design to disk or to a stream. After saving the design, get an IReportRunnable handle for the modified design in order to generate a report.

How to change a simple property of a report item

The code sample in Listing 13-14 uses a method on LabelHandle to change the text in a label. The variable, design, is a ReportDesignHandle object. This sample accesses the label by name. You can also access a report item by navigating the report structure.

Listing 13-14   Changing the text property of a label report item

```
// Access the label by name.
LabelHandle headerLabel =
    ( LabelHandle ) design.findElement( "Header Label" );
try {
    headerLabel.setText( "Updated " + headerLabel.getText( ) );
} catch ( Exception e ) {
    // Handle the exception
}
```

Accessing and setting complex properties

Complex properties use BIRT handle objects to access data structures. For example, a DimensionHandle object provides access to size and position properties, such as the absolute value and the units of the width of a report item.

Some String properties on a handle object, such as font style and text alignment on a style handle, have restricted values defined by constants in the interface, DesignChoiceConstants in the org.eclipse.birt.report.model.api.elements package. For example, the font style property can have only one of the values, FONT_STYLE_ITALIC, FONT_STYLE_NORMAL, and FONT_STYLE_OBLIQUE.

Using a property handle

To access complex properties, you use getter methods on the report item. For example, to access the width of a report item, call the method ReportItemHandle.getWidth( ). This method returns a DimensionHandle object. To work with complex properties, you use getter and setter methods on the handle object. For example, to get and set the size of a dimension, you use DimensionHandle.getMeasure( ) and DimensionHandle.setAbsolute( ), respectively.

When you set a value on a complex property, the change to the handle object affects the report item straight away. You do not call an additional setter method on the report item itself.

Using styles on a report item

The StyleHandle class provides access to many fundamental properties of a report item, such as margin size, text alignment, background color, borders, font, and so on. StyleHandle provides a full set of getter methods for each style property. For simple properties, StyleHandle provides setter methods. To modify complex properties, you use setter methods on the property handle object, not on the style handle itself.

A report item can use two styles: a private style and a shared style. The handle classes for these styles are PrivateStyleHandle and SharedStyleHandle, respectively. Both classes derive from StyleHandle.

A private style contains the settings that the report developer chose in the property editor when designing the report. Shared styles appear in the Outline view in BIRT Report Designer. You use shared styles to apply the same appearance to multiple items in a report design. Changes to a shared style affect all report items that use the style. Style settings in a private style override the settings in a shared style.

How to change a complex property of a report item

The code sample in Listing 13-15 shows how to use PrivateStyleHandle and ColorHandle objects to change the background color of a label. The variable, design, is a ReportDesignHandle object. This sample accesses the label by name. You can also access a report item by navigating the report structure.

Listing 13-15   Changing a complex property of a report item

```
// Access the label by name.
LabelHandle headerLabel =
  ( LabelHandle ) design.findElement( "Header Label" );
try {
  // To prepare to change a style property, get a
  StyleHandle.
  StyleHandle labelStyle = headerLabel.getPrivateStyle();
  // Update the background color.
  ColorHandle bgColor = labelStyle.getBackgroundColor();
```

```
      bgColor.setRGB( 0xFF8888 );
} catch ( Exception e ) {
    // Handle any exception
}
```

Adding a report item to a report design programmatically

A reporting application can use a simple report design or a template to create more complex designs. The application can add extra report items to the design's structure based on external conditions. For example, based on the user name of the user requesting generation of a report, you can add extra information to the report for that category of user. You use the same techniques to add content to a new design if you create a design entirely with the API.

The class that creates new elements, such as report items, in a report design is ElementFactory. This class provides methods of the form, newXXX( ), where XXX is the report item or element to create. The method newElement( ) is a generic method that creates an element of any type. To access the element factory, call the ReportDesign.getElementFactory( ) method.

You can place new report items at the top level of the report design, directly in the Body slot, within containers such as a cell in a table or grid, or on the master page. You can add a simple item, such as a label, or complex items, such as a table with contents in its cells. Wherever you add the new report item, the location is a slot, such as the body slot of the report design or a cell slot in a row in a table. To add a report item to a slot, you use one of the SlotHandle.add( ) methods. The method has two signatures that support adding the report item to the end of a slot, or to a particular position in a slot.

Table and list elements are container items that iterate over the rows that a data set provides. For these report items to access the data rows, you must bind them to a data set. The table or list element provides data rows to the report items that it contains. For this reason, you usually bind only the container item to a data set, as described later in this chapter.

How to add a grid item and label item to a report design

The code sample in Listing 13-16 creates a grid item, then adds a label item to one of the cells in the grid. An application can create any other report item in a similar manner. The variable, design, is a ReportDesignHandle object.

Listing 13-16   Adding a container item to the Body slot

```
// Instantiate an element factory.
ElementFactory factory = design.getElementFactory( );
try {
    // Create a grid element with 2 columns and 1 row.
    GridHandle grid = factory.newGridItem( "New grid", 2, 1 );
    // Set a simple property on the grid, the width.
    grid.setWidth( "50%" );
    // Create a new label and set its properties.
```

```
        LabelHandle label = factory.newLabel( "Hello Label" );
        label.setText( "Hello, world!" );
        // Get the first row of the grid.
        RowHandle row = ( RowHandle ) grid.getRows( ).get( 0 );
        // Add the label to the second cell in the row.
        CellHandle cell = ( CellHandle ) row.getCells( ).get( 1 );
        cell.getContent( ).add( label );
        // Get the Body slot. Add the grid to the end of the slot.
        design.getBody( ).add( grid );
    } catch ( Exception e ) {
        // Handle any exception
    }
```

Accessing a data source and data set with the API

This section shows how to use ROM elements that are not report items. To use
other ROM elements, such as the libraries that the report design uses, you
employ similar techniques.

You access the report design's data sources and data sets from methods on the
ReportDesignHandle instance, in a similar way to other report elements. The
model classes that define a data source and data set are DataSourceHandle and
DataSetHandle, respectively. A data set provides a report item such as a table
with data from a data source. For a report item to access the data set, use the
setDataSet( ) method.

You can use a finder method on the report design handle to access a data source
or data set by name. The finder methods are findDataSource( ) and
findDataSet( ), respectively.

Alternatively, to access all the data sources or data sets, you can use a getter
method that returns a slot handle. The getter methods are getDataSources( ) and
getDataSets( ), respectively. To access the individual data sources or data sets in
a slot handle, you iterate over the contents of the slot handle in the same way as
for any other slot handle.

About data source classes

DataSourceHandle is a subclass of ReportElementHandle. You get and set
report item properties for a data source in the same way as for any other report
element. DataSourceHandle also provides methods to access the scripting
methods of the data source.

The two subclasses of DataSourceHandle, OdaDataSourceHandle and
ScriptDataSourceHandle, provide the functionality for the two families of BIRT
data sources. For more information about ODA data sources, see the Javadoc for
the ODA API, in Open Data Access (ODA) 3.0.0 API Reference. The scripting
methods for a scripted data source fully define the data source, as described
earlier in this book.

About data set classes

DataSetHandle is a subclass of ReportElementHandle. You get and set properties for a data set in the same way as for any other report element. DataSetHandle also provides methods to access properties specific to a data set, such as the data source, the data set fields, and the scripting methods of the data set.

The two subclasses of DataSetHandle, OdaDataSetHandle and ScriptDataSetHandle, provide the functionality for the two families of BIRT data sets. For more information about ODA data sets, see the Javadoc for the ODA API.

Using a data set programmatically

Typically, a reporting application uses data sets and data sources already defined in the report design. You can use the data set's setDataSource( ) method to change the data source of a data set. For example, based on the name of the user of the reporting application, you can report on the sales database for a particular geographical region, such as Europe or for North America.

Changing the properties of a data set

Changing the properties of a data set requires consideration of the impact on the report design. If you change the data source of a data set, the type of the data source must be appropriate for the type of the data set. You must also be certain that the new data source can provide the same fields as the original data source.

How to change the data source for a data set

The code sample in Listing 13-17 shows how to check for a particular data source and data set in a report design, then changes the data source for the data set. The code finds the data source and data set by name.

Alternatively, use the getDataSets( ) and getDataSources( ) methods. Then use the technique for iterating over the contents of a slot handle. The variable, design, is a ReportDesignHandle object.

Listing 13-17   Modifying a data set

```
// Find the data set by name.
DataSetHandle ds = design.findDataSet( "Customers" );
// Find the data source by name.
DataSourceHandle dso = design.findDataSource( "EuropeSales" );
// Check for the existence of the data set and data source.
if (dso == null) || ( ds == null )
{
   System.err.println( "EuropeSales or Customers not found" );
   return;
}
// Change the data source of the data set.
```

```
try
{
    ds.setDataSource( dso );
} catch ( SemanticException e1 ) {
    e1.printStackTrace( );
}
```

Changing the data set binding of a report item

You can also use the report item's setDataSet( ) method to set or change the data
set used by a report item. If you change the data set used by a report item, you
must ensure that the contents of the report item access only data bindings that
are supplied by the new data set. If necessary, you must change the references to
data bindings in data elements, text elements, and scripting methods. If the data
bindings in the old data set do not match the names or data types of the fields
that the new data set provides, you must correct the data bindings before you
generate a report from the modified report design. Use the ReportItemHandle
method, columnBindingsIterator( ), to iterate over the column bindings that the
report item uses. The items in the list are of type ComputedColumnHandle.
This class provides methods to access the name, expression, and data type of the
column binding.

To access the data set column and expression that a data item uses, call the
methods, getResultSetColumn( ) and getResultSetExpression( ). You can
compare the data type and name with the result set columns that the data set
returns.

How to bind a data set to a table

The code sample in Listing 13-18 shows how to check for a particular data set in
a report design, then changes the data set for a table. The code finds the table
and data set by name. Alternatively, use slot handles to navigate the report
design structure. The variable, design, is a ReportDesignHandle object.

Listing 13-18   Binding a data set to a report item

```
// Find the table by name.
TableHandle table =
    ( TableHandle ) design.findElement( "Report Data" );
// Find the data set by name.
DataSetHandle ds = design.findDataSet( "EuropeanCustomers" );
// Check for the existence of the table and the data set.
if (table == null) || ( ds == null ) {
    System.err.println( "Incorrect report structure" );
    return;
}
// Change the data set for the table.
try {
    table.setDataSet( ds );
```

```
} catch (Exception e) {
    System.err.println( "Could not set data set for table" );
}
```

Saving a report design programmatically

After making changes to an existing report design or creating a new report design, you can choose to save the design for archival purposes, or for future use. To overwrite an existing report design to which the application has made changes, use the ReportDesignHandle.save( ) method. To save a new report design or to keep the original report design after making changes, use the ReportDesignHandle.saveAs( ) method.

Alternatively, if you do not need to save the changes to the report design, use the ReportDesignHandle.serialize( ) method. This method returns an output stream. The report engine can generate a report by opening a stream as an input stream.

If you do not need to make any further changes to the report design, use the ReportDesignHandle.close( ) method to close the report design.

How to save a report design

The following code saves the open report design. The variable, design, is a ReportDesignHandle object.

```
design.saveAs( "sample.rptdesign" );
design.close( );
```

Creating a report design programmatically

You can build a report design and generate the report output in an application without using BIRT Report Designer. You use the createDesign( ) method on the session handle class, SessionHandle, to create a report design. You use the other model classes to create its contents.

How to create a new report design

The following code creates a report design.

```
SessionHandle session = DesignEngine.newSession( null );
ReportDesignHandle design = session.createDesign( );
```

14

Programming with the BIRT Charting APIs

This chapter describes the basic requirements of a charting application and illustrates the use of BIRT charting API classes and interfaces for modifying an existing chart definition and for creating a new chart.

The BIRT charting API allows you to:

- Write Java applications with bar charts, pie charts, line charts, scatter charts, area charts, dial charts, and stock charts.

- Customize a chart in many ways to fit the requirements of the application.

- Modify an existing chart item in a BIRT report design or add a chart to an existing report design.

While this chapter illustrates how to customize an existing chart and create a new chart within a BIRT application, describing how to use the charting API in a stand-alone application is beyond the scope of this book. However, creating a chart in a stand-alone application is not significantly different from creating a chart in a BIRT application.

Although there are more than 400 classes and interfaces in the BIRT charting API, this chapter discusses only the most important classes and interfaces. For detailed information about the complete set of charting API classes and interfaces, see the BIRT online help. For examples of completed charting applications, download the BIRT samples from the BIRT web site.

About the environment for building a charting application

The minimum requirements for creating a basic charting application are:

- The BIRT run-time engine

  The run-time engine is only required for an application that runs within the BIRT report context.

- The BIRT run-time charting engine
- Java JDK 1.4.2 or later
- The following JAR files and folders within the Java classpath:
  - From BIRT runtime/Chart Engine
    - org.eclipse.birt.chart.device.extension_2.1.0.jar
    - org.eclipse.birt.chart.device.svg_2.1.0.jar
    - org.eclipse.birt.chart.engine.extension_2.1.0.jar
    - org.eclipse.birt.chart.engine_2.1.0.jar
    - org.eclipse.birt.core.ui_2.1.0.jar
    - org.eclipse.birt.core_2.1.0.jar
  - From BIRT runtime/Report Engine
    - org.mozilla.rhino_1.6.0 folder
    - org.apache.commons.codec_1.3.0 folder
    - org.eclipse.emf.common_2.2.0.jar
    - org.eclipse.emf.ecore_2.1.0.jar
    - org.eclipse.emf.ecore.xmi_2.1.0.jar
  - From eclipse/plugins
    - org.eclipse.birt.chart.device.swt_2.1.0.jar
    - org.eclipse.birt.chart.ui.extension_2.1.0.jar
    - org.apache.batik_1.6.0 folder
    - org.apache.batik.pdf_1.6.0 folder
    - org.apache.xerces_2.8.0 folder
  - Any custom extension plug-in JAR files of your own creation

Your application may require additional JAR files in the Java classpath. You can be certain that you have all the necessary BIRT-related JAR files for an application if you add the following JAR files to your Java classpath:

- $RUNTIME/Chart Engine /*.jar
- $RUNTIME/Report Engine/plugins/*.jar

In addition to the JAR files that are installed with the BIRT run-time engine, you might need to include itext-1.3.jar in the Java classpath. itext-1.3.jar is an auxiliary JAR file that you have to download as described in the instructions in the chapter on BIRT requirements. itext-1.3.jar is used only for the generation of a PDF report.

Verifying the development environment for charting applications

Listing 14-1 illustrates the creation of the most basic charting application it is possible to write. The output of the example program is an XML file that describes a chart that has no data binding, no labels, no series, and no titles.

Although the output of this example is not useful, by compiling and running the program, you can verify that your environment is correctly configured for compiling and running a charting application.

Listing 14-1   Basic charting application

```java
import java.io.*;
import org.eclipse.birt.chart.model.*;
import org.eclipse.birt.chart.model.impl.*;

public class MyFirstChartProg {
   public static void main( String[] args ) {
      Chart myChart = ChartWithAxesImpl.create( );
      Serializer si = SerializerImpl.instance( );
      try {
         si.write( myChart, new FileOutputStream( new File
            ( "C:\\myChart.chart" ) ) );
      }
      catch ( IOException e ) {e.printStackTrace( );}
   }
}
```

When this program compiles and executes without errors, it creates a file called myChart.chart containing several hundred lines of XML code representing a basic chart definition.

Using the charting API to modify an existing chart

A Java program can open an existing BIRT report design file and alter the content of the report before displaying or saving the report. The chapter on programming BIRT describes how to open a report file using the BIRT engine API. This section describes how to modify an existing chart within the report design by using the charting API. The following sections contain code examples for each step in the process.

Getting a Chart object from the report design

To get a report item from a report design, you must first get a ReportDesignHandle object. Listing 14-2 illustrates how to get a ReportDesignHandle object and then get a Chart object from it. The code in Listing 14-2 assumes that the chart that you want to modify is the first report item of a list and that the list is the first report item in the report.

Listing 14-2   Getting a ReportDesignHandle object and a Chart object

```
SessionHandle sessionHandle = DesignEngine.newSession( null );
ReportDesignHandle designHandle = null;
try {
   designHandle = sessionHandle.openDesign( designFileName );
} catch ( DesignFileException e1 ) {
        e1.printStackTrace( );
}
ListHandle li =  ( ListHandle )
   designHandle.getBody( ).getContents( ).get( 0 );
ExtendedItemHandle eihChart1 =
   ( ExtendedItemHandle )
   li.getSlot( 0 ).getContents( ).get( 0 );
ChartReportItemImpl crii = null;
try {
   crii = ( ChartReportItemImpl ) eihChart1.getReportItem( );
}
catch ( ExtendedElementException e2 ) {
   e2.printStackTrace( );
}
Chart chart = ( Chart ) crii.getProperty( "chart.instance" );
```

Modifying chart properties

When you have the chart you want to modify, you can change the chart's properties, as shown in the following code example.

```
chart.setDimensions( ChartDimension.TWO_DIMENSIONAL_LITERAL );
chart.getTitle( ).getLabel( ).getCaption( ).setValue
   ( "North America" );
```

```
chart.getTitle( ).getLabel( ).getCaption( ).getFont( )
   .setRotation( 5 );
```

Modifying axes properties

To modify the properties of one or more axes of a chart, it is first necessary to cast the Chart object to a type of ChartWithAxes, as shown in the following statement.

```
chart = ( ChartWithAxes ) chart;
```

Listing 14-3 illustrates the technique for getting the axes of a chart and setting their properties.

Listing 14-3   Getting an axis and setting its properties

```
Axis xAxisPrimary = chart.getPrimaryBaseAxes( )[0];
xAxisPrimary.getLabel( ).getCaption( ).getFont( ).setRotation
   ( 45 );
xAxisPrimary.getTitle( ).getCaption( ).setValue( "Months" );
Axis yAxisPrimary =
   chart.getPrimaryOrthogonalAxis( xAxisPrimary );
yAxisPrimary.getMajorGrid( ).setTickStyle
   ( TickStyle.LEFT_LITERAL );
yAxisPrimary.setType( AxisType.LINEAR_LITERAL );
yAxisPrimary.getLabel( ).getCaption( ).getFont( ).setRotation
   ( 90 );
yAxisPrimary.getTitle( ).getCaption( )
   .setValue( "Sales Growth" );
yAxisPrimary.setFormatSpecifier
   ( JavaNumberFormatSpecifierImpl.create( "$" ) );
```

Modifying plot properties

The following code illustrates how to get the chart plot and how to modify its properties.

```
Plot plot = chart.getPlot( );
plot.getClientArea( ).setBackground( ColorDefinitionImpl.CREAM
   ( ) );
plot.getOutline( ).setVisible( true );
```

Modifying the legend properties

You can also get the chart legend and modify its properties using code similar to the following code.

```
Legend legend = cm.getLegend( );
legend.getText( ).getFont( ).setSize( 16 );
legend.getInsets( ).set( 10, 5, 0, 0 );
legend.setAnchor( Anchor.NORTH_LITERAL );
```

Modifying the series properties

The following code illustrates how to get a series from an axis and how to change the properties of the series.

```
SeriesDefinition seriesDefX = SeriesDefinitionImpl.create( );
seriesDefX = ( SeriesDefinition )
   xAxisPrimary.getSeriesDefinitions( ).get( 0 );
seriesDefX.getSeriesPalette( ).update( 0 );
```

Adding a series to a chart

You can add a new series to a chart. Listing 14-4 illustrates how to create a second series, set some of its properties, assign data to the series, and add the series to an axis.

Listing 14-4   Creating a series, setting its properties, and adding the series to an axis

```
SeriesDefinition seriesDefY = SeriesDefinitionImpl.create( );
seriesDefY.getSeriesPalette( ).update( ColorDefinitionImpl
   .YELLOW( ) );
BarSeries barSeries2 = ( BarSeries ) BarSeriesImpl.create( );
barSeries2.setSeriesIdentifier( "Q2" );
barSeries2.setRiserOutline( null );
barSeries2.getLabel( ).setVisible( true );
barSeries2.setLabelPosition( Position.INSIDE_LITERAL );

// Assign data to the series

Query query2 = QueryImpl.create( "row[\"Value2\"]" );
barSeries2.getDataDefinition( ).add( query2 );
seriesDefY.getSeries( ).add( barSeries2 );
seriesDefY.getQuery( ).setDefinition( "\"Q2\"" );

// Add the new series to the y-axis

yAxisPrimary.getSeriesDefinitions( ).add( seriesDefY );
```

Adding a chart event handler to a charting application

There are two kinds of chart event handlers that you can add to a charting application: a Java event handler or a JavaScript event handler.

Adding a Java chart event handler to a charting application

To add a Java event handler, you must first create a separate Java class file containing your new event handler method or methods. The process for creating a Java event handler class is identical to the process for creating a Java event handler class for any other report item. For more information about creating a Java event handler class, see the chapter on scripting with Java.

To register a Java class in the charting application code, use the setScript( ) method of the chart instance object, as shown in the following statement.

```
chart.setScript
( "com.MyCompany.eventHandlers.ChartEventHandlers" );
```

In the preceding statement, the string passed to the setScript( ) method is the fully qualified name of the Java class. Notice that the .class extension is not included in the class name.

Adding a JavaScript chart event handler to a charting application

To add a JavaScript event handler, you must code the script as one long string and pass that string to the setScript( ) method of the chart instance object. You must include a function for every event handler method of the chart. For example, the Java statement in Listing 14-5 passes a string to chart.setScript( ) containing event handler scripts for two event handler methods.

Listing 14-5   Adding an event handler script to a chart

```
cwaBar.setScript(
   "function beforeDrawDataPointLabel"
   + "(dataPoints, label, scriptContext)"
   + "{val = dataPoints.getOrthogonalValue( );"
   + "clr = label.getCaption( ).getColor( );"
   + "if ( val < -10 ) clr.set( 32, 168, 255 );"
   + "else if ( ( val >= -10 ) & ( val <=10 ) )"
   + "clr.set( 168, 0, 208 );"
   + "else if ( val > 10 ) clr.set( 0, 208, 32 );}"
```

Line breaks in the JavaScript code are indicated by backslash n (\n), and quotes within the script are indicated by a backslash quote (\"). The JavaScript code in Listing 14-5 consists of several strings concatenated together to form a single string. This technique helps make the script more readable.

Using the charting APIs to create a new chart

You can add a new chart to an existing report design or to a new report design. In either case, your program must perform a series of tasks. Creating a new chart and adding the chart to a report design requires performing the following tasks:

■ Creating the chart instance object

The chart instance object contains the properties of the chart, such as its title, its axes, and its series.

- Setting the properties of the chart instance object

  The properties of the chart include everything about the chart except the data set to which it is bound and the chart's ultimate display size.

- Getting an ElementFactory object

  You use the ElementFactory object to create a new report element.

- Creating sample data

  Sample data is useful for the correct display of a chart element in BIRT Report Designer.

- Getting an ExtendedItemHandle object

  The ExtendedItemHandle object is similar to a standard report item handle. The item handle is the object with which you access the report item instance. The handle is also the object that binds to a data set and the object that you add to the report design.

- Setting the chart.instance property on the report item

  The chart.instance property of the report item identifies the chart instance object. This property provides the link between the report item and the chart instance object.

- Getting a data set from the report design

  A chart must bind to data in order to have meaning. The report design provides access to one or more data sets that the report developer defined. The program also can create a data set and add it to the design.

- Binding a chart to the data set

  To bind a chart to a data set, you specify the data set as a property of the extended item handle object.

- Adding the new chart to the report design

  The last step is to add the chart to the report design by adding the extended item handle object to the report design.

- Optionally saving the report design

  An application program that creates or modifies a BIRT report design can also save the new or modified report design.

The following sections describe the preceding steps in more detail and provide code examples for every step.

Creating the chart instance object

To create a chart instance object, you use a static method of one of the chart implementation classes. Depending on which chart implementation object you use, you can either create a chart with or without axes. The following line of code creates a chart with axes.

```
ChartWithAxes newChart = ChartWithAxesImpl.create( );
```

Setting the properties of the chart instance object

You define the characteristics of the chart by setting the properties of the chart instance object. The following sections describe setting various properties of the chart.

Setting the chart color and bounds

To set the chart's color and bounds, use setter methods of the chart instance object.

```
newChart.getBlock( ).setBackground
    ( ColorDefinitionImpl.WHITE );
newChart.getBlock( ).setBounds( BoundsImpl.create( 0, 0, 400,
    250 ) );
newChart.getTitle( ).getLabel( ).getCaption( ).setValue
    ( "Europe" );
```

Setting plot properties

To set properties of the plot, first get a Plot object from the chart instance object, then use a setter method of a component of the Plot object.

```
Plot p = newChart.getPlot( );
p.getClientArea( ).setBackground( ColorDefinitionImpl.create
    ( 255, 255, 225 ) );
```

Setting legend properties

To set properties of the chart legend, first get a Legend object from the chart instance object, then use a setter method of a component of the Legend object.

```
Legend lg = newChart.getLegend( );
lg.getText( ).getFont( ).setSize( 16 );
lg.getInsets( ).set( 1, 1, 1, 1 );
lg.getOutline( ).setVisible( false );
lg.setAnchor( Anchor.NORTH_LITERAL );
```

Setting legend line properties

To set properties of the legend line, first get a LineAttribute object from the Legend object.

```
LineAttributes lia = lg.getOutline( );
lia.setStyle( LineStyle.SOLID_LITERAL );
```

Setting axes properties

A chart with axes always has at least two axes, the primary base axis and the axis orthogonal to the base axis. There can be more than one primary base axis, but for every base axis there is one axis that is orthogonal to it. To get a primary base axis, use the getPrimaryBaseAxes( ) method of the chart instance. This method returns an array. If there is only one primary base axis, get the zeroth element of the array, as shown in the following code.

```
Axis xAxisPrimary = newChart.getPrimaryBaseAxes( )[0];
```

The following code sets the properties of the primary base axis.

```
xAxisPrimary.setType( AxisType.TEXT_LITERAL );
xAxisPrimary.getMajorGrid( ).setTickStyle
   ( TickStyle.BELOW_LITERAL );
xAxisPrimary.getOrigin( ).setType
   ( IntersectionType.VALUE_LITERAL );
xAxisPrimary.getTitle( ).setVisible( false );
```

To get the axis orthogonal to the primary base axis, use the getPrimaryOrthogonalAxis( ) method of the chart instance object, as shown in the following code:

```
Axis yAxisPrimary =
   newChart.getPrimaryOrthogonalAxis( xAxisPrimary );
yAxisPrimary.getMajorGrid( ).setTickStyle
   ( TickStyle.LEFT_LITERAL );
yAxisPrimary.getScale( ).setMax( NumberDataElementImpl.create
   ( 160 ) );
yAxisPrimary.getScale( ).setMin( NumberDataElementImpl.create
   ( -50 ) );
yAxisPrimary.getTitle( ).getCaption( ).setValue
   ( "Sales Growth" );
```

Creating a category series

To create a chart series, use the static create( ) method of the SeriesImpl class.

```
Series seriesCategory = SeriesImpl.create( );
```

Once you have a Series object, you must create a query and add the query to the series data definition, as shown in the following code:

```
Query query = QueryImpl.create( "row[\"Category\"]" );
seriesCategory.getDataDefinition( ).add( query );
```

Creating a y-series

To create a y-series, use the static create( ) method of one of the subclasses of the SeriesImpl class. You can create series of various types using the create( ) method of one of the following classes:

- AreaSeriesImpl

- BarSeriesImpl

- DialSeriesImpl

- LineSeriesImpl

- PieSeriesImpl

- ScatterSeriesImpl

- StockSeriesImpl

Because a chart can have multiple series of differing types, it is not always possible to classify a chart as a single type.

The following example creates a bar series and a line series.

```
BarSeries bs1 = ( BarSeries ) BarSeriesImpl.create( );
bs1.setSeriesIdentifier( "Q1" );
LineSeries ls1 = ( LineSeries ) LineSeriesImpl.create( );
ls1.setSeriesIdentifier( "Q2" );
```

Defining the y-series queries

To set the data values for the y-series, you must create Query objects and add the queries to the LineSeries objects as shown in the following code.

```
Query query1 = QueryImpl.create( "row[\"Value1\"]" );
Query query2 = QueryImpl.create( "row[\"Value2\"]" );
bs1.getDataDefinition( ).add( query1 );
ls1.getDataDefinition( ).add( query2 );
```

Setting the y-series properties

To set the properties of the y-series, use getter and setter methods of the LineSeries objects, as shown in Listing 14-6.

Listing 14-6   Setting the properties of a series

```
ls1.getLineAttributes( ).setColor
   ( ColorDefinitionImpl.RED( ) );
ls1.getMarker( ).setType( MarkerType.TRIANGLE_LITERAL );
ls1.getLabel( ).setVisible( true );
ls1.getLabel( ).getCaption( ).setValue( "Q1" );
ls2.getLineAttributes( ).setColor
   ( ColorDefinitionImpl.YELLOW( ) );
bs1.getMarker( ).setType( MarkerType.TRIANGLE_LITERAL );
bs1.getLabel( ).setVisible( true );
bs1.getLabel( ).getCaption( ).setValue( "Q2" );
```

Setting the properties of the x- and y-series

To set the properties of either the x- or y-series, you must first use the static create( ) method of the SeriesDefinitionImpl class to get a SeriesDefinition object, as shown in the following code.

```
SeriesDefinition sdX = SeriesDefinitionImpl.create( );
SeriesDefinition sdY1 = SeriesDefinitionImpl.create( );
SeriesDefinition sdY2 = SeriesDefinitionImpl.create( );
```

To set the color of a series, get a SeriesPalette object and call its update( ) method, as shown in the following code.

```
sdX.getSeriesPalette( ).update( 0 );
sdY1.getSeriesPalette( ).update( 0 );
sdY2.getSeriesPalette( ).update( 0 );
```

Adding a series definition to the Axis object

After setting the properties of a SeriesDefinition object, you must add the SeriesDefinition object to the Axis object's collection of series definitions, as shown in the following code.

```
xAxisPrimary.getSeriesDefinitions( ).add( sdX );
yAxisPrimary.getSeriesDefinitions( ).add( sdY1 );
yAxisPrimary.getSeriesDefinitions( ).add( sdY2 );
```

Adding series, queries, and categories to the series definitions

To add the line series to the series definition's collection of series, get the series from the SeriesDefinition object and add the line series to it, as shown in the following examples.

```
sdY1.getSeries( ).add( ls1 );
sdY2.getSeries( ).add( bs1 );
```

To add a query to the series definition, get the query from the SeriesDefinition object and pass the query to the setDefinition( ) method, as shown in the following code.

```
sdY1.getQuery( ).setDefinition( "\"Q1\"" );
sdY2.getQuery( ).setDefinition( "\"Q2\"" );
```

To add a category to the SeriesDefinition object, get the series from the SeriesDefinition object and add the category to it, as shown in the following statement:

```
sdX.getSeries( ).add( seriesCategory );
```

Creating sample data

This section describes an optional step in the creation of a chart. If you omit the code in Listing 14-7, the chart renders correctly at run time but not in the BIRT Report Designer.

Listing 14-7   Adding sample data to a chart

```
SampleData sdt = DataFactory.eINSTANCE.createSampleData( );
BaseSampleData sdBase =
   DataFactory.eINSTANCE.createBaseSampleData( );
sdBase.setDataSetRepresentation( "A" );
sdt.getBaseSampleData( ).add( sdBase );
OrthogonalSampleData sdOrthogonal =
   DataFactory.eINSTANCE.createOrthogonalSampleData( );
sdOrthogonal.setDataSetRepresentation( "1" );
sdOrthogonal.setSeriesDefinitionIndex( 0 );
sdt.getOrthogonalSampleData( ).add( sdOrthogonal );
newChart.setSampleData( sdt );
```

Getting an element factory object

You must have an ElementFactory object to create the next object in the chain. To get an ElementFactory object, use the getElementFactory( ) method of the ReportDesignHandle object.

```
ElementFactory ef = designHandle.getElementFactory( );
```

Getting an extended item handle object

You use the ElementFactory object to create an ExtendedItemHandle object. Because the chart report item is an extended report item, you use the newExtendedItem( ) method of the ElementFactory object to create the ExtendedItemHandle object.

```
ExtendedItemHandle chartHandle = ef.newExtendedItem( null,
   "Chart" );
```

Setting the chart.instance property on the report item

You must set the chart.instance property of the report item object so that it contains the chart instance object. You get the report item from the extended item handle object, as shown in the following code.

```
try{
   chartHandle.getReportItem( ).setProperty( "chart.instance",
   newChart );
} catch( ExtendedElementException e )
{
   e.printStackTrace( );
}
```

Getting a data set from the report design

The new chart is still not bound to a data set. To bind a chart to a data set, you must get a data set from the report design, as shown in the following code.

```
OdaDataSetHandle dataSet =
   ( OdaDataSetHandle ) designHandle.getDataSets( ).get( 0 );
```

Binding the chart to the data set

Use the extended item handle to bind the chart to the data set. This is also a good place to set the dimensions of the report item.

```
try {
   chartHandle.setDataSet( dataSet );
   chartHandle.setHeight( "250pt" );
   chartHandle.setWidth( "400pt" );
}
catch ( SemanticException e ) {
   e.printStackTrace( );
}
```

Adding the new chart to the report design

Once the properties of the chart are properly set and the chart is bound to a data set, it is time to add the new chart to the report design. The following code adds the chart to the footer of a list item.

```
ListHandle li =  ( ListHandle )
   designHandle.getBody( ).getContents( ).get( 0 );
try {
   li.getFooter( ).add( chartHandle );
}
catch ( ContentException e3 ) {
   e3.printStackTrace( );
}
catch ( NameException e3 ) {
   e3.printStackTrace( );
}
```

Saving the report design after adding the chart

Although the previous step is the final step in creating the chart and adding it to the report, you still have to save the design. It is a good idea to save the modified report design with a new name in order not to destroy the original report design file.

```
try {
   designHandle.saveAs( "./Test_modified.rptdesign" );
}
```

```
catch ( IOException e ) {
   e.printStackTrace( );
}
designHandle.close( );
```

Putting it all together

The application in Listing 14-8 uses many of the techniques illustrated in this section and unites them in a coherent Java application.

Listing 14-8   Adding a chart to the report design

```
import java.io.IOException;
import java.util.HashMap;
import org.eclipse.birt.report.engine.api.*;
import org.eclipse.birt.chart.model.*;
import org.eclipse.birt.chart.model.attribute.*;
import org.eclipse.birt.chart.model.attribute.impl.*;
import org.eclipse.birt.chart.model.component.*;
import org.eclipse.birt.chart.model.component.impl.*;
import org.eclipse.birt.chart.model.data.*;
import org.eclipse.birt.chart.model.data.impl.*;
import org.eclipse.birt.chart.model.layout.*;
import org.eclipse.birt.chart.model.type.*;
import org.eclipse.birt.chart.model.type.impl.*;
import org.eclipse.birt.chart.reportitem.*;


/**
 * Reads a BIRT report design file, adds a chart and writes a
 * new report design file containing the added chart.
 * Run this application with the following command line:
 * java ChartReportApp origDesing modifiedDesign
 */

public class ChartReportApp
{
private EngineConfig config;

ChartReportApp () {

   // Get an EngineConfig object with which to specify
   // the home of the BIRT report engine.
   config = new EngineConfig( );

   // Alter this path to the location of your Eclipse
   // installation.
```

```
      config.setEngineHome(
        "C:/birt-runtime-2_1_0/Report Engine" );
   }


   /****************************************************************
    * Give default values to the original design, the new design,
    * and the output format.
    * Extract command line values, if any.
    * Create an instance of this class, build a chart,
    * and run the report
    ****************************************************************/

   public static void main(String[] args)
   {

      String reportDesign = "./test.rptdesign";
      String newReportDesign = "./Test_modified.rptdesign";
      String format = HTMLRenderOption.OUTPUT_FORMAT_HTML;
      boolean showInfo = true;

      if(args.length > 0){
         reportDesign = args[0];
      }
      if(args.length > 1){
         newReportDesign = args[1];
      }

      ChartReportApp cra = new ChartReportApp( );

      cra.build( reportDesign, newReportDesign );
      cra.run( newReportDesign, format );
   }


   /**************************************************************
    * Build a chart
    **************************************************************/
   public void build ( String origDesign, String newDesign )
   {
      // Get a new DesignEngine session
      SessionHandle sessionHandle = DesignEngine.newSession(
         null );

      // Get a handle to the original report design
      ReportDesignHandle designHandle = null;
      try {
         designHandle = sessionHandle.openDesign( origDesign );
      } catch ( DesignFileException e1 ) {
         e1.printStackTrace( );
```

```
}

// Creaate a new chart instance object
ChartWithAxes newChart = ChartWithAxesImpl.create( );

// Set the properties of the chart
newChart.setType( "Line Chart" );
newChart.setSubType( "Overlay" );
newChart.getBlock().setBackground(
   ColorDefinitionImpl.WHITE() );
newChart.getBlock().setBounds(
   BoundsImpl.create( 0, 0, 400, 250 ) );
Plot p = newChart.getPlot();
p.getClientArea().setBackground(
   ColorDefinitionImpl.create( 255, 255, 225 ));
newChart.getTitle().getLabel().getCaption().
   setValue( "Europe" );

Legend lg = cwaLine.getLegend();
LineAttributes lia = lg.getOutline();
lg.getText().getFont().setSize( 16 );
lia.setStyle( LineStyle.SOLID_LITERAL );
lg.getInsets().set( 1, 1, 1, 1 );
lg.getOutline().setVisible( false );
lg.setAnchor( Anchor.NORTH_LITERAL );

Axis xAxisPrimary = newChart.getPrimaryBaseAxes()[0];
xAxisPrimary.setType( AxisType.TEXT_LITERAL );
xAxisPrimary.getMajorGrid().setTickStyle(
TickStyle.BELOW_LITERAL );
xAxisPrimary.getOrigin().setType(
IntersectionType.VALUE_LITERAL );
xAxisPrimary.getTitle().setVisible( false );

Axis yAxisPrimary = cwaLine.getPrimaryOrthogonalAxis(
   xAxisPrimary );
yAxisPrimary.getMajorGrid().setTickStyle(
   TickStyle.LEFT_LITERAL );
yAxisPrimary.getScale().setMax(
   NumberDataElementImpl.create( 160 ));
yAxisPrimary.getScale().setMin(NumberDataElementImpl.
   create( -50 ));
yAxisPrimary.getTitle().getCaption().
   setValue( "Sales Growth" );

// Create sample data.
SampleData sdt = DataFactory.eINSTANCE.createSampleData();
BaseSampleData sdBase =
   DataFactory.eINSTANCE.createBaseSampleData();
```

```
sdBase.setDataSetRepresentation("A");
sdt.getBaseSampleData().add( sdBase );
OrthogonalSampleData sdOrthogonal =
  DataFactory.eINSTANCE.createOrthogonalSampleData();
sdOrthogonal.setDataSetRepresentation( "1" );
sdOrthogonal.setSeriesDefinitionIndex(0);
sdt.getOrthogonalSampleData().add( sdOrthogonal );
newChart.setSampleData(sdt);

// Create the category series
Series seCategory = SeriesImpl.create();

// Set data value for X-Series
Query query = QueryImpl.create( "row[\"Category\"]" );
seCategory.getDataDefinition().add( query );

// Create the primary data set
LineSeries ls1 = ( LineSeries ) LineSeriesImpl.create();
ls1.setSeriesIdentifier("Q1");

// Set data value for Y-Series
Query query1 = QueryImpl.create("row[\"Value1\"]");
ls1.getDataDefinition().add(query1);
ls1.getLineAttributes().setColor(
  ColorDefinitionImpl.RED());
ls1.getMarker().setType(MarkerType.TRIANGLE_LITERAL);
ls1.getLabel().setVisible(true);
ls1.getLabel().getCaption().setValue( "Q1" );
LineSeries ls2 = (LineSeries) LineSeriesImpl.create();
ls2.setSeriesIdentifier( "Q2" );

// Set data value for Y-Series
Query query2 = QueryImpl.create( "row[\"Value2\"]" );
ls2.getDataDefinition().add( query2 );

ls2.getLineAttributes().setColor(
  ColorDefinitionImpl.YELLOW() );
ls2.getMarker().setType( MarkerType.TRIANGLE_LITERAL );
ls2.getLabel().setVisible( true );
ls2.getLabel().getCaption().setValue( "Q2" );

SeriesDefinition sdX = SeriesDefinitionImpl.create();
sdX.getSeriesPalette().update( 0 );
xAxisPrimary.getSeriesDefinitions().add( sdX );

SeriesDefinition sdY1 = SeriesDefinitionImpl.create();
sdY1.getSeriesPalette().update( 0 );
sdY1.getSeries().add( ls1 );
sdY1.getQuery().setDefinition( "\"Q1\"" );
```

```
yAxisPrimary.getSeriesDefinitions().add( sdY1 );

SeriesDefinition sdY2 = SeriesDefinitionImpl.create();
sdY2.getSeriesPalette().update( 0 );
sdY2.getSeries().add( ls2 );
sdY2.getQuery().setDefinition( "\"Q2\"" );
yAxisPrimary.getSeriesDefinitions().add( sdY2 );
sdX.getSeries().add(seCategory);


// Get a chart implementation object and set its
// chart.instance property
ElementFactory ef = designHandle.getElementFactory( );
ExtendedItemHandle extendedItemHandle =
   ef.newExtendedItem( null, "Chart" );

try{
   ChartReportItemImpl chartItem =
      (ChartReportItemImpl)extendedItemHandle.
      getReportItem( );
   chartItem.setProperty("chart.instance", newChart);
} catch(ExtendedElementException e){ e.printStackTrace( ); }

// Get an ODA data set and bind it to the chart
OdaDataSetHandle dataSet = ( OdaDataSetHandle )
   designHandle.getDataSets( ).get( 0 );
try {
   extendedItemHandle.setDataSet( dataSet );
   extendedItemHandle.setHeight( "250pt" );
   extendedItemHandle.setWidth( "400pt" );
} catch ( SemanticException e ) {
    e.printStackTrace( );
}

// Add the chart to the report design
ListHandle li =  (ListHandle) designHandle.
   getBody( ).getContents( ).get( 0 );
try {
    li.getFooter( ).add( extendedItemHandle );
  } catch ( ContentException e3 ) {
    e3.printStackTrace( );
  } catch ( NameException e3 ) {
    e3.printStackTrace( );
}

// Save the  report design that now contains a chart
try {
   designHandle.saveAs( newDesign );
} catch ( IOException e ) {
```

```
        e.printStackTrace( );
      }
      designHandle.close();
   }

   /**************************************************************
    *  Run the report design that contains the new chart.
    *  Depending on format parameter, this method creates either
    *  an HTML report or a PDF report.
    **************************************************************/
   public void run( String reportDesign, String format )
   {
      // Create an image handler object
      IHTMLImageHandler imageHandler = new
        HTMLServerImageHandler();

      // Create an emitter config object and set the image
      // handler on it.
      HTMLEmitterConfig hc = new HTMLEmitterConfig();
      hc.setImageHandler( imageHandler );

      // Create a rendering context object and set its image
      // directories.
      HTMLRenderContext renderContext = new HTMLRenderContext( );
      renderContext.setImageDirectory( "./images" );
      renderContext.setBaseImageURL( "./images" );

      // Create the report engine.
      ReportEngine engine = new ReportEngine( config );

      // Creaet a runnable report from the reportDesign.
      IReportRunnable report = null;
      try
      {
         report = engine.openReportDesign( reportDesign );
      }
      catch ( EngineException e )
      {
         System.err.println( "Report " + reportDesign +
           " not found!\n" );
         engine.destroy( );
         return;
      }

      // Create a task to run the report
      IRunAndRenderTask task = engine.
        createRunAndRenderTask( report );
      HTMLRenderOption options = new HTMLRenderOption( );
```

```
                // Set the output format, either HTML or PDF
                options.setOutputFormat( format );

                // Give the report the same name as the design,
                // except give it the appropriate extension
                String output = reportDesign.replaceFirst( ".rptdesign",
                    "." + format );
                options.setOutputFileName( output );

                // Set the render options on the RunAndRenderTask object
                task.setRenderOption( options );

                // Create an application context HashMap and add the
                // render context to it
                HashMap appContext = new HashMap( );
                appContext.put(
                    EngineConstants.APPCONTEXT_HTML_RENDER_CONTEXT,
                    renderContext );

                // Set the application context on the task
                task.setAppContext( appContext );


                // Run the report.
                try {
                    task.run( );
                }
                catch ( EngineException e1 )
                {
                    System.err.println( "Report " + reportDesign +
                        " run failed.\n" );
                    System.err.println( e1.toString( ) );
                }
                engine.destroy( );
        }
    }
```

Using the BIRT charting API in a Java Swing application

The BIRT charting API does not rely on the BIRT design engine or the BIRT report engine. You can use the BIRT charting API to generate a chart in any Java application.

The program shown in Listing 14-9 uses the BIRT charting API to build a chart in a Java Swing application. The application does not use the BIRT design engine or the BIRT report engine, and it does not process a BIRT report design file.

Listing 14-9   Java Swing charting application

```
import java.awt.BorderLayout;
import java.awt.Color;
import java.awt.Container;
import java.awt.Dimension;
import java.awt.FlowLayout;
import java.awt.Font;
import java.awt.FontMetrics;
import java.awt.Graphics;
import java.awt.Graphics2D;
import java.awt.GridLayout;
import java.awt.Rectangle;
import java.awt.Toolkit;
import java.awt.event.ActionEvent;
import java.awt.event.ActionListener;
import java.awt.event.ComponentEvent;
import java.awt.event.ComponentListener;
import java.util.HashMap;
import java.util.Map;
import javax.swing.JFrame;
import javax.swing.JPanel;

import org.eclipse.birt.chart.device.IDeviceRenderer;
import org.eclipse.birt.chart.device.IUpdateNotifier;
import org.eclipse.birt.chart.exception.ChartException;
import org.eclipse.birt.chart.factory.GeneratedChartState;
import org.eclipse.birt.chart.factory.Generator;
import org.eclipse.birt.chart.model.Chart;
import org.eclipse.birt.chart.model.ChartWithAxes;
import org.eclipse.birt.chart.model.attribute.AxisType;
import org.eclipse.birt.chart.model.attribute.Bounds;
import org.eclipse.birt.chart.model.attribute.impl.BoundsImpl;
import org.eclipse.birt.chart.model.component.Axis;
import org.eclipse.birt.chart.util.PluginSettings;
import org.eclipse.birt.chart.model.impl.ChartWithAxesImpl;
import org.eclipse.birt.chart.model.attribute.impl.
    ColorDefinitionImpl;
import org.eclipse.birt.chart.model.layout.Plot;
import org.eclipse.birt.chart.model.layout.Legend;
import org.eclipse.birt.chart.model.attribute.
    IntersectionType;
import org.eclipse.birt.chart.model.attribute.LegendItemType;
import org.eclipse.birt.chart.model.attribute.TickStyle;
```

```java
import org.eclipse.birt.chart.model.data.NumberDataSet;
import org.eclipse.birt.chart.model.data.impl.
   NumberDataSetImpl;
import org.eclipse.birt.chart.model.data.TextDataSet;
import org.eclipse.birt.chart.model.component.Series;
import org.eclipse.birt.chart.model.data.SeriesDefinition;
import org.eclipse.birt.chart.model.type.BarSeries;
import org.eclipse.birt.chart.model.data.impl.
   SeriesDefinitionImpl;
import org.eclipse.birt.chart.model.attribute.Position;
import org.eclipse.birt.chart.model.data.impl.TextDataSetImpl;
import org.eclipse.birt.chart.model.type.impl.BarSeriesImpl;
import org.eclipse.birt.chart.model.component.impl.SeriesImpl;

/* The selector of charts in Swing JPanel.
 *
 */
public final class SwingChartingApp extends JPanel implements
     IUpdateNotifier,
     ComponentListener
{

   private static final long serialVersionUID = 1L;
   private boolean bNeedsGeneration = true;
   private GeneratedChartState gcs = null;
   private Chart cm = null;
   private IDeviceRenderer idr = null;
   private Map contextMap;

   /* Contructs the layout with a container for displaying
    * chart
    */
   public static void main( String[] args )
   {
     SwingChartingApp scv = new SwingChartingApp( );
     JFrame jf = new JFrame( );
     jf.setDefaultCloseOperation( JFrame.DISPOSE_ON_CLOSE );
     jf.addComponentListener( scv );
     Container co = jf.getContentPane( );
     co.setLayout( new BorderLayout( ) );
     co.add( scv, BorderLayout.CENTER );
     Dimension dScreen = Toolkit.
        getDefaultToolkit( ).getScreenSize( );
     Dimension dApp = new Dimension( 800, 600 );
     jf.setSize( dApp );
     jf.setLocation( ( dScreen.width - dApp.width ) / 2,
          ( dScreen.height - dApp.height ) / 2 );
     jf.setTitle( scv.getClass( ).getName( ) + " [device="
          + scv.idr.getClass( ).getName( )
```

```
                   + "]" );//$NON-NLS-1$
       jf.show( );
   }

   /* Get the connection with SWING device to render the
    * graphics.
    */
   SwingChartingApp( )
   {
      contextMap = new HashMap( );
      final PluginSettings ps = PluginSettings.instance( );
      try
      {
         idr = ps.getDevice( "dv.SWING" );//$NON-NLS-1$
      }
      catch ( ChartException ex )
      {
         ex.printStackTrace( );
      }
      cm = createBarChart( );
   }

   /* Build a simple bar chart */
      public static final Chart createBarChart( )
      {
         ChartWithAxes cwaBar = ChartWithAxesImpl.create( );

      /* Plot */
         cwaBar.getBlock( ).
            setBackground( ColorDefinitionImpl.WHITE( ) );
         cwaBar.getBlock( ).getOutline( ).setVisible( true );
         Plot p = cwaBar.getPlot( );
         p.getClientArea( ).
            setBackground(
               ColorDefinitionImpl.create( 255,
                  255,
                  225 ) );
         p.getOutline( ).setVisible( false );

         /* Title */
         cwaBar.getTitle( ).getLabel( ).getCaption( ).
            setValue( "Bar Chart" );

         /* Legend */
         Legend lg = cwaBar.getLegend( );
         lg.getText( ).getFont( ).setSize( 16 );
         lg.setItemType( LegendItemType.CATEGORIES_LITERAL );

         /* X-Axis */
```

```
        Axis xAxisPrimary = cwaBar.getPrimaryBaseAxes( )[0];
        xAxisPrimary.setType( AxisType.TEXT_LITERAL );
        xAxisPrimary.getMajorGrid( ).
           setTickStyle( TickStyle.BELOW_LITERAL );
        xAxisPrimary.getOrigin( ).
           setType( IntersectionType.VALUE_LITERAL );
        xAxisPrimary.getTitle( ).setVisible( true );

        /* Y-Axis */
        Axis yAxisPrimary = cwaBar.
           getPrimaryOrthogonalAxis( xAxisPrimary );
        yAxisPrimary.getMajorGrid( ).
           setTickStyle( TickStyle.LEFT_LITERAL );
        yAxisPrimary.setType( AxisType.LINEAR_LITERAL );
        yAxisPrimary.getLabel( ).getCaption( ).
           getFont( ).setRotation( 90 );

        /* Data Set */
        TextDataSet categoryValues =
           TextDataSetImpl.create( new String[]{
              "Item 1", "Item 2", "Item 3"} );
        NumberDataSet orthoValues = NumberDataSetImpl.
           create( new double[]{
              25, 35, 15
              } );

        /* X-Series */
        Series seCategory = SeriesImpl.create( );
        seCategory.setDataSet( categoryValues );
        SeriesDefinition sdX = SeriesDefinitionImpl.create( );
        sdX.getSeriesPalette( ).update( 0 );
        xAxisPrimary.getSeriesDefinitions( ).add( sdX );
        sdX.getSeries( ).add( seCategory );

        /* Y-Series */
        BarSeries bs = (BarSeries) BarSeriesImpl.create( );
        bs.setDataSet( orthoValues );
        bs.setRiserOutline( null );
        bs.getLabel( ).setVisible( true );
        bs.setLabelPosition( Position.INSIDE_LITERAL );
        SeriesDefinition sdY = SeriesDefinitionImpl.create( );
        yAxisPrimary.getSeriesDefinitions( ).add( sdY );
        sdY.getSeries( ).add( bs );
        return cwaBar;
    }

public void regenerateChart( )
{
    bNeedsGeneration = true;
```

```
      repaint( );
   }

   public void repaintChart( )
   {
      repaint( );
   }

   public Object peerInstance( )
   {
      return this;
   }

   public Chart getDesignTimeModel( )
   {
      return cm;
   }

   public Object getContext( Object key )
   {
      return contextMap.get( key );
   }

   public Object putContext( Object key, Object value )
   {
      return contextMap.put( key, value );
   }

   public Object removeContext( Object key )
   {
      return contextMap.remove( key );
   }

   public Chart getRunTimeModel( )
   {
      return gcs.getChartModel( );
   }

   public void paint( Graphics g )
   {
      super.paint( g );
      Graphics2D g2d = (Graphics2D) g;
      idr.setProperty( IDeviceRenderer.GRAPHICS_CONTEXT, g2d );
      idr.setProperty( IDeviceRenderer.UPDATE_NOTIFIER, this );
      Dimension d = getSize( );
      Bounds bo = BoundsImpl.create( 0, 0, d.width, d.height );
      bo.scale( 72d / idr.getDisplayServer( ).
         getDpiResolution( ) );
```

```
        Generator gr = Generator.instance( );

        if ( bNeedsGeneration )
        {
          bNeedsGeneration = false;
          try
          {
            gcs = gr.build( idr.getDisplayServer( ),
                  cm,
                  bo,
                  null,
                  null,
                  null );
          }
          catch ( ChartException ex )
          {
            System.out.println( ex );
          }
        }

        try
        {
          gr.render( idr, gcs );
        }
        catch ( ChartException ex )
        {
          System.out.println( ex );
        }
      }

      public void componentHidden( ComponentEvent e )
      {
      }

      public void componentMoved( ComponentEvent e )
      {
      }

      public void componentResized( ComponentEvent e )
      {
        bNeedsGeneration = true;
      }

      public void componentShown( ComponentEvent e )
      {
      }
    }
```

Understanding the chart programming examples

The org.eclipse.birt.chart.examples plug-in is a collection of chart programming examples. The root directory of the chart programming examples is:

```
C:\eclipse\plugins\org.eclipse.birt.chart.examples
```

The individual examples in the chart examples plug-in are located in a subdirectory under the examples root directory, called EXAMPLES_ROOT. Most of the examples consist of one or more Java applications that use either Java Swing or Eclipse SWT. The application classes are called viewer applications and their class names end in Viewer. Most of the examples also have one or more additional classes that the viewer class uses. The additional classes are usually where the chart is built.

The following sections provide brief summaries of the examples in the chart examples plug-in.

DataCharts

The DataCharts example consists of DataChartsViewer, a Java Swing application that uses the DataCharts class to build a chart. Depending on user selection, the application builds any of the following three kinds of charts:

- A pie chart with a minimum slice
- A bar chart with multiple y-axes
- A bar chart with multiple Y series

GroupOnXSeries

The GroupOnXSeries example is a Java application that processes a BIRT report design and modifies it. The original report design contains a chart report item that does not group on the X series. The GroupOnXSeries Java application modifies the design so that the chart report item does group on the X series. The application modifies the design it reads from NonGroupOnXSeries.rptdesign and it saves a new BIRT report design named GroupOnXSeries.rptdesign.

GroupOnYAxis

The GroupOnYAxis example is a Java application that processes a BIRT report design and modifies it. The original report design contains a chart report item that does not group on the y-axis. The GroupOnYAxis Java application modifies the design so that the chart report item does group on the y-axis. The application modifies the design it reads from NonGroupOnYAxis.rptdesign and it saves a new BIRT report design named GroupOnYAxis.rptdesign.

AutoDataBinding

The AutoDataBinding example is an Eclipse SWT application that consists of the AutoDataBindingViewer and DataRowExpressionEvaluator classes. The AutoDataBindingViewer creates a SWT Display widget and adds a chart to it. The application binds data to the chart and renders the chart.

FormatCharts

The FormatCharts example is a Java Swing application that consists of the FormatChartsViewer and FormatCharts Java classes. The FormatChartsViewer class calls any of several methods in FormatCharts to add a chart to the application. FormatCharts has methods to build the following kinds of charts based on user selection:

- Axis format
- Colored by category
- Legend title
- Percentage value
- Plot format
- Series format

InteractivityCharts

There are three viewer applications for the InteractivityCharts example, SvgInteractivityViewer, SwingInteractivityViewer, and SwtInteractivityViewer. Each of the viewer applications uses a different Java framework, as indicated by the name of the viewer. All three applications do the same thing, offering the user a choice of type of interactivity chart and calling the corresponding method in the InteractivityCharts class. The four types of interactivity illustrated in these charts are:

- Click to highlight series
- Mouse over data points to show tooltips
- Click line series to toggle visibility
- Click pie slice to redirect URL

PDFChartGenerator

The PDFChartGenerator example is a Java application that builds a simple chart and renders it as a PDF file. The PDFChartGenerator example consists of ChartModels and PDFChartGenerator. ChartModels has a single method that builds a simple chart. PDFChartGenerator uses the BIRT charting API to get the PDF renderer and the chart generator.

StyleProcessor

The StyleProcessor example builds a simple chart and applies styles to several elements of the chart. The example consists of StyleChartViewer, an Eclipse SWT application, and StyleProcessor class, an implementation of the IStyleProcessor interface.

ScriptViewer

The ScriptViewer example consists of two applications, JavaScriptViewer and JavaViewer. Both applications are SWT applications that illustrate the techniques for creating charts with report element event handlers. JavaScriptViewer builds charts that have JavaScript event handlers. JavaViewer builds charts that have Java event handlers. Both applications use the ScriptCharts class to build charts.

The ScriptCharts class has methods to create charts with report element event handlers written in JavaScript and four methods that create charts with report element event handlers written in Java.

Each JavaScript event handler is defined as a single string in ScriptCharts. The Java event handlers are Java classes that are located in EXAMPLES_ROOT/api/script/java. The ScriptCharts methods that add a Java event handler pass a string containing the path of the Java class.

Viewer

The Viewer example is a set of six Eclipse applications that create a wide variety of charts. There are two Java Swing applications and four Eclipse SWT applications. The following list includes the viewers and the kinds of charts that they can create:

- Chart3DViewer
  - 3D bar chart
  - 3D line chart
  - 3D area chart
- CurveFittingViewer
  - Curve fitting bar chart
  - Curve fitting line chart
  - Curve fitting stock chart
  - Curve fitting area chart
- DialChartViewer
  - Single dial multiregion chart
  - Multidial multiregion chart

- Single dial single region chart
- Multidial single region chart
- SwingChartViewersSelector
  - Bar chart
  - Bar chart with 2 series
  - Pie chart
  - Pie chart with 4 series
  - Line chart
  - Bar/Line stacked chart
  - Scatter chart
  - Area chart
- SwingLiveChartViewer
  - Live animated chart with scrolling data
- SWTchartViewerSelector
  - Bar chart
  - Bar chart with 2 series
  - Pie chart
  - Pie chart with 4 series
  - Line chart
  - Bar/Line stacked chart
  - Scatter chart
  - Area chart

ChartWizardLauncher

The ChartWizardLauncher example consists of two Java classes, ChartWizardLauncher and DefaultDataServiceProviderImpl. ChartWizardLauncher attempts to read a chart from testCharts.chart. If the file exists, it modifies that file. If the file does not exist, the application creates a new file. The ChartWizardLauncher uses the BIRT chart wizard to create a wizard for the chart. DefaultDataServiceProviderImpl provides a basic implementation for a simulated data service.

Report

There are three report examples, all of which are Java applications that have no user interface. The three report examples use the BIRT design engine to build a BIRT report design file from scratch. All three report examples use the BIRT charting API to add a chart to the report design. All of the report examples do add the following elements to the report design file:

- Master pages
- Data sources
- Data sets
- A body section

The MeterChartExample example adds a meter chart to the body of the report. The SalesReport example creates styles and adds a pie chart to the body of the report. The StockReport example adds a stock chart to the body of the report.

Preference

The preference example illustrates how a Java servlet can process URL parameters to set style preferences for a chart. The servlet, PreferenceServlet, uses ChartModels to generate the chart. The servlet uses the LabelStyleProcessor class to use the style parameters to affect the style of a label in the chart. The example also includes a help page that explains how to do the following things:

- Set up Eclipse to work with Tomcat
- Run the Preference example
- Develop chart pages using JSPs and servlets

V

Working with the Extension Framework

Building the BIRT Project

This chapter explains how to download the BIRT 2.1 source code and build the
BIRT project. This information is primarily for contributors to the BIRT open
source project. You do not need to build BIRT to extend BIRT or write scripts for
BIRT.

About building the BIRT project

Building the BIRT project consists of the following tasks:

- Assuring that you have the correct software on your system

  Your Eclipse version and your Java JDK must be compatible with the version
  of BIRT you are building. BIRT also requires several additional Eclipse
  plug-ins.

- Configuring your Eclipse workspace to compile BIRT code

  You must configure your Eclipse workspace correctly to be able to build
  BIRT. Switching workspaces causes the Eclipse preferences to change, so it is
  necessary to confirm the workspace settings whenever you switch
  workspaces.

- Downloading and compiling the BIRT source code from the Eclipse web site

  You use the Eclipse CVS system to download the BIRT source code. The
  downloaded code compiles automatically when the download is complete.

- Building the web viewer

  You must build the web viewer separately from building BIRT.

Assuring that you have the correct software on your system

To assure that you have all the components that are necessary for building BIRT, install Eclipse and all the related components necessary for running BIRT, as explained in the installation chapters. By creating a complete, functioning BIRT installation, you insure that you have all the correct software on your system necessary for building BIRT.

Configuring the Eclipse workspace to compile BIRT

The BIRT source code uses some features that are only present in JDK version 1.4 and higher. In order for BIRT to build successfully, you need to set the Eclipse compiler compliance to 1.4. You can set this version for your Eclipse workspace by starting Eclipse and setting Eclipse preferences. If you create a new workspace or switch to a different workspace, you can lose the compiler settings, in which case you must reset them as described in the following instructions.

How to set Eclipse workspace preferences

1 Choose Window→Preferences. Preferences appears, as shown in Figure 15-1.

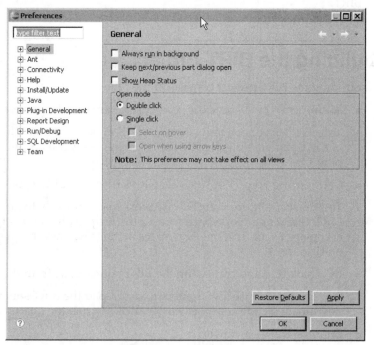

Figure 15-1   The Preferences dialog

2 Expand the Java entry in the tree and select Compiler, as shown in Figure 15-2.

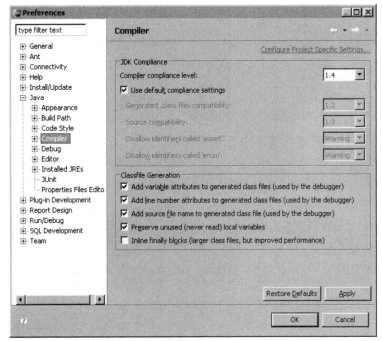

Figure 15-2   Compiler preferences

3 In JDK Compliance:

- Select 1.4 in Compiler compliance level.

- Deselect Use default compliance settings.

- In Generated .class files compatibility, select 1.4.

- In Source compatibility, select 1.4.

- In Classfile Generation, accept the default settings, shown in Figure 15-3.

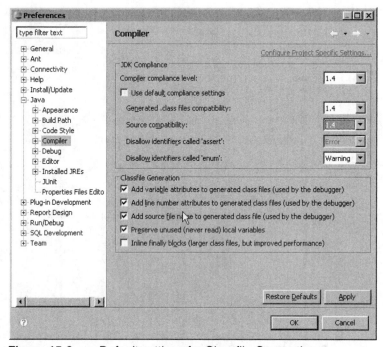

Figure 15-3   Default settings for Classfile Generation

Choose OK. The message shown in Figure 15-4 appears.

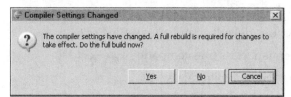

Figure 15-4   Compiler settings prompt

4 Choose Yes.

Creating Eclipse projects

To build BIRT, you must download the source code. You use the CVS client in Eclipse to specify the Eclipse CVS repository site location and to download the source from the remote site. When you check out code from the Eclipse CVS site, Eclipse downloads the source code to the current Eclipse workspace on your local system. Every project you check out creates a corresponding Eclipse project in your current workspace. There are no restrictions or special requirements to download the source code. It is freely available from the Eclipse open source site.

Specifying the repository locations

The following instructions describe how to specify the repository location for the BIRT source.

How to specify a CVS repository location for the BIRT project

1   In Eclipse, choose Window→Open Perspective→Other→CVS Repository Exploring. The Eclipse desktop changes to the CVS perspective, similar to Figure 15-5.

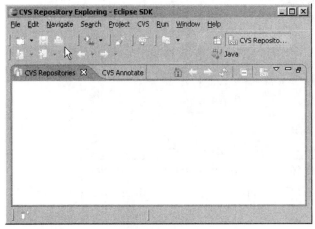

Figure 15-5   The CVS perspective

2   Right-click in CVS Repositories and choose New→Repository Location.

Add CVS Repository appears, as shown in Figure 15-6.

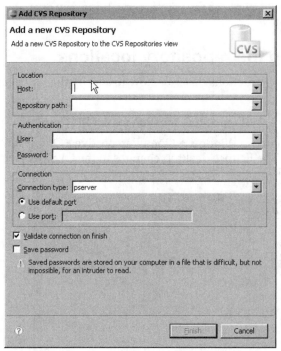

Figure 15-6   The Add CVS Repository dialog

3 On Add CVS Repository, set the values that appear in Table 15-1.

Table 15-1   Values for Add CVS Repository fields

Field	Value
Host	dev.eclipse.org
Repository path	/home/birt
User	anonymous
Connection type	pserver
Use default port	Selected
Validate connection on finish	Selected
Save password	Deselected

4 Choose Finish.

A new node appears in CVS Repositories, as shown in Figure 15-7. This node is named :pserver:anonymous@dev.eclipse.org:/cvsroot/birt.

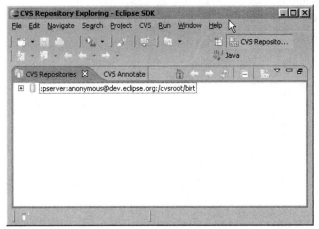

Figure 15-7   BIRT project repository in CVS Repositories

Checking out the BIRT source

You use the CVS source code checkout procedure to check out BIRT source code.

How to check out the BIRT source

1 If Eclipse is not already set to the CVS Repositories perspective, choose Window→Open Perspective→Other→CVS Repository Exploring.

2 If the Problems view is not already visible, choose Basic→Problems in Show View.

   Note any exisisting problems.

3 In the CVS Repositories tree, expand the following nodes:

   ■ :pserver:anonymous@dev.eclipse.org/cvsroot/birt

   ■ Branches

   ■ BIRT_2_1_0_Branch

   ■ sourceBIRT_2_1_0_Branch

   The CVS Repositories tree appears, as shown in Figure 15-8.

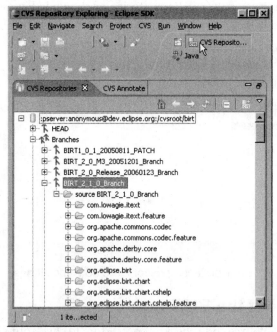

Figure 15-8   The BIRT release in CVS Repositories

4 In the BIRT repository, at:

```
:pserver:anonymous@dev.eclipse.org:/cvsroot/
    birt➤Branches➤BIRT_2_1_0_Branch➤
    sourceBIRT_2_1_0_Branch
```

select all nodes.

5 Some of the nodes in CVS are extraneous for building BIRT and can create compile errors. While the compile errors are not serious, it is easier to verify that you have a good build if you have no compiler errors. The following nodes are unnecessary and can be deselected:

- org.eclipse.birt.chart.tests

- org.eclipse.birt.report.data.oda.flatfile

- org.eclipse.birt.report.data.oda.flatfile.nl

- org.eclipse.birt.report.data.oda.flatfile.ui

- org.eclipse.birt.report.data.oda.flatfile.ui.nl

- org.eclipse.birt.report.designer.rcp.ui

- org.eclipse.birt.report.designer.tests

- org.eclipse.birt.report.tests.chart

- org.eclipse.birt.report.tests.engine

- org.eclipse.birt.report.tests.model

- org.eclipse.birt.test.performance

- org.eclipse.birt.tests.core

- org.eclipse.birt.tests.data

6 From the context menu, choose Check Out.

The entire BIRT source tree now downloads and builds. The building phase of this operation can take a long time. There is a progress meter in the bottom- right corner of the Eclipse window that provides percentage build completion information.

7 Check the Problems view for errors.

You should see more problems now than before you checked out the BIRT source. You must add one JAR file to eliminate the new errors, as described in the following section.

Adding the extra JAR file

There is one extra JAR file, itext-1.3.jar, that BIRT requires to complete the build process. This JAR file is not in the repository and you must download it separately.

You can download itext_1.3.jar from:

```
http://prdownloads.sourceforge.net/itext/itext-1.3.jar
```

The following section describes how to add itext-1.3.jar to the com.lowagie.text project.

How to add itext-1.3.jar to the com.lowagie.text project

1 Copy itext-1.3.jar into com.lowagie.itext/lib, located in the current Eclipse workspace.

2 If the Package Explorer view is not visible, perform the following steps:

    1 Choose Window➤Show View➤Other.

    2 In Show View, select Java➤Package Explorer.

3 In Package Explorer, select the com.lowagie.itext folder.

4 Choose File➤Refresh.

Eclipse rebuilds the workspace after every change to a project. When BIRT finishes rebuilding the workspace, the Problems view should show only the errors that existed before starting the BIRT build, if any.

Building the web viewer

Once you have a successful BIRT build, you are ready to build the BIRT report viewer and the web viewer. Except for the choice of the build script, the process for building the two viewers is identical. However, you must build the report viewer before building the web viewer. Both viewer build scripts are Ant scripts located in org.eclipse.birt.report.viewer.

How to build the report viewer and the web viewer

1 Choose Window→Open Perspective→Java to change your Eclipse perspective to Java. Package Explorer appears on the Eclipse workbench, as shown in Figure 15-9.

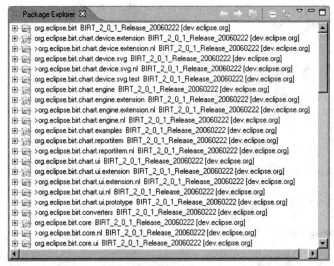

Figure 15-9   Package Explorer

2 In Package Explorer, expand org.eclipse.birt.report.viewer, as shown in Figure 15-10.

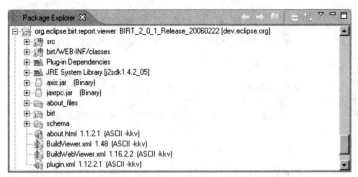

Figure 15-10   Contents of org.eclipse.birt.report.viewer

3 Right-click BuildViewer.xml and choose Run As➤2 Ant Build from the context menu, as shown in Figure 15-11. There are two Ant Build choices on the context menu. Be sure to choose 2 Ant Build.

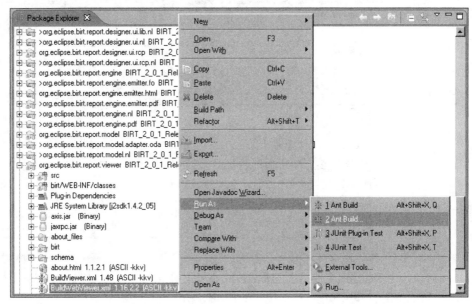

Figure 15-11 Selecting 2 Ant Build

Modify attributes and launch appears.

4 Choose the Targets tab and deselect all the targets except JAR (default), as shown in Figure 15-12.

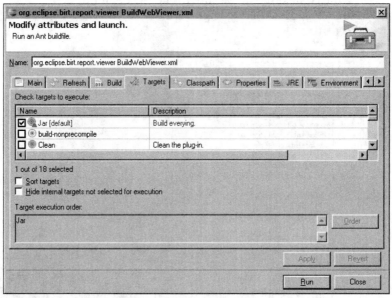

Figure 15-12 The Modify attributes and launch dialog

5 Choose the Properties tab. Modify attributes and launch—Properties appears.

6 Deselect Use global properties as specified in the Ant run-time preferences and choose Add Property. Add Property appears, as shown in Figure 15-13.

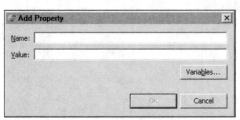

Figure 15-13 Add Property

7 In Name, type:

```
eclipse.home
```

8 In Value, type the path to your Eclipse home directory. Choose OK.

Properties appears, as shown in Figure 15-14.

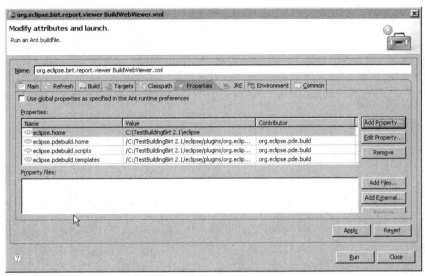

Figure 15-14   The Properties page, showing eclipse.home

9 Choose Run. Console appears, as shown in Figure 15-15.

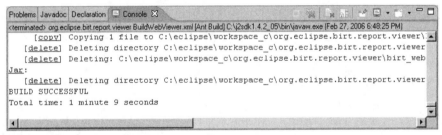

Figure 15-15   The Console page

Assuming that there were no errors in the web viewer build, a folder is created named:

```
$ECLIPSE_WORKSPACE/org.eclipse.birt.report.viewer/birt_web
```

10 Repeat step 3 through step 9, substituting BuildWebViewer.xml for BuildViewer.xml in step 3.

16

Extending BIRT

This chapter provides an overview of the BIRT extension framework and shows how to create and deploy a BIRT extension using the Eclipse Plug-in Development Environment (PDE).

Overview of the extension framework

The Eclipse platform is an open source, integrated system of application development tools that you implement and extend using a plug-in interface. Eclipse provides a set of core plug-ins that configure the basic services for the platform's framework. A platform developer can build and integrate new tools in this application development system.

BIRT is a set of plug-in extensions that enable a developer to add reporting functionality to an application. The BIRT APIs define extension points that allow a developer to add custom functionality to the BIRT framework. Eclipse makes BIRT source code available to the developer community in the CVS repository.

In the Eclipse installation, the name of a plug-in directory contains an appended version number. This book omits the version number from the names of the plug-in directories. For example, the book abbreviates the name of the plug-in directory, org.eclipse.birt.report.data.oda.jdbc_2.1.0.N20060628-1351, to org.eclipse.birt.report.data.oda.jdbc.

The following sections provide a general description of how to make an extension to a defined extension point in the BIRT release 2.1 framework using the Eclipse PDE.

Understanding the structure of a BIRT plug-in

An Eclipse plug-in implements the following components:

- Extension point schema definition

  An XML document that specifies a grammar that you must follow when defining the elements of a plug-in extension in the Eclipse PDE

- Plug-in manifest

  An XML document that describes the plug-in's activation framework to the Eclipse run-time environment

- Plug-in run-time class

  A Java class that defines the methods for starting, managing, and stopping a plug-in instance

The following sections provide detailed descriptions of these Eclipse plug-in components.

Understanding an extension point schema definition file

A plug-in directory typically contains an XML extension point schema definition (.exsd) file in a schema subdirectory. The XML schema documents the elements, attributes, and types used by the extension point. The Eclipse PDE uses this information to describe the elements and attributes in the property editors and other facilities of the Eclipse platform.

You use the Eclipse PDE to develop the plug-in content, test, and deploy a plug-in. The Eclipse PDE automatically generates the plugin.xml, build.properties, and run-time archive files.

The file, $INSTALL_DIR\eclipse\plugins\org.eclipse.birt.report.designer.ui \schema\reportitemUI.exsd, documents the settings for a report item extension to the BIRT Report Designer user interface. The XML schema file, reportitemUI.exsd, has the following structure:

- <schema> is the root element that sets the target namespace and contains all other elements and their attributes.

- <annotation> contains the following attributes:

  - <appinfo> provides the following items:

    - Machine-readable metadata that Eclipse uses to identify the plug-in

    - Text-based information that appears in the PDE Extensions page and HTML extension point description

- <documentation> provides user information that appears in the PDE's HTML extension point description.

■ <element> declares a reference for the model and optional user interface extensions, such as figure, label, image, builder, property page, palette, editor, outline, and description. Each extension element is a complex type containing attributes and annotations, as described below:

  ■ model is an extension element that specifies the Report Object Model (ROM) name for the report item extension.

  ■ Each user interface extension element specifies the following items:

    ❑ Extension element name.

    ❑ Fully qualified name of the Java class implementing the interface specified for the extension element. For example, builder implements the interface, org.eclipse.birt.report.designer.ui.extensions .IReportItemBuilderUI.

Listing 16-1 is a partial schema example showing reportitemUI.exsd. The ellipses (...) mark the places in the code where lines are omitted.

Listing 16-1   Partial example schema for Report Item UI

```
<?xml version='1.0' encoding='UTF-8'?>
<!-- Schema file written by PDE -->
<schema targetNamespace="org.eclipse.birt.report.designer.ui">
   <annotation>
      <appInfo>
         <meta.schema
            plugin="org.eclipse.birt.report.designer.ui"
            id="reportitemUI"
            name="Report Item UI Extension Point"/>
      </appInfo>
      <documentation>
         This extension point is used in conjunction with the
         Report Item extension point defined in the model. It
         is used to register the GUI to be used for the
         Extended report item.
      </documentation>
   </annotation>
   <element name="extension">
      <complexType>
         <sequence>
            ...
            <element ref="model"/>
            <element ref="builder" minOccurs="0" maxOccurs="1"/>
            <element ref="propertyPage" minOccurs="0"
               maxOccurs="1"/>
            <element ref="palette" minOccurs="0" maxOccurs="1"/>
            <element ref="editor" minOccurs="0" maxOccurs="1"/>
            <element ref="outline" minOccurs="0" maxOccurs="1"/>
```

```
            <element ref="description" minOccurs="0"
                maxOccurs="1"/>
        </sequence>
        <attribute name="point" type="string" use="required">
            ...
        </attribute>
    </complexType>
</element>
<element name="model">
    <complexType>
        <attribute name="extensionName" type="string"
            use="required">
            <annotation>
                <documentation>
                    The ROM Report Item Extension name that maps
                    to this UI
                </documentation>
            </annotation>
        </attribute>
    </complexType>
</element>
...
<element name="builder">
    <annotation>
        <documentation>
            Optional Builder for the element inside the Editor.
            Instantiated when a new item is dragged from the
            palette inside the editor.
        </documentation>
    </annotation>
    <complexType>
        <attribute name="class" type="string">
            <annotation>
                <documentation>
                    a fully qualified name of the Java class
                    implementing org.eclipse.birt.report
                    .designer.ui.extensions.IReportItemBuilderUI
                </documentation>
                <appInfo>
                    <meta.attribute kind="java"/>
                </appInfo>
            </annotation>
        </attribute>
    </complexType>
</element>
...
</schema>
```

Understanding a plug-in manifest file

You install an Eclipse plug-in in a subdirectory of the $INSTALL_DIR/eclipse/ plugins directory. The plug-in manifest file, plugin.xml, describes the plug-in's activation framework to the Eclipse run-time environment.

At run time, Eclipse scans the subdirectories in $INSTALL_DIR/eclipse/ plugins, parses the contents of each plug-in manifest file, and caches the information in the plug-in registry. If the Eclipse run time requires an extension, Eclipse lazily loads the plug-in, using the registry information to instantiate the plug-in's objects. The run-time environment for the BIRT Report Engine functions in a similar way.

The plug-in manifest file declares the plug-in's required code and extension points to the plug-in registry. The plug-in run-time class provides the code segment. By lazily loading the plug-in's code segment, the run-time environment minimizes start-up time and conserves memory resources.

The plug-in manifest file, plugin.xml, has the following structure:

- <plugin> is the root element.

- <extension> specifies the extension points and the related elements and attributes that define the processing capabilities of the plug-in component.

Listing 16-2 shows the contents of the plug-in manifest file, org.eclipse.birt.sample.reportitem.rotatedlabel\plugin.xml. This file describes the required classes and extension points for the BIRT report item extension sample, rotated label.

Listing 16-2   Sample plug-in manifest file

```xml
<?xml version="1.0" encoding="UTF-8"?>
<?eclipse version="3.2"?>
<plugin>
   <extension
     id="rotatedLabel"
     name="Rotated Label Extension"
     point="org.eclipse.birt.report.designer.ui
        .reportitemUI">
     <reportItemLabelUI
       class="org.eclipse.birt.sample.reportitem
          .rotatedlabel.RotatedLabelUI"/>
     <model extensionName="RotatedLabel"/>
     <palette icon="icons/rotatedlabel.jpg"/>
     <editor
       canResize="true"
       showInDesigner="true"
       showInMasterPage="true"/>
     <outline icon="icons/rotatedlabel.jpg"/>
     <propertyPage
```

```
        class="org.eclipse.birt.sample.reportitem
           .rotatedlabel.RotatedLabelPropertyEditUIImpl"/>
  </extension>
  <extension
     id="rotatedLabel"
     name="Rotated Label Extension"
     point="org.eclipse.birt.report.model.reportItemModel">
     <reportItem
        class="org.eclipse.birt.sample.reportitem
           .rotatedlabel.RotatedLabelItemFactoryImpl"
        extensionName="RotatedLabel">
        <property
           defaultDisplayName="Rotation Angle"
           defaultValue="-45"
           name="rotationAngle"
           type="integer"/>
        <property
           defaultDisplayName="Display Text"
           defaultValue="Rotated Label"
           name="displayText"
           type="string"/>
     </reportItem>
  </extension>
  <extension
     id="rotatedLabel"
     name="Rotated Label Extension
     point="org.eclipse.birt.report.engine.reportitem
        Presentation">
     <reportItem
        class="org.eclipse.birt.sample.reportitem.rotated
           label.RotatedLabelPresentationImpl"
        name="RotatedLabel"/>
  </extension>
</plugin>
```

Understanding a plug-in run-time class

A plug-in runs within an instance of a plug-in run-time class. A plug-in
run-time class extends org.eclipse.core.runtime.Plugin, the abstract superclass
for all plug-in run-time class implementations. The Plugin run-time class
defines the methods for starting, managing, and stopping a plug-in instance.

The Plugin run-time class typically contains a reference to an Open Services
Gateway Initiative (OSGi) resource bundle that manages the execution context.
Plugin implements the interface, org.osgi.framework.BundleActivator, which
installs, starts, stops, and uninstalls the OSGi resource bundle. The OSGi
resource bundle implements a service registry to support the following services:

■ Installing the resource bundle

- Subscribing to an event

- Registering a service object

- Retrieving a service reference

The OSGi platform provides a secure, managed, extensible Java framework for deploying, downloading, and managing service applications. For more information about the OSGi platform, visit the OSGi Alliance web site at http://www.osgi.org/. For more information about the Java run-time and OSGi APIs, see the reference documentation for the Platform Plug-in Developer Guide in Eclipse Help.

Listing 16-3 is a code example showing the life-cycle and resource bundle methods for the report item plug-in, rotated label.

Listing 16-3 Sample code for the rotated label report item plug-in

```
package org.eclipse.birt.sample.reportitem.rotatedlabel;

import org.eclipse.core.runtime.Plugin;
import org.osgi.framework.BundleContext;
import java.util.*;

/**
 * The main plugin class to be used in the desktop.
 */
public class RotatedLabelPlugin extends Plugin {
   // The Plugin ID
   public final static String ID =
      "org.eclipse.birt.sample.reportitem.rotatedlabel";
   //The shared instance.
   private static RotatedLabelPlugin plugin;
   //Resource bundle.
   private ResourceBundle resourceBundle;

   /**
    * The constructor.
    */
   public RotatedLabelPlugin() {
      super();
      plugin = this;
      try {
         resourceBundle = ResourceBundle.getBundle
            ("org.eclipse.birt.sample.reportitem.rotatedlabel
               .RotatedLabelPluginResources" );
      } catch (MissingResourceException x) {
         resourceBundle = null;
      }
   }
```

```java
/**
 * This method is called upon plug-in activation
 */
public void start(BundleContext context) throws Exception {
    super.start(context);
}

/**
 * This method is called when the plug-in is stopped
 */
public void stop(BundleContext context) throws Exception {
    super.stop(context);
}

/**
 * Returns the shared instance.
 */
public static RotatedLabelPlugin getDefault() {
    return plugin;
}

/**
 * Returns the string from the plugin's resource bundle,
 * or 'key' if not found.
 */
public static String getResourceString(String key) {
    ResourceBundle bundle =
        RotatedLabelPlugin.getDefault().getResourceBundle();
    try {
        return (bundle != null) ? bundle.getString(key) : key;
    } catch (MissingResourceException e) {
        return key;
    }
}

/**
 * Returns the plugin's resource bundle,
 */
public ResourceBundle getResourceBundle() {
    return resourceBundle;
}
}
```

Working with the Eclipse PDE

The Eclipse PDE is an integrated design tool that you use to create, develop, test, debug, and deploy a plug-in. The PDE provides wizards, editors, views, and launchers to assist you in developing a plug-in.

The Eclipse PDE provides a wizard to assist you in setting up a plug-in project and creating the framework for a plug-in extension. In the Plug-in Development perspective, you can use the New Plug-in Project wizard to assist you in setting up a plug-in project and creating the framework for a plug-in extension. The PDE wizard automatically generates the plug-in manifest file, plugin.xml, and, optionally, the Java plug-in run-time class.

How to choose the Plug-in Development perspective

To access the PDE, you must choose the Plug-in Development perspective. To open the Plug-in Development perspective, perform the following tasks:

1 From the Eclipse menu, choose Window→Open Perspective→Other. Open Perspective appears.

2 Select Plug-in Development, as shown in Figure 16-1.

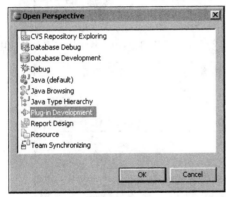

Figure 16-1   Selecting a perspective

Choose OK. The Plug-in Development perspective appears.

How to set up a new plug-in project

To access the New Plug-in Project wizard and create a project, perform the following tasks:

1 From the PDE menu, choose File→New→Project. New Project appears.

2 In Wizards, expand Plug-in Development, and select Plug-in Project, as shown in Figure 16-2.

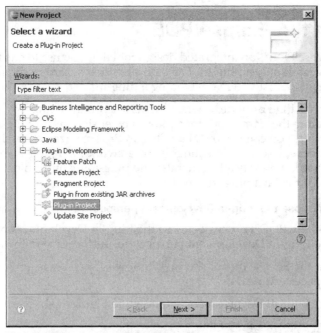

Figure 16-2   New Project

Choose Next. New Plug-in Project appears, as shown in Figure 16-3.

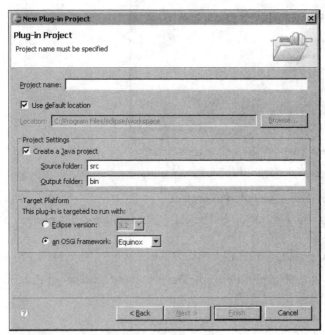

Figure 16-3   New Plug-in Project

Understanding plug-in project properties

Using the New Plug-in Project wizard, you can define the following properties for the plug-in:

- Project settings

  - Name

  - Location

  - Source and output folders

  - Plug-in format, such as the Eclipse version and whether to create an OSGi bundle manifest

- Plug-in content

  - Properties such as ID, version, name, provider, and the run-time library classpath

  - Choose to generate an activator, a Java class that controls the plug-in's life cycle

  - Create a rich client application

- Plug-in components such as an editor, property page, view, menu, or other components from a series of templates

In Eclipse 3.2, opting to create an OSGi bundle manifest, MANIFEST.MF, offers significant advantages. The OSGi bundle manifest, META-INF/MANIFEST.MF, contains a set of manifest headers that provide descriptive information about a bundle.

Eclipse 3.2 uses an implementation of the OSGi R4 framework specification. This framework defines the directives that specify the access rules for an exported package and the headers that facilitate class loading, start-up time, filtering, and other features.

BIRT release 2.1 uses the OSGi framework that comes with the Eclipse 3.2 platform. You must implement any plug-in that extends a BIRT release 2.1 extension point as an OSGi bundle.

Inside the Eclipse environment, you can develop and deploy a plug-in for BIRT Report Designer. Outside of the Eclipse environment, you can develop and deploy a plug-in for BIRT Web Viewer. BIRT Web Viewer is a J2EE web application consisting of servlets and JSPs that encapsulates the BIRT Report Engine API to generate reports.

Understanding the Eclipse PDE Workbench

The Eclipse PDE supports host and run-time instances of the workbench project. The host instance provides the development environment. The run-time instance allows you to launch a plug-in to test it.

Figure 16-4 shows the project for the report item extension sample, rotated label, in the host instance of the PDE Workbench. In the host instance, the PDE Workbench provides the following view and editor components:

- Package Explorer provides an expandable view of the plug-in package.

- Outline provides an expandable view of the project settings.

- PDE Manifest Editor displays a page containing the project settings for the currently selected item in Outline.

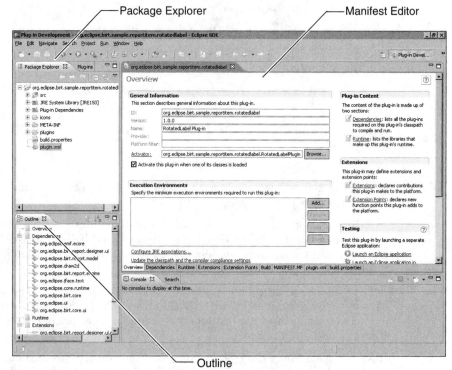

Figure 16-4 The host instance of the PDE Workbench

In PDE Manifest Editor, you specify project settings and edit related files to create the plug-in framework on the following pages:

- Overview

  Lists general information such as the plug-in ID, version, name, provider, platform filter, and activator class. This page also contains sections that link to the plug-in content pages, extensions, launchers for testing and debugging, deployment wizards, and the settings for the execution environment. In Figure 16-4, PDE Manifest Editor displays the Overview page.

- Dependencies

  Lists the plug-ins that must be on the classpath to compile and run.

- Runtime

  Declares the packages that the plug-in exposes to clients, the package visibility to other plug-ins, and the libraries and folders in the plug-in classpath.

- Extensions

  Declares the extensions that the plug-in makes to the platform.

- Extension Points

  Declares the new extension points that the plug-in adds to the platform.

- Build

  Displays the build configuration settings. A change to a setting on this page updates the file, build.properties.

- MANIFEST.MF

  Displays an editable page containing the header settings for the manifest file, MANIFEST.MF, that provide descriptive information about an OSGi bundle.

- Plug-in.xml

  Displays an editable page containing the settings for the plug-in manifest file, plugin.xml.

- Build.properties

  Displays an editable page containing the settings for the file, build.properties.

A modification to a setting in a PDE Manifest Editor page automatically updates the corresponding plug-in manifest or build properties file.

Creating the structure of a plug-in extension

Use the host instance of the PDE Workbench to create the basic structure of a plug-in extension by performing the following tasks:

- Specifying the plug-in dependencies
- Verifying the plug-in run-time archive
- Specifying the plug-in extension

How to specify the plug-in dependencies

1 On PDE Manifest Editor, choose Overview.

2 In Plug-in Content, choose Dependencies.

3 In Required Plug-ins, choose Add. Plug-in Selection appears, as shown in Figure 16-5.

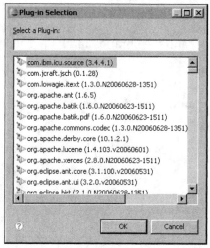

Figure 16-5   Plug-in Selection

4 In Plug-in Selection, select a plug-in, such as the following example:

```
org.eclipse.birt.report.designer.ui
```

Choose OK.

5 Repeat steps 2 and 3 to add more plug-ins to the list of required plug-ins in the Dependencies page.

In Required Plug-ins, the order of the list determines the sequence in which a plug-in loads at run time. Use Up and Down to change the loading order as necessary.

Figure 16-6 shows an example of a list of dependencies for a plug-in extension.

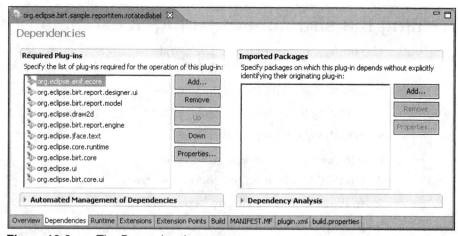

Figure 16-6   The Dependencies page

How to verify the plug-in run-time archive

1 On PDE Manifest Editor, choose Runtime. Runtime appears, as shown in Figure 16-7.

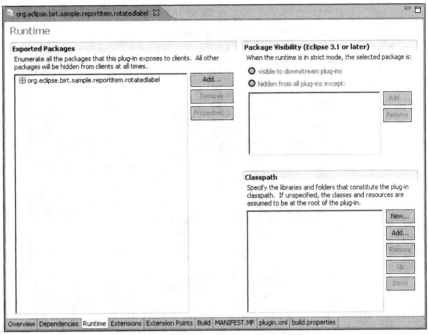

Figure 16-7   The Runtime page

2 In Runtime, perform the following tasks:

- In Exported Packages, list all the packages that the plug-in exposes to clients.

- In Package Visibility, when the plug-in is in strict run-time mode, indicate whether a selected package is one of the following options:

  - Visible to downstream plug-ins

  - Hidden except for the specified plug-ins

- In Classpath, choose Add to add the name of an archive file or folder to the classpath manually.

How to specify the plug-in extension

1 On PDE Manifest Editor, choose Extensions.

2 In All Extensions, choose Add. New Extension appears.

3 On Extension Point Selection, in Extension Points, select a plug-in, such as the following example:

```
org.eclipse.birt.report.designer.ui.reportitemUI
```

New Extension appears, as shown in Figure 16-8.

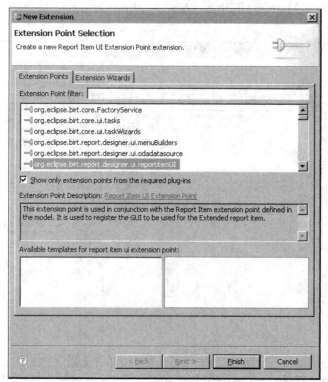

Figure 16-8   New Extension—Extension Point Selection

Choose Finish. Extensions appears, as shown in Figure 16-9.

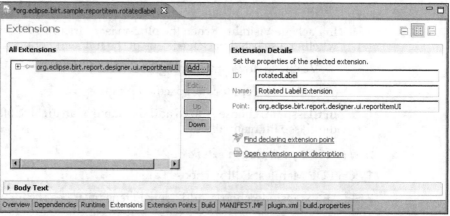

Figure 16-9   The Extensions page

4 Repeat steps 2 and 3 to add more plug-ins to the list of required extension points in the Extensions page.

Creating the plug-in extension content

The XML schema specifies a grammar that you must follow when creating an extension in the Eclipse PDE. When you select an element of an extension in the Extensions page of the PDE, Eclipse uses the XML schema to populate the Extension Element Details section with the list of valid attributes and values for the element.

On Extensions, if you choose Find declaring extension point, the PDE searches for an extension point that matches the criteria. If you choose Open extension point description, the PDE generates an HTML page containing the information documented in the XML schema and displays the page in a viewer.

This section discusses the following tasks:

- Searching for and viewing extension point information
- Specifying plug-in extension content
- Specifying a build configuration

How to search for and view extension point information

1   In the Eclipse PDE, select a plug-in extension in All Extensions.

2   In Extension Details, choose Find declaring extension point.

Search appears. In Figure 16-10, Search lists one match, org.eclipse.birt.report.designer.ui.reportitemUI.

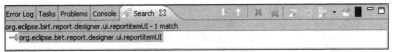

Figure 16-10   Search, showing a single match

3   In Search, double-click on the match, such as org.eclipse.birt.report .designer.ui.reportitemUI. In PDE Manifest Editor, a window appears, displaying the contents of the file, org.eclipse.birt.report.designer.ui/ plugin.xml, as shown in Figure 16-11.

Figure 16-11   Plugin.xml, showing three extension points

Plugin.xml describes the extension points, odadatasource, reportItemUI, and menu Builders.

4 In PDE Manifest Editor, close the window displaying contents of the plugin.xml file. Choose Extensions.

5 In Extension Details, choose Open extension point description.

A viewer opens, displaying the HTML document for the extension point. In Figure 16-12, the viewer displays Report Item UI Extension Point, containing information extracted from the XML schema, $INSTALL_DIR\eclipse\ plugins\org.eclipse.birt.report.designer.ui\schema\reportitemUI.exsd.

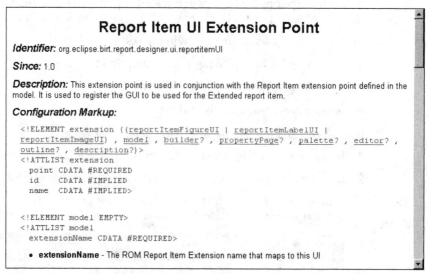

Figure 16-12 Extension point description

In the HTML document, Configuration Markup displays the attribute list for the extension point. Scroll down to view all the contents of the HTML document, including the optional set of user interface elements for the report item extension, such as builder, property page, palette, editor, outline, and description.

How to specify plug-in extension content

1 In PDE Manifest Editor, choose Extensions.

2 In All Extensions, right-click on an extension point such as org.eclipse.birt.report.designer.ui.reportItemLabelUI, and choose New→<extension point element>.

Figure 16-13 shows how to select the extension point element, reportItemLabelUI.

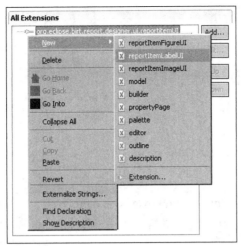

Figure 16-13 Context menu for selecting an extension point element

Extensions appears, displaying the extension element and its details, as shown in Figure 16-14.

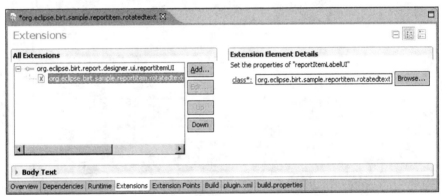

Figure 16-14 The Extensions page

In this example, All Extensions lists the extension, org.eclipse.birt.sample .reportitem.rotatedlabel.RotatedLabelUI (rotatedItemLabelUI), and Extension Element Details lists rotatedItemLabelUI properties. In Extension Element Details, the label for a required attribute, such as class, contains an asterisk.

3 To view the annotation for a property listed in Extension Element Details, hover the cursor over the property label.

A ToolTip appears, displaying the annotation for the property from the XML schema. Figure 16-15 shows the annotation for the class property for the example extension element, rotatedItemLabelUI.

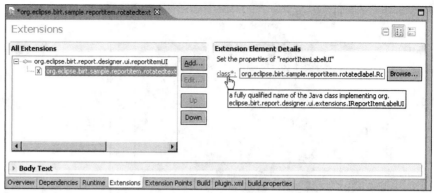

Figure 16-15   Annotation for an extension element

4 To specify the class attributes for an extension element, choose class in Extension Element Details.

If no class file exists, Java Attribute Editor appears, as shown in Figure 16-16. If the class file exists, the class file opens in PDE Manifest Editor.

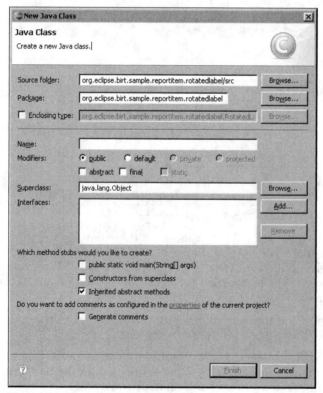

Figure 16-16   Java Attribute Editor

On Java Attribute Editor, you can modify or add to the settings for the following class properties:

- Source folder

- Package

- Enclosing type

- Class name

- Modifiers, such as public, default, private, protected, abstract, final, and static

- Superclass

- Interfaces

- Method stubs, such as main, constructors, and inherited abstract methods

- Comments

Choose Finish.

5 To add more elements and attributes to a selected extension point, repeat steps 1 and 2.

Figure 16-17 shows the full list of extension points required for the sample report item extension, org.eclipse.birt.sample.reportitem.rotatedlabel.

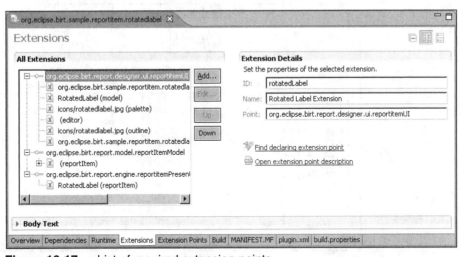

Figure 16-17 List of required extension points

Building a plug-in extension

In Eclipse PDE Manifest Editor, Build allows you to specify the build configuration, including the following items:

- Runtime Information

  Defines the libraries, the source folders to compile into each library, and the compilation order.

- Binary Build

  Selects the files and folders to include in the binary build.

- Source Build

  Selects the files and folders to include in the source build. Source Build is not typically required. Source Build uses the org.eclipse.pde.core.source extension point that allows the PDE to find source archives for libraries in other Eclipse plug-ins.

How to specify a build configuration

1 On PDE Manifest Editor, choose Build. Build Configuration appears. Figure 16-18 shows Build Configuration.

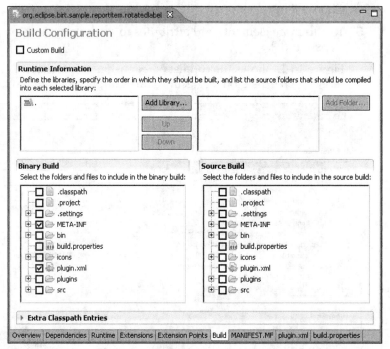

Figure 16-18   Build Configuration

2 In Runtime Information, add a new library by choosing Add Library.

Add Entry appears.

Enter the new library name or select a run-time library from the list, as shown in Figure 16-19. Choose OK.

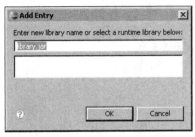

Figure 16-19   Add Entry

3 To change the compilation order of a library, change its position in the list. In Runtime Information, select the library and choose Up or Down.

Figure 16-20 shows Runtime Information with mylibrary.jar selected and Down enabled.

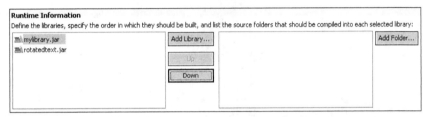

Figure 16-20   Changing the compilation order of a library

4 To add a folder to a library, choose Add Folder. New Source Folder appears, as shown in Figure 16-21.

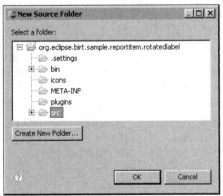

Figure 16-21   New Source Folder

Select a folder, such as src, and choose OK. Runtime Information appears, as shown in Figure 16-22.

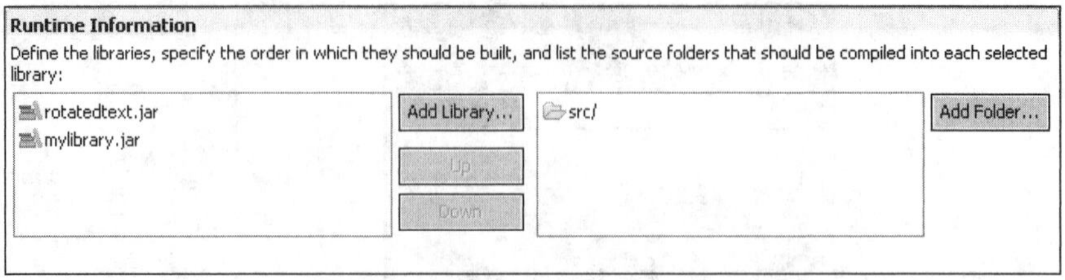

Figure 16-22   Runtime Information

5   In Binary Build, include a folder in the binary build by selecting the folder. Figure 16-23 shows the icons folder selected.

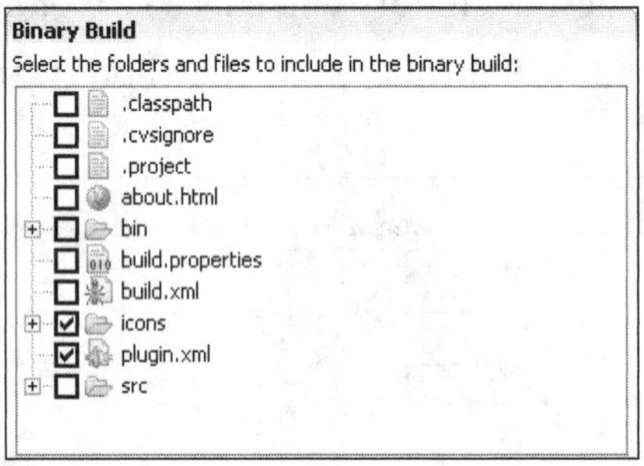

Figure 16-23   Binary Build

6   From the Eclipse menu, choose Project→Build All, to build a project.

Alternatively, you can choose Project→Build Automatically to continually build the project as you make changes to the code.

Generating an Ant build script

The Eclipse PDE can generate an Ant build script for compiling plug-in code, based on the settings in the build.properties file. The generated script is an XML file in which the elements are the required tasks for the build operation. The Ant build tool compiles the project, using the specified Java compiler.

Ant is an open source Java application available from the Apache Software Foundation. For more information on Ant and the Apache Software Foundation, visit the web site at http://ant.apache.org.

How to generate an Ant build script

In Package Explorer, right-click the project's plugin.xml file and choose PDE Tools→Create Ant Build File. PDE Tools creates an Ant script file, build.xml, in the project folder.

Testing a plug-in extension

You can launch an instance of the run-time workbench to test and debug the plug-in extension.

How to launch a run-time workbench

1   On PDE Manifest Editor, choose Overview. Overview appears as shown in Figure 16-24.

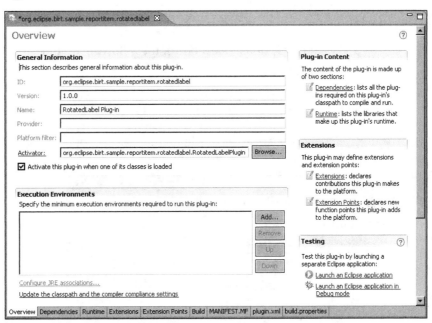

Figure 16-24   Overview, showing testing and debugging options

2   In Testing, choose Launch an Eclipse application. Eclipse launches the run-time workbench.

In the report item extension example, Report Design—Eclipse SDK appears. In the run-time workbench, you must create a new report design project to use the report label extension.

Deploying the extension plug-in

You can use the Export Wizard to produce a distributable archive file that contains the plug-in code and other resources. A user can find a software update and extract the contents of the archive file to an Eclipse installation using the Feature Updates and Product Configuration managers. A plug-in developer can create and manage an update site using the Update Site Editor in the Eclipse PDE.

How to deploy a plug-in extension

1 In the Eclipse PDE Manifest Editor, choose Overview.

2 In Exporting, choose Export Wizard. Export appears.

3 In Available Plug-ins and Fragments, select the plug-in to export. For example, select org.eclipse.birt.sample.reportitem.rotatedlabel.

4 In Export Destination, specify Archive file or Directory. For example, in Directory, type:

```
C:\Program Files\eclipse
```

5 In Export Options, select one of the following options, if necessary:

- Include source code

- Package plug-ins as individual JAR archives

- Save as Ant script

Export appears as shown in Figure 16-25. Choose Finish to export the plug-in to the specified destination.

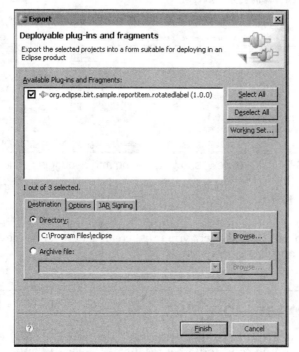

Figure 16-25   Exporting a plug-in

Installing feature updates and managing the Eclipse configuration

If all the dependent resources are available in the new environment, Eclipse can discover and activate the plug-in in the run-time environment. In this type of unmanaged distribution and installation, the user must find and install updates to the plug-in if a release occurs in the future.

A plug-in developer can also use a more structured approach and group plug-ins into features. A feature is a set of plug-ins that you install and manage together.

Features contain information that allow the Feature Updates and Product Configuration managers to locate published updates and discover new related features. Updates are typically published in a special internet directory called an update site, created and managed by a plug-in developer using the Update Site Editor.

How to install feature updates and manage the Eclipse configuration

The Eclipse PDE provides wizards and editors that support the use of features and update sites. Choose Help→Software Updates→Find and Install to access Feature Updates. Feature Updates allows you to search for updates and new features, as shown in Figure 16-26.

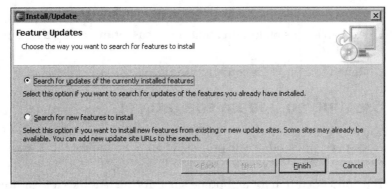

Figure 16-26   Searching for feature updates

Choose Help→Software Updates→Manage Configuration to access Product Configuration. Figure 16-27 shows Product Configuration.

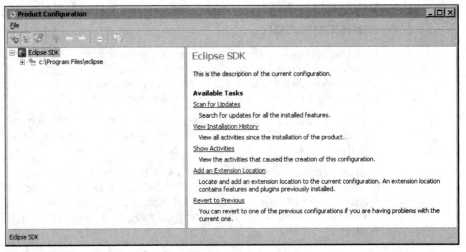

Figure 16-27   Product Configuration

Product Configuration allows you to perform the following tasks:

- Scan for updates.

- View installation history.

- Show activities that created the current configuration.

- Add an extension location that contains features and plug-ins previously installed.

- Revert to a previous configuration.

Creating an update site project

You create an update site by building an update site project in the Eclipse PDE workspace. The update site project contains a manifest file, site.xml, that lists the features and plug-ins packages.

The build operation for an update site puts the JAR files for features in a features folder and the JAR files for plug-ins in a plug-ins folder. The Eclipse PDE also provides support for uploading an update site to a remote server or local file system for distribution.

How to create an update site project

1 From the Eclipse menu, choose File→New→Project. New Project appears.

2 In Wizards, open Plug-in Development and select Update Site Project, as shown in Figure 16-28. Choose Next. Update Site Project appears.

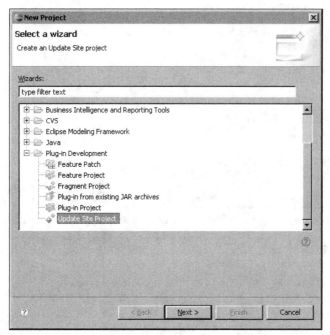

Figure 16-28   Selecting Update Site Project wizard

3 On Update Site Project, specify the following items:

- Project name

- Project contents directory, such as C:\Program Files\eclipse\workspace\ BIRT Update Site

- Web resources

  ❑ Select Generate web page listing of all available features within the site

  Creates index.html, site.css, and site.xls files for displaying the contents of the update site.

  ❑ Web resources location

  Change this setting to the web resources location. The default value is web.

Update Site Project appears as shown in Figure 16-29. Choose Finish. Update Site Map appears as shown in Figure 16-30.

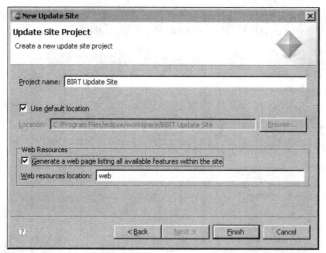

Figure 16-29   Creating a new update site project

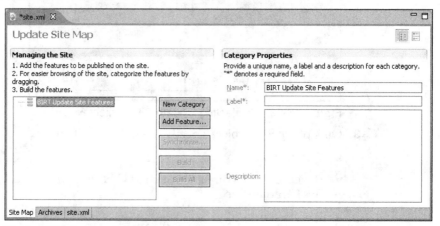

Figure 16-30   Update Site Map

4 Choose New Category to create a feature category.

5 Choose Add Feature to add a feature to a selected category.

For more information about deploying a plug-in, installing features, managing a product configuration, and building an update site, see the documentation for the Platform Plug-in Developer Guide in Eclipse Help.

Downloading the code for the extension examples

This book provides examples for the following types of BIRT extensions:

- Report item

  The example shows how to build a rotated label report item plug-in and add the report item to the BIRT Report Designer using the defined extension points. This plug-in renders the label of a report item as an image. The extension rotates the image in a report design to display the label at a specified angle.

- Report rendering

  The example shows how to extend the emitter interfaces to build and deploy a report rendering plug-in that runs in the BIRT Report Engine environment. The CSV extension example is a plug-in that writes the table data in a report to a file in CSV format.

- ODA drivers

  The CSV ODA driver example is a plug-in that reads data from a CSV file. The Hibernate ODA driver example uses HQL to provide a SQL-transparent extension that makes the ODA extension portable to all relational databases.

  These examples also show how to develop an ODA extension to the BIRT Report Designer 2.1 user interface so that a report developer can select an extended ODA driver.

You can download the source code for these extension examples at http://www.actuate.com/birt/contributions.

Developing a Report Item Extension

This chapter describes how to create a BIRT extension in the Eclipse PDE using the sample report item extension, rotated label. You learn about creating a BIRT report item extension in the following sections:

- Understanding a report item extension
- Developing the sample report item extension
- Understanding the sample report item extension
- Building, deploying, and testing the rotated label report item plug-in

Understanding a report item extension

A report item extension adds a new type of report item to the BIRT framework by implementing multiple extension points. A plug-in that defines an extension point typically contains an XML extension point schema definition (.exsd) file in a schema subdirectory. This XML schema describes the elements, attributes, and types used by the extension point to the Eclipse PDE environment.

To add a new report item, a report item extension implements the following extension points:

- Report item model

  org.eclipse.birt.report.model.reportItemModel specifies the report item extension point for the ROM. The XML schema file, org.eclipse.birt.report.model/schema/reportItemModel.exsd, describes this extension point.

- Report item user interface

  org.eclipse.birt.report.designer.ui.reportitemUI specifies the report item extension point for the user interface in the report layout editor and report item palette. The XML schema file, org.eclipse.birt.report.designer.ui/ schema/reportitemUI.exsd, describes this extension point.

- Report item query (optional)

  org.eclipse.birt.report.engine.reportitemQuery specifies the extension point for query preparation support in the BIRT designer and report engine. A query preparation extension is optional. If the report item does not require query preparation, you can omit the query extension. The XML schema file, org.eclipse.birt.report.engine/schema/reportitemQuery.exsd, describes this extension point.

- Report item run time

  org.eclipse.birt.report.engine.reportitemGeneration specifies the extension point for instantiating, processing, and persisting a new report item at report generation time. The XML schema file, org.eclipse.birt.report.engine/ schema/reportitemGeneration.exsd, describes this extension point.

  org.eclipse.birt.report.engine.reportitemPresentation specifies the extension point for instantiating, processing, and rendering a new report item at report presentation time. The XML schema file, org.eclipse.birt.report.engine/ schema/reportitemPresentation.exsd, describes this extension point.

- Report item emitter (optional)

  org.eclipse.birt.report.engine.emitters specifies the extension point for support of a new output format in the presentation engine. The XML schema file, org.eclipse.birt.report.engine/schema/emitters.exsd, describes this extension point.

At run time, the BIRT Report Engine performs the following processing on a report item before rendering the final output:

- Query preparation

  Gathers the data binding information and expressions defined for the report, passing the information to the report engine. The data engine prepares the data access strategy based on this information.

- Generation

  Creates the instances of report items and fetches the data.

- Presentation

  Renders the report item to a supported data primitive, such as an image, string, HTML segment, or custom data component.

- Emitter

  Converts the output to a specified format, such as HTML or PDF.

This chapter provides an example of a custom report item extension, org.eclipse.birt.sample.reportitem.rotatedlabel. The sample code for the rotated label report item extension creates a text element that renders label text at a specified angle.

The standard report item plug-in, chart, is a more complex example of a report item extension. The BIRT chart plug-in implements user interface and report engine extensions that support a report design using any of the following chart types:

- Bar
- Line
- Pie
- Scatter
- Stock

For reference documentation for the report item API, see the Javadoc for the org.eclipse.birt.report.engine.extension package in BIRT Programmer Reference in Eclipse Help.

Developing the sample report item extension

The Report Item extension framework allows a report developer to create a customized report item in the palette of BIRT Report Designer. You can use a report item extension in a report design in the same way as a standard report item, such as Label, Text, Grid, Table, or Chart.

The sample code for the rotated label report item extension creates a label element that renders text at a specified angle. This section describes the steps required to implement the org.eclipse.birt.sample.reportitem.rotatedlabel sample. To implement the rotated label report item extension, perform the following tasks:

- Configure the plug-in project.

  You can build the rotated label report item plug-in manually by following the instructions in this chapter.

- Add the report item to the Report Designer UI.

  Extend the Report Item UI extension point, org.eclipse.birt.report.designer .ui.reportItemUI.

- Add the report item definition to the ROM.

  Extend the Report Item Model extension point, org.eclipse.birt.report.model .reportItemModel.

- Add rendering behavior to the report item.

Extend the Report Item Presentation extension point, org.eclipse.birt.report .engine.reportItemPresentation.

- Deploy the report item extension.

Export the rotated label report item plug-in folder from your workspace to the eclipse\plugins folder. You do not need to export the plug-in folder to test the extension when you launch it as an Eclipse application in the PDE.

You can download the source code for the rotated label report item extension example at http://www.actuate.com/birt/contributions.

Downloading BIRT source code from the CVS repository

Eclipse makes BIRT source code available to the developer community in the CVS repository. You work only with the Java classes in the org.eclipse.birt.sample.reportitem.rotatedlabel plug-in.

To compile, you do not need the source code for any required plug-ins. You can configure the system to use the JAR files in the $INSTALL_DIR\eclipse\plugin folder.

These plug-ins must be in the classpath to compile successfully. To debug, you may need the source code for all the required BIRT plug-ins.

The rotated label report item extension depends on the following Eclipse plug-ins:

- org.eclipse.emf.ecore
- org.eclipse.birt.report.designer.ui
- org.eclipse.birt.report.model
- org.eclipse.draw2d
- org.eclipse.birt.report.engine
- org.eclipse.jface.text
- org.eclipse.core.runtime
- org.eclipse.birt.core
- org.eclipse.ui
- org.eclipse.birt.core.ui

Creating a rotated label report item plug-in project

Create a new plug-in project for the rotated label report item extension in the Eclipse PDE.

How to create the plug-in project

1 In the Eclipse PDE, choose File→New→Project. New Project appears.

2 In Select a wizard, select Plug-in Project. Choose Next. New Plug-in Project appears.

3 In Plug-in Project, modify the settings, as shown in Table 17-1.

Table 17-1   Settings for Plug-in Project fields

Section	Option	Value
Plug-in Project	Project name	org.eclipse.birt.sample .reportitem.rotatedlabel
	Use default location	Selected
	Location	Not available when you select Use default location.
Project Settings	Create a Java project	Selected
	Source folder	src
	Output folder	bin
Target Platform	Eclipse version	3.2
	OSGi framework	Selected Equinox

Plug-in Project appears, as shown in Figure 17-1.

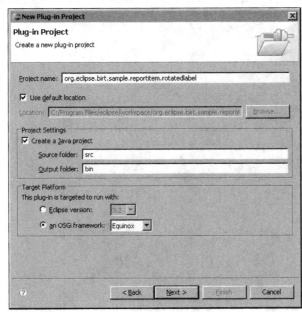

Figure 17-1   Plug-in Project settings

Choose Next. Plug-in Content appears.

4 In Plug-in Content, modify the settings as shown in Table 17-2.

Table 17-2   Plug-in Content settings

Section	Option	Value
Plug-in Properties	Plug-in ID	org.eclipse.birt.sample .reportitem.rotatedlabel
	Plug-in Version	1.0.0
	Plug-in Name	RotatedLabel Plug-in
	Plug-in Provider	yourCompany.com or leave blank
	Classpath	rotatedLabel.jar or leave blank
Plug-in Options	Generate an activator, a Java class that controls the plug-in's life cycle	Selected
	Activator	org.eclipse.birt.sample .reportitem.rotatedlabel .RotatedLabelPlugin
	This plug-in will make contributions to the UI	Deselected
Rich Client Application	Would you like to create a rich client application?	No

New Plug-in Content appears, as shown in Figure 17-2. Choose Finish.

Figure 17-2   Plug-in Content, showing settings for a new plug-in project

The rotated label report item extension project appears in the Eclipse PDE Workbench, as shown in Figure 17-3.

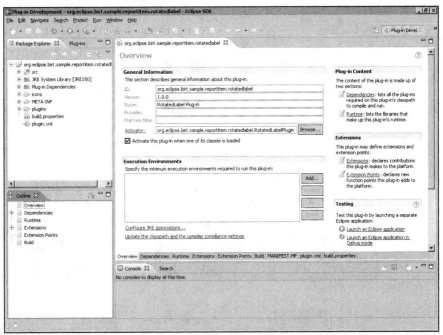

Figure 17-3   Plug-in project in the Eclipse PDE Workbench

Defining the dependencies for the rotated label report item extension

In this task, you specify the list of plug-ins that must be available on the classpath of the rotated label report item extension to compile and run.

How to specify the dependencies

1 On PDE Manifest Editor, choose Overview.

2 In Plug-in Content, choose Dependencies. Required Plug-ins contains the following plug-ins:

```
org.eclipse.ui
org.eclipse.core.runtime
```

3 In Required Plug-ins, perform the following tasks:

    1 Select org.eclipse.ui and choose Remove.

    2 Select org.eclipse.core.runtime and choose Remove.

    org.eclipse.core.runtime and org.eclipse.ui no longer appear in Required Plug-ins.

4 In Required Plug-ins, choose Add. Plug-in Selection appears.

5 In Plug-in Selection, hold down CTRL and select the following plug-ins:

- org.eclipse.emf.ecore
- org.eclipse.birt.report.designer.ui
- org.eclipse.birt.report.model
- org.eclipse.draw2d
- org.eclipse.birt.report.engine
- org.eclipse.jface.text
- org.eclipse.core.runtime
- org.eclipse.birt.core
- org.eclipse.ui
- org.eclipse.birt.core.ui

Choose OK. Dependencies appears, as shown in Figure 17-4.

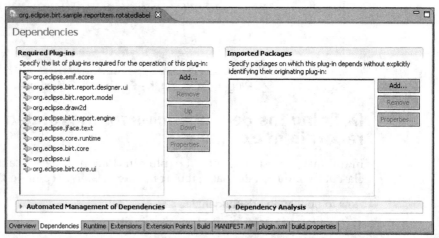

Figure 17-4   Dependencies, showing required plug-ins

The order of the list determines the sequence in which a plug-in loads at run time. Use Up and Down to change the loading order as necessary, as shown in Figure 17-4. The rotated label report item extension does not require any changes to the loading order if you selected the required plug-ins in the order listed in step 5.

Specifying the run-time package for the rotated label report item extension

On Runtime, you specify exported packages, package visibility, the libraries, and folders on the plug-in classpath. In the rotated label report item plug-in, the only package that you must make visible to other plug-ins is org.eclipse.birt .sample.reportitem.rotatedlabel.

On PDE Manifest Editor, choose Runtime. On Runtime, in Exported Packages, verify that the org.eclipse.birt.sample.reportitem.rotatedlabel package appears in the list.

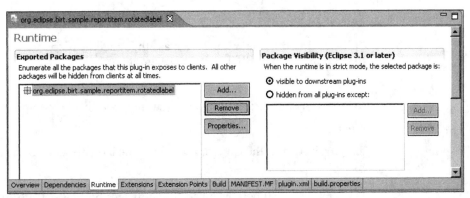

Figure 17-5   The Runtime page

Declaring the report item extension points

In this next step, you specify the extension points required to implement the rotated label report item extension and add the extension element details. The Eclipse PDE uses the XML schema defined for each extension point to provide the list of valid attributes and values specified for the extension elements.

The rotated label report item extension implements the following extension points:

- org.eclipse.birt.report.designer.ui.reportitemUI

  Registers the graphical user interface (GUI) to use for the report item extension

- org.eclipse.birt.report.model.reportItemModel

  Specifies how to represent and persist the report item extension in the ROM

- org.eclipse.birt.report.engine.reportitemPresentation

  Specifies how to instantiate, process, and render the report item extension

The XML schema specifies the following properties that identify each extension point in the run-time environment:

- ID

  Optional identifier of the extension instance

- Name

  Optional name of the extension instance

- Point

  Fully qualified identifier of the extension point

The extension point, org.eclipse.birt.report.designer.ui.reportitemUI, specifies the following extension elements:

- reportItemLabelUI

  Fully qualified name of the Java class that gets the display text for the report item component in BIRT Report Designer

- model

  ROM report item extension name that maps to this UI component

- palette

  Icon to show and the category in which the icon appears in the Palette

- editor

  Flags indicating whether the editor shows in the MasterPage and Designer UI and is resizable in the Editor

- outline

  Icon to show in the Outline View

- propertyPage

  Optional Property Edit Page to use for the report item extension in the Property Edit View

The extension point, org.eclipse.birt.report.model.reportItemModel, specifies reportItem and the following extension element properties:

- extensionName

  Internal unique name of the report item extension

- class

  Fully qualified name of the Java class that implements the org.eclipse.birt.report.model.api.extension.IReportItemFactory interface

- defaultStyle

  Predefined style to use for the report item extension

- isNameRequired

Field indicating whether the report item instance name is required

- displayNameID

  Resource key for the display name

reportItem also specifies the following property extension elements:

- rotationAngle
- displayText

rotationAngle and displayText each specify the following properties:

- name

  Internal unique name of the property extension element

- type

  Data type, such as integer or string

- displayNameID

  Resource key for the display name

- canInherit

  Flag indicating whether the property extension element can inherit properties

- detailType

  Detail data type, such as Boolean or string

- defaultValue

  Default value of the property extension element

- isEncryptable

  Flag indicating whether the property is encrypted

- defaultDisplayName

  Display name to use if no localized I18N display name exists

The extension point, org.eclipse.birt.report.engine.reportitemPresentation, specifies the following reportItem extension elements:

- name

  Unique name of the report item extension

- class

  Fully qualified name of the Java class that implements the org.eclipse.birt.report.engine.extension.IReportItemPresentation interface

- supportedFormats

Supported rendering formats for this extended item. The value for this attribute is a comma-separated string, such as "HTML,PDF". The string is case-insensitive.

How to specify the extension points

1 On PDE Manifest Editor, choose Extensions.

2 In All Extensions, choose Add. New Extension appears.

3 On New Extension—Extension Points, in Available extension points, select the following plug-in:

```
org.eclipse.birt.report.designer.ui.reportitemUI
```

New Extension—Extension Points appears, as shown in Figure 17-6. Choose Finish.

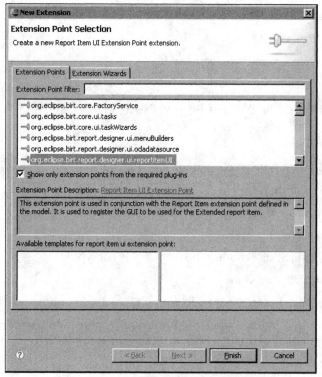

Figure 17-6   Extension points in New Extension

4 Repeat steps 2 and 3 to add the following extension points to the list of required extension points in the Extensions page:

■ org.eclipse.birt.report.model.reportItemModel

■ org.eclipse.birt.report.engine.reportitemPresentation

Figure 17-7 shows the list of extension points required for the report item extension example.

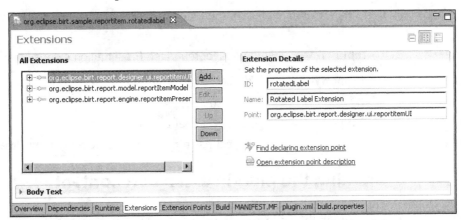

Figure 17-7 Required extension points for a report item extension

How to add the extension details

Perform the following tasks:

1 On Extensions, in All Extensions, select org.eclipse.birt.report.designer.ui .reportitemUI.

2 In Extension Details, set the following property values as shown in Table 17-3.

Table 17-3 Properties for reportItemUI extension

Property	Value
ID	rotatedLabel
Name	Rotated Label Extension
Point	org.eclipse.birt.report.designer.ui.reportitemUI

3 In All Extensions, select org.eclipse.birt.report.model.reportItemModel

4 In Extension Details, set the following property values as shown in Table 17-4.

Table 17-4 Properties for reportItemModel extension

Property	Value
ID	rotatedLabel
Name	Rotated Label Extension
Point	org.eclipse.birt.report.model.reportItemModel

5 In All Extensions, select
org.eclipse.birt.report.engine.reportitemPresentation

6 In Extension Details, set the following property values as shown in
Table 17-5.

Table 17-5   Properties for reportitemPresentation extension

Property	Value
ID	rotatedLabel
Name	Rotated Label Extension
Point	org.eclipse.birt.report.engine.reportitemPresentation

Creating the plug-in extension content

The XML schema specifies a grammar that you must follow when creating an
extension in the Eclipse PDE. When you select an element of an extension in the
Extensions page of the PDE, Eclipse uses the XML schema to populate the
Extension Element Details section with the list of valid attributes and values for
the element.

How to specify the plug-in extension content

1 In PDE Manifest Editor, choose Extensions.

2 In All Extensions, right-click org.eclipse.birt.report.designer.ui.reportItemUI
and choose New→reportItemLabelUI, as shown in Figure 17-8.

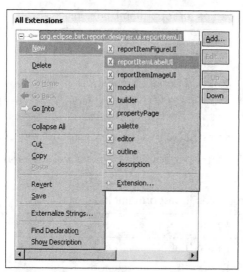

Figure 17-8   Selecting an extension element

All Extensions lists the extension, org.eclipse.birt.sample.reportitem
.rotatedlabel.ReportItemLabelUI (rotatedItemLabelUI), and Extension
Element Details lists rotatedItemLabelUI properties.

3 In Extension Element Details, type the following fully qualified class name:

```
org.eclipse.birt.sample.reportitem.rotatedlabel
    .RotatedLabelUI
```

Extensions appears, as shown in Figure 17-9.

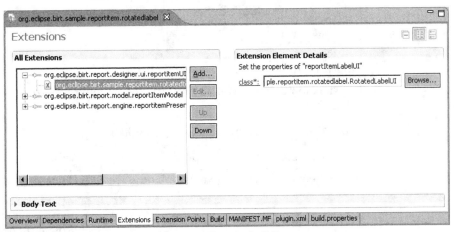

Figure 17-9   Properties for rotatedItemLabelUI

4 In All Extensions, right-click org.eclipse.birt.report.designer.ui.reportitemUI
again and repeatedly choose New→<extension element> to add the
following extension elements, corresponding extension element properties,
and values, as shown in Table 17-6.

Table 17-6   Properties for other reportitemUI extension elements

Extension element	Property	Value
model	extensionName	RotatedLabel
palette	icon	icons/rotatedlabel.jpg
editor	showInMasterPage	true
	showInDesigner	true
	canResize	true
outline	icon	icons/rotatedlabel.jpg
propertyPage	class	org.eclipse.birt.sample .reportitem.rotated label.RotatedLabel PropertyEditUIImpl

5 In All Extensions, right-click org.eclipse.birt.report.model.reportItemModel and choose New→reportItem, as shown in Figure 17-10.

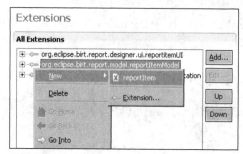

Figure 17-10   Choosing a new report item

6 In Extension Element Details, add the reportItem properties shown in Table 17-7.

Table 17-7   Property values for reportItem

Extension element	Property	Value
reportItem	extensionName	RotatedLabel
	class	org.eclipse.birt.sample .reportitem.rotatedlabel .RotatedLabelItem FactoryImpl

7 In All Extensions, in org.eclipse.birt.report.model.reportItemModel, perform the following tasks:

1 Right-click reportItem and choose New→property to add the extension element properties shown in Table 17-8.

Table 17-8   Property values for rotationAngle

Extension element	Property	Value
property	name	rotationAngle
	type	integer
	defaultValue	-45
	defaultDisplayName	Rotation Angle

2 Right-click reportItem again and choose New→property to add the extension element properties shown in Table 17-9.

Table 17-9   Property values for displayText

Extension element	Property	Value
property	name	displayText
	type	string
	defaultValue	Rotated Label
	defaultDisplayName	Display Text

8 In All Extensions, right-click org.eclipse.birt.report.engine
.reportitemPresentation and choose New→reportItem, as shown in
Figure 17-11.

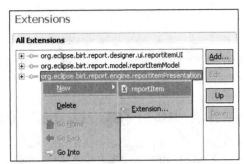

Figure 17-11   Choosing reportItem

9 In Extension Element Details, add the reportItem properties shown in
Table 17-10.

Table 17-10   Property values for reportItem

Extension element	Property	Value
reportItem	name	RotatedLabel
	class	org.eclipse.birt.sample .reportitem.rotated label.RotatedLabel PresentationImpl

Figure 17-12 shows the full list of extension points and elements required for the
example, org.eclipse.birt.sample.reportitem.rotatedlabel.

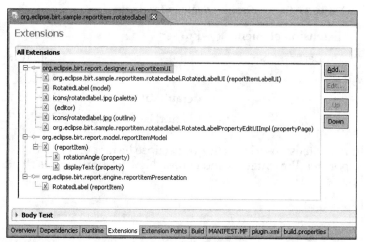

Figure 17-12   Extension points for rotated label report item extension

Understanding the rotated label report item extension

The rotated label report item plug-in provides the functionality required at run time to render the label of a report item as an image and rotate the image in the report design to display the label at the specified angle. The following sections provide a general description of the code-based extensions a developer must make to complete the development of the rotated report item extension after defining the plug-in framework in the Eclipse PDE.

The rotated label report item extension implements the following interfaces and classes:

- org.eclipse.birt.report.designer.ui.extensions

  Specifies the following interfaces:

  - IPropertyTabUI

    Represents a new tab in the Property Editor view, creating the UI, updating property values on request, and notifying the BIRT framework of any UI-based property change. PropertyTabUIAdapter is the adapter class that implements this interface.

  - IReportItemLabelProvider

    Defines the interface for the accessor method that provides the label text. ReportItemLabelProvider is the adapter class that implements this interface.

  - IReportItemPropertyEditUI

    Provides the interface for defining tabs in the Property Editor. No default adapter class exists for this interface in BIRT release 2.1.

- org.eclipse.birt.report.designer.ui.views.attributes.providers .PropertyProcessor

  Provides accessor methods for processing general property information.

- org.eclipse.birt.report.engine.extension

  - IRowSet

    Defines the interface to a row set. Provides metadata, grouping level, and row navigation methods.

  - IReportItemPresentation

    Defines the interface for presentation of a report item extension. IReportItemPresentation sets the locale, resolution, output, and image formats, and processes the extended item in the report presentation environment. ReportItemPresentationBase is the adapter class that implements this interface.

- org.eclipse.birt.report.model.api

  - DesignElementHandle

    Functions as the base class for all report elements. DesignElementHandle provides a high-level interface to the BIRT report model. The class provides the generic services for all elements. Derived classes provide specialized methods for each element type. DesignElementHandle implements the interface, org.eclipse.birt.report.model.elements .interfaces.IDesignElementModel.

  - DesignEngine

    Provides an interface to the BIRT design engine. DesignEngine instantiates a session handle to use when creating a new design, opening an existing design, and managing design processing. The session handle contains the report design's state. DesignEngine implements the interface, IDesignEngine interface.

  - ExtendedItemHandle

    Provides a handle to an extended item that appears in a section of a report. The extended report item can have properties such as size, position, style, visibility rules, or a binding to a data source. ExtendedItemHandle extends ReportItemHandle, an abstract base class that extends DesignElementHandle.

- org.eclipse.birt.report.model.elements.Style

  Extends org.eclipse.birt.report.model.core.StyleElement, the base class for report elements with a style, and implements org.eclipse.birt.report.model .elements.interfaces.IStyleModel, the interface for storing style element constants.

- org.eclipse.birt.report.model.api.extension

  Specifies the following interfaces:

  - IMessages

    Defines the interface for getting a localized message from a message file using a resource key.

  - IPropertyDefinition

    Defines the interface for the accessor methods that describe a property. PropertyDefinition is the adapter class that implements this interface.

  - IReportItem

    Defines the interface for an instance of an extended report element. There is a one-to-one correspondence between the BIRT report item and this implementation. ReportItem is the adapter class that implements this interface.

  - IReportItemFactory

    Defines the interface for the factory that creates an instance of the extended element, IReportItem. IReportItem stores the model data and serializes the model state. ReportItemFactory is the adapter class that implements this interface.

- org.eclipse.birt.report.model.metadata.PropertyType

  Functions as the base class for the meta-data of a property type. A property type provides the display name, data validation and conversion methods, XML name, and other processing. PropertyType implements the interface, org.eclipse.birt.report.model.api.metadata.IPropertyType.

- org.eclipse.core.runtime.Plugin

  Defines the basic methods for starting, managing, and stopping the plug-in instance.

The following sections contain implementation details for the most important classes in the rotated label report item extension.

Understanding RotatedLabelItemFactoryImpl

The RotatedLabelItemFactoryImpl class instantiates a new report item when the user drags a rotated label report item from the Palette and drops the report item in the BIRT Report Designer Editor. RotatedLabelItemFactoryImpl extends the adapter class, org.eclipse.birt.report.model.api.extension.ReportItemFactory.

The newReportItem( ) method receives a reference to DesignElementHandle, which provides the interface to the BIRT report model. The newReportItem( ) method instantiates the new report item, as shown in Listing 17-1.

Listing 17-1   The newReportItem( ) method

```
public class RotatedTextItemFactoryImpl
   extends ReportItemFactory implements IMessages
{
   public IReportItem newReportItem( DesignElementHandle deh )
   {
      return new RotatedTextReportItemImpl( deh );
   }
   ...
}
```

Understanding RotatedLabelUI

In the RotatedLabelUI class, the RotatedLabelUI.getLabel( ) method provides the text representation for the label to BIRT Report Designer. RotatedLabelUI extends the adapter class, org.eclipse.birt.report.designer .ui.extensions.ReportItemLabelProvider. Listing 17-2 shows the code for the getLabel( ) method.

Listing 17-2   The getLabel( ) method

```
public class RotatedLabelUI extends ReportItemLabelProvider
{
   public String getLabel( ExtendedItemHandle handle )
   {
      if ( handle.getProperty( "displayText" ) != null ) {
         return ( String ) handle.getProperty( "displayText" );
      } else {
         return "Rotated Label";
      }
   }
}
```

Understanding RotatedLabelPresentationImpl

The RotatedLabelPresentationImpl class specifies how to process and render the report item at presentation time. RotatedLabelPresentationImpl extends the org.eclipse.birt.report.engine.extension.ReportItemPresentationBase class.

The method, onRowSets( ), renders the rotated label report item as an image, rotated by the angle specified in the report design, as shown in Listing 17-3.

Listing 17-3   The onRowSets( ) method

```
public Object onRowSets(IRowSet[ ] rowSets) throws
   BirtException
{
   if ( modelHandle == null )
   {
      return null;
   }
```

```
        graphicsUtil = new GraphicsUtil( );
        org.eclipse.swt.graphics.Image rotatedImage =
          graphicsUtil.createRotatedText( modelHandle );
        ImageLoader imageLoader = new ImageLoader( );
        imageLoader.data = new ImageData[ ]
          { rotatedImage.getImageData() };
        ByteArrayOutputStream baos =
          new ByteArrayOutputStream();
        imageLoader.save( baos, SWT.IMAGE_JPEG );
        return baos.toByteArray();
    }
```

Understanding RotatedLabelReportItemImpl

In the RotatedLabelReportItemImpl class, the method,
getPropertyDefinitions( ), instantiates RotatedLabelPropertyDefinitionImpl
objects for the displayText and rotationAngle properties.
RotatedLabelReportItemImpl extends the adapter class,
org.eclipse.birt.report.model.api.extension.ReportItem. Listing 17-4 shows the
code for the getPropertyDefinitions( ) method.

Listing 17-4   The getPropertyDefinitions( ) method

```
public IPropertyDefinition[ ] getPropertyDefinitions( )
{
   if ( rt == null )
   {
      return null;
   }
   return new IPropertyDefinition[ ]{
         new RotatedLabelPropertyDefinitionImpl( null,
               "displayText", "property.label.displayText",
               false,
               PropertyType.STRING_TYPE,
               null,null,null,true),
         new RotatedLabelPropertyDefinitionImpl( null,
               "rotationAngle",
               "property.label.rotationAngle",
               false,
               PropertyType.INTEGER_TYPE,
               null,null,null,true),
   }
}
```

Understanding RotatedLabelPropertyEditUIImpl

The RotatedLabelPropertyEditUIImpl class builds the UI using the
RotatedLabelGeneralTabUIImpl class to set up the controls for the UI.
RotatedLabelPropertyEditUIImpl implements the org.eclipse.birt.report
.designer.ui.extensions.IReportItemPropertyEditUI interface.

In the RotatedLabelPropertyEditUIImpl class, the getCategoryTabs( ) method instantiates the RotatedLabelGeneralTabUIImpl class, as shown in Listing 17-5.

Listing 17-5   The getCateoryTabs( ) method

```
public class RotatedLabelGeneralTabUIImpl implements
   IReportItemPropertyEditUI {
   public IPropertyTabUI[ ] getCategoryTabs( ) {
      return new IPropertyTabUI[ ]{
         new RotatedLabelGeneralTabUIImpl( ),
      };
   }
}
```

The RotatedLabelGeneralTabUIImpl class contains an internal class, GeneralCategoryWrapper, which creates the UI contents, as shown in Listing 17-6.

Listing 17-6   The GeneralCategoryWrapper class

```
static class GeneralCategoryWrapper
   extends AttributesUtil.PageWrapper {
   static String CATEGORY_NAME = "General";

   public void buildContent( Composite parent,
      Map propertyMap ) {
      parent.setLayout( createGridLayout( 2 ) );
      buildGridControl( parent,
           propertyMap,
           ReportDesignConstants.EXTENDED_ITEM,
           ReportItemHandle.NAME_PROP,
           1,
           false,
           new TextPropertyDescriptor
             ( new PropertyProcessor
             ( ReportDesignConstants.EXTENDED_ITEM,
               ReportItemHandle.NAME_PROP ) ),
           true,
           150);
           . . .
```

Understanding GraphicsUtil

The GraphicsUtil class creates the image containing the specified text and rotates the text image to the specified angle, using the following methods:

- createRotatedText( )

  This method performs the following operations:

  - Gets the display text and rotation angle properties

- Sets the display text font and determines the font metrics
- Creates an image the same size as the display text String
- Draws the display text as an image
- Calls the rotateImage( ) method to rotate the image at the specified angle
- Disposes of the operating system resources used to render the image
- Returns the image object

Listing 17-7 shows the code for createRotatedText( ) method.

Listing 17-7   The createRotatedText( ) method

```
public Image createRotatedText( ExtendedItemHandle
   modelHandle )
{
   Image stringImage;
   Image image;
   GC gc;
      String text = "";
   if ( modelHandle.getProperty( "displayText" ) != null ) {
      text = ( String ) modelHandle.getProperty
         ( "displayText" );
   }
      Integer angle = null;
   if ( modelHandle.getProperty( "rotationAngle" ) != null ) {
      angle = ( Integer ) modelHandle.getProperty
         ( "rotationAngle" );
   }
      String fontFamily = "Arial";
   if ( modelHandle.getProperty(Style.FONT_FAMILY_PROP ) !=
      null ) {
      fontFamily = ( String ) modelHandle.getProperty
         ( Style.FONT_FAMILY_PROP );
   }
      if ( display == null ) SWT.error
         ( SWT.ERROR_THREAD_INVALID_ACCESS );

   FontData fontData = new FontData( fontFamily, 14, 0 );
   Font font = new Font( display, fontData );
   try
   {
      gc = new GC( display );
      gc.setFont( font );
      gc.getFontMetrics( );
      Point pt = gc.textExtent( text );
      gc.dispose( );
      stringImage = new Image( display, pt.x, pt.y );
      gc = new GC( stringImage );
```

```
      gc.setFont( font );
      gc.drawText( text, 0, 0 );
      image = rotateImage( stringImage, angle.doubleValue( ) );
      gc.dispose( );
      stringImage.dispose( );
      return image;
   }
   catch( Exception e )
   {
      e.printStackTrace( );
   }
   return null;
}
```

- rotateImage( )

This method rotates the image and determines the width, height, and point of origin for the image, as shown in Listing 17-8.

Listing 17-8   The rotateImage( ) method

```
private Image rotateImage ( Image img, double degrees )
{
   double positiveDegrees = ( degrees % 360 ) +
      ( ( degrees < 0 ) ? 360 : 0 );
   double degreesMod90 = positiveDegrees % 90;
   double radians = Math.toRadians( positiveDegrees );
   double radiansMod90 = Math.toRadians( degreesMod90 );
   if ( positiveDegrees == 0 )
      return img;
   int quadrant = 0;
   if ( positiveDegrees < 90 )
      quadrant = 1;
   else if ( ( positiveDegrees >= 90 ) &&
      ( positiveDegrees < 180 ) )
      quadrant = 2;
   else if ( ( positiveDegrees >= 180 ) &&
      ( positiveDegrees < 270 ) )
      quadrant = 3;
   else if ( positiveDegrees >= 270 )
      quadrant = 4;
   int height = img.getBounds().height;
   int width = img.getBounds().width;
   double side1 = ( Math.sin( radiansMod90 ) * height ) +
      ( Math.cos( radiansMod90 ) * width );
   double side2 = ( Math.cos( radiansMod90 ) * height ) +
      ( Math.sin( radiansMod90 ) * width );
   double h = 0;
   int newWidth = 0, newHeight = 0;
   if ( ( quadrant == 1 ) || ( quadrant == 3) ) {
```

```
        h = ( Math.sin( radiansMod90) * height );
        newWidth = ( int )side1;
        newHeight = ( int )side2;
    } else {
        h = ( Math.sin( radiansMod90 ) * width );
        newWidth = ( int )side2;
        newHeight = ( int )side1;
    }
    int shiftX = ( int )( Math.cos( radians ) * h ) -
        ( ( quadrant == 3 ) || ( quadrant == 4 )
            ? width : 0 );
    int shiftY = ( int )( Math.sin( radians ) * h ) +
        ( ( quadrant == 2) || ( quadrant == 3 )
            ? height : 0 );
    Image newImg = new Image( display, newWidth, newHeight );
    GC newGC = new GC( newImg );
    Transform tr = new Transform( display );
    tr.rotate( ( float )positiveDegrees );
    newGC.setTransform( tr );
    newGC.setBackground( display.getSystemColor
        ( SWT.COLOR_WHITE ) );
    newGC.drawImage( img, shiftX, -shiftY );
    newGC.dispose( );
    return newImg;
}
```

Deploying and testing the rotated label report item plug-in

After building the plug-in, the Eclipse PDE provides support for deploying and testing the plug-in in a run-time environment. The following sections describe the steps to deploy and test the rotated label report item plug-in example.

Deploying a report item extension

To deploy the rotated label report item plug-in and integrate the extension with the BIRT Report Designer, use the Export wizard or manually copy the org.eclipse.birt.sample.reportitem.rotatedtext plug-in from your workspace to the eclipse\plugins folder.

Launching the rotated label report item plug-in

On PDE Manifest Editor, in Overview, the Testing section contains links to launch a plug-in as a separate Eclipse application in either Run or Debug mode. Figure 17-13 shows Overview for the rotated label report item extension example in the host instance of the PDE Workbench.

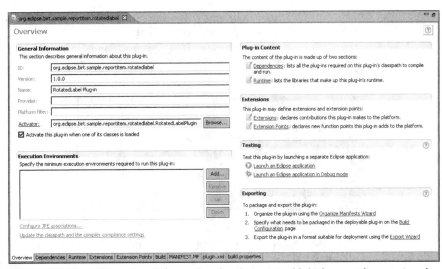

Figure 17-13   Overview information for the rotated label report item extension

How to launch a run-time workbench

1   On PDE Manifest Editor, choose Overview. In Testing, choose Launch an Eclipse application. Eclipse launches the run-time workbench.

2   In Report Design, choose File→New→Project. New Project appears. In Wizards, choose Report Project, as shown in Figure 17-14.

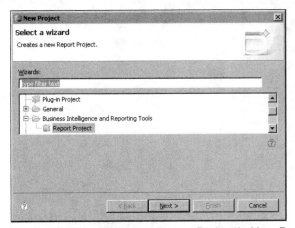

Figure 17-14   Selecting Report Project in New Project

Choose Next. New Report Project appears.

3   In Project name, type:

```
sample report item
```

Choose Finish. Sample report item appears in the Navigator.

4 In Report Design—Eclipse Platform, choose File➤New➤Report. New
Report appears, as shown in Figure 17-15.

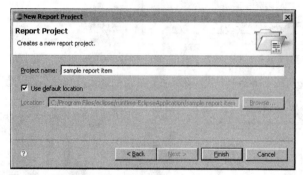

Figure 17-15   New Report

5 In File name, type a file name if you want to change the default file name.
Choose Next. New Report displays the report templates.

6 In Report templates, choose Blank Report. Choose Finish. The layout editor
displays the report design, new_report.rptdesign. Palette contains the
RotatedText report item.

7 From Palette, drag RotatedLabel to Layout, as shown in Figure 17-16.

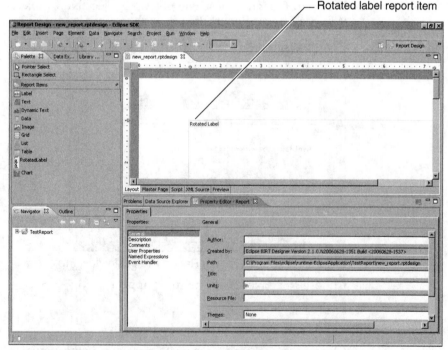

Figure 17-16   Rotated label report item in the report design

8 In new_report.rptdesign, choose Preview. The preview appears, displaying the rotated label report item, as shown in Figure 17-17.

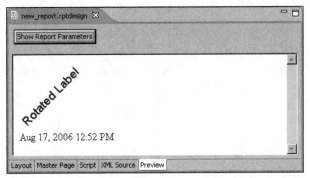

Figure 17-17   The rotated label in the report preview

Developing a Report Rendering Extension

This chapter describes how to develop a report rendering extension using the Eclipse PDE with a sample CSV report rendering extension as the example. You learn how to develop a BIRT report rendering extension in the following sections:

- Understanding a report rendering extension
- Developing the CSV report rendering extension
- Understanding the sample CSV report rendering extension
- Testing the CSV report rendering plug-in

Understanding a report rendering extension

BIRT Report Engine provides report rendering extensions that render a report in HTML and PDF. In BIRT release 2.1, the BIRT report rendering extension API supports rendering a report in a customized format, such as CSV.

This chapter provides a sample implementation of a customized CSV report rendering extension, org.eclipse.birt.report.engine.emitter.csv. The sample code creates a BIRT plug-in that writes the data contents of a report to a file. For reference documentation on the BIRT report rendering API, see the Javadoc for the org.eclipse.birt.report.engine.emitter and org.eclipse.birt.report.engine.content packages in BIRT Programmer Reference in Eclipse Help.

The BIRT Report Engine does not run as an Eclipse plug-in. BIRT implements a separate plug-in loading framework in the report engine environment. This framework runs independently of the Eclipse run-time environment, giving the BIRT Report Engine complete control of report execution.

A BIRT engine plug-in typically loads and runs in the BIRT Report Engine environment rather than the Eclipse run-time environment. A BIRT engine plug-in extension is functionally similar to an Eclipse plug-in extension.

A rendering extension adds an emitter to the BIRT framework by implementing the extension point, org.eclipse.birt.report.engine.emitters. This extension point enables support for a new output format in the presentation engine. The BIRT plug-in registry uses this extension point to discover all supported output formats specified in the report engine environment. The XML schema file, org.eclipse.birt.report.engine/schema/emitters.exsd, describes the extension point.

Developing the CSV report rendering extension

The CSV report rendering extension extends the functionality defined by the org.eclipse.birt.report.engine.emitter package. This package is part of the org.eclipse.birt.report.engine plug-in. In developing the CSV report rendering extension, you perform the following tasks:

- Download the required BIRT source code from the Eclipse CVS repository.
- Create a CSV report rendering extension project in the Eclipse PDE.
- Define the dependencies.
- Declare the emitters extension point.
- Implement the emitter interfaces.
- Test the extension in the run-time environment.

You can download the source code for the CSV report rendering extension example at http://www.actuate.com/birt/contributions.

Downloading BIRT source code from the CVS repository

The CSV report rendering extension depends on the following BIRT plug-ins:

- org.eclipse.birt.core
- org.eclipse.birt.report.engine
- org.eclipse.birt.report.model

The CSV report rendering extension requires changes to the org.eclipse.birt .report.engine plug-in, so you must download the source code for this plug-in from the CVS repository.

To compile, you do not need the source code for the other required plug-ins. You can configure the system to use the JAR files in the $INSTALL_DIR\eclipse\ plugins folder.

These plug-ins must be in the classpath to compile successfully. To debug, you may need the source code for all required BIRT plug-ins.

Creating a CSV report rendering plug-in project

Create a new plug-in project for the CSV report rendering extension using the Eclipse PDE.

How to create the CSV report rendering plug-in project

1 From the Eclipse PDE menu, choose File→New→Project. New Project appears.

2 On New Project, select Plug-in Project. Choose Next. New Plug-in Project appears.

3 In Plug-in Project, modify the settings, as shown in Table 18-1.

Table 18-1   Values for Plug-in Project fields

Section	Option	Value
Plug-in Project	Project name	org.eclipse.birt.report .engine.emitter.csv
	Use default location	Selected
	Location	Not available when you select Use default location
Project Settings	Create a Java project	Selected
	Source folder	src
	Output folder	bin
Target Platform	Eclipse version	3.2
	an OSGi framework	Selected Equinox

Plug-in Project appears as shown in Figure 18-1. Choose Next. Plug-in Content appears.

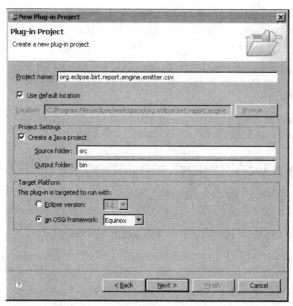

Figure 18-1   Values for Plug-in Project

4 In Plug-in Content, modify the settings, as shown in Table 18-2.

Table 18-2   Values for Plug-in Content fields

Section	Option	Value
Plug-in Properties	Plug-in ID	org.eclipse.birt.report.engine.emitter.csv
	Plug-in Version	1.0.0
	Plug-in Name	BIRT CSV Emitter
	Plug-in Provider	yourCompany.com or leave blank
	Classpath	csvEmitter.jar or leave blank
Plug-in Options	Generate an activator, a Java class that controls the plug-in's life cycle	Selected
	Activator	org.eclipse.birt.report.engine.emitter.csv.CsvPlugin
	This plug-in will make contributions to the UI	Deselected
Rich Client Application	Would you like to create a rich client application?	No

Plug-in Content appears as shown in Figure 18-2. Choose Finish.

Figure 18-2   Values for Plug-in Content

The CSV report rendering extension project appears in the Eclipse PDE workbench, as shown in Figure 18-3.

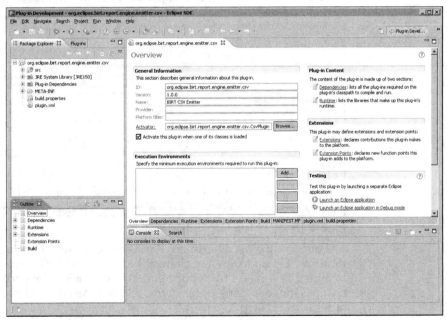

Figure 18-3   CSV report rendering extension project

Defining the dependencies for the CSV report rendering extension

To compile and run the CSV report rendering example, you need to specify the list of plug-ins that must be available on the classpath of the extension.

How to specify the dependencies

1 On PDE Manifest Editor, choose Overview.

2 In Plug-in Content, choose Dependencies. Required Plug-ins contains the following plug-in:

```
org.eclipse.core.runtime
```

3 In Required Plug-ins, perform the following tasks:

    1 Select org.eclipse.core.runtime and choose Remove.

    org.eclipse.core.runtime no longer appears in Required Plug-ins.

    2 Choose Add. Plug-in Selection appears.

    3 In Plug-in Selection, hold down CTRL and select the following plug-ins:

      ❑ org.eclipse.birt.core

      ❑ org.eclipse.birt.report.model

      ❑ org.eclipse.birt.report.engine

    Choose OK. Dependencies appears as shown in Figure 18-4.

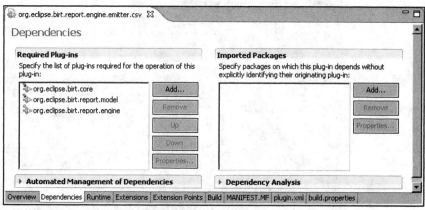

Figure 18-4   The Dependencies page

The order of the list determines the sequence in which a plug-in loads at run time. Use Up and Down to change the loading order as necessary, as shown in Figure 18-4. The CSV report rendering extension does not require any changes to the loading order if you selected the required plug-ins in the order listed in step 3.

Declaring the emitters extension point

In this step, you specify the extension point required to implement the CSV report rendering extension and add the extension element details. The extension point, org.eclipse.birt.report.engine.emitters, specifies the following properties that identify the extension point:

- ID

  Optional identifier of the extension instance

- Name

  Optional name of the extension instance

- Point

  Fully qualified identifier of the extension point

The extension point defines an emitter that specifies the output format for the plug-in, requiring you to define the following extension element properties:

- class

  Java class that implements the IContentEmitter interface

- format

  Output format that the emitter supports, such as csv

- mimeType

  MIME type for the supported output format, such as text/csv

- id

  Optional identifier of the emitter extension

You specify the extension point and extension element details using the Eclipse PDE.

How to specify the extension point

1 On PDE Manifest Editor, choose Extensions.

2 In All Extensions, choose Add. New Extension—Extension Point Selection appears.

3 In Available extension points, select the following plug-in:

```
org.eclipse.birt.report.engine.emitters
```

Choose Finish. Extensions appears, as shown in Figure 18-5.

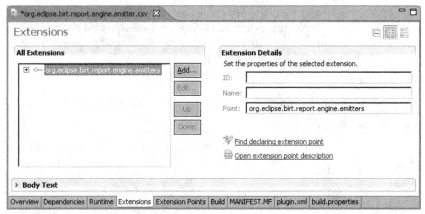

Figure 18-5   Emitter plug-in extension on the Extensions page

All Extensions lists the extension point, org.eclipse.birt.report.engine
.emitters. Extension Details contains the list of extension details specified in
the XML schema file, emitters.exsd.

4 In All Extensions, right-click the extension point, org.eclipse.birt.report
.engine.emitters, and choose the extension element, emitter, as shown in
Figure 18-6.

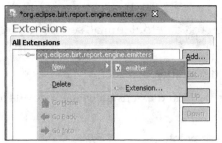

Figure 18-6   Selecting the emitter extension element

Extension element, emitter, appears in All Extensions.

5 In Extension Element Details, specify the properties for the emitter extension
element, emitter, as shown in Table 18-3.

Table 18-3   Property values for the emitter extension element

Property	Value
class	org.eclipse.birt.report.engine.emitter.csv.CSVReportEmitter
format	csv
mimeType	text/csv
id	org.eclipse.birt.report.engine.emitter.csv

Extensions appears as shown in Figure 18-7. PDE Manifest Editor automatically updates plugin.xml.

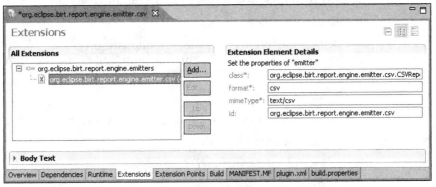

Figure 18-7   Property values for the emitter extension

Understanding the sample CSV report rendering extension

The CSV report rendering extension described in this chapter is a simplified example that illustrates how to create a report rendering plug-in using the Eclipse PDE. The extension extends the report emitter interfaces and XML writer in org.eclipse.birt.report.engine.emitter. The example is based on the plug-in, org.eclipse.report.engine.emitter.html, which is part of the BIRT framework. BIRT release 2.1 also provides a data extraction feature built into the UI that can export data from a report document in CSV, tab-separated values (TSV), and Extensible Markup Language (XML) formats.

The CSV report rendering extension example exports only the data in the table controls to the CSV output file. The lines of the CSV output file contain only column data separated by commas. The sample CSV report design cannot contain images, charts, or hyperlinks.

The extension example creates the CSV output file in the same folder as the exported report. The output file name is the name of the report with a .csv extension. The extension provides only limited error checking.

The following section provides a general description of the code-based extensions a developer must make to complete the development of the CSV report rendering extension after defining the plug-in framework in the Eclipse PDE.

Implementing the emitter interfaces

The org.eclipse.birt.report.engine.emitter plug-in defines the report emitter interfaces that XML writer uses to render the elements of the report items in a report container, such as a page, table, row, column, cell, label, image, or extended item. The CSV report rendering extension implements parts of the following interfaces and classes in the emitter plug-in:

- IContentEmitter

  Defines the interface for the start and end processing that renders the report items. ContentEmitterAdapter is the adapter class that implements this interface.

- IEmitterServices

  Defines the interface an emitter uses to access the following items:

  - Emitter configuration

    Provides information on the engine emitter configuration

  - Rendering context

    Provides information on the engine rendering context

  - Rendering options

    Implements the org.eclipse.birt.report.engine.api.IRenderOption interface, specifying the following output items:

    - Format, such as PDF or HTML
    - File name to use for output
    - Stream for writing to the output file
    - Miscellaneous settings

  - Runnable report design

    Defines the methods that get the report design handle, images, and property values, such as report name, title, and description. Specified by an implementation of the interface, org.eclipse.birt.report.engine.api .IReportRunnable.

  - Engine task

    Defines the set of operations specified for a unit of work. Implements the org.eclipse.birt.report.engine.api interface, providing access to the following items:

    - Task identifier
    - Locale
    - Application context
    - Parameters
    - Report engine
    - Scriptable Java object

EngineEmitterServices is the adapter class that implements this interface.

- XMLWriter

  Outputs content in XML format. CSV report rendering extension extends XMLWriter to write in CSV format. Performs the following operations:

  - Opens and closes the output stream, using an instance of java.io.PrintWriter class

  - Starts and finishes the java.io.PrintWriter processing

  - Returns encoding information

  - Opens and closes the printing of an XML tag, including any attributes and encoded content

  - Sets up the java.util.logging.Logger object and logs messages at the specified logging levels

As a best practice, Eclipse recommends extending the adapter class rather than implementing an interface directly. An adapter class provides stub implementations of all the methods in the interface. If you implement an interface directly and the interface changes, you must add any new methods to the code to avoid compiler errors even if you do not plan to use the methods. Extending the adapter class insulates the developer from this problem. A class that extends an adapter compiles, but does not provide the new behavior automatically. You must be aware of the changes to the interface to take advantage of the new functionality and extend the code.

Implementing the content interfaces

The package, org.eclipse.birt.report.engine.content, defines the interfaces for BIRT report items that BIRT Report Engine uses to pass content to an emitter. These content interfaces provide a common protocol for rendering an instance of a content object.

The CSV report rendering extension implements some of these interfaces. Each interface defines accessor methods for properties depending on the type of the content object, as shown in Table 18-4.

Table 18-4 Interfaces that pass content to an emitter

Interface	Properties
IBandContent	Header and footer content in a table or group.
ICellContent	Row and column spans.
IContainerContent	No defined fields or methods. Inherits fields and methods from the superinterfaces, IContent, IElement, and CSSStylableElement.
IDataContent	Label and help keys, text, and values.

(continues)

Table 18-4   Interfaces that pass content to an emitter *(continued)*

Interface	Properties
IElement	Parent or children of a content element.
IForeignContent	Raw types and values not handled by BIRT Report Engine.
IImageContent	URI, MIME type, image source, image map, help key, extension, alternative key and text.
ILabelContent	Label and help keys and text.
IPageContent	Page number, dimensions, orientation, and content style.
IRowContent	Table, group, band, and row.
ITableBandContent	Table and group headers and footers, and band detail.
ITableContent	Table band content, caption, column, and column count.
ITextContent	Text.

Most of the interfaces in the org.eclipse.birt.report.engine.content package, with the exception of interfaces such as IContentVisitor, IElement, and IReportContent, inherit from the superinterface, org.eclipse.birt.report.engine .content.IContent. IContent specifies methods that provide access to the following additional interfaces and properties in the package:

- IContentVisitor

  Defines a visitor interface, typically used by a buffered emitter. The visitor design pattern separates content objects and their operations into different classes. Implementing a visitor design pattern allows a developer to change the operations performed on a collection of objects without changing the structure of the objects and recompiling the object code.

- IBounds

  Describes the geometric properties of the content.

- ContentType

  Lists the constant field values used to identify content types.

- IHyperlinkAction

  Defines the interface that allows BIRT Report Engine to pass hyperlink information to an emitter.

The following interfaces define additional functionality in the org.eclipse.birt.report.engine.content package:

- IStyle

  Defines the accessor methods for ROM style properties

- IReportContent

  Creates report item content, using the following components:

  - Report design

    An instance of org.eclipse.birt.report.engine.ir.Report

  - Table of contents (TOC) node

    An instance of org.eclipse.birt.report.engine.api.TOCNode

  - CSS engine

    An instance of org.eclipse.birt.report.engine.css.engine.CSSEngine

Understanding the CSV report rendering extension package

The implementation package for the CSV report rendering extension example, org.eclipse.birt.report.engine.emitter.csv, contains the following classes:

- CSVReportEmitter

  Extends org.eclipse.birt.report.engine.emitter.ContentEmitterAdapter. CSVReportEmitter handles the start and end processing that renders the report container.

- CSVTags.java

  Defines the comma and new line Strings used when writing to the CSV file.

- CSVWriter

  Extends org.eclipse.birt.report.engine.emitter.XMLWriter. CSVWriter performs the following operations:

  - Overrides XMLWriter.closeTag( ) to set up for CSV output processing

  - Prints CSV content, using a call to java.io.PrintWriter.print( )

- CSVPlugin

  Defines the methods for starting, managing, and stopping a plug-in instance.

The following section contains more specific information about the implementation details for the classes in the CSV report rendering extension package.

Understanding CSVReportEmitter

CSVReportEmitter is the class that extends ContentEmitterAdapter to output the text content of the report items to a CSV file. CSVReportEmitter instantiates the writer and emitter objects.

CSVReportEmitter implements the following methods:

- CSVReportEmitter( ) instantiates the CSV report emitter class as an org.eclipse.birt.report.engine.presentation.ContentEmitterVisitor object, to perform emitter operations, as shown in Listing 18-1.

Listing 18-1   The CSVReportEmitter( ) constructor

```
public CSVReportEmitter( )
{
    contentVisitor = new ContentEmitterVisitor( this );
}
```

- initialize( ) performs the following operations required to create an output stream that writes the text contents of the report to the CSV file:

  - Obtains a reference to the IEmitterServices interface. Instantiates the file and output stream objects, using the specified settings.

  - Instantiates the CSV writer object.

Listing 18-2 shows the initialize( ) method.

Listing 18-2   The initialize( ) method

```
public void initialize( IEmitterServices services )
{
    this.services = services;
    Object fd = services.getOption
        ( RenderOptionBase.OUTPUT_FILE_NAME );
    File file = null;
    try
    {
        if ( fd != null )
        {
            file = new File( fd.toString( ) );
            File parent = file.getParentFile( );
            if ( parent != null && !parent.exists( ) )
            {
                parent.mkdirs( );
            }
            out = new BufferedOutputStream( new
                FileOutputStream( file ) );
        }
    }
    catch ( FileNotFoundException e )
    {
        logger.log( Level.WARNING, e.getMessage( ), e );
    }
    if ( out == null )
    {
```

```
        Object value = services.getOption
           ( RenderOptionBase.OUTPUT_STREAM );
        if ( value != null && value instanceof OutputStream )
        {
           out = (OutputStream) value;
        }
        else
        {
          try
          {
             file = new File( REPORT_FILE );
             out =
                new BufferedOutputStream
                   ( new FileOutputStream( file ) );
          }
          catch ( FileNotFoundException e )
          {
             logger.log( Level.SEVERE, e.getMessage( ), e );
          }
        }
      }
      writer = new CSVWriter( );
   }
```

- start( ) performs the following operations:

  - Obtains a reference to the IReportContent interface, containing accessor methods that get the interfaces to the report content emitters

  - Sets a logging level and writes to the log file

  - Opens the output file and specifies the encoding scheme as UTF-8

  - Starts the CSV writer

Listing 18-3 shows the start( ) method.

Listing 18-3   The start( ) method

```
public void start( IReportContent report )
{
   logger.log( Level.FINE,
      "[CSVReportEmitter] Start emitter." );
   this.report = report;
   writer.open( out, "UTF-8" );
   writer.startWriter( );
}
```

- end( ) performs the following operations:

  - Sets a logging level and writes to the log file

  - Ends the write process and closes the CSV writer

■ Closes the output file

Listing 18-4 shows the end( ) method.

Listing 18-4   The end( ) method

```
public void end( IReportContent report )
{
   logger.log( Level.FINE,
     "[CSVReportEmitter] End report." );
   writer.endWriter( );
   writer.close( );
   if( out != null )
   {
      try
      {
         out.close( );
      }
      catch ( IOException e )
      {
         logger.log( Level.WARNING, e.getMessage( ), e );
      }
   }
}
```

Understanding the other CSVReportEmitter methods

The CSVReportEmitter class defines the following additional methods, called at different phases of the report generation process, that identify hidden content and provide access to emitters, render options, and style information to facilitate BIRT Report Engine processing:

■ push( ), pop( ), and peek( )

The CSV plug-in does not export hidden report elements. You can use the IStyle interface to obtain information about the visible format of a content object by pushing and popping this object on and off a stack.

In Listing 18-5, while the IStyle object is on the stack, peek( ) uses IStyle.getVisibleFormat( ) to examine the visible format property. peek( ) determines if the current content object is visible and returns the Boolean variable, isHidden, to indicate the status of the item.

Listing 18-5   The peek( ) method

```
public boolean peek( IStyle style )
{
   boolean isHidden = false;
   if ( !stack.empty( ) )
   {
      isHidden =
         ( (Boolean) stack.peek( ) ).booleanValue( );
```

```
    }
    if ( !isHidden )
    {
        String formats = style.getVisibleFormat( );
        if ( formats != null
            && ( formats.indexOf
                ( EngineIRConstants.FORMAT_TYPE_VIEWER ) >=
                0 || formats.indexOf
                    ( BIRTConstants.BIRT_ALL_VALUE ) >= 0 ) )
        {
            isHidden = true;
        }
    }
    return isHidden;
}
```

- startTable( )

When writing to the CSV file, the CSV rendering extension must consider the cell position in the row because all the cells end with a comma except the last cell in the row.

startTable( ) uses ITableContent.getColumnCount( ) to get information about table column numbers and to initialize the protected columnNumbers variable, as shown in Listing 18-6.

Listing 18-6   The startTable( ) method

```
public void startTable( ITableContent table )
{
    assert table != null;
    columnNumbers = table.getColumnCount();
    ...
}
```

- startRow( )

At the start of each row, startRow( ) performs the following operations:

- Calls isRowInFooterBand( ) to determine if the row is in the header or footer band of a table or group

- Sets the currentColumn indicator to 0

Listing 18-7 shows the startRow( ) code.

Listing 18-7   The startRow( ) method

```
public void startRow( IRowContent row )
{
    assert row != null;
    if ( isRowInFooterBand( row ) )
        exportTableElement = false;
```

```
IStyle mergedStyle = row.getStyle( );
push( mergedStyle );
if ( isHidden( ) )
{
   return;
}
currentColumn = 0;
}
```

■ isRowInFooterBand( )

If the row is an instance of band content, isRowInFooterBand( ) checks the band type. If the band type is a footer, the method returns true, as shown in Listing 18-8.

Listing 18-8   The isRowInFooterBand( ) method

```
boolean isRowInFooterBand( IRowContent row )
{
   IElement parent = row.getParent( );
   if ( !( parent instanceof IBandContent ) )
   {
      return false;
   }
   IBandContent band = ( IBandContent )parent;
   if ( band.getBandType( ) == IBandContent.BAND_FOOTER )
   {
      return true;
   }
   return false;
}
```

■ startText( )

If the element is exportable and not hidden, startText( ) writes the text value to the CSV output file, as shown in Listing 18-9.

Listing 18-9   The startText( ) method

```
public void startText( ITextContent text )
{
   IStyle mergedStyle = text.getStyle( );
   if ( peek( mergedStyle ) )
   {
      return;
   }
   logger.log( Level.FINE,
      "[CSVReportEmitter] Start text" );
```

```
      String textValue = text.getText( );

      if ( exportTableElement )
      {
         writer.text( textValue );
      }
   }
```

- endCell( )

   If the current cell is not the last column in the row and the element is
   exportable and not hidden, endCell( ) writes a comma to the CSV output file,
   as shown in Listing 18-10.

   Listing 18-10   The endCell( ) method

```
public void endCell( ICellContent cell )
{
   if ( isHidden( ) )
   {
      return;
   }
   logger.log( Level.FINE,
      "[CSVReportEmitter] End cell." );

   if ( ( currentColumn < columnNumbers )
      && exportTableElement )
   {
      writer.closeTag( CSVTags.TAG_COMMA );
   }
}
```

- endRow( )

   At the end of each row, if the element is exportable and not hidden,
   endRow( ) writes a new line or carriage return to the CSV output file, as
   shown in Listing 18-11.

   Listing 18-11   The endRow( ) method

```
public void endRow( IRowContent row )
{
   if ( pop( ) )
   {
      return;
   }
   if ( exportTableElement )
   writer.closeTag( CSVTags.TAG_CR );
   exportTableElement = true;
}
```

Understanding CSVTags

The CSVTags class defines the contents of the comma and new line tags, as shown in Listing 18-12.

Listing 18-12 The CSVTags class

```
public class CSVTags
{
   public static final String TAG_COMMA = "," ;
   public static final String TAG_CR = "\n" ;
}
```

Understanding CSVWriter

The CSVWriter class extends org.eclipse.birt.report.engine.emitter.XMLWriter, overwriting the closeTag( ) method to write the closing tags defined in CSVTags, as shown in Listing 18-13.

Listing 18-13 The closeTag( ) method

```
public void closeTag( String tagName )
{
   super.printWriter.print( tagName );
}
```

Understanding the BIRT report engine API package

In addition to the rendering classes, implementing the CSV report rendering extension requires making changes to the org.eclipse.birt.report .engine.api package. The following changes create and expose the API for the CSV rendering option developed in the org.eclipse.birt.report.engine .emitter.csv package:

- RenderOptionBase

  Add the CSV output format to the format definitions in RenderOptionBase.

- CSVRenderOption

  Create the class, org.eclipse.birt.report.engine.api.CSVRenderOption, to integrate the plug-in with BIRT Report Engine. This class defines CSV as an option in BIRT Report Engine.

- EngineConstants

  Add the CSV render context to the list in EngineConstants.

The following section contains more specific information about the implementation details for the classes in the org.eclipse.birt.report.engine.api package.

Understanding RenderOptionBase

The org.eclipse.birt.report.engine.api.RenderOptionBase class implements the IRenderOption interface, which defines the rendering options for emitters. The accessor methods for this interface provide access to the following output options:

- File name
- Format
- Stream

Add the new CSV format to the format definitions in org.eclipse.birt.report .engine.api.RenderOptionBase class, as shown in Listing 18-14.

Listing 18-14   The RenderOptionBase class

```
public class RenderOptionBase implements IRenderOption {
    ...
    public static final String OUTPUT_FORMAT_HTML = "html";
    public static final String OUTPUT_FORMAT_PDF = "pdf";
    public static final String OUTPUT_FORMAT_FO = "fo";
    public static final String OUTPUT_FORMAT_CSV = "csv";
    ...
```

Understanding CSVRenderOption

The org.eclipse.birt.report.engine.api.CSVRenderOption class extends RenderOptionBase to add the CSV rendering option, as shown in Listing 18-15.

Listing 18-15   The CSVRenderOption class

```
package org.eclipse.birt.report.engine.api;

public class CSVRenderOption extends RenderOptionBase {

    public static final String CSV = "CSV";

    public CSVRenderOption( ) {
    }
}
```

Understanding EngineConstants

The org.eclipse.birt.report.engine.api.EngineConstants class defines the CSV rendering context options to add the CSV rendering context option, as shown in Listing 18-16.

Listing 18-16   The EngineConstants class
___

```
public class EngineConstants {
    public final static String APPCONTEXT_HTML_RENDER_CONTEXT =
        "HTML_RENDER_CONTEXT";
    public final static String APPCONTEXT_PDF_RENDER_CONTEXT =
        "PDF_RENDER_CONTEXT";
    public final static String APPCONTEXT_CSV_RENDER_CONTEXT =
        "CSV_RENDER_CONTEXT";
    ...
}
```
___

Testing the CSV report rendering plug-in

To test the CSV report rendering example, you create a Java application that runs a report design in an installation of the BIRT run-time engine. BIRT provides a run-time engine that runs in a stand-alone J2EE application server environment and a preview engine that runs in the BIRT Report Designer.

To test the CSV report rendering plug-in, you perform the following tasks:

- Build the org.eclipse.birt.report.engine.emitter.csv and org.eclipse.birt .report.engine.api plug-ins.

- Deploy the plug-ins to the BIRT run-time engine directory.

- Launch a run-time instance of the Eclipse PDE.

- Create a Java application that runs a report design and writes the report's table data to a CSV file.

- Create a report design containing a table that maps to a data source and data set.

- Run the application and examine the output in the CSV file.

You must have previously installed the BIRT run-time engine in the test environment. For more information about downloading and installing the BIRT run-time engine, see the sections on installing the BIRT system earlier in this book or visit the Eclipse BIRT web site at http://www.eclipse.org/birt.

The following sections describe the steps required to build and export the plug-ins, launch the Eclipse PDE run-time environment, create the Java application and report design, and test the plug-in example.

How to build and export the org.eclipse.birt.report.engine.emitter.csv plug-in

On PDE Manifest Editor, perform the following tasks:

1 On Build, specify the binary build configuration for the plug-in for org.eclipse.birt.report.engine.emitter.csv to include the following items:

- plugin.xml

- bin\org.eclipse.birt.report.engine.emitter.csv
- META-INF\MANIFEST.MF

2 On Overview, in Exporting, choose the Export Wizard and perform the following tasks:

    1 In Options, choose Package plug-ins as individual JAR archives, as shown in Figure 18-8.

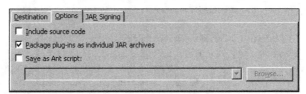

Figure 18-8   Exporting a plug-in option

    2 In Destination, choose the directory, $INSTALL_DIR\birt-runtime-2_1_0\Report Engine, as shown in Figure 18-9. Choose Finish.

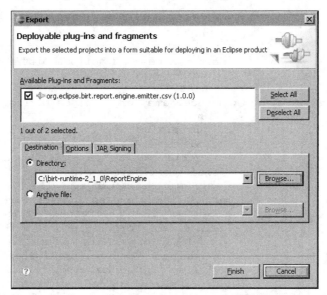

Figure 18-9   Exporting a plug-in to BIRT run-time engine

How to build and deploy the org.eclipse.birt.report.engine plug-in

1 Using Ant with the following BuildEngineAPI.xml file, create an archive containing the org.eclipse.birt.report.engine.api package with the modifications required to run the CSV emitter example.

BuildEngineAPI.xml has two target operations:

- Jar creates the engineapi.jar file from a defined file set.

- Clean removes any objects created by previous build and archive operations, deleting the bin directory and engineapi.jar file.

Listing 18-17 shows the BuildEngineAPI.xml code.

Listing 18-17   The BuildEngineAPI.xml code

```xml
<project name="BIRT Engine Project" default="Jar"
   basedir=".">
   <description>BIRT Engine Project.</description>

   <property name="bin" location="bin"/>
   <property name="lib" location="lib"/>

   <target name="Jar"  description="package engine files">
      <jar destfile="engineapi.jar">
         <fileset dir="${bin}">
            <include
               name="org/eclipse/birt/report/engine/api/
               *.class"/>
            <include name="org/eclipse/birt/report/engine/
               util/
               *.class"/>
            <include name="org/eclipse/birt/report/engine/
               i18n/
               *.class"/>
            <include name="org/eclipse/birt/report/engine/
               i18n/
               *.properties"/>
            <include name="org/eclipse/birt/report/engine/
               api/impl/CascadingParameterGroupDefn.class"/>
            <include name="org/eclipse/birt/report/engine/
               api/impl/ParameterDefn.class"/>
            <include name="org/eclipse/birt/report/engine/
               api/impl/ParameterDefnBase.class"/>
            <include name="org/eclipse/birt/report/engine/
               api/impl/ParameterGroupDefn.class"/>
            <include name="org/eclipse/birt/report/engine/
               api/impl/ParameterSelectionChoice.class"/>
            <include name="org/eclipse/birt/report/engine/
               api/impl/ScalarParameterDefn.class"/>
         </fileset>
      </jar>
   </target>

   <!-- Clean removes any objects created by
        previous build and archive operations -->
   <target name="Clean" description="clean up">
      <!-- Delete the ${bin} directory -->
      <delete dir="${bin}"/>
      <!-- Delete the engineapi.jar file /-->
```

```
        <delete dir="engineapi.jar"/>
    </target>

</project>
```

2 Copy engineapi.jar to $INSTALL_DIR\birt-runtime-2_1_0\Report Engine\lib.

Launching the CSV report rendering plug-in

On PDE Manifest Editor, in Overview, the Testing section contains links to launch a plug-in as a separate Eclipse application in either Run or Debug mode. Figure 18-10 shows Overview for the CSV report rendering extension example in the host instance of the PDE workbench.

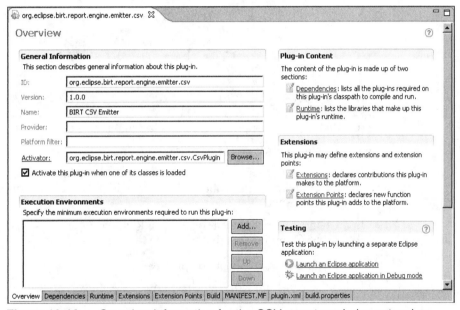

Figure 18-10 Overview information for the CSV report rendering extension

When the Eclipse PDE launches an Eclipse application, it creates the working directory, $INSTALL_DIR\eclipse\runtime-EclipseApplication, by default if the directory does not exist. For testing purposes, you can create a Java project in this workspace to run and render a report in CSV format. You can change the location of the working directory when you create the launch configuration for the Java application.

To execute, the report execution project must include the archive, org.eclipse.birt .report.engine.emitter.csv in $INSTALL_DIR\birt-runtime-2_1_0\Report Engine\plugins, and the archive, engineapi.jar, in lib. Figure 18-11 shows the Eclipse run-time workbench with the report execution project completely specified, after a successful execution.

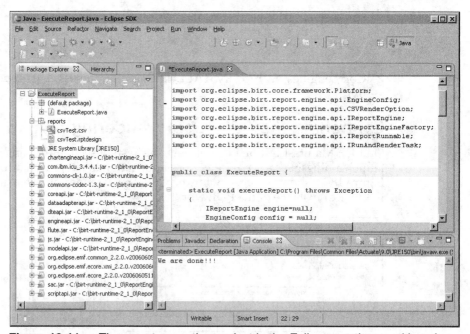

Figure 18-11   The report execution project in the Eclipse run-time workbench

How to launch the CSV report rendering plug-in

1   On Eclipse PDE Manifest Editor, in the Testing section of Overview, choose Launch an Eclipse application. The Eclipse PDE launches a run-time instance of the workbench.

2   In the run-time instance of the Eclipse PDE workbench, choose Window➤Open Perspective➤Java. Java opens.

How to create the report execution project

1   In Eclipse run-time workbench, choose File➤New➤Project. New Project appears.

2   In New Project—Select a wizard, perform the following tasks:

    1   In Wizards, choose Java Project. Choose Next. Create a Java Project appears.

    2   In Create a Java Project, perform the following tasks:

        1   In Project name, type:

            ExecuteReport

        2   In Contents, select Create new project in workspace. Choose Next. Java Settings—Source appears.

        3   In Java Settings, choose Libraries. Java Settings—Libraries appears.

4 In Libraries, perform the following tasks:

    1 Choose Add External JARS. JAR Selection opens.

    2 On JAR Selection, in Look in, navigate to $INSTALL_DIR\birt -runtime-2_1_0\Report Engine\lib and, holding down CTRL, select the following libraries:

       ❏ chartengineapi.jar

       ❏ com.ibm.icu_3.4.4.1.jar

       ❏ commons-cli-1.0.jar

       ❏ commons-codec-1.3.jar

       ❏ coreapi.jar

       ❏ dataadapterapi.jar

       ❏ dteapi.jar

       ❏ engineapi.jar

       ❏ flute.jar

       ❏ js.jar

       ❏ modelapi.jar

       ❏ org.eclipse.emf.common_2.2.0.jar

       ❏ org.eclipse.emf.ecore.xmi_2.2.0.jar

       ❏ org.eclipse.emf.ecore_2.2.0.jar

       ❏ sac.jar

       ❏ scriptapi.jar

    Choose Open. Choose Finish. In Package Explorer, the ExecuteReport project appears.

How to create the Java report execution class

1 In Eclipse run-time workbench, choose File→New→Class. New Java Class appears.

2 On New Java Class, perform the following tasks:

    1 In Source folder, type:

```
ExecuteReport
```

    2 In Which method stubs would you like to create?, perform the following tasks:

       1 Select Public static void main(Strings[ ] args).

       2 Deselect Constructors from superclass.

3   Deselect Inherited abstract methods.

Choose Finish.

In Package Explorer, ExecuteReport.java appears in the ExecuteReport project.

3 Open ExecuteReport.java in Java Editor, and add the required code. The ExecuteReport code is discussed later in this chapter.

4 In Eclipse run-time workbench, compile the project by choosing Project→Build Project.

How to run the CSV report rendering extension

To run the CSV report rendering extension, using the ExecuteReport application, perform the following tasks:

1 In Eclipse run-time workbench, right-click ExecuteReport, and choose Run As→Run from the menu. Run appears.

2 On Run, perform the following tasks:

1   In Java Application, select ExecuteReport, as shown in Figure 18-12.

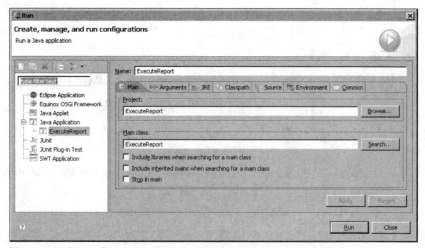

Figure 18-12   Selecting ExecuteReport

2 To change the working directory for the launch configuration, perform the following tasks:

1   On Run, choose (x) = Arguments.

2   In Working Directory, choose Other. Choose File System. Browse for Folder appears. Select the working directory that contains the ExecuteReports project for the launch configuration. Choose OK.

3   On Run, choose Apply.

3 To run the Java application using the launch configuration, choose Run.

How to view the CSV report rendering extension file output

1 Navigate to the directory containing the CSV output file. This CSV report rendering extension example writes the CSV file to the following location:

```
C:\Program Files\eclipse\runtime-EclipseApplication\
   ExecuteReport\reports
```

2 Using a text editor or other tool, open the file, and view its contents.

Figure 18-13 shows the CSV output.

```
1969 Harley Davidson Ultimate Chopper,7933,95.7
1952 Alpine Renault 1300,7305,214.3
1996 Moto Guzzi 1100i,6625,118.94
2003 Harley-Davidson Eagle Drag Bike,5582,193.66
1972 Alfa Romeo GTA,3252,136
1962 LanciaA Delta 16V,6791,147.74
1968 Ford Mustang,68,194.57
2001 Ferrari Enzo,3619,207.8
```

Figure 18-13 CSV output

The XML source code for the report design used in this example is discussed later in this chapter.

About ExecuteReport class

The ExecuteReport class runs a BIRT report and renders the output in CSV format, writing the text-based elements of the report to a file. The ExecuteReport class performs the following operations:

- Configures the report engine
- Sets the log configuration and logging level
- Starts the platform and loads the plug-ins
- Gets the report engine factory object from the platform and creates the report engine
- Opens the report design
- Creates a task to run and render the report
- Set the rendering options, such as the output file and format
- Runs the report and destroys the engine
- Shuts down the engine

Listing 18-18 shows the code for the ExecuteReport class in the CSV report rendering extension example.

Listing 18-18 The ExecuteReport class code

```
import java.util.logging.Level;
import org.eclipse.birt.core.framework.Platform;
import org.eclipse.birt.report.engine.api.EngineConfig;
import org.eclipse.birt.report.engine.api.CSVRenderOption;
import org.eclipse.birt.report.engine.api.IReportEngine;
import
   org.eclipse.birt.report.engine.api.IReportEngineFactory;
import org.eclipse.birt.report.engine.api.IReportRunnable;
import org.eclipse.birt.report.engine.api.IRunAndRenderTask;

public class ExecuteReport {

   static void executeReport( ) throws Exception
   {
      IReportEngine engine=null;
      EngineConfig config = null;
      config = new EngineConfig( );
      config.setEngineHome
         ( "C:/birt-runtime-2_1_0/ReportEngine" );
      config.setLogConfig( "c:/birt/logs", Level.FINE );
      Platform.startup( config );
      IReportEngineFactory factory =
         ( IReportEngineFactory ) Platform.createFactoryObject
         ( IReportEngineFactory
            .EXTENSION_REPORT_ENGINE_FACTORY );
      engine = factory.createReportEngine( config );
      engine.changeLogLevel( Level.WARNING );

      IReportRunnable design =
         engine.openReportDesign
            ( "reports/csvTest.rptdesign" );
      IRunAndRenderTask task =
         engine.createRunAndRenderTask( design );
      String format = CSVRenderOption.OUTPUT_FORMAT_CSV;
      if ( format.equals( CSVRenderOption.OUTPUT_FORMAT_CSV ))
      {
         CSVRenderOption csvOptions = new CSVRenderOption( );
         csvOptions.setOutputFormat( format );
         csvOptions.setOutputFileName( "reports/csvTest.csv" );
         task.setRenderOption( csvOptions );
      }

      task.run( );
      task.close( );
      engine.shutdown( );
      Platform.shutdown( );
      System.out.println("We are done!!!");
```

```
  }
  public static void main(String[] args) {
     try
     {
        executeReport( );
     }
     catch ( Exception e )
     {
        e.printStackTrace();
     }
  }
}
```

About the report design XML code

The XML file for the report design, csvTest.reportdesign, contains the following source code settings, as specified in the report design:

- Data sources, including the ODA plug-in extension ID, driver class, URL, and user

- Data sets, including the ODA JDBC plug-in extension ID, result set properties, and query text

- Page setup, including the page footer

- Body, containing the table structure and properties for the bound data columns, including the header, footer, and detail rows

The report design example specifies a data source that connects to org.eclipse.birt.report.data.oda.sampledb, the BIRT Classic Models sample database. Listing 18-19 shows the XML source code for the report design used to test the CSV rendering example. The sample application runs the report from the reports subfolder in the ExecuteReport project.

Listing 18-19   The report design XML code

```
<?xml version="1.0" encoding="UTF-8"?>
<!-- Written by Eclipse BIRT 2.0 -->
<report xmlns="http://www.eclipse.org/birt/2005/design"
   version="3.2.2" id="1">
   <property name="createdBy">
      Eclipse BIRT Designer Version 1.0.1
      Build &lt;20050729-0746></property>
   <property name="units">in</property>
   <data-sources>
      <oda-data-source
         extensionID=
         "org.eclipse.birt.report.data.oda.sampledb"
         name="Data Source" id="2">
```

```xml
        <property
          name="odaDriverClass">
          org.eclipse.birt.report.data.oda.sampledb.Driver
        </property>
        <property
          name="odaURL">jdbc:classicmodels:sampledb
        </property>
        <property name="odaUser">ClassicModels</property>
    </oda-data-source>
  </data-sources>
  <data-sets>
    <oda-data-set
      extensionID=
        "org.eclipse.birt.report.data.oda.jdbc
          .JdbcSelectDataSet" name="Data Set" id="3">
        <structure name="cachedMetaData">
          <list-property name="resultSet">
            <structure>
              <property name="position">1</property>
              <property name=
                "name">PRODUCTNAME
              </property>
              <property
                name="dataType">string
              </property>
            </structure>
            <structure>
              <property name="position">2</property>
              <property
                name="name">QUANTITYINSTOCK
              </property>
              <property
                name="dataType">integer
              </property>
            </structure>
            <structure>
              <property name="position">3</property>
              <property name="name">MSRP</property>
              <property name="dataType">float</property>
            </structure>
          </list-property>
        </structure>
        <property name="dataSource">Data Source</property>
        <property name="queryText">
          select CLASSICMODELS.PRODUCTS.PRODUCTNAME,
                 CLASSICMODELS.PRODUCTS.QUANTITYINSTOCK,
                 CLASSICMODELS.PRODUCTS.MSRP
          from CLASSICMODELS.PRODUCTS</property>
    </oda-data-set>
  </data-sets>
  <page-setup>
    <simple-master-page name="Simple MasterPage" id="4">
```

```
<page-footer>
   <text id="5">
      <property name="contentType">html</property>
      <text-property name="content">
         <![CDATA[<value-of>new Date()</value-of>]]>
      </text-property>
   </text>
</page-footer>
   </simple-master-page>
</page-setup>
<body>
   <table id="6">
      <property name="width">100%</property>
      <property name="dataSet">Data Set</property>
      <list-property name="boundDataColumns">
         <structure>
            <property name="name">PRODUCTNAME</property>
            <expression
               name="expression">dataSetRow["PRODUCTNAME"]
            </expression>
         </structure>
         <structure>
            <property
               name="name">QUANTITYINSTOCK
            </property>
            <expression
               name="expression">
               dataSetRow["QUANTITYINSTOCK"]
            </expression>
         </structure>
         <structure>
            <property name="name">MSRP</property>
            <expression
               name="expression">dataSetRow["MSRP"]
            </expression>
         </structure>
      </list-property>
      <column id="28"/>
      <column id="29"/>
      <column id="30"/>
      <header>
         <row id="7">
            <cell id="8">
               <property name="colSpan">3</property>
               <property name="rowSpan">1</property>
               <property name="textAlign">center</property>
                  <label id="9">
                     <property
                        name="fontSize">x-large
                     </property>
                     <property
                        name="fontWeight">bold
                     </property>
```

```xml
                <property
                   name="textAlign">center
                </property>
                <text-property
                   name="text">Report
                </text-property>
              </label>
            </cell>
          </row>
          <row id="10">
            <cell id="11">
              <label id="12">
                <text-property
                   name="text">PRODUCTNAME
                </text-property>
              </label>
            </cell>
            <cell id="13">
              <label id="14">
                <text-property
                   name="text">QUANTITYINSTOCK
                </text-property>
              </label>
            </cell>
            <cell id="15">
              <label id="16">
                <text-property
                   name="text">MSRP
                </text-property>
              </label>
            </cell>
          </row>
        </header>
        <detail>
          <row id="17">
            <cell id="18">
              <data id="19">
                <property
                   name="resultSetColumn">PRODUCTNAME
                </property>
              </data>
            </cell>
            <cell id="20">
              <data id="21">
                <property
                   name="resultSetColumn">QUANTITYINSTOCK
                </property>
              </data>
            </cell>
            <cell id="22">
              <data id="23">
                <property
                   name="resultSetColumn">MSRP
```

```
                </property>
              </data>
            </cell>
          </row>
        </detail>
        <footer>
          <row id="24">
            <cell id="25"/>
            <cell id="26"/>
            <cell id="27"/>
          </row>
        </footer>
      </table>
    </body>
  </report>
```

BIRT Report Engine can render a report design for output using a standard emitter extension or a customized emitter extension, such as this CSV rendering example.

19

Developing an ODA Extension

This chapter describes how to develop an ODA extension. BIRT uses the Eclipse Data Tools Platform (DTP) ODA API to build a driver that connects to a data source and retrieves data for a report. The API defines interfaces and classes that manage the following tasks:

- Connecting to a data source
- Preparing and executing a query
- Handling data and metadata in a result set
- Mapping between the object representation of data and the data source

Eclipse DTP also provides tools and support for SQL development, locales, logging, and other special types of processing. For more information about the Eclipse DTP project, see http://www.eclipse.org/datatools.

This chapter shows how to develop an ODA extension using examples that access the following data sources:

- CSV file

  Uses the source code from the DTP ODA flat file plug-in, org.eclipse.datatools.connectivity.oda.flatfile, as the template for the classes in the CSV ODA plug-in project. The DTP ODA interfaces are similar to a JDBC interface with extensions that support retrieving data from non-relational database sources.

- Relational database

  Uses Hibernate Core for Java, an object-oriented software system for generating SQL and handling JDBC result sets. Hibernate Query Language

(HQL) provides a SQL-transparent extension that makes the DTP ODA extension portable to all relational databases. Hibernate also supports developing a query in the native SQL dialect of a database.

Hibernate is free, open-source software licensed under the GNU Lesser General Public License (LGPL). For more information about Hibernate, see http://www.hibernate.org/.

Understanding an ODA extension

A BIRT report design specifies the type of data access and data transformations required to generate a report. All data comes from an external data source. The BIRT data engine supports the DTP ODA framework. The DTP ODA framework provides access to standard and custom data sources using an open API.

The ODA extension point makes it possible to create a plug-in driver to any external data source. BIRT adopts DTP ODA extension points for the report designer and report generation environments.

A DTP ODA extension adds a new data source driver to the BIRT framework by implementing the following extension points:

- ODA data source

  org.eclipse.datatools.connectivity.oda.dataSource supports the extension of BIRT design-time and run-time data source access. The XML schema file, org.eclipse.datatools.connectivity.oda/schema/dataSource.exsd, describes this extension point.

- ODA user interface

  org.eclipse.datatools.connectivity.oda.design.ui.dataSource supports optionally adding an integrated user interface for an ODA driver to BIRT Report Designer. The plug-in can provide user interface support that allows a user to specify the data source and edit the data set. The XML schema file, org.eclipse.datatools.connectivity.oda.design.ui/schema/dataSource.exsd, describes this extension point.

For more information on the DTP ODA APIs, see the Javadoc for the org.eclipse.datatools.connectivity.oda package hierarchy. The Javadoc is in the DTP Software Development Kit (SDK) available from the Eclipse Data Tools Platform project at http://www.eclipse.org/datatools.

Developing the CSV ODA driver extensions

You develop the CSV ODA extensions by performing the following tasks:

- Download the required BIRT source code from the Eclipse CVS repository.

- Create two new projects in the Eclipse PDE to implement the following plug-ins:

  - CSV ODA driver to access the data source

  - CSV ODA user interface (UI) to select the data file and available data columns in BIRT Report Designer

- Extend the source code in the CSV ODA plug-in projects by adding new functionality at the defined extension points.

- Test and deploy the extensions in the run-time environment.

You can download the source code for the CSV ODA driver extension examples at http://www.actuate.com/birt/contributions.

About the CSV ODA plug-ins

The CSV ODA extensions require the following two plug-ins:

- org.eclipse.birt.report.data.oda.csv

  The CSV ODA data source plug-in extends the functionality defined by the extension point, org.eclipse.datatools.connectivity.oda.dataSource, to create the CSV ODA driver. The first row of the CSV input file contains the column names. The remaining rows, separated by new line markers, contain the data fields, separated by commas. The org.eclipse.birt.report.data.oda.csv plug-in contains the database classes and data structures, such as data types, result set, metadata result set, and query used to handle data in a BIRT report.

  The org.eclipse.datatools.connectivity.oda.dataSource extension point is in the Eclipse DTP project and is part of the org.eclipse.datatools .connectivity.oda plug-in. This plug-in is available from the CVS repository in /home/datatools.

- org.eclipse.birt.report.data.csv.ui

  The CSV ODA UI plug-in extends the functionality defined by the org.eclipse.datatools.connectivity.connectionProfile, org.eclipse.ui .propertyPages, and org.eclipse.datatools.connectivity.oda.design.ui .dataSource extension points. The UI consists of the following two pages:

  - The data source page specifies and validates the path and name of the CSV file.

  - The data set page shows the selected data file and columns available in the file. By default, the UI selects all the columns in the data set.

Downloading BIRT source code from the CVS repository

The CSV ODA driver plug-in, org.eclipse.birt.report.data.oda.csv, requires the following Eclipse plug-ins:

- org.eclipse.core.runtime

- org.eclipse.datatools.connectivity.oda

The CSV ODA UI extension, org.eclipse.birt.report.data.csv.ui, requires the following Eclipse plug-ins:

- org.eclipse.core.runtime

- org.eclipse.ui

- org.eclipse.datatools.connectivity.oda.design.ui

- org.eclipse.birt.report.data.oda.csv

For the org.eclipse.birt.report.data.oda.csv plug-in, you extend only the Java classes in the org.eclipse.datatools.connectivity.oda plug-in. For the org.eclipse.birt.report.data.csv.ui plug-in, you extend the Java classes in the org.eclipse.datatools.connectivity.oda.design.ui plug-in.

Eclipse makes source code available to the developer community in the CVS repository. To compile, you do not need the source code for the plug-ins. You can configure the system to use the JAR files in the eclipse\plugins folder. To debug, you may need the source code for all the required BIRT and DTP plug-ins.

Implementing the CSV ODA driver plug-in

This section describes how to implement an ODA driver plug-in, using the CSV ODA driver plug-in as an example. To create an ODA driver plug-in, perform the following tasks:

- Create the ODA driver plug-in project.

- Define the dependencies.

- Specify the run-time archive.

- Declare the ODA extension points.

You can create the CSV ODA driver plug-in project, org.eclipse.birt.report .data.oda.csv, in the Eclipse PDE. This section describes how to create the plug-in project using the New Plug-in Project wizard.

How to create the CSV ODA driver plug-in project

1 From the Eclipse PDE menu, choose File➤New➤Plug-in Project.

2 On New Project—Select a wizard, select Plug-in Project. Choose Next. New Plug-in Project appears.

3 In Plug-in Project, modify the settings as shown in Table 19-1. Choose Next. Plug-in Content appears.

Table 19-1 Settings for Plug-in Project options

Section	Option	Value
Plug-in Project	Project name	org.eclipse.birt.report.data.oda.csv
	Use default location	Selected
	Location	Not available when you select Use default location
Project Settings	Create a Java project	Selected
	Source folder	src
	Output folder	bin
Target Platform	Eclipse version	3.2
	OSGi framework	Selected Equinox

4 In Plug-in Content, modify the settings as shown in Table 19-2. Choose Finish.

Table 19-2 Settings for Plug-in Content options

Section	Option	Value
Plug-in Properties	Plug-in ID	org.eclipse.birt.report.data.oda.csv
	Plug-in Version	1.0.0
	Plug-in Name	CSV ODA Driver
	Plug-in Provider	yourCompany.com or leave blank
	Classpath	csvODA.jar
Plug-in Options	Generate an activator, a Java class that controls the plug-in's life cycle	Selected
	Activator	org.eclipse.birt.report.data.oda.csv.CsvPlugin
	This plug-in will make contributions to the UI	Deselected
Rich Client Application	Would you like to create a rich client application?	No

Defining the dependencies for the CSV ODA driver extension

In this step, you specify the list of plug-ins that must be available on the classpath of the CSV ODA driver extension to compile and run.

How to specify the dependencies

1 On PDE Manifest Editor, choose Overview.

2 In Plug-in Content, choose Dependencies. In Required Plug-ins, choose Add. Plug-in Selection appears.

3 In Plug-in Selection, hold down CTRL and select the following plug-ins:

   - org.eclipse.core.runtime

   - org.eclipse.datatools.connectivity.oda

Choose OK. Dependencies appears, as shown in Figure 19-1.

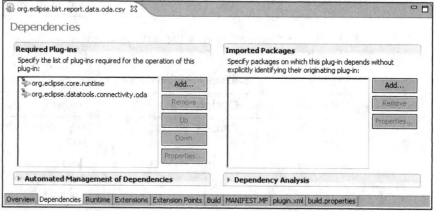

Figure 19-1   The Dependencies page

The order of the list determines the sequence in which a plug-in loads at run time. Use Up and Down to change the loading order as necessary. The CSV ODA driver extension does not require any changes to the loading order if you selected the required plug-ins in the order listed in step 3.

Specifying the run-time settings for the CSV ODA driver extension

On PDE Manifest Editor, choose Runtime. On Runtime, you specify exported package visibility and the libraries and folders on the plug-in classpath.

In Exported Packages, verify that the org.eclipse.birt.report.data.oda.csv package appears in the list. In Classpath, verify that the archive file you specified in the New Plug-in Project wizard, csvODA.jar, appears in the library list.

Declaring the ODA data source extension point

In this next step, you specify the extension point used to implement the CSV ODA driver extension and add the extension element details. The ODA data source extension point supports extending design-time and run-time data source access for an application. The extension must implement the ODA Java run-time interfaces defined in the org.eclipse.datatools.connectivity.oda plug-in.

The extension point, org.eclipse.datatools.connectivity.oda.dataSource, specifies the following properties that identify the extension in the run-time environment:

- ID

  Optional identifier of the extension instance

- Name

  Optional name of the extension instance

- Point

  Fully qualified identifier of the extension

The extension point requires you to define the following extension elements and extension element details for the CSV ODA driver:

- Datasource

  Defines an ODA data source extension type to use at design time and run time, containing the following elements and element details:

  - id

    Fully qualified identifier of an ODA data source extension.

  - driverClass

    Java class that implements the org.eclipse.datatools.connectivity.oda .IDriver interface. This interface provides the entry point for the ODA run-time driver extension.

  - odaVersion

    Version of the ODA interfaces. Specify version 3.0 for an ODA driver developed for BIRT release 2.1.

  - defaultDisplayName

    Display name of the ODA data source extension. The value can be localized using the plugin.properties mechanism. The default display name is the extension id.

  - setThreadContextClassLoader

    Indicates whether the consumer of the ODA run-time extension plug-in must set the thread context class loader before calling an ODA interface method. The OSGi class loader that loads the ODA run-time plug-in is not designed to load additional classes. To load additional classes, an ODA run-time plug-in must provide its own java.net.URLClassLoader object and switch the thread context class loader as required.

The dataSource element also specifies a property, HOME, containing the following extension element details:

- name

  Unique name of a property group.

- defaultDisplayName

  Default display name of a property group. The value can be localized using the plugin.properties mechanism. The default display name is the id.

- type

  Data type of the property.

- canInherit

  Flag indicating whether the property extension element can inherit properties.

- defaultValue

  Default value of the property extension element.

- isEncryptable

  Flag indicating whether the property is encrypted.

- dataSet

  Defines a type of data set supported by a dataSource extension, containing the following elements and element details:

  - id

    Required identifier of the ODA data set extension.

  - defaultDisplayName

    Display name of the ODA data set extension. The value can be localized using the plugin.properties mechanism. The default display name is the element id.

The dataSet element also specifies a complex data type, dataTypeMapping, which defines a sequence of data type mappings containing the following properties:

- nativeDataTypeCode

  Integer value that must match one of the data type codes returned in the implementation for the ODA driver interface.

- nativeDataType

  String value specifying the data source native data type.

- odaScalarDataType

  ODA scalar data type that maps to the native type. Supported ODA data types include Date, Double, Integer, String, Time, Timestamp, Decimal, BLOB, and CLOB.

How to specify the data source extension point

1 On PDE Manifest Editor, choose Extensions.

2 In All Extensions, choose Add. New Extension appears.

3 On New Extension—Extension Points, in the list of extension points, select the following plug-in:

```
org.eclipse.datatools.connectivity.oda.dataSource
```

New Extension—Extension Points appears as shown in Figure 19-2. Choose Finish.

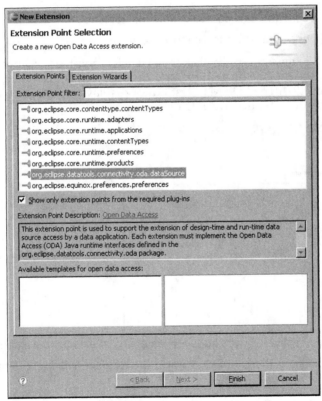

Figure 19-2   Selecting the dataSource extension point

Extensions appears as shown in Figure 19-3.

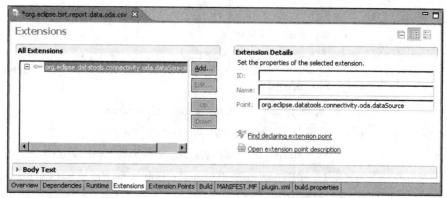

Figure 19-3   The dataSource extension point on Extensions page

All Extensions lists the extension point, org.eclipse.datatools.connectivity
.oda.dataSource. Extensions Details contains the list of extension details
specified in the XML schema file, dataSource.exsd.

How to specify the data source extension element

1   On PDE Manifest Editor, choose Extensions.

In All Extensions, right-click the extension point, org.eclipse.datatools
.connectivity.oda.dataSource, and choose New➤dataSource, as shown in
Figure 19-4. The PDE Manifest Editor displays org.eclipse.birt.report.data
.oda.csv.dataSource in All Extensions.

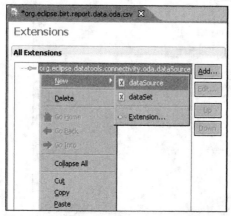

Figure 19-4   Choosing a new data source extension element

2   In Extension Element Details, add the extension element details for the
extension element, dataSource, as shown in Table 19-3.

Table 19-3 Property values for the dataSource extension element

Property	Value
id	org.eclipse.birt.report.data.oda.csv
driverClass	org.eclipse.birt.report.data.oda.csv.CSVFileDriver
odaVersion	3.0
defaultDisplayName	CSV Data Source
setThreadContextClassLoader	false

3 The property values for the dataSource extension element appear as shown in Figure 19-5.

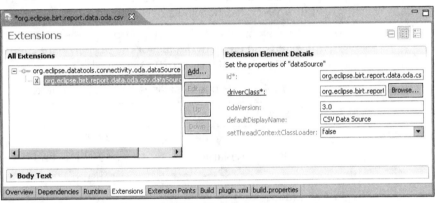

Figure 19-5 Property settings for the new extension element

4 Specify the extension element details for org.eclipse.datatools .connectivity.oda.dataSource by performing the following tasks:

1 In All Extensions, right-click the dataSource extension element and choose New→properties, as shown in Figure 19-6. PDE Manifest Editor displays properties in All Extensions.

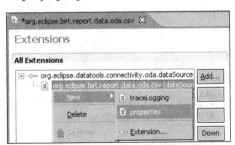

Figure 19-6 Choosing properties

2 Right-click properties and choose New→property, as shown in Figure 19-7. PDE Manifest Editor displays property in All Extensions.

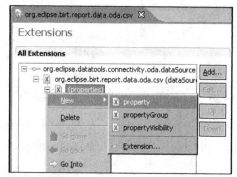

Figure 19-7   Choosing a new property

3 Add the element details for the property, as shown in Table 19-4. When the extension element details for the property are complete, All Extensions appears as shown in Figure 19-8.

Table 19-4   Property settings for HOME property

Property	Value
name	HOME
defaultDisplayName	CSV File Full Path
type	string
canInherit	true

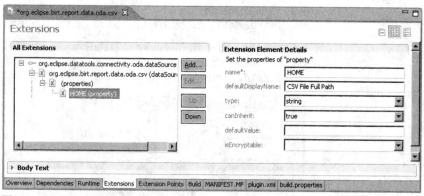

Figure 19-8   HOME property settings in Extensions

How to specify the data set extension

1 On PDE Manifest Editor, choose Extensions.

2 In All Extensions, right-click the extension point, org.eclipse.datatools .connectivity.oda.dataSource, and choose the extension element, New→dataSet, as shown in Figure 19-9.

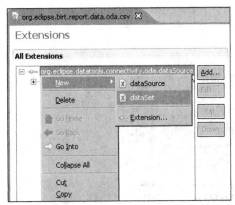

Figure 19-9   Choosing the dataSet extension

The Eclipse PDE displays org.eclipse.birt.report.data.oda.csv.dataSet in All Extensions. In Extension Element Details, add the details for the extension, dataSet, as shown in Table 19-5. Extensions appears as shown in Figure 19-10.

Table 19-5   Property values for the dataSet extension

Property	Value
id	org.eclipse.birt.report.data.oda.csv .dataSet
defaultDisplayName	CSV Data Set

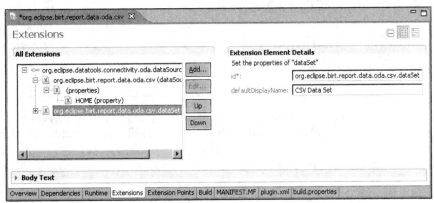

Figure 19-10   Property settings for dataSet, in Extensions

3 In All Extensions, right-click the extension point, org.eclipse.birt
.report.data.oda.csv.dataSet and choose New➔dataTypeMapping, as shown
in Figure 19-11.

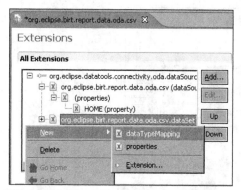

Figure 19-11   Choosing a new data type mapping

Repeat step 3 eight times to add more dataTypeMapping elements.

4 In Extension Element Details, add the extension element details for the list of
dataTypeMapping elements, as shown in Table 19-6.

Table 19-6   Settings for dataTypeMapping elements

nativeDataType	nativeDataTypeCode	odaScalarDataType
INTEGER	4	Integer
DOUBLE	8	Double
BIGDECIMAL	2	Decimal
STRING	12	String
DATE	91	Date
TIME	92	Time
TIMESTAMP	93	Timestamp
BLOB	2004	String
CLOB	2005	String

When the extension element details for all the dataTypeMappings are
complete, All Extensions appears as shown in Figure 19-12.

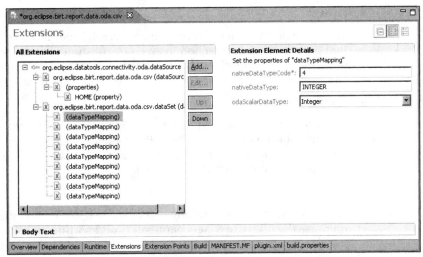

Figure 19-12   Data type mappings in All Extensions

PDE Manifest Editor automatically updates plugin.xml with extension element information.

Understanding the sample CSV ODA driver extension

BIRT Data Engine supports the Eclipse DTP ODA framework. The DTP ODA framework supports creating an extension that can plug any external data source into BIRT Report Engine.

The DTP ODA API specifies the interfaces for a run-time driver. BIRT Data Engine uses the data source and data set definitions in a report design to access the ODA run-time driver to execute a query and retrieve data.

The DTP ODA interfaces are similar to JDBC interfaces with extensions that support retrieving data from non-RDBMS sources. An extended ODA driver can implement these interfaces to wrap the API for another data source, such as a CSV file, to retrieve a result set containing data rows.

The CSV ODA driver extension described in this chapter is a simplified example that illustrates how to create an ODA plug-in using the Eclipse PDE. The following section describes the code-based extensions a developer must make to complete the development of the CSV ODA driver extension after defining the plug-in framework in the Eclipse PDE.

Implementing the DTP ODA interfaces

The ODA plug-in, org.eclipse.datatools.connectivity.oda, defines the run-time interfaces used to retrieve data from a data source. The CSV ODA driver extension implements the following interfaces in the ODA plug-in:

- IDriver

  The entry point to an ODA run-time driver. IDriver is the connection factory that generates the connection to an ODA run-time driver. An IDriver implementation provides the IConnection object used to establish a connection to a data source.

- IConnection

  The interface that establishes a connection to a data source. An IConnection implementation opens and closes the connection, returns an IQuery object for a data set, and optionally commits or rolls back all changes made since the last commit or rollback operation.

- IQuery

  The base interface for handling a query. The IQuery implementation prepares the query text, sets parameters and sorting specifications, executes the query, returns metadata for the result set, and closes the query.

- IResultSet

  The interface used to access the result set retrieved by an IQuery object. An IResultSet implementation opens and closes a cursor that points to the current data row, and moves the cursor forward to the next row, until there are no more rows or MaxRows limit is reached. Accessor methods get the value for specified columns in the current row as specific data types. A query can retrieve one or more IResultSet instances.

- IResultSetMetaData

  The interface that contains the metadata for an IResultSet object. An IResultSetMetaData implementation contains metadata describing each column in a result set, including the following information:

  - Column count in the result set
  - Display length
  - Label
  - Name
  - Data type
  - Precision
  - Scale
  - Permits null

- IDataSetMetaData

  An interface that describes the features and capabilities of a data set type, including the following attributes:

  - Indicates whether the data set type supports the following features:

- Input, output, or named parameters
- Named or multiple result sets
- Multiple open result sets
  - Provides the following information:
    - Version of the data source provider
    - Sort mode for columns, such as none, single, or multiple sort order
  - Returns references to the following components:
    - Data source connection
    - Collection of objects in the data source provider catalog
- IParameterMetaData

  An interface that provides information on the parameters defined in a prepared statement, including count, data type, precision, scale, or whether a parameter allows null.

- IAdvancedQuery

  An extended interface for a query that has complex input and output parameters or returns multiple result sets.

Understanding the CSV ODA extension package

The package for the CSV ODA extension example, org.eclipse.birt.report .data.oda.csv, uses the following classes to implement the ODA plug-in interfaces:

- CSVFileDriver

  Implements the IDriver interface. Instantiates the connection object for the CSV ODA driver and sets up the log configuration and application context.

- Connection

  Implements the IConnection interface. Opens and closes the connection to the CSV file and instantiates the IQuery object.

- CSVFileQuery

  Implements the IQuery interface. Handles the processing that performs the following operations:

  - Sets up the java.io.File object, containing the file and path names
  - Fetches the data rows from the data file, using the internal class, CSVBufferReader
  - Trims the column data, removing extraneous characters such as commas and quotes
  - Prepares the result set metadata, containing the table and column names

- ResultSet

  Implements the IResultSet interface. Handles the processing that transforms the String value for a column to the specified data type.

- ResultSetMetaData

  Implements the IResultSetMetaData interface. Describes the metadata for each column in the result set.

- DataSetMetaData

  Implements the IDataSetMetaData interface. Describes the features and capabilities of the data set.

- Messages

  Defines the exception messages for the CSV ODA driver.

- DataTypes

  Defines, validates, and returns the data types supported by the CSV ODA driver.

- CommonConstant

  Defines the constants used in the package, such as the driver name, ODA version, query keywords, and delimiters.

Understanding CSVFileDriver

The CSVFileDriver class instantiates the connection object for the CSV ODA driver and sets up the log configuration and application context. Listing 19-1 shows the getConnection( ) method.

Listing 19-1   The getConnection( ) method

```
public IConnection getConnection( String odaDataSourceId )
    throws OdaException
{
    return new Connection( );
}
```

Understanding CSVFileQuery

In the CSVFileQuery class, the constructor sets up the java.io.File object, containing the file and path names. The constructor allows the application to submit the home directory parameter, homeDir, as a file name as well as a path. CSVFileQuery( ) configures the data source property based on the value of the HOME property specified in the report design, as shown in Listing 19-2.

Listing 19-2   The Statement class

```
CSVFileQuery ( String homeDir, IConnection host )
    throws OdaException
```

```
{
   if ( homeDir == null || host == null )
      throw new OdaException(Messages.getString
         ("Common.ARGUMENT_CANNOT_BE_NULL"));
   File file = new File(homeDir);
   if (file.isDirectory( )
      this.homeDirectory = homeDir;
   else if (file.isFile( )
      this.homeDirectory = file.getParent( );
   this.connection = host;
}
```

The CSVFileQuery class prepares and executes a query, then retrieves the data. CSVFileQuery implements the following additional methods:

- prepare( ) performs the following operations:

    - Formats the query String, eliminating redundant spaces and converting all keywords to uppercase, by calling formatQueryText( )

    - Validates the query by calling validateQueryText( )

    - Prepares the metadata required for the execution of the query and retrieval of the query results by calling prepareMetaData( )

Listing 19-3 shows the prepare( ) method.

Listing 19-3   The prepare( ) method

```
public void prepare( String queryText ) throws OdaException
{
   validateOpenConnection( );
   String formattedQuery = formatQueryText( queryText );
   validateQueryText( formattedQuery );
   prepareMetaData( formattedQuery );
}
```

- prepareMetaData( ) acquires the following metadata:

  - Table name

  - Actual column names read from data file

  - Query column names, including prepared column names that use wildcards

  - Query data types

If the command column list contains a wild card, prepareMetaData( ) sets the array of command column names equal to the array of actual column names.

prepareMetaData( ) then instantiates and sets up the ResultSetMetaData object. Listing 19-4 shows the prepareMetaData( ) method.

Listing 19-4   The prepareMetaData( ) method

```
private void prepareMetaData( String queryText )
   throws OdaException
{
   String[ ] queryFragments =
      parsePreparedQueryText( queryText );
   String tableName =
      getPreparedTableNames( queryFragments );
   String[] allColumnNames =
      discoverActualColumnMetaData( tableName,
      NAME_LITERAL );
   String[ ] allColumnTypes = null;
   String[ ] queryColumnNames = null;
   String[ ] queryColumnTypes = null;
   if ( isWildCard
      ( getPreparedColumnNames( queryFragments ) ) )
   {
      queryColumnNames = allColumnNames;
      queryColumnTypes = allColumnTypes;
   }
   else
   {
      queryColumnNames =
         getPreparedColumnNames( queryFragments )
            .split( CommonConstants.DELIMITER_COMMA );
   }

   this.resultSetMetaData =
      new ResultSetMetaData( queryColumnNames,
         queryColumnTypes,
         getColumnLabels( queryFragments ) );
   this.currentTableName = tableName;
}
```

- executeQuery( ) performs the following operations:

  - Fetches the data from the file to a Vector object

  - Transfers the data from the Vector to a two-dimensional String array

  - Returns the data rows and metadata in a single ResultSet object

  Listing 19-5 shows the executeQuery( ) method.

Listing 19-5   The executeQuery( ) method

```
public IResultSet executeQuery( ) throws OdaException
{
   Vector v = fetchQueriedDataFromFileToVector( );
   String[ ][ ] rowSet =
      copyDataFromVectorToTwoDimensionArray( v );
```

```
      return new ResultSet( rowSet, this.resultSetMetaData );
   }
```

■ The internal class, CSVBufferReader, fetches the data rows from the data file. Listing 19-6 shows the readLine( ) method.

Listing 19-6   The readLine( ) method

```
public String readLine( ) throws IOException
{
   if ( isLastCharBuff( ) && needRefillCharBuff( ) )
      return null;
   if ( needRefillCharBuff( ) )
   {
      charBuffer = newACharBuff( );
      int close = reader.read( charBuffer );
      if ( close == -1 )
         return null;
      if ( close != CHARBUFFSIZE )
         this.eofInPosition = close;
      this.startingPosition = 0;
   }
   String candidate = "";
   int stopIn = CHARBUFFSIZE;
   if ( isLastCharBuff( ) )
   {
      stopIn = this.eofInPosition;
   }
   for ( int i = this.startingPosition; i < stopIn; i++ )
   {
      if ( this.charBuffer[i] == '\n' )
      {
         return readALine( candidate, stopIn, i );
      }
   }
   if ( isLastCharBuff( ) )
   {
      return readLastLine( candidate );
   }
   return readExtraContentOfALine( candidate );
}
```

Understanding ResultSet

The ResultSet class performs the following operations:

■ Provides the cursor processing that fetches forward into the buffered result set rows

■ Transforms the String value for a column to the specified data type

ResultSet implements the following methods:

- ResultSet( ), the constructor, sets up a two-dimensional array that contains the table data and metadata, as shown in Listing 19-7.

Listing 19-7   The ResultSet( ) constructor

```
ResultSet( String[ ][ ] sData, IResultSetMetaData rsmd )
{
    this.sourceData = sData;
    this.resultSetMetaData = rsmd;
}
```

- getRow( ) returns the cursor, indicating the position of the row in the result set, as shown in Listing 19-8.

Listing 19-8   The getRow( ) method

```
public int getRow( ) throws OdaException
{
    validateCursorState( );
    return this.cursor;
}
```

- next( ) increments the cursor to point to the next row, as shown in Listing 19-9.

Listing 19-9   The next( ) method

```
public boolean next( ) throws OdaException
{
    if ( (this.maxRows <= 0? false:cursor >=
        this.maxRows - 1) || cursor >=
        this.sourceData.length - 1 )
    {
        cursor = CURSOR_INITIAL_VALUE;
        return false;
    }
    cursor++;
    return true;
}
```

- getInt( ) returns the data type value for a column in the row at the column position specified in the result set, as shown in Listing 19-10.

Listing 19-10   The getInt( ) method

```
public int getInt( int index ) throws OdaException
{
    return stringToInt( getString( index ) );
}
```

- stringToInt( ) converts the String value of the column to the specified data type, as shown in Listing 19-11.

Listing 19-11   The stringToInt( ) method

```
private int stringToInt( String stringValue )
{
   if ( stringValue != null )
   {
      try
      {
         return new Integer( stringValue ).intValue( );
      }
      catch ( NumberFormatException e )
      {
         this.wasNull = true;
      }
   }
   return 0;
}
```

Understanding ResultSetMetaData

The ResultSetMetaData class describes the metadata for a column in the result set, including the following information:

- Column count in the result set
- Display length
- Label
- Name
- Data type
- Precision
- Scale
- Permits null

getColumnName( ) returns the column name for a column at the row, column position specified in the result set, as shown in Listing 19-12.

Listing 19-12   The getColumnName( ) method

```
public String getColumnName( int index ) throws OdaException
{
   validateColumnIndex( index );
   return this.columnName[index - 1].trim( );
}
```

Understanding DataSetMetaData

The DataSetMetaData class describes the features and capabilities of the data set, including:

- Indicating whether the data set supports multiple result sets
- Providing information about the sort mode for columns
- Returning a reference to the data source connection

getConnection( ) returns a reference to a data source connection, as shown in Listing 19-13.

Listing 19-13 The getConnection( ) method

```
public IConnection getConnection( ) throws OdaException
{
   return connection;
}
```

Understanding Messages

The Messages class defines the exception messages for the CSV ODA driver.

getString( ) returns a message from the resource bundle using the key value, as shown in Listing 19-14.

Listing 19-14 The getString( ) method

```
public static String getString(String key) {
   try {
   return RESOURCE_BUNDLE.getString(key);
   } catch (MissingResourceException e) {
      return '!' + key + '!';
   }
}
```

Understanding DataTypes

The DataTypes class defines, validates, and returns the data types supported by the CSV ODA driver. DataTypes sets up a map, correlating the names of data types with a specific integer value, as shown in Listing 19-15.

Listing 19-15 The DataTypes class

```
public final class DataTypes
{
   public static final int INT = Types.INTEGER;
   public static final int DOUBLE = Types.DOUBLE;
   public static final int STRING = Types.VARCHAR;
   . . .
   private static HashMap typeStringIntPair = new HashMap( );
```

```
static
{
   typeStringIntPair.put( "INT", new Integer( INT ) );
   typeStringIntPair.put( "DOUBLE", new Integer( DOUBLE ) );
   typeStringIntPair.put( "STRING", new Integer( STRING ) );
...
}
```

getTypeCode( ) returns the integer value for a type based on the type name parameter, as shown in Listing 19-16.

Listing 19-16   The getType( ) method

```
public static int getTypeCode( String typeName ) throws
   OdaException
{
   String preparedTypeName = typeName.trim( ).toUpperCase( );
   if ( typeStringIntPair.containsKey( preparedTypeName ) )
      return
         ( ( Integer ) typeStringIntPair
            .get( preparedTypeName ) ).intValue( );
   throw new OdaException( Messages.getString
      ( "DataTypes.TYPE_NAME_INVALID" ) + typeName );
}
```

Understanding CommonConstant

The CommonConstant class defines the constants used in the package, such as the driver name, ODA version, query keywords, and delimiters. Listing 19-17 shows these definitions.

Listing 19-17   The CommonConstant class

```
final class CommonConstant
{
   public static final String DELIMITER_COMMA = ",";
   public static final String DELIMITER_SPACE = " ";
   public static final String DELIMITER_DOUBLEQUOTE = "\"";
   public static final String KEYWORD_SELECT = "SELECT";
   public static final String KEYWORD_FROM = "FROM";
   public static final String KEYWORD_AS = "AS";
   public static final String KEYWORD_ASTERISK = "*";
   public static final String DRIVER_NAME =
      "ODA CSV FILE DRIVER";
   public static final int MaxConnections = 0;
   public static final int MaxStatements = 0;
   public static final String CONN_HOME_DIR_PROP = "HOME";
   public static final String CONN_DEFAULT_CHARSET = "UTF-8";
   public static final String PRODUCT_VERSION = "3.0";
}
```

Developing the CSV ODA UI extension

The data source extension point, org.eclipse.datatools.connectivity.oda.design
.ui.dataSource, supports adding a new data source to a user interface, such as
BIRT Report Designer. For each data source, the extension implements the
following optional components:

- A wizard for creating the data source

- A set of pages for editing the data source

- The list of data sets that the data source supports

For each data set, the extension implements the following optional components:

- A wizard for creating the data set

- A set of pages for editing the data set

The data source editor page must implement the extension point, org.eclipse.ui
.propertyPages, by extending the abstract class, org.eclipse.datatools
.connectivity.oda.design.ui.wizards.DataSourceEditorPage. The data set editor
page must implement the extension point, org.eclipse.ui.propertyPages, by
extending the abstract class, org.eclipse.datatools.connectivity.oda.design
.ui.wizards.DataSourceEditorPage. The ODA data source and data set UI
extensions extend these base classes to create customized property pages with
page control and other behavior.

This section describes how to implement a BIRT ODA UI plug-in, using the CSV
ODA driver plug-in as an example. To create an ODA driver plug-in, perform
the following tasks:

- Create the CSV ODA UI plug-in project.

- Define the dependencies.

- Specify the run-time archive.

- Declare the ODA UI extension points.

Creating the CSV ODA UI plug-in project

You can create the CSV ODA UI plug-in project, org.eclipse.birt.report.data
.oda.csv.ui, using the Eclipse PDE. The following section describes how to create
the plug-in project using the New Plug-in Project wizard.

How to create the CSV ODA UI plug-in project

1 From the Eclipse menu, choose File→New→Plug-in Project. New Project
   appears.

2 On New Project—Select a wizard, select Plug-in Project. Choose Next. New
   Plug-in Project appears.

3 In Plug-in Project, modify the settings as shown in Table 19-7. Choose Next. Plug-in Content appears.

Table 19-7   Settings for Plug-in Project options

Section	Option	Value
Plug-in Project	Project name	org.eclipse.birt.report .data.oda.csv.ui
	Use default location	Selected
	Location	Not available when you select Use default location
Project Settings	Create a Java project	Selected
	Source folder	src
	Output folder	bin
Target Platform	Eclipse version	3.2
	OSGi framework	Selected Equinox

4 In Plug-in Content, modify the settings as shown in Table 19-8. Choose Finish.

Table 19-8   Settings for Plug-in Content options

Section	Option	Value
Plug-in Properties	Plug-in ID	org.eclipse.birt.report .data.oda.csv.ui
	Plug-in Version	1.0.0
	Plug-in Name	%plugin.name
	Plug-in Provider	yourCompany.com or leave blank
	Classpath	csvOdaUI.jar
Plug-in Options	Generate an activator, a Java class that controls the plug-in's life cycle	Selected
	Activator	org.eclipse.birt.report.data .oda.csv.ui.UiPlugin
	This plug-in will make contributions to the UI	Selected
	This plug-in will make contributions to the UI	Deselected

(continues)

Table 19-8   Settings for Plug-in Content options *(continued)*

Section	Option	Value
Rich Client Application	Would you like to create a rich client application?	No

Defining the dependencies for the CSV ODA UI extension

In this step, you specify the list of plug-ins that must be available on the classpath of the CSV ODA UI extension to compile and run.

How to specify the dependencies

1 On PDE Manifest Editor, choose Overview.

2 In Plug-in Content, choose Dependencies.

3 In Required Plug-ins, choose Add. Plug-in Selection appears.

4 In Plug-in Selection, hold down CTRL and select the following plug-ins:

   ■ org.eclipse.core.runtime

   ■ org.eclipse.ui

   ■ org.eclipse.datatools.connectivity.oda.design.ui

   ■ org.eclipse.birt.report.data.oda.csv

Choose OK. Dependencies appears as shown in Figure 19-13.

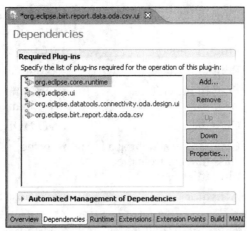

Figure 19-13   Selected plug-ins in Dependencies

The order of the list determines the sequence in which a plug-in loads at run time. Use Up or Down to change the loading order as necessary. The CSV ODA UI extension does not require any changes to the loading order, if you selected the required plug-ins in the order listed in step 4.

Specifying the run-time settings for the CSV ODA UI extension

On PDE Manifest Editor, choose Runtime. On Runtime, you specify exported package visibility and the libraries and folders on the plug-in classpath.

In Exported Packages, verify that the org.eclipse.birt.report.data.oda.csv.ui and org.eclipse.birt.report.data.oda.csv.ui.wizards packages appear in the list. In Classpath, verify that the archive file you specified in the New Plug-in Project wizard, csvODAui.jar, appears in the library list.

Declaring the ODA data source UI extension point

In this next step, you specify the extension points used to implement the CSV ODA UI extension and add the extension element details. The CSV ODA UI plug-in extends the functionality defined by the following extension points:

- org.eclipse.datatools.connectivity.connectionProfile

  Provides support for adding a connection profile

- org.eclipse.ui.propertyPages

  Adds a property page that displays the properties of an object in a dialog box

- org.eclipse.datatools.connectivity.oda.design.ui.dataSource

  Extends the ODA Designer UI framework to support creating a dialog page that allows a user to specify an ODA data source and a related data set

The extension points specify the following properties that identify the extensions in the run-time environment:

- ID

  Optional identifier of the extension instance

- Name

  Optional name of the extension instance

- Point

  Fully qualified identifier of the extension point

The connectionProfile extension point specifies the following extension elements:

- category

  Identifies the category. Supports grouping of connection profile types, such as related database connection profiles.

- connectionProfile

  Defines a connection profile type. Specifies properties such as id, display name, category, icon, connection factory, and property persistence.

- connectionFactory

  Defines a connection factory that creates a connection to a server using the properties stored in a connection profile.

- newWizard

  Defines a wizard that creates a connection profile.

The propertyPages extension point specifies the following extension elements:

- page

  Defines a property page. Specifies properties such as id, display name, category, icon, object class, and filter.

- filter

  Specifies an action filter that evaluates the attributes of each object in a current selection. If an object has the specified attribute state, a match occurs. Each object must implement the org.eclipse.ui.IActionFilter interface.

The dataSource extension point specifies the following extension elements:

- dataSourceUI

  Adds UI support for specifying an extended data source

- dataSetUI

  Adds UI support for specifying a data set from an extended data source

The dataSourceUI extension element requires you to define the following extension elements and details:

- id

  Fully qualified name of the data source, such as org.eclipse.birt.report .data.oda.csv. This name must be the same as the name for ODA extension driver.

- newDataSourceWizard

  Wizard class that allows a report developer to specify a data source in the UI. This class must use or extend org.eclipse.datatools.connectivity.oda.design .ui.wizards.NewDataSourceWizard.

The dataSetUI extension element requires you to define the following extension elements and details:

- id

  Fully qualified name of the data set, such as org.eclipse.birt.report.data .oda.csv.dataSet. This name must be the same as the name for the ODA extension driver data set.

- dataSetWizard

  Wizard class that allows a report developer to specify a data set in the BIRT Report Designer UI. This class must use or extend org.eclipse.datatools .connectivity.oda.design.ui.wizards.DataSetWizard.

- dataSetPage

  Specifies an editor page to add to the editor dialog for a data set. The data set UI adds editor pages to a dialog in the order the pages are defined. This class must use or extend org.eclipse.datatools.connectivity.oda.design.ui.wizards .DataSetWizardPage.

How to specify the CSV ODA UI extension points

1 On the PDE Manifest Editor, choose Extensions.

2 In All Extensions, choose Add. New Extension appears.

3 On New Extension—Extension Points, in the list of extension points, select the following plug-in:

```
org.eclipse.datatools.connectivity.connectionProfile
```

Choose Finish.

4 Repeat steps 2 and 3 to add the following extension points to the list to the Extensions page:

- org.eclipse.ui.propertyPages

- org.eclipse.datatools.connectivity.oda.design.ui.dataSource

Figure 19-14 shows the list of extension points required for the CSV ODA UI extension example.

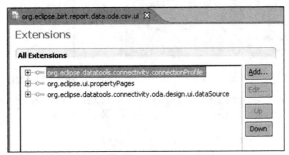

Figure 19-14   Required extension points for the CSV ODA UI extension

How to add the extension details

1 In All Extensions, select org.eclipse.datatools.connectivity.connectionProfile.

2 In Extension Details, to specify point property value for connectionProfile, type:

```
org.eclipse.datatools.connectivity.connectionProfile
```

3 In All Extensions, select org.eclipse.ui.propertyPages.

4 In Extension Details, to specify the point property value for propertyPages, type:

```
org.eclipse.ui.propertyPages
```

5 In All Extensions, select org.eclipse.datatools.connectivity.oda.design.ui .dataSource.

6 In Extension Details, to specify the point property value for dataSource, type:

```
org.eclipse.datatools.connectivity.oda.design.ui.dataSource
```

Leave the values for ID and Name properties blank for these three extension points blank.

How to specify the connectionProfile extension elements

1 In All Extensions, right-click the extension point, org.eclipse.datatools .connectivity.connectionProfile, and choose New→category, as shown in Figure 19-15. The Eclipse PDE displays category in All Extensions.

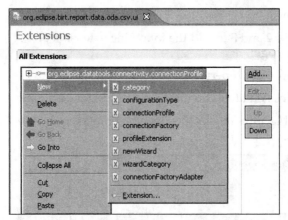

Figure 19-15 Choosing a connectionProfile extension element

2 In Extension Element Details, specify the extension element details for the extension element, category, as shown in Table 19-9.

Table 19-9 Property settings for category

Property	Value
id	%oda.data.source.id
parentCategory	%oda.parent.category.id
name	%oda.data.source.name

3 Add the following additional extension elements to the connectionProfile extension point on the Extensions page:

- connectionProfile
- connectionFactory
- newWizard

1 To add the connectionProfile properties, in All Extensions, right-click the extension point, org.eclipse.datatools.connectivity.connectionProfile, and choose New➤connectionProfile. In Extension Element Details, specify the extension element details for connectionProfile, as shown in Table 19-10.

Table 19-10   Property settings for connectionProfile

Property	Value
id	%oda.data.source.id
category	%oda.data.source.id
name	%connection.profile.name
icon	icons/file.gif
pingFactory	org.eclipse.datatools.connectivity.oda.profile .OdaConnectionFactory

2 To add the connectionFactory properties, in All Extensions, right-click the extension point, org.eclipse.datatools.connectivity.connectionProfile, and choose New➤connectionFactory. In Extension Element Details, specify the extension element details for connectionFactory, as shown in Table 19-11.

Table 19-11   Property settings for connectionFactory

Property	Value
id	org.eclipse.datatools.connectivity.oda .IConnection
class	org.eclipse.datatools.connectivity.oda.profile .OdaConnectionFactory
profile	%oda.data.source.id
name	%oda.connection.factory.name

3 To add the newWizard properties, in All Extensions, right-click the extension point, org.eclipse.datatools.connectivity.connectionProfile, and choose New➤newWizard. In Extension Element Details, specify the extension element details for newWizard, as shown in Table 19-12.

Table 19-12   Property settings for newWizard

Property	Value
id	%oda.data.source.id
name	%newwizard.name
class	org.eclipse.datatools.connectivity.oda.design.ui .wizards.NewDataSourceWizard
profile	%oda.data.source.id
icon	icons/fieldlist.ico
description	%newwizard.description

Figure 19-16 shows the complete list of extension points and extension elements required for the connectionProfile extension.

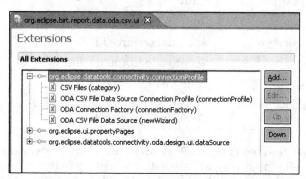

Figure 19-16   connectionProfile extension points and elements

How to specify the propertyPages extension elements

1 In All Extensions, right-click the extension point, org.eclipse.ui.propertyPages, and choose New➤page, as shown in Figure 19-17. The Eclipse PDE displays page in All Extensions.

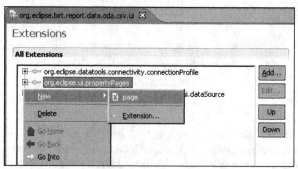

Figure 19-17   Choosing a propertyPages extension element

2 In Extension Element Details, specify the extension element details for page, as shown in Table 19-13.

Table 19-13   Property settings for page

Property	Value
id	%oda.data.source.id
name	%profile.propertypage.name
class	org.eclipse.datatools.connectivity.oda.design.ui.pages .impl.DefaultDataSourcePropertyPage
objectClass	org.eclipse.datatools.connectivity.IConnectionProfile

3 In All Extensions, right-click the extension element, page, and choose New➤filter, as shown in Figure 19-18. The Eclipse PDE displays filter in All Extensions.

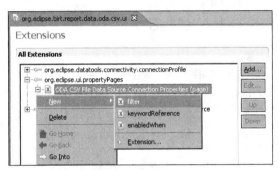

Figure 19-18   Choosing a filter extension element

4 In Extension Element Details, specify the extension element details for filter, as shown in Table 19-14.

Table 19-14   Property settings for filter

Property	Value
name	org.eclipse.datatools.profile.property.id
value	%oda.data.source.id

Figure 19-19 shows the complete list of extension points and extension elements required for the propertyPages extension.

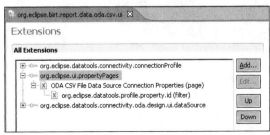

Figure 19-19   propertyPages extension points and elements

How to specify the dataSource extension elements

1 In All Extensions, right-click the extension point, org.eclipse.datatools
.connectivity.oda.design.ui.dataSource, and choose New➤dataSourceUI, as
shown in Figure 19-20. The Eclipse PDE displays dataSourceUI in All
Extensions.

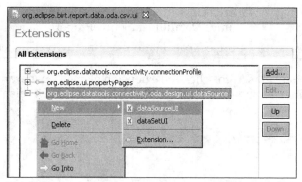

Figure 19-20   Choosing a dataSourceUI extension element

2 In Extension Element Details, specify the extension element details for
dataSourceUI, as shown in Table 19-15.

Table 19-15   Property setting for dataSourceUI

Property	Value
id	%oda.data.source.id

3 In All Extensions, right-click the extension element, dataSourceUI, and
choose New➤newDataSourceWizard, as shown in Figure 19-21. The Eclipse
PDE displays newDataSourceWizard in All Extensions.

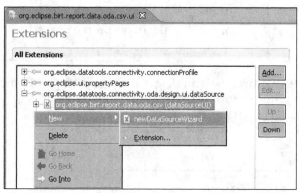

Figure 19-21   Choosing a newDataSourceWizard extension element

4 In Extension Element Details, specify the extension element details for newDataSourceWizard, as shown in Table 19-16.

Table 19-16 Property settings for newDataSourceWizard

Property	Value
pageClass	org.eclipse.datatools.connectivity.oda.design.ui.pages .impl.DefaultDataSourceWizardPage
windowTitle	%wizard.window.title
includes Progress Monitor	false
pageTitle	%datasource.selectfile

5 In All Extensions, right-click the extension point, org.eclipse.datatools .connectivity.oda.design.ui.dataSource, and choose New→dataSetUI, as shown in Figure 19-22. The Eclipse PDE displays dataSetUI in All Extensions.

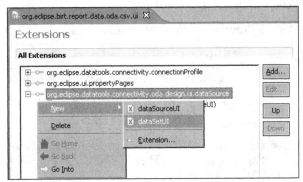

Figure 19-22 Choosing a dataSetUI extension element

6 In Extension Element Details, specify the extension element details for dataSetUI, as shown in Table 19-17.

Table 19-17 Property settings for dataSetUI

Property	Value
id	org.eclipse.birt.report.data.oda.csv.dataSet
initialPageId	oda.csv.ui.tablePage
supportsIn Parameters	false
supportsOut Parameters	false

7 In All Extensions, right-click the extension element, dataSetUI, and choose New→dataSetWizard, as shown in Figure 19-23. The Eclipse PDE displays dataSetWizard in All Extensions.

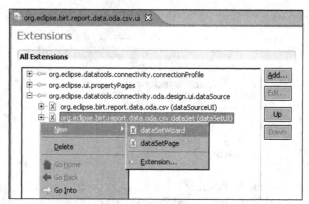

Figure 19-23   Choosing a dataSetWizard extension element

8 In Extension Element Details, specify the extension element details for dataSetWizard, as shown in Table 19-18.

Table 19-18   Property settings for dataSetWizard

Property	Value
class	org.eclipse.datatools.connectivity.oda.design.ui.wizards .DataSetWizard
windowTitle	%dataset.selectcolumns

9 In All Extensions, right-click the extension element, dataSetUI, and choose New→dataSetPage, as shown in Figure 19-24. The Eclipse PDE displays dataSetPage in All Extensions.

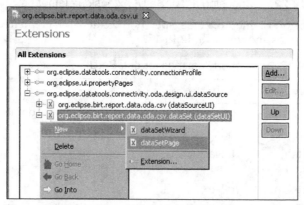

Figure 19-24   Choosing a dataSetPage extension element

10 In Extension Element Details, specify the extension element details for the extension element, dataSetPage, as shown in Table 19-19.

Table 19-19   Property settings for dataSetPage

Property	Value
id	oda.csv.ui.tablePage
wizardPage Class	org.eclipse.birt.report.data.oda.csv.ui.wizards .FileSelectionWizardPage
displayName	%dataset.selectcolumns
path	/
icon	icons/file.gif

Figure 19-25 shows the complete list of extension points and extension elements required for the org.eclipse.datatools.connectivity.oda.design .ui.dataSource extension point.

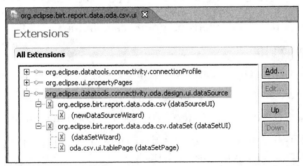

Figure 19-25   dataSource extension points and elements

PDE Manifest Editor automatically updates plugin.xml with the extension element information.

Understanding the sample CSV ODA UI extension

The CSV ODA UI extension described in this chapter illustrates how to create an ODA UI plug-in using the Eclipse PDE. The following section describes the code-based extensions a developer must make to complete the development of the CSV ODA UI extension, after defining the plug-in framework in the Eclipse PDE.

The CSV ODA UI plug-in contains the following packages:

■ org.eclipse.birt.report.data.oda.csv.ui

Contains the following files:

- UiPlugin class is automatically generated by the PDE Manifest Editor when you create the plug-in project.

- Messages class and the properties file, messages.properties, generate the messages displayed in the UI. The localized versions for these messages are in files, using the following naming syntax:

  ```
  messages_<locale>.msg
  ```

- org.eclipse.birt.report.data.oda.csv.ui.wizards

  The wizards package contains the classes that create the user interface pages used to choose a data source and data set in BIRT Report Designer. For more details about these classes, see "Understanding the org.eclipse.birt .report.data.oda.csv.ui.wizards package," later in this chapter.

Implementing the ODA data source and data set wizards

In BIRT release 2.1, BIRT Report Designer adopted the Eclipse Data Tools Platform (DTP) ODA design-time framework. The DTP ODA framework defines two of the three extension points used in the CSV ODA UI plug-in:

- Connection profile

  Defined in org.eclipse.datatools.connectivity.connectionProfile

- Data source and data set wizards

  Defined in org.eclipse.datatools.connectivity.oda.design.ui.dataSource

The CSV ODA UI plug-in also uses the extension point for property pages defined in org.eclipse.ui.propertyPages.

The CSV ODA UI plug-in uses the following classes in the org.eclipse.datatools .connectivity.oda.design.ui.wizards package to create the wizards that specify the data source and data set pages. An ODA UI plug-in must extend these classes to provide the wizard pages with page control and related behavior:

- DataSourceEditorPage

  The abstract base class that provides the framework for implementing an ODA data source property page

- DataSourceWizardPage

  The abstract base class that provides the framework for implementing an ODA data source wizard page

- DataSetWizardPage

  The abstract base class that provides the framework for implementing an ODA data set wizard page

The CSV ODA UI plug-in must also implement the org.eclipse.ui.propertyPages extension point. The propertyPages extension point requires a class attribute

specifying the fully qualified name of the class that implements org.eclipse.ui
.IWorkbenchPropertyPage.

Understanding the org.eclipse.birt.report.data.oda .csv.ui.wizards package

The org.eclipse.birt.report.data.oda.csv.ui.wizards package in the CSV ODA UI
extension example implements the following classes:

- Constants

  Defines the constants for the data source connection properties defined in
  org.eclipse.birt.report.data.oda.csv.

- CSVFilePropertyPage

  Extends DataSourceEditorPage. This class creates and initializes the editor
  controls for the property page used to specify the ODA data source. The class
  updates the connection profile properties with the values collected from the
  page.

- CSVFileSelectionPageHelper

  Specifies the page layout and sets up the control that listens for user input
  and verifies the location of the CSV data source file.

- CSVFileSelectionWizardPage

  Extends DataSourceWizardPage. This class creates and initializes the
  controls for the data source wizard page. The class sets the select file message
  and collects the property values.

- FileSelectionWizardPage

  Extends DataSetWizardPage. This class creates and initializes the controls for
  the data set wizard page and specifies the page layout. The class connects to
  the data source, executes a query, retrieves the metadata and result set, and
  updates the date-set design.

Understanding Constants

The Constants class defines the following variables for the data source
connection properties defined in org.eclipse.birt.report.data.oda.csv:

- ODAHOME specifies the CSV ODA file path constant, HOME.

- ODA_DEFAULT_CHARSET specifies the default character set as 8-bit
  Unicode Transformation Format (UTF-8).

Listing 19-18 shows the code for the Constants class.

Listing 19-18 The Constants class

```
public class Constants {
```

```
public static String ODAHOME="HOME";
public static String ODA_DEFAULT_CHARSET = "UTF-8";
}
```

Understanding CSVFilePropertyPage

CSVFilePropertyPage extends the DataSourceEditorPage class, implementing
the following methods to provide page editing functionality for the CSV ODA
data source property page:

- createAndInitCustomControl( ) method performs the following tasks:

  - Instantiates a CSVFileSelectionPageHelper object

  - Specifies the page layout and sets up the editing control by calling
    CSVFileSelectionPageHelper.createCustomControl( ) method

Listing 19-19 shows the code for the createAndInitCustomControl( ) method.

Listing 19-19   The createAndInitCustomControl( ) method

```
protected void createAndInitCustomControl
  ( Composite parent, Properties profileProps )
{
  if( m_pageHelper == null )
    m_pageHelper =
      new CSVFileSelectionPageHelper( this );
  m_pageHelper.createCustomControl( parent );
  m_pageHelper.initCustomControl( profileProps );
  if( ! isSessionEditable( ) )
    getControl( ).setEnabled( false );
}
```

- collectCustomProperties( ) updates the connection profile properties with
  the values collected from the page by calling CSVFileSelectionPageHelper
  .collectCustomProperties( ) method, as shown in Listing 19-20.

Listing 19-20   The collectCustomProperties( ) method

```
public Properties collectCustomProperties
  ( Properties profileProps )
{
  if( m_pageHelper == null )
    return profileProps;
  return m_pageHelper.collectCustomProperties
    ( profileProps );
}
```

Understanding CSVFileSelectionPageHelper

CSVFileSelectionPageHelper provides auxiliary processing for the
CSVFilePropertyPage and CSVFileSelectionWizardPage classes.
CSVFileSelectionPageHelper implements the following methods:

- createCustomControl( ) performs the following tasks:
  - Sets up the composite page layout
  - Calls the setupFileLocation( ) method that sets up a control to listen for user input and verify the location of the CSV data source file

Listing 19-21 shows the code for the createCustomControl( ) method.

Listing 19-21   The createCustomControl( ) method

```
void createCustomControl( Composite parent )
{
    Composite content = new Composite( parent, SWT.NULL );
    GridLayout layout = new GridLayout( 2, false );
    content.setLayout(layout);
    setupFileLocation( content );
}
```

- setupFileLocation( ) performs the following tasks:
  - Sets up the label and the grid data object in the page layout
  - Sets up the control that listens for user input and verifies the location of the CSV data source file

Listing 19-22 shows the code for the setupFileLocation( ) method.

Listing 19-22   The setupFileLocation( ) method

```
private void setupFileLocation( Composite composite )
{
    Label label = new Label( composite, SWT.NONE );
    label.setText( Messages.getString
        ( "label.selectFile" ) );
    GridData data = new GridData( GridData.FILL_HORIZONTAL );
    fileName = new Text( composite, SWT.BORDER );
    fileName.setLayoutData( data );
    setPageComplete( false );
    fileName.addModifyListener
        ( new ModifyListener( )
            {
                public void modifyText( ModifyEvent e )
                {
                    verifyFileLocation();
                }
            } );
}
```

- collectCustomProperties( ) sets the data source directory property in the connection profile, as shown in Listing 19-23.

Listing 19-23 The collectCustomProperties( ) method

```
Properties collectCustomProperties( Properties props )
{
   if( props == null )
     props = new Properties( );
     props.setProperty( CommonConstants.CONN_HOME_DIR_PROP,
       getFolderLocation( ) );
   return props;
}
```

- initCustomControl( ) initializes the data source wizard control to the location of the data source file, as shown in Listing 19-24.

Listing 19-24 The initCustomControl( ) method

```
void initCustomControl( Properties profileProps )
{
   if( profileProps == null || profileProps.isEmpty() ||
     fileName == null )
   return;
   String folderPath = profileProps.getProperty
     ( CommonConstants.CONN_HOME_DIR_PROP );
   if( folderPath == null )
     folderPath = EMPTY_STRING;
     fileName.setText( folderPath );
     verifyFileLocation( );
}
```

Understanding CSVFileSelectionWizardPage

The CSVFileSelectionWizardPage class extends the DataSourceWizardPage class, implementing the following methods to provide the functionality for the CSV ODA data source wizard page:

- The createPageCustomControl( ) method performs the following tasks:

  - Instantiates a CSVFileSelectionPageHelper object

  - Specifies the page layout and sets up the wizard page control by calling CSVFileSelectionPageHelper.createCustomControl( ) method

  - Calls CSVFileSelectionPageHelper.initCustomControl( ) to initialize the control to the location of the data source file

Listing 19-25 shows the code for the createPageCustomControl( ) method.

Listing 19-25 The createPageCustomControl( ) method

```
public void createPageCustomControl( Composite parent )
{
```

```
                if( m_pageHelper == null )
                    m_pageHelper =
                        new CSVFileSelectionPageHelper( this );
                m_pageHelper.createCustomControl( parent );
                m_pageHelper.initCustomControl( m_csvFileProperties );
            }
```

■ The collectCustomProperties( ) method instantiates a Properties object to
contain the CSV data source properties information, as shown in
Listing 19-26.

Listing 19-26   The collectCustomProperties( ) method

```
public Properties collectCustomProperties( )
{
    if( m_pageHelper != null )
        return m_pageHelper.collectCustomProperties
            ( m_csvFileProperties );
    return ( m_csvFileProperties != null ) ?
        m_csvFileProperties : new Properties( );
}
```

Understanding FileSelectionWizardPage

The FileSelectionWizardPage class extends the DataSetWizardPage class,
implementing the following methods to provide the functionality for the CSV
ODA data set wizard page:

■ The createPageControl( ) method performs the following tasks:

    ■ Specifies the page layout and sets up the wizard page control

    ■ Gets the data source properties

    ■ Calls populateAvailableList( ) to update the data set design

Listing 19-27 shows the code for the createPageControl( ) method.

Listing 19-27   The createPageControl( ) method

```
private Control createPageControl( Composite parent )
{
    Composite composite = new Composite( parent, SWT.NULL );
    FormLayout layout = new FormLayout( );
    composite.setLayout( layout );
    FormData data = new FormData( );
    data.left = new FormAttachment( 0, 5 );
    data.top = new FormAttachment( 0, 5 );
    fileName = new Text( composite, SWT.BORDER );
    fileName.setLayoutData( data );
    Properties dataSourceProps =
    getInitializationDesign( ).getDataSourceDesign( )
        .getPublicProperties( );
    fileName.setText( ( String )
```

```
        ( dataSourceProps.getProperty( Constants.ODAHOME )));
    data = new FormData();
    data.top = new FormAttachment
        ( fileName, 10, SWT.BOTTOM );
    data.left = new FormAttachment( 0, 5 );
    data.right = new FormAttachment( 47, -5 );
    data.bottom = new FormAttachment( 100, -5 );
    data.width = DEFAULT_WIDTH;
    data.height = DEFAULT_HEIGHT;
    m_availableList = new List( composite,
        SWT.MULTI | SWT.BORDER |
        SWT.H_SCROLL | SWT.V_SCROLL );
    m_availableList.setLayoutData( data );
    m_selectedFile =
        new File(( String )
        (dataSourceProps.getProperty( Constants.ODAHOME )));
    populateAvailableList( );
    return composite;
}
```

- getQuery( ) method builds the query for the data set by performing the following tasks:

  - Gets the table name from the file object

  - Appends the table name to a query that selects all the columns using a wildcard

  - Appends the column list then the table name to a query that selects specific columns

  - Returns the query text

Listing 19-28 shows the code for the getQuery( ) method.

Listing 19-28   The getQuery( ) method

```
private String getQuery( )
{
    String tableName = null;
    StringBuffer buf = new StringBuffer( );
    File file = m_selectedFile;
    if(file != null)
    {
        tableName = file.getName( );
    }
    if(tableName != null)
    {
        if(m_availableList.getItemCount( ) == 0)
        {
            buf.append("select * from ").append(tableName);
        }
        else
```

```
      {
         buf.append("select ");
         String[ ] columns = m_availableList.getItems();
         for(int n = 0; n < columns.length; n++)
         {
            buf.append(columns[n]);
            if(n < columns.length - 1)
            {
               buf.append(", ");
            }
         }
         buf.append(" from ").append(tableName);
      }
   }
   return buf.toString( );
   }
```

- getQueryColumnNames( ) method performs the following tasks:

  - Instantiates the CSVFileDriver

  - Prepares the query and gets the results set metadata using the CSV ODA
    run-time driver and data source connection properties settings

  - Gets the column count

  - Iterates through the metadata results to get the column names and return
    the results

Listing 19-29 shows the code for the getQueryColumnNames( ) method.

Listing 19-29   The getQueryColumnNames( ) method

```
private String[ ] getQueryColumnNames
   ( String queryText, File file )
{
   IDriver ffDriver = new CSVFileDriver( );
   IConnection conn = null;
   try
   {
      conn = ffDriver.getConnection( null );
      IResultSetMetaData metadata =
            getResultSetMetaData( queryText, file, conn );
      int columnCount = metadata.getColumnCount( );
      if( columnCount == 0 )
         return null;
      String[ ] result = new String[columnCount];
      for( int i = 0; i < columnCount; i++ )
         result[i] = metadata.getColumnName( i + 1 );
      return result;
   }
   catch( OdaException e )
   {
      setMessage( e.getLocalizedMessage( ), ERROR );
      disableAll( );
```

```
        return null;
    }
    finally
    {
        closeConnection( conn );
    }
}
```

- getResultSetMetaData( ) method performs the following tasks:

  - Sets up the Properties object with the location of the data source file

  - Opens the connection to the data source

  - Sets up a Query object and prepares the query text

  - Executes the query

  - Returns the metadata

Listing 19-30 shows the code for the getResultSetMetaData( ) method.

Listing 19-30   The getResultSetMetaData( ) method

```
private IResultSetMetaData getResultSetMetaData
    ( String queryText, File file, IConnection conn )
    throws OdaException
{
    java.util.Properties prop = new java.util.Properties( );
    prop.put( CommonConstants.CONN_HOME_DIR_PROP,
            file.getParent( ) );
    conn.open( prop );
    IQuery query = conn.newQuery( null );
    query.setMaxRows( 1 );
    query.prepare( queryText );
    query.executeQuery( );
    return query.getMetaData( );
}
```

- setResultSetMetaData( ) method updates the data set page design with
  metadata returned by the query by performing the following tasks:

  - Calls the DesignSessionUtil.toResultSetColumnsDesign( ) method to
    convert the run-time metadata to a design-time ResultSetColumns object

  - Obtains a ResultSetDefinition object from the design factory to use in
    populating the data set page design with the metadata definitions

  - Calls the resultSetDefn.setResultSetColumns( ) method to set the
    reference to ResultSetColumns object, containing the metadata content

  - Assigns the result set definition to the data set design

Listing 19-31 shows the code for the setResultSetMetaData( ) method.

Listing 19-31 The setResultSetMetaData( ) method

```
private void setResultSetMetaData
   ( DataSetDesign dataSetDesign, IResultSetMetaData md )
   throws OdaException
{
   ResultSetColumns columns =
      DesignSessionUtil.toResultSetColumnsDesign( md );
   ResultSetDefinition resultSetDefn =
      DesignFactory.eINSTANCE.createResultSetDefinition();
   resultSetDefn.setResultSetColumns( columns );
   dataSetDesign.setPrimaryResultSet( resultSetDefn );
   dataSetDesign.getResultSets().setDerivedMetaData( true );
}
```

- savePage( ) method performs the following tasks:

  - Instantiates the CSVFileDriver

  - Gets the result set metadata

  - Updates the data set design with the metadata

  - Closes the connection

Listing 19-32 shows the code for the savePage( ) method.

Listing 19-32 The savePage( ) method

```
private void savePage( DataSetDesign dataSetDesign )
{
   String queryText = getQuery( );
   dataSetDesign.setQueryText( queryText );
   IConnection conn = null;
   try
   {
      IDriver ffDriver = new CSVFileDriver();
      conn = ffDriver.getConnection( null );
      IResultSetMetaData metadata =
         getResultSetMetaData( queryText, m_selectedFile,
         conn );
      setResultSetMetaData( dataSetDesign, metadata );
   }
   catch( OdaException e )
   {
      dataSetDesign.setResultSets( null );
   }
   finally
   {
      closeConnection( conn );
   }
}
```

Testing the CSV ODA UI plug-in

On PDE Manifest Editor, in Overview, the Testing section contains links to launch a plug-in as a separate Eclipse application in either Run or Debug mode.

How to launch the CSV report rendering plug-in

1 On the Eclipse PDE Manifest Editor, in the Testing section of Overview, choose Launch an Eclipse application. The Eclipse PDE launches a run-time instance of the workbench.

2 In the run-time instance of the Eclipse PDE workbench, choose Window→Open Perspective→Other. Select Perspective appears.

3 In Select Perspective, select Report Design. Choose OK. Report Design appears.

How to create a report design

1 In Report Design, choose File→New→Project.

2 Expand Business Intelligence and Reporting Tools and choose Report Project. Choose Next. New Report Project appears.

3 In Report Project, perform the following tasks:

1 In Project name, type:

```
CSV_ODA_Reports
```

In Project contents, select Use default location. Choose Finish. In Navigator, CSV_ODA_Reports appears.

4 In Navigator, right-click CSV_ODA_Reports and choose File→New→Report. New Report appears.

5 On New Report, perform the following tasks:

1 In Enter or select the parent folder, select CSV_ODA_Reports.

2 In file name, type:

```
new_report_1.rptdesign
```

Choose Next.

3 In Report Templates, select Blank Report. Choose Finish. In Navigator, new_report_1.rptdesign appears in the CSV_ODA_Reports project folder.

6 Right-click new_report_1.rptdesign and choose Open. new_report_1.rptdesign appears in Report Design, as shown in Figure 19-26.

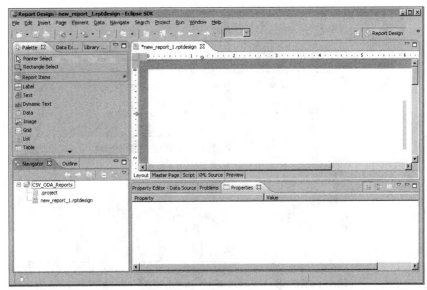

Figure 19-26   new_report_1.rptdesign in the report design environment

How to specify a data source

1   In Data Explorer, right-click Data Sources and choose New Data Source, as shown in Figure 19-27. New Data Source appears.

Figure 19-27   Choosing New Data Source

2 On New Data Source, choose CSV Data Source, as shown in Figure 19-28. Choose Next. Select File appears.

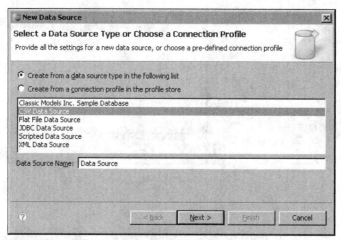

Figure 19-28 Choosing CSV Data Source

3 In Select File, enter the path and file name of the directory that contains the CSV data source file, as shown in Figure 19-29. Choose Finish. Report Design appears.

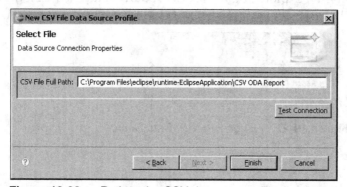

Figure 19-29 Path to the CSV data source file directory

How to select a new data set

1 In Report Design, choose Data→New Data Set. New Data Set appears, as shown in Figure 19-30. Choose Next. Select Columns appears.

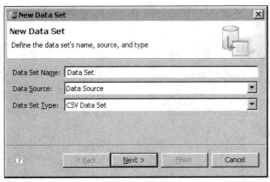

Figure 19-30   New Data Set

2   On Select Columns, select all the columns, as shown in Figure 19-31. Choose Finish.

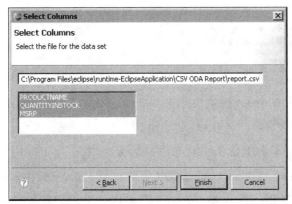

Figure 19-31   Selecting columns

Edit Data Set appears, as shown in Figure 19-32.

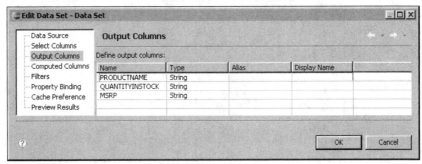

Figure 19-32   Edit Data Set

3 Choose Preview Results. Preview Results appears as shown in Figure 19-33. Choose OK.

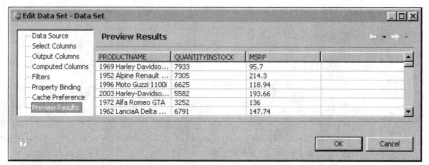

Figure 19-33 Data preview

4 On Data Explorer, expand Data Sets. Data Explorer appears as shown in Figure 19-34.

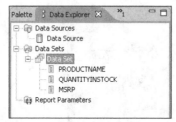

Figure 19-34 Data Set in Data Explorer

How to run a report design using CSV ODA UI and driver extensions

1 To build the report, drag Data Set from Data Explorer to the layout editor. Layout appears as shown in Figure 19-35.

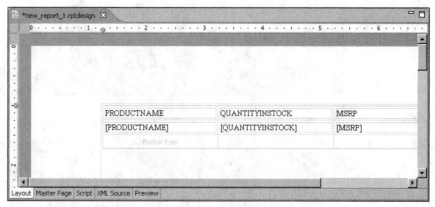

Figure 19-35 Report design in the layout editor

2 To run the report design, choose Preview. new_report_1.rptdesign runs, displaying the data set from the CSV data source, as shown in Figure 19-36.

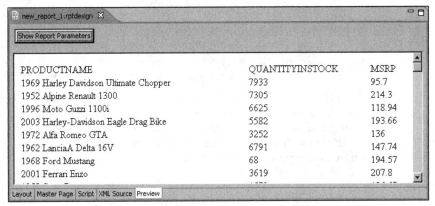

Figure 19-36 Preview of the data set from the CSV data source

Developing a Hibernate ODA extension

You develop the Hibernate ODA extension by creating two new projects in the Eclipse PDE that implement the following plug-ins:

- org.eclipse.birt.report.data.oda.hibernate

  The Hibernate ODA driver accesses a relational data source using HQL. The Hibernate ODA data source plug-in extends the functionality defined by the org.eclipse.datatools.connectivity.oda.dataSource extension point to create the Hibernate ODA driver.

- org.eclipse.birt.report.data.oda.hibernate.ui

  The Hibernate ODA UI plug-in for BIRT Report Designer selects a Hibernate data source and allows the user to create an HQL statement to retrieve data from the available tables and columns. The Hibernate ODA UI plug-in extends the functionality defined by the org.eclipse.datatools.connectivity .oda.design.ui.dataSource, org.eclipse.ui.propertyPages, and org.eclipse .datatools.connectivity.connectionProfile extension points.

The UI consists of the following pages:

- Data source page

  Includes the Hibernate data source in the list of available data sources. The Hibernate ODA driver contains preconfigured Hibernate configuration and mapping files that connect to the MySQL version of the BIRT demonstration database, ClassicModels.

- Data set page

  Creates an HQL statement that selects the data set and embeds the HQL statement in the report design.

In BIRT Report Designer, the Hibernate ODA data source wizard allows the report developer to select a Hibernate ODA driver containing preconfigured Hibernate configuration and mapping files. The Hibernate ODA driver searches for these configuration and mapping files in the plug-in's hibfiles directory.

The Hibernate ODA driver also searches in the hibfiles directory for JAR and ZIP files and the org.eclipse.birt.report.data.oda.jdbc plug-in for JDBC drivers to add to the classpath. This approach prevents the need to copy drivers to multiple locations. Note that changing the configuration causes the Hibernate ODA driver plug-in to rebuild the Hibernate SessionFactory, which is a machine-intensive operation.

Once the Hibernate ODA driver creates the data source configuration, you can create a data set. The Hibernate data set wizard allows the user to enter HQL statements. The Hibernate ODA UI example only supports simple queries, such as the following types of statements:

```
From Customer
```

or

```
Select ord.orderNumber,cus.customerNumber, cus.customerName
   from Orders as ord, Customer as cus
   where ord.customerNumber = cus.customerNumber and
   cus.customerNumber = 363
```

In the Hibernate ODA plug-in, there is an exampleconfig directory. This directory contains a sample Hibernate configuration file, mapping files, and Java classes that connect to the BIRT sample MySQL database. You can test using these files by performing the following tasks:

- Modify the hibernate.cfg.file to connect to your database configuration.

- Copy these files to the hibfiles directory.

- Create a JAR file containing the Java classes.

You can test and deploy the extensions in the Eclipse PDE run-time environment.

The following sections describe how to create and deploy the Hibernate ODA driver and UI plug-in projects. You can download the source code for the Hibernate ODA driver and UI extension examples at http://www.actuate.com/birt/contributions.

Creating the Hibernate ODA driver plug-in project

Create the Hibernate ODA driver plug-in project, org.eclipse.birt.report .data.oda.hibernate, using the New Plug-in Project wizard in the Eclipse PDE.

How to create the Hibernate ODA driver plug-in project

1 From the Eclipse PDE menu, choose File➤New➤Plug-in Project.

2 On New Project—Select a wizard, select Plug-in Project. Choose Next. New Plug-in Project appears.

3 In Plug-in Project, modify the settings as shown in Table 19-20.

Table 19-20 Settings for Plug-in Project options

Section	Option	Value
Plug-in Project	Project name	org.eclipse.birt.report.data .oda.hibernate
	Use default location	Selected
	Location	Not available when you select Use default location
Project Settings	Create a Java project	Selected
	Source folder name	src
	Output folder name	bin
Target Platform	Eclipse version	3.2
	OSGi framework	Selected Equinox

4 On Plug-in Content, modify the settings as shown in Table 19-21.

Table 19-21 Settings for Plug-in Content options

Section	Option	Value
Plug-in Properties	Plug-in ID	org.eclipse.birt.report.data .oda.hibernate
	Plug-in Version	2.0.0
	Plug-in Name	BIRT ODA-Hibernate Driver
	Plug-in Provider	yourCompany.com or leave blank
	Classpath	odahibernate.jar
Plug-in Options	Generate an activator, a Java class that controls the plug-in's life cycle	Selected
	Activator	org.eclipse.birt.report.data .oda.hibernate.Activator
	This plug-in will make contributions to the UI	Deselected

(continues)

Table 19-21   Settings for Plug-in Content options *(continued)*

Section	Option	Value
Rich Client Application	Would you like to create a rich client application?	No

Choose Finish. The Hibernate ODA driver plug-in project appears in the Eclipse PDE workbench.

How to specify the properties of the Hibernate ODA plug-in project

1 Using the Eclipse PDE Manifest Editor, in Dependencies, specify the following required plug-ins in the following order:

- org.eclipse.core.runtime

- org.eclipse.birt.report.data.oda.jdbc

- org.eclipse.datatools.connectivity.oda

Dependencies appears as shown in Figure 19-37.

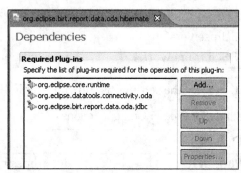

Figure 19-37   Required plug-ins, in Dependencies

2 On Runtime, in Exported Packages, verify that the org.eclipse.birt.report .data.oda.hibernate package appears in the list, as shown in Figure 19-38.

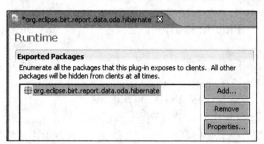

Figure 19-38   Runtime exported packages

3 On Runtime, in Classpath, add the following JAR files to the plug-in classpath:

- lib/hibernate3.jar
- lib/ant-antlr-1.6.5.jar
- lib/antlr-2.7.6.rc1.jar
- lib/asm.jar
- lib/asm-attrs.jar
- lib/cglib-2.1.3.jar
- lib/dom4j-1.6.1.jar
- lib/ehcache-1.1.jar
- lib/jta.jar
- lib/commons-collections-2.1.1.jar
- lib/commons-logging-1.0.4.jar

Classpath appears as shown in Figure 19-39.

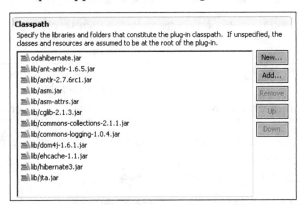

Figure 19-39 Runtime classpath

You must have previously imported these JAR files into the lib directory in the Hibernate ODA plug-in. You can also put these JAR files in a new plug-in that the Hibernate ODA plug-in references.

4 On Extensions, add the extension point, org.eclipse.datatools.connectivity .oda.dataSource, and the following elements and details for:

- dataSource

Add the extension element details, as shown in Table 19-22.

Table 19-22   Property settings for the dataSource extension element

Property	Value
id	org.eclipse.birt.report.data.oda.hibernate
driverClass	org.eclipse.birt.report.data.oda.hibernate.HibernateDriver
odaVersion	3.0
defaultDisplayName	Hibernate Data Source
setThreadContextClassLoader	true

The dataSource extension has an attribute named setThreadContextClassLoader, which, if set to true, sets the thread context class loader to the Hibernate ODA plug-in class loader. In this example, this attribute is set to true to avoid potential class conflicts with classes loaded with the Eclipse Tomcat plug-in.

- dataSet

   Add the extension element details, as shown in Table 19-23.

Table 19-23   Property settings for the dataSet extension element

Property	Value
id	org.eclipse.birt.report.data.oda.hibernate.dataSet
defaultDisplayName	Hibernate Data Set

5 On Extensions, select dataSource and add the following properties and element details:

- HIBCONFIG, as shown in Table 19-24.

Table 19-24   HIBCONFIG property settings

Property	Value
name	HIBCONFIG
defaultDisplayName	Hibernate Configuration File
type	string
canInherit	true

- MAPDIR, as shown in Table 19-25.

Table 19-25   MAPDIR property settings

Property	Value
name	MAPDIR
defaultDisplayName	Hibernate Mapping Directory
type	string
canInherit	true

6 On Extensions, select dataSet and add the list of dataTypeMapping elements, as shown in Table 19-26.

Table 19-26   Settings for dataTypeMapping elements

nativeDataType	nativeDataTypeCode	odaScalarDataType
BIT	-7	Integer
TINYINT	-6	Integer
SMALLINT	5	Integer
INTEGER	4	Integer
BIGINT	-5	Decimal
FLOAT	6	Double
REAL	7	Double
DOUBLE	8	Double
NUMERIC	2	Decimal
DECIMAL	3	Decimal
CHAR	1	String
VARCHAR	12	String
LONGVARCHAR	-1	String
DATE	91	Date
TIME	92	Time
TIMESTAMP	93	Timestamp
BINARY	-2	String
VARBINARY	-3	String
LONGVARBINARY	-4	String
BOOLEAN	16	Integer
BLOB	2004	Blob
CLOB	2005	Clob

Extensions appears as shown in Figure 19-40.

Figure 19-40 Extensions

Understanding the sample Hibernate ODA driver extension

The package for the Hibernate ODA extension example, org.eclipse.birt .report.data.oda.hibernate, implements the following classes using the ODA plug-in interfaces defined in the DTP plug-in, org.eclipse.datatools .connectivity.oda, and the extension points defined in the XML Schema file, datasource.exsd. The package implements the following classes:

- HibernateDriver

  Implements the IDriver interface. Instantiates the connection object for the Hibernate ODA driver. This is the entry point for the Hibernate ODA plug-in.

- Connection

  Implements the IConnection interface. Opens and closes the connection to the Hibernate ODA data source and instantiates the IQuery object.

- Statement

  Implements the IQuery interface. Prepares the result set metadata containing the table and column names, executes the query, and fetches the data rows from the data source.

- ResultSet

  Implements the IResultSet interface. Provides access to the data rows in the result set, maintaining a cursor that points to the current row. Handles the processing that gets the value for a column as the specified data type.

- ResultSetMetaData

  Implements the IResultSetMetaData interface. Describes the metadata for each column in the result set.

- DataSetMetaData

  Implements the IDataSetMetaData interface. Describes the features and capabilities of the driver for the data set.

- Messages

  Defines the exception messages for the Hibernate ODA driver.

- DataTypes

  Defines, validates, and returns the data types supported by the Hibernate ODA driver.

- CommonConstant

  Defines the constants used in the package, such as the driver name, ODA version, query keywords, and delimiters.

- HibernateUtil

  Manages the Hibernate SessionFactory that provides the session or run-time interface between the Hibernate service and the ODA driver. This class is built based on the example HibernateUtil, available at `http://www.hibernate.org`.

  The Hibernate ODA driver plug-in supports specifying the Hibernate configuration file and mapping files directory in the data source wizard. The plug-in creates the Hibernate SessionFactory from these settings. The example project has an exampleconfig directory that contains a Hibernate configuration and mapping files for use with the BIRT MySQL example database, ClassicModels.

The following sections describe the classes where there are important differences between the implementation of Hibernate ODA driver and the earlier example, the CSV ODA driver.

Understanding HibernateDriver

The HibernateDriver class instantiates the Connection object for the Hibernate ODA driver. This class implements the IDriver interface, but does not provide any processing for the methods that configure logging and set the application context. Listing 19-33 shows the getConnection( ) method.

Listing 19-33   The getConnection( ) method

```
public IConnection getConnection( String connectionClassName )
    throws OdaException
{
    return new Connection( );
}
```

getMaxConnections( ) returns 0, imposing no limit on the number of connections to the ODA data source from the application. Listing 19-34 shows the getMaxConnections( ) method.

Listing 19-34   The getMaxConnections( ) method

```
public int getMaxConnections( ) throws OdaException
{
    return( 0 );
}
```

Understanding Connection

The Connection class implements the following methods:

■ open( )

Opens a Hibernate session and sets the Boolean variable, isOpen, to true. The open( ) method uses the HibernateUtil class to obtain a session from a Hibernate SessionFactory, providing the run-time interface between the Hibernate service and the ODA driver.

The open( ) method retrieves the locations for the Hibernate configuration file and mapping files directory from connection properties. The open( ) method calls HibernateUtil.constructSessionFactory( ), which attempts to build the SessionFactory with these settings. If the SessionFactory already exists, the plug-in does not recreate the SessionFactory unless the Hibernate configuration file or the mapping directory have changed.

Listing 19-35 shows the code for the open( ) method.

Listing 19-35   The open( ) method

```
public void open( Properties connProperties )
    throws OdaException
{
try
{
```

```
      configfile =
      connProperties.getProperty( "HIBCONFIG" );
      mapdir = connProperties.getProperty( "MAPDIR" );
      HibernateUtil
      .constructSessionFactory( configfile, mapdir );
      Session testSession = HibernateUtil.currentSession( );
      this.isOpen = true;
   }catch( Exception e )
   {
      throw new OdaException( e.getLocalizedMessage( ) );
   }
   }
```

- newQuery( )

  Opens a new query by returning an instance of a Statement object, the class
  that implements the IQuery interface. The connection can handle multiple
  result set types, but the Hibernate ODA example uses only one and ignores
  the dataSetType parameter, as shown in Listing 19-36.

  Listing 19-36   The newQuery( ) method

  ```
  public IQuery newQuery( String dataSetType )
     throws OdaException
  {
     if ( !isOpen( ) )
        throw new OdaException( Messages.getString
           ( "Common.CONNECTION_IS_NOT_OPEN" ) );
     return new Statement( this );
  }
  ```

- getMetaData( )

  Returns an IDataSetMetaData object of the data set type, as shown in
  Listing 19-37.

  Listing 19-37   The getMetaData( ) method

  ```
  public IDataSetMetaData getMetaData( String dataSetType )
     throws OdaException
  {
     return new DataSetMetaData( this );
  }
  ```

- getMaxQueries( )

  Indicates the maximum number of queries the driver supports. The
  getMaxQueries( ) method returns 1, indicating that the Hibernate ODA
  driver does not support concurrent queries, as shown in Listing 19-38.

Listing 19-38   The getMaxQueries( ) method

```
public int getMaxQueries( ) throws OdaException
{
return 1;
}
```

- commit( ) and rollback( )

Handle transaction processing. The Hibernate ODA driver example does not support transaction operations. In the Connection class, the commit( ) and rollback( ) methods throw UnsupportedOperationException. Listing 19-39 shows the code for the commit( ) method.

Listing 19-39   The commit( ) method

```
public void commit( ) throws OdaException
{
throw new UnsupportedOperationException ( );
}
```

- close( )

Closes the Hibernate session, as shown in Listing 19-40.

Listing 19-40   The close( ) method

```
public void close( ) throws OdaException
{
   this.isOpen = false;
   try{
      HibernateUtil.closeSession( );
   }catch(Exception e){
      throw new OdaException( e.getLocalizedMessage( ) );
   }
}
```

Understanding DataSetMetaData

The DataSetMetaData class describes the features and capabilities of the data source for the specified data set. The Hibernate ODA driver example returns true or false to indicate support for a feature. The Hibernate ODA driver example does not support input or output parameters, named parameters, or multiple result sets.

The following code example indicates that the Hibernate ODA driver does not support multiple result sets, as shown in Listing 19-41.

Listing 19-41   The supportsMultipleResultSets( ) method

```
public boolean supportsMultipleResultSets( ) throws
   OdaException
{
```

```
    return false;
}
```

A method such as getSQLStateType( ), which has no implementation, simply
throws UnsupportedOperationException, as shown in Listing 19-42.

Listing 19-42   The getSQLStateType( ) method

```
public int getSQLStateType( ) throws OdaException
{
    throw new UnsupportedOperationException ( );
}
```

Understanding Statement

The Statement class implements the IQuery interface. This class prepares and
executes the query. Statement also handles parameters and retrieves the result
set and result set metadata.

The Statement class implements the following methods:

- prepare( )

  The ODA framework calls the prepare( ) method before executing the query.
  The ODA framework uses the query saved in the report design.

  The Hibernate ODA UI plug-in also calls prepare( ) to verify the columns
  used in the report design. The UI plug-in passes an HQL statement that gets
  the columns from the result set object.

  prepare( ) sets up the result-set metadata and stores the query in an object
  variable for use by the executeQuery( ) method. The ODA run time uses the
  result-set metadata to retrieve the data. BIRT Report Designer also uses the
  result-set metadata to display the columns in the UI.

  The prepare( ) method performs the following operations:

  - Sets up array lists to contain the columns, column types, and column
    classes

  - Trims the query String

  - Creates a Hibernate Query object, using the HQL query

  - Gets the Hibernate column names, types, and classes for the query

  - Instantiates a ResultSetMetaData object, passing in the column names
    and data types

  - Saves the query for execution

  Listing 19-43 shows the code for the prepare( ) method.

  Listing 19-43   The prepare( ) method

```
public void prepare( String query ) throws OdaException
```

```
{
Query qry = null;
testConnection( );
ArrayList arColsType = new ArrayList( );
ArrayList arCols = new ArrayList( );
ArrayList arColClass = new ArrayList( );

String[ ] props = null;
try
{
   Session hibsession = HibernateUtil.currentSession( );
   query = query.replaceAll( "[\\n\\r]+"," " );
   query = query.trim( );
   qry = hibsession.createQuery( query );
   Type[ ] qryReturnTypes = qry.getReturnTypes( );
   if( qryReturnTypes.length > 0
   && qryReturnTypes[0].isEntityType( ) )
   {
   for( int j=0; j< qryReturnTypes.length; j++ )
   {
      String clsName=qryReturnTypes[j].getName( );
      props =
      HibernateUtil.getHibernateProp( clsName );
      for( int x = 0; x < props.length; x++ )
      {
      String propType =
         HibernateUtil.getHibernatePropTypes
         ( clsName, props[x] );
      if( DataTypes.isValidType( propType ))
      {
         arColsType.add( propType );
         arCols.add( props[x] );
         arColClass.add( clsName );
      }
      else
      {
         throw new OdaException
         ( Messages.getString
         ( "Statement.SOURCE_DATA_ERROR" ) );
      }
      }
   }
   }
   else
   {
      props = extractColumns( qry.getQueryString( ) );
      for( int t=0; t < qryReturnTypes.length; t++)
      {
```

```
              if( DataTypes.isValidType
                 (qryReturnTypes[t].getName( )))
              {
                 arColsType.add( qryReturnTypes[t].getName( ));
                 arCols.add( props[t] );
              }
              else
              {
                 throw new OdaException
                    ( Messages.getString
                       ("Statement.SOURCE_DATA_ERROR") );
              }
           }
        }
     }
     catch( Exception e )
     {
        throw new OdaException( e.getLocalizedMessage( ) );
     }
     this.resultSetMetaData = new ResultSetMetaData
        (( String[ ])arCols.toArray
           ( new String[arCols.size( )] ),
         (String[ ])arColsType.toArray
           ( new String[arColsType.size( )] ),
         (String[ ])arCols.toArray
           ( new String[arCols.size( )] ),
         (String[ ])arColClass.toArray
           ( new String[arColClass.size( )] ));
     this.query = query;
  }
```

■ getMetaData( )

The BIRT framework calls getMetaData( ) after the prepare( ) method to
retrieve the metadata for a result set. The BIRT framework uses the metadata
to create the data set in the report.

Listing 19-44 shows the code for the getMetaData( ) method.

Listing 19-44   The getMetaData( ) method

```
public IResultSetMetaData getMetaData( ) throws OdaException
{
   return this.resultSetMetaData;
}
```

■ executeQuery( )

The executeQuery( ) method executes the prepared query and retrieves the
results. The executeQuery( ) method returns an IResultSet object, which is
created using the list results, result-set metadata, and Hibernate types
returned from the HQL query. The ODA framework uses the IResultSet
object to iterate over the results.

The executeQuery( ) method performs the following operations:

- Sets up an array of org.hibernate.type.Type to map Java types to JDBC datatypes
- Sets up a list to contain the results set
- Trims the query String
- Instantiates a Hibernate Query object, creating the HQL query
- Executes the HQL query, returning the query result set in a List
- Gets the Hibernate types for the query result set
- Instantiates a ResultSet object, passing in the data, metadata, and Hibernate types

Listing 19-45 shows the code for the executeQuery( ) method.

Listing 19-45 The executeQuery( ) method

```
public IResultSet executeQuery( ) throws OdaException
{
   Type[ ] qryReturnTypes = null;
   List rst = null;
   try
   {
      Session hibsession = HibernateUtil.currentSession( );
      String qryStr = this.query;
      qryStr = qryStr.replaceAll( "[\\n\\r]+"," " );
      qryStr.trim( );
      Query qry = hibsession.createQuery( qryStr );
      rst = qry.list( );
      qryReturnTypes = qry.getReturnTypes( );


   }
   catch( Exception e )
   {
      throw new OdaException( e.getLocalizedMessage( ) );
   }
   return new ResultSet
      ( rst, getMetaData( ), qryReturnTypes );
}
```

- close( )

The close( ) method clears the Connection and ResultSetMetaData objects. In the Connection object, the close( ) method closes the Hibernate session.

Listing 19-46 shows the code for the Statement.close( ) method.

Listing 19-46 The Statement.close( ) method

```
public void close( ) throws OdaException
```

```
    {
        connection = null;
        resultSetMetaData = null;
    }
```

Understanding ResultSet

The ResultSet class implements the IResultSet interface. When this class is instantiated, it stores the list.iterator( ) passed from the Statement object. It uses the iterator when the ODA driver framework calls the next( ) method.

The iterator points to the next available row of data from the HQL query results. The framework calls the accessor methods that get the data types for the columns in the current row. For example, if the first column is a String, the framework calls getString( ). This method calls the getResult( ) method, which interprets the HQL query results.

The getResult( ) method parses the results in one of the following ways, depending on whether the query returns a Hibernate EntityType or just an array of values:

- If the query uses HQL and each return type is an EntityType, getResult( ) gets each Column class and uses the Hibernate ClassMetaData methods to retrieve the value.

- If the query returns standard data types, getResult( ) gets each value or values, returning an Object containing the simple value or an array of Objects containing the multiple values.

Listing 19-47 shows the code for the getResult( ) method.

Listing 19-47   The getResult( ) method

```
private Object getResult( int rstcol ) throws OdaException
    {
        Object obj = this.currentRow;
        Object value = null;
        try
            {
            if( qryReturnTypes.length >
              0 && qryReturnTypes[0].isEntityType( ))
            {
                String checkClass =
                (( ResultSetMetaData )getMetaData( ))
                    .getColumnClass(rstcol);
                Object myVal =
                HibernateUtil.getHibernatePropVal( obj,
                    checkClass,
                    getMetaData( ).getColumnName( rstcol ));
                value = myVal;
            }
            else
            {
```

```
                    if( getMetaData( ).getColumnCount( ) == 1)
                    {
                    value = obj;
                }
                    else
                    {
                        Object[ ] values = ( Object[ ])obj;
                        value = values[rstcol-1];
                }
                }
            }
            catch( Exception e )
            {
                throw new OdaException( e.getLocalizedMessage( ) );
            }
        return( value );
    }
```

Understanding HibernateUtil

HibernateUtil is a utility class that provides the run-time interface between the
Hibernate service and the application. The HibernateUtil class example derives
from the class provided with the Hibernate documentation. HibernateUtil
performs the following operations:

- Initializes the SessionFactory

- Builds the Hibernate SessionFactory

- Opens and closes a session

- Returns information on Hibernate classes and properties

- Registers the JDBC driver with the DriverManager

The Connection.open( ) method calls HibernateUtil.constructSessionFactory( ),
which creates a SessionFactory if one does not already exist. The
constructSessionFactory( ) method closes and rebuilds the SessionFactory if the
location of the configuration file or mapping files directory has changed.

The SessionFactory construction process creates the ClassLoader. The
ClassLoader adds the drivers directory in the org.eclipse.birt.report.data.oda
.jdbc plug-in and the hibfiles directory in the Hibernate ODA plug-in to
classpath. This process also registers the JDBC driver specified in the Hibernate
config file with the DriverManager.

The HibernateUtil class implements the following methods:

- initSessionFactory( )

    This method creates the SessionFactory object from the configuration
    settings in the hibernate.cfg.xml file. Listing 19-48 shows the code for the
    initSessionFactory( ) method.

Listing 19-48 shows the code for the initSessionFactory( ) method.

Listing 19-48   The initSessionFactory( ) method

```
private static synchronized void initSessionFactory
    ( String hibfile, String mapdir)
    throws HibernateException
    {
        if( sessionFactory == null)
        {
            Thread thread = Thread.currentThread( );
            try
            {
                oldloader = thread.getContextClassLoader( );
                refreshURLs( );
                ClassLoader changeLoader = new URLClassLoader
                    ( ( URL [ ])URLList.toArray
                        ( new URL[0]),thread
                            .getContextClassLoader( ));
                thread.setContextClassLoader( changeLoader );
                Configuration cfg =
                    buildConfig( hibfile,mapdir );
                Class driverClass =
                    changeLoader.loadClass( cfg.getProperty
                        ( "connection.driver_class" ));
                Driver driver =
                    ( Driver ) driverClass.newInstance( );
                WrappedDriver wd =
                    new WrappedDriver( driver,
                        cfg.getProperty
                        ( "connection.driver_class" ));
                boolean foundDriver = false;
                Enumeration drivers =
                    DriverManager.getDrivers( );
                while ( drivers.hasMoreElements( ))
                {
                    Driver nextDriver =
                        ( Driver )drivers.nextElement( );
                    if ( nextDriver.getClass( ) == wd.getClass( ))
                    {
                        if( nextDriver.toString( )
                            .equals(wd.toString( )) )
                        {
                            foundDriver = true;
                            break;
                        }
                    }
                }
                if( !foundDriver )
                {
                    DriverManager.registerDriver( wd );
                }
                sessionFactory = cfg.buildSessionFactory( );
```

```
                   configuration = cfg;
                   HibernateMapDirectory = mapdir;
                   HibernateConfigFile = hibfile;
               }
               catch( Exception e)
               {
                  e.printStackTrace( );
                  throw new HibernateException
                     ( "No Session Factory Created " +
                        e.getLocalizedMessage( ));
               }
               finally
               {
                  thread.setContextClassLoader( oldloader );
               }
            }
         }
```

- constructSessionFactory

This method checks to see if a configuration change occurred. If a change occurred, the method closes the session and SessionFactory and calls the initSessionFactory to rebuild the SessionFactory.

Listing 19-49 shows the code for the constructSessionFactory( ) method.

Listing 19-49 The constructSessionFactory( ) method

```
   public static void constructSessionFactory
      ( String hibfile, String mapdir)
      throws HibernateException
      {
         if( hibfile == null)
         {
            hibfile = "";
         }
         if( mapdir == null)
         {
            mapdir = "";
         }
         if( sessionFactory == null)
         {
            initSessionFactory( hibfile, mapdir);
            return;
         }
         if( HibernateMapDirectory.equalsIgnoreCase
            ( mapdir ) && HibernateConfigFile
               .equalsIgnoreCase( hibfile ))
         {
            return;
         }
         synchronized( sessionFactory )
         {
```

```
            Session s = ( Session ) session.get( );
            if ( s != null )
            {
                closeSession( );
            }
            if ( sessionFactory != null &&
                !sessionFactory.isClosed( ))
            {
                closeFactory( );
            }
            sessionFactory = null;
            initSessionFactory( hibfile, mapdir);
        }
```

- currentSession( )

    This method opens a session when called by the Connection.open( ) method, as shown in Listing 19-50.

    Listing 19-50   The currentSession( ) method

    ```
    public static Session currentSession( )
        throws HibernateException {
        Session s = ( Session ) session.get( );
        if ( s == null ) {
            s = sessionFactory.openSession( );
            session.set( s );
        }
            return s;
        }
    ```

Other methods in this class return information on a particular class and its properties. The getHibernateProp( ) method returns the properties for a class. The getHibernatePropTypes( ) method returns the data type for a property of a class.

Building the Hibernate ODA driver plug-in

To build and deploy the org.eclipse.birt.report.data.oda.hibernate plug-in using the Eclipse PDE Manifest Editor, perform the following tasks:

- On Build, specify the Build Configuration to include the following items:

    - In Runtime Information, add the odahibernate.jar file.

    - In Binary Build, select the following files and folders:

        - META-INF

        - exampleconfig

        - hibfiles

        - lib

❏ plugin.xml

Build Configuration appears, as shown in Figure 19-41.

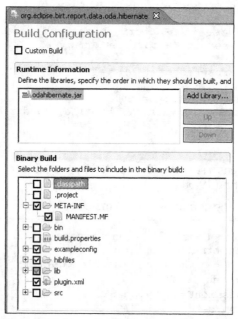

Figure 19-41   Build Configuration settings

- On Overview, in Exporting, choose Export Wizard and perform the following tasks:

   - In Options, verify that Package plug-ins as individual JAR archives is not selected.

   - In Destination, choose the directory, $INSTALL_DIR\birt-runtime-2_1_0\Report Engine, as shown in Figure 19-42.

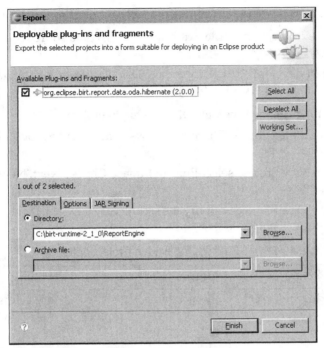

Figure 19-42   Using the Export wizard

The Hibernate ODA example uses MySQL as the database. The BIRT sample database and the MySQL installation scripts can be downloaded from http://www.eclipse.org/birt/db. For information about the required Hibernate libraries, please refer to the Hibernate web site at http://www.hibernate.org.

Developing the Hibernate ODA UI extension

To use the data retrieved by the Hibernate ODA driver in a BIRT report design, you must extend the DTP design UI. To implement the Hibernate ODA UI, you extend the following extension points:

- org.eclipse.datatools.connectivity.oda.design.ui.dataSource

  The dataSource extension point defines and implements the UI for new data source and data set wizards. These wizards use the Hibernate ODA driver plug-in to extend the functionality available in the Data Explorer of BIRT Report Designer.

- org.eclipse.ui.propertyPages

  The propertyPage extension displays and manipulates the Hibernate configuration file and mapping files directory locations.

- org.eclipse.datatools.connectivity.connectionProfile

  The connectionProfile extension shares a data source connection between applications.

To start developing the Hibernate ODA UI plug-in, create the plug-in project, org.eclipse.birt.report.data.oda.hibernate.ui.

How to create the Hibernate ODA UI plug-in project

1 From the Eclipse PDE menu, choose File➤New➤Plug-in Project. New Project appears.

2 On New Project, select Plug-in Project. Choose Next. New Plug-in Project appears.

3 In Plug-in Project, modify the settings as shown in Table 19-27. Choose Next. Plug-in Content appears.

Table 19-27   Settings for Plug-in Project options

Section	Option	Value
Plug-in Project	Project name	org.eclipse.birt.report.data .oda.hibernate.ui
	Use default location	Selected
	Location	Not available when you select Use default location
Project Settings	Create a Java project	Selected
	Source folder name	src
	Output folder name	bin
Target Platform	Eclipse version	3.2
	OSGi framework	Selected Equinox

4 In Plug-in Content, modify the settings as shown in Table 19-28. Choose Finish.

Table 19-28   Settings for Plug-in Content options

Section	Option	Value
Plug-in Properties	Plug-in ID	org.eclipse.birt.report.data .oda.hibernate.ui
	Plug-in Version	2.0.0
	Plug-in Name	BIRT Hibernate UI Plug-in
	Plug-in Provider	yourCompany.com or leave blank
	Classpath	hibernateui.jar

Table 19-28 Settings for Plug-in Content options *(continued)*

Section	Option	Value
Plug-in Options	Generate an activator, a Java class that controls the plug-in's life cycle	Selected
	Activator	org.eclipse.birt.report.data .oda.hibernate.ui .Activator
	This plug-in will make contributions to the UI	Deselected
Rich Client Application	Would you like to create a rich client application?	No

The Hibernate ODA UI plug-in project appears in the Eclipse PDE workbench.

How to specify the Hibernate ODA UI dependencies

1 On the Eclipse PDE Manifest Editor, in Dependencies, specify the required plug-ins in the following order:

- org.eclipse.core.runtime

- org.eclipse.ui

- org.eclipse.datatools.connectivity.oda.design.ui

- org.eclipse.birt.report.data.oda.hibernate

Dependencies appears as shown in Figure 19-43.

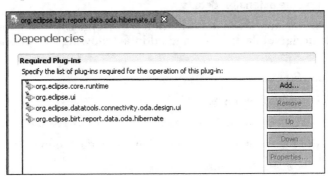

Figure 19-43 Required plug-ins for the Hibernate ODA UI plug-in project

How to specify the Hibernate ODA UI runtime

On Runtime, in Exported Packages, add org.eclipse.birt.report.oda.hibernate.ui to the list of packages that this plug-in exposes to clients.

Runtime appears as shown in Figure 19-44.

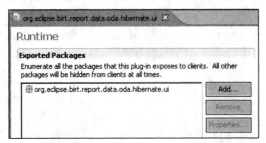

Figure 19-44 Exported packages for the Hibernate ODA UI plug-in project

How to specify the Hibernate ODA UI extension points

1 On the PDE Manifest Editor, choose Extensions.

2 In All Extensions, choose Add. New Extension appears.

3 On New Extension—Extension Points, in the list of extension points, select the following plug-in:

```
org.eclipse.datatools.connectivity.oda.design.ui.dataSource
```

Choose Finish.

4 Repeat steps 2 and 3 to add the following extension points to the list on the Extensions page:

   ■ org.eclipse.ui.propertyPages

   ■ org.eclipse.datatools.connectivity.connectionProfile

How to add the extension details

1 On Extensions, select the extension point, org.eclipse.datatools.connectivity .oda.design.ui.dataSource, and add the following elements and element details:

   ■ dataSourceUI

   Add the following id:

   ```
   org.eclipse.birt.report.data.oda.hibernate
   ```

   Add the following extension element to dataSourceUI:

   ```
   newDataSourceWizard
   ```

   Add the extension element details for the extension element, newDataSourceWizard, as shown in Table 19-29.

Table 19-29   Property settings for newDataSourceWizard

Property	Value
pageClass	org.eclipse.birt.report.data.oda .hibernate.ui.HibernateDataSourceWizard
windowTitle	Hibernate Data Source
includesProgressMonitor	false
pageTitle	Hibernate Data Source

■ dataSetUI

Add the extension element details for the extension element, dataSetUI, as shown in Table 19-30.

Table 19-30   Property settings for the dataSetUI extension element

Property	Value
id	org.eclipse.birt.report.data.oda .hibernate.dataSet
initialPageId	org.eclipse.birt.report.data.oda .hibernate.ui.HibernatePage
supportsInParameters	true
supportsOutParameters	false

2 On Extensions, select dataSetUI, org.eclipse.birt.report.data.oda.hibernate .dataSet, and add the following properties and element details:

■ dataSetWizard, as shown in Table 19-31

Table 19-31   Property settings for the dataSetWizard extension element

Property	Value
class	org.eclipse.datatools.connectivity .oda.design.ui.wizards.DataSetWizard
windowTitle	Hibernate Data Set

■ dataSetPage, as shown in Table 19-32

Table 19-32   Property settings for the dataSetPage extension element

Property	Value
id	org.eclipse.birt.report.data.oda .hibernate.ui.HibernatePage

(continues)

Table 19-32   Property settings for the dataSetPage extension
element *(continued)*

Property	Value
wizardPageClass	org.eclipse.birt.report.data.oda .hibernate.ui .HibernateHqlSelectionPage
displayName	Enter HQL
path	/

3 On Extensions, select org.eclipse.ui.propertyPages and add the following property and extension element details for page, as shown in Table 19-33.

Table 19-33   Property settings for the page extension element

Property	Value
id	org.eclipse.birt.report.data.oda.hibernate.
name	ODA Hibernate Data Source Connection Properties
class	org.eclipse.birt.report.data.oda.hibernate.ui .HibernatePropertyPage
objectClass	org.eclipse.datatools.connectivity .IConnectionProfile

4 On Extensions, select page and add the following property and extension element details for filter, as shown in Table 19-34.

Table 19-34   Property settings for the filter extension element

Property	Value
name	org.eclipse.datatools.profile.property.id
value	org.eclipse.birt.report.data.oda.hibernate

5 On Extensions, select org.eclipse.datatools.connectivity.connectionProfile, and add the following properties and element details:

- category, as shown in Table 19-35

Table 19-35   Property settings for the filter extension element

Property	Value
id	org.eclipse.birt.report.data.oda.hibernate
parentCategory	org.eclipse.datatools.connectivity.oda .profileCategory
name	Hibernate Data Source

- connectionProfile, as shown in Table 19-36

Table 19-36   Property settings for the connectionProfile extension element

Property	Value
id	org.eclipse.birt.report.data.oda.hibernate
category	org.eclipse.birt.report.data.oda.hibernate
name	ODA Hibernate Data Source Connection Profile
pingFactory	org.eclipse.datatoools.connectivity.oda .profile.OdaConnectionFactory

- connectionFactory, as shown in Table 19-37

Table 19-37   Property settings for the connectionFactory extension element

Property	Value
id	ogr.eclipse.datatools.connectivity.oda .IConnection
class	ogr.eclipse.datatools.connectivity.oda .profile.OdaConnectionFactory
profile	org.eclipse.birt.report.data.oda.hibernate
name	ODA Connection Factory

- newWizard, as shown in Table 19-35

Table 19-38   Property settings for the newWizard extension element

Property	Value
id	org.eclipse.birt.report.data.oda.hibernate
name	ODA Hibernate Data Source
class	org.eclipse.datatools.connectivity .oda.design.ui.wizards .NewDataSourceWizard
profile	org.eclipse.birt.report.data.oda.hibernate
description	Create an ODA Hibernate connection profile

Extensions appears as shown in Figure 19-45.

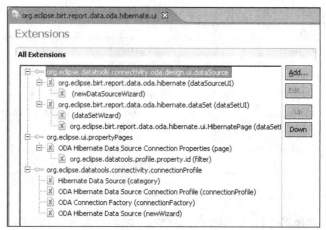

Figure 19-45 Extensions for the Hibernate ODA UI

Understanding the sample Hibernate ODA UI extension

The following sections describe the code-based extensions a developer must make to complete the development of the Hibernate ODA UI extension, after defining the plug-in framework in the Eclipse PDE.

The Hibernate ODA UI plug-in implements the following classes:

- HibernatePropertyPage

  Creates and initializes the editor controls for the property page that specify the ODA data source. This class updates the connection profile properties with the values collected from the page. HibernatePropertyPage extends org.eclipse.datatools.connectivity.oda.design.ui.wizards .DataSourceEditorPage, the abstract base class for implementing a customized ODA data source property page.

- HibernatePageHelper

  Implements the user interface that specifies data source properties. This utility class specifies the page layout, sets up the controls that listen for user input, verifies the location of the Hibernate configuration file, and sets up the location of the mapping directory. The HibernateDataSourceWizard and HibernatePropertyPage classes use HibernatePageHelper. HibernatePageHelper also extends org.eclipse.datatools.connectivity.oda .design.ui.wizards.DataSourceEditorPage.

- HibernateDataSourceWizard

  Creates and initializes the controls for the data source wizard page. The class sets the configuration file message and collects the property values. In the extension element settings for newDataSourceWizard, the pageClass property specifies this class as the implementation class for the dataSourceUI wizard. The HibernateDataSourceWizard class extends org.eclipse.datatools.connectivity.oda.design.ui.wizards.DataSourceWizardPage, the abstract base class for implementing a customized ODA data source wizard page.

■ HibernateHqlSelectionPage

Creates the user interface that specifies an HQL statement. The Hibernate ODA UI plug-in calls HibernateHqlSelectionPage when creating or modifying the data set for a data source. In the extension element settings for dataSetPage, the wizardPageClass property specifies this class as the implementation class for the dataSetUI page wizard. HibernateHqlSelectionPage also extends org.eclipse.datatools.connectivity.oda.design.ui.wizards.DataSourceWizardPage.

■ Messages

This class and the related properties file, messages.properties, generate the messages displayed in the Hibernate ODA UI.

Understanding HibernatePageHelper

This class creates the components that select the Hibernate configuration file and a mapping files directory using the following methods:

■ createCustomControl( )

Builds the user interface for the data source

■ initCustomControl( )

Sets the initial property values

■ collectCustomProperties( )

Returns the modified properties to the ODA framework

When the data source page displays, the Finish button becomes available when the setPageComplete( ) method indicates the page is complete.

HibernateDataSourceWizard.createPageCustomControl( ) and HibernatePropertyPage.createAndInitCustomControl( ) call HibernatePageHelper. The createCustomControl( ) method is the entry point for this class.

Listing 19-51 shows the code for the createCustomControl( ) method.

Listing 19-51 The createCustomControl( ) method

```
void createCustomControl( Composite parent )
   {
     Composite content = new Composite( parent, SWT.NULL );
     GridLayout layout = new GridLayout( 3, false );
     content.setLayout(layout);
```

```
        setupConfigLocation( content );
        setupMapLocation( content );
    }
```

The setupConfigLocation( ) method sets up the configuration file location. The setupMapLocation( ) method sets up the mapping folder. These two methods perform similar tasks.

Listing 19-52 shows the code for the setupConfigLocation( ) method. This method adds a label, a text entry component, and a button. The text entry component has a ModifyListener( ) method, which verifies that the file selected exists, and the button has a SelectionAdapter( ) method, which uses the FileDialog( ) method to access the configuration file.

Listing 19-52   The setupConfigLocation( ) method

```
private void setupConfigLocation( Composite composite )
    {
        Label label = new Label( composite, SWT.NONE );
        label.setText("Select Hibernate Config File" );
        GridData data =
          new GridData( GridData.FILL_HORIZONTAL );
        m_configLocation = new Text( composite, SWT.BORDER );
        m_configLocation.setLayoutData( data );
        setPageComplete( true );
        m_configLocation.addModifyListener
          ( new ModifyListener( )
              {
                public void modifyText( ModifyEvent e )
                {
                    verifyConfigLocation( );
                }
              } );
    m_browseConfigButton = new Button( composite, SWT.NONE );
    m_browseConfigButton.setText( "..." );
    m_browseConfigButton.addSelectionListener
      ( new SelectionAdapter( )
        {
          public void widgetSelected( SelectionEvent e )
          {
            FileDialog dialog = new FileDialog
               ( m_configLocation.getShell( ) );
            if( m_configLocation.getText( ) != null &&
              m_configLocation.getText( )
                .trim( ).length( ) > 0 )
              {
                dialog.setFilterPath
                   ( m_configLocation.getText() );
              }
            dialog.setText
               ( "Select Hibernate Config File" );
            String selectedLocation = dialog.open( );
            if( selectedLocation != null )
```

```
            {
                m_configLocation.setText
                    ( selectedLocation );
            }
        }
    } );
}
```

The initCustomControl( ) method initializes the properties settings. The plug-in
passes the properties to the method from the createPageCustomControl( ) and
setInitialProperties( ) methods of the HibernateDataSourceWizard class and the
createAndInitCustomControl( ) method of the HibernatePropertyPage class.

The initCustomControl( ) method retrieves the properties for the Hibernate
configuration file and mapping files directory and sets text component values.

Listing 19-53 shows the code for the initCustomControl( ) method.

Listing 19-53   The initCustomControl( ) method

```
void initCustomControl( Properties profileProps )
    {
        setPageComplete( true );
        setMessage( DEFAULT_MESSAGE, IMessageProvider.NONE );
        if( profileProps == null || profileProps.isEmpty() ||
            m_configLocation == null )
            return;
        String configPath =
            profileProps.getProperty( "HIBCONFIG" );
        if( configPath == null )
        configPath = EMPTY_STRING;
        m_configLocation.setText( configPath );
        String mapPath = profileProps.getProperty( "MAPDIR" );
        if( mapPath == null )
            mapPath = EMPTY_STRING;
        m_mapLocation.setText( mapPath );
        verifyConfigLocation( );
    }
```

When the user presses the Finish or Test Connection button, the plug-in calls the
collectCustomProperties( ) method to retrieve the new values for the Hibernate
configuration file and mapping files directory. The HibernateDataSourceWizard
and HibernatePropertyPage classes call the
HibernatePageHelper.collectCustomProperties( ) method from their
collectCustomProperties( ) methods.

Listing 19-54 shows the code for the collectCustomProperties( ) method.

Listing 19-54   The collectCustomProperties( ) method

```
Properties collectCustomProperties( Properties props )
    {
        if( props == null )
            props = new Properties( );
```

```
        props.setProperty( "HIBCONFIG",
            getConfig( ) );
        props.setProperty( "MAPDIR", getMapDir( ) );
        return props;
    }
```

Understanding HibernateDataSourceWizard

The HibernateDataSourceWizard class extends the DTP
DataSourceWizardPage, by implementing three methods that the ODA
framework calls:

- createPageCustomControl( )

  Constructs the user interface

- setInitialProperties( )

  Sets the initial values of the user interface

- collectCustomProperties( )

  Retrieve the modified values

This class creates the HibernatePageHelper class, and uses the methods
described earlier to handle these three methods. The ODA framework uses this
class to create a new data source.

Understanding HibernatePropertyPage

The HibernatePropertyPage class extends the DTP DataSourceEditorPage by
implementing two methods that the ODA framework calls:

- createAndInitCustomControl( )

  Constructs the user interface and sets the initial values

- collectCustomProperties( )

  Retrieves the modified values

This class creates the HibernatePageHelper class and uses the methods
described earlier to handle these two methods. The ODA framework uses this
class to create a new data source.

Understanding HibernateHqlSelectionPage

The HibernateHqlSelectionPage class extends DataSetWizardPage to define the
page controls and related functionality for the Hibernate ODA data set wizard.
HibernateHqlSelectionPage allows the user to create an HQL statement that
selects the data set and embeds the HQL statement in the report design. This
page links to the Hibernate ODA through the wizardPageClass attribute of the
dataSetPage element within the dataSource extension.

The HibernateHqlSelectionPage class implements the following methods:

- createPageControl( )

  This method performs the following operations:

  - Sets up a composite set of controls using a series of GridLayout and GridData objects to create the data set editor UI

  - Sets the user prompt to enter an HQL statement and verify the query

  - Adds a text control to allow the user to enter and modify text

  - Adds a ModifyListener to the text control to detect user input

  - Sets up the Verify Query button and adds a SelectionListener to detect when the user selects the button

  - Returns the composite page control

  Listing 19-55 shows the code for the createPageControl( ) method.

Listing 19-55   The createPageControl( ) method

```
public Control createPageControl( Composite parent )
  {
  Composite composite = new Composite
    ( parent, SWT.NONE );
  GridLayout layout = new GridLayout( );
  layout.numColumns = 1;
  composite.setLayout( layout );
  Label label = new Label( composite, SWT.NONE );
  label.setText( Messages.getString
    ( "wizard.title.selectColumns" ));
  GridData data = new GridData( GridData.FILL_BOTH );
  queryText = new Text( composite,SWT.MULTI |
    SWT.WRAP | SWT.V_SCROLL );
  queryText.setLayoutData( data );
  queryText.addModifyListener( new ModifyListener( ){
    public void modifyText( ModifyEvent e )
    {
      if( m_initialized == false)
      {
        setPageComplete(true);
        m_initialized = true;
      }
      else
      {
        setPageComplete(false);
      }
    }
  } );
  setPageComplete( false );
  Composite cBottom = new Composite
    ( composite, SWT.NONE );
  cBottom.setLayoutData
```

```
                ( new GridData( GridData.FILL_HORIZONTAL ) );
        cBottom.setLayout( new RowLayout( ) );
        queryButton = new Button( cBottom, SWT.NONE );
        queryButton.setText(Messages.getString
            ( "wizard.title.verify" ));
        queryButton.addSelectionListener
            ( new SelectionAdapter( ))
        {
        public void widgetSelected( SelectionEvent event )
        {
             verifyQuery( );
        }
        } );
        return composite;
        }
```

- initializeControl( )

  The plug-in calls this method to retrieve the HQL query from the current
  design and initializes the HQL text component with this value.
  initializeControl( ) also reads the Hibernate configuration file and mapping
  files directory from the report design and stores them in member variables
  for use when building a query.

  Listing 19-56 shows the code for the initializeControl( ) method.

  Listing 19-56 The initializeControl( ) method

```
    private void initializeControl( )
      {
          Properties dataSourceProps =
            getInitializationDesign( ).getDataSourceDesign( )
              .getPublicProperties( );
           m_hibconfig =
               dataSourceProps.getProperty( "HIBCONFIG" );
          m_mapdir = dataSourceProps.getProperty( "MAPDIR" );
          DataSetDesign dataSetDesign =
              getInitializationDesign( );
          if( dataSetDesign == null )
              return;
          String queryTextTmp = dataSetDesign.getQueryText( );
          if( queryTextTmp == null )
             return;
          queryText.setText( queryTextTmp );
          this.m_initialized = false;
          setMessage( "", NONE );
      }
```

- verifyQuery( )

  This method is the selection event called when the user chooses the Verify
  Query button. verifyQuery performs the following operations:

  - Opens a connection to the run-time environment.

- Instantiates a Query object and gets the query text entered by the user.
- Prepares the query.
- Checks the column to determine if the query prepare was successful. Depending on the success of the query prepare, verifyQuery( ) indicates that page processing is complete or incomplete.
- Re-enables the Verify Query button.
- Closes the connection.

Listing 19-57 shows the code for the verifyQuery( ) method.

Listing 19-57   The verifyQuery( ) method

```
boolean verifyQuery( )
{
   setMessage( "Verifying Query", INFORMATION );
   setPageComplete( false );
   queryButton.setEnabled( false );
   Connection conn = new Connection( );
   try
   {
      Properties prop = new Properties( );
      if( m_hibconfig == null)m_hibconfig = "";
      if( m_mapdir == null)m_mapdir = "";
      prop.put("HIBCONFIG", m_hibconfig );
         prop.put("MAPDIR", m_mapdir);
      conn.open( prop );
      IQuery query = conn.newQuery( "" );
      query.prepare( queryText.getText( ) );
      int columnCount =
         query.getMetaData( ).getColumnCount( );
      if ( columnCount == 0 )
      {
         setPageComplete( false );
         return false;
      }
      setPageComplete( true );
      return true;
   }
   catch ( OdaException e )
   {
      System.out.println( e.getMessage( ) );
      showError( "ODA Verify Exception", e.getMessage( ) );
      setPageComplete( false );
      return false
   }
   catch ( Exception e )
   {
      System.out.println( e.getMessage( ) );
      showError( "Verify Exception", e.getMessage( ) );
      setPageComplete( false );
      return false;
```

```
        }
        finally
        {
          try
          {
            queryButton.setEnabled( true );
            conn.close( );
          }
          catch ( OdaException e )
          {
            System.out.println( e.getMessage( ) );
            setMessage( e.getLocalizedMessage( ),
              ERROR );e.getMessage( ) );
            setPageComplete( false );
            return false;
          }
        }
      }
```

■ canLeave( )

When the user chooses OK or attempts to leave the page, the plug-in calls the canLeave( ) method. If the HQL statement verifies or is unchanged, the plug-in permits the user to leave the page, and saves the HQL in the report. If the page is not complete the plug-in prompts the user to verify the query.

Listing 19-58 shows the code for the canLeave( ) method.

Listing 19-58   The canLeave( ) method

```
public boolean canLeave( )
{
if ( !isPageComplete( ) )
{
  setMessage( Messages.getString
  ( "error.selectColumns" ), ERROR );
  return false;
}
return true;
}
```

■ savePage( )

The savePage( ) method is called when the ODA framework calls the collectDataSetDesign( ) method. This action occurs when the user presses the Finish button on the new data set wizard or the OK button on the data set editor is pressed. The savePage( ) method saves the query to the report, as shown in Listing 19-59.

Listing 19-59   The savePage( ) method

```
private boolean savePage( )
{
IConnection conn = null;
```

```
try
{
   IDriver hqDriver = new HibernateDriver( );
   conn = hqDriver.getConnection( null );
   IResultSetMetaData metadata =
   getResultSetMetaData( dataSetDesign
      .getQueryText( ), conn );
   setResultSetMetaData( dataSetDesign, metadata );
}
catch( OdaException e )
{
   dataSetDesign.setResultSets( null );
}
finally
{
   closeConnection( conn );
}
}
```

- getResultSetMetaData( )

The savePage( ) method calls the getResultSetMetaData( ) method when saving the report design. This method retrieves the query metadata that setResultSetMetaData( ) uses to create the data set columns.

Listing 19-60 shows the code for the getResultSetMetaData( ) method.

Listing 19-60   The getResultSetMetaData( ) method

```
private IResultSetMetaData getResultSetMetaData
   ( String queryText, IConnection conn )
   throws OdaException
{
    java.util.Properties prop =
   new java.util.Properties( );
   if( m_hibconfig == null)m_hibconfig = "";
   if( m_mapdir == null)m_mapdir = "";
   prop.put( "HIBCONFIG", m_hibconfig );
   prop.put( "MAPDIR", m_mapdir );
   conn.open( prop );
   IQuery query = conn.newQuery( null );
   query.prepare( queryText );
   return query.getMetaData( );
}
```

- setResultSetMetaData( )

The savePage( ) method calls the setResultSetMetaData( ) method when saving the report design. This method uses the DataSetDesign and the ResultSetMetaData objects for the query to create the columns in the data set for use in the report design.

Listing 19-61 shows the code for the setResultSetMetaData( ) method.

Listing 19-61   The setResultSetMetaData( ) method

```
private void setResultSetMetaData
  ( DataSetDesign dataSetDesign,
    IResultSetMetaData md ) throws OdaException
{
  ResultSetColumns columns =
    DesignSessionUtil.toResultSetColumnsDesign( md );
  ResultSetDefinition resultSetDefn =
    DesignFactory.eINSTANCE
    .createResultSetDefinition( );
  resultSetDefn.setResultSetColumns( columns );
  dataSetDesign.setPrimaryResultSet( resultSetDefn );
  dataSetDesign.getResultSets().setDerivedMetaData( true );
}
```

- collectDataSetDesign( )

  The plug-in calls this method when creating or modifying the query finishes. The plug-in passes the current design to this method. collectDataSetDesign( ) then verifies that a query exists and sets the design query to the value of the query text. The savePage( ) method saves the design and creates the columns in the data set.

  Listing 19-62 shows the code for the collectDataSetDesign( ) method.

Listing 19-62   The collectDataSetDesign( ) method

```
protected DataSetDesign collectDataSetDesign
  ( DataSetDesign design )
{
  if( ! hasValidData( ) )
    return design;
  design.setQueryText( queryText.getText( ) );
  savePage( design );
  return design;
}
```

Building the Hibernate ODA UI plug-in

To build and deploy the org.eclipse.birt.report.data.oda.hibernate.ui plug-in using the Eclipse PDE Manifest Editor, perform the following tasks:

- On Build, specify the Build Configuration to include the following items:

  - In Runtime Information, add the hibernateodaui.jar file.

  - In Binary Build, select the following files and folders:

    - META-INF

    - plugin.xml

  Build Configuration appears, as shown in Figure 19-46.

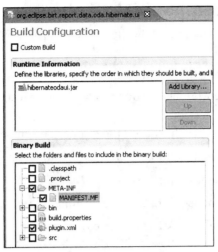

Figure 19-46   Build Configuration settings

- On Overview, in Exporting, choose Export Wizard and perform the following tasks:

  - In Options, verify that Package plug-ins as individual JAR archives is not selected.

  - In Destination, choose the directory, $INSTALL_DIR\birt-runtime-2_1_0\Report Engine, as shown in Figure 19-47.

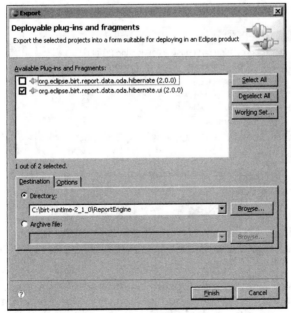

Figure 19-47   Using the Export wizard

Testing the Hibernate ODA UI plug-in

You can test the Hibernate ODA UI plug-in using a run-time instance of the
Eclipse PDE workbench.

How to launch the Hibernate ODA UI plug-in

1 On the Eclipse PDE Manifest Editor, in Overview—Testing, choose Launch
   an Eclipse application.

2 In the run-time workbench, choose the Report Design perspective.

3 In Report Design, create a new report project and create a new blank report.

How to specify a data source and data set

1 In Report Design, choose Data Explorer. Data Explorer appears.

2 In Data Explorer, right-click Data Sources and choose New Data Source, as
   shown in Figure 19-48. New Data Source appears.

Figure 19-48 Choosing New Data Source

On New Data Source, choose Create from a data source type in the following
list and select Hibernate Data Source as the data source type, as shown in
Figure 19-49. Choose Next.

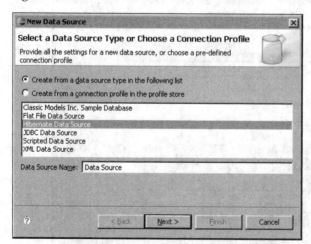

Figure 19-49 Selecting Hibernate Data Source

Hibernate Data Source appears, as shown in Figure 19-50. On Hibernate
Data Source, select the Hibernate configuration file and mapping directory
or leave these items blank if you use the hibfiles directory. Choose Finish.

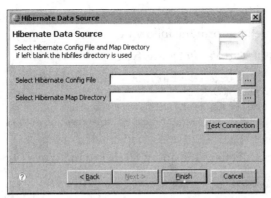

Figure 19-50   Configuring the Hibernate Data Source

Data Explorer appears with the new data source in Data Sources, as shown in Figure 19-51.

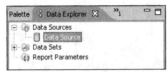

Figure 19-51   New data source in Data Explorer

3 In Data Explorer, right-click Data Sets and choose New Data Set, as shown in Figure 19-52.

Figure 19-52   Choosing New Data Set

New Data Set appears, as shown in Figure 19-53.

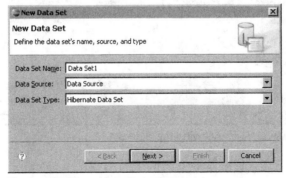

Figure 19-53   New Data Set

Choose Next. Hibernate Data Set appears.

4 On Edit Data Set, perform the following tasks:

1 In Enter HQL and Verify Query, type:

```
select ord.orderNumber, cus.customerNumber,
    cus.customerName
from Orders as ord, Customer as cus
where  ord.customerNumber = cus.customerNumber
and cus.customerNumber = 363
```

Edit Data Set displays the query, as shown in Figure 19-54.

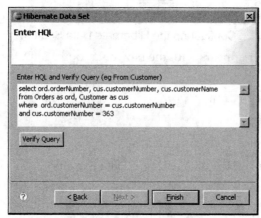

Figure 19-54 Editing the HQL query

2 Choose Verify Query.

3 Choose Finish. Edit Data Set appears. Choose Preview Results. Preview Results appears as shown in Figure 19-55.

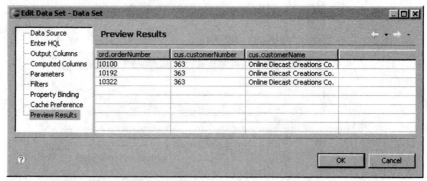

Figure 19-55 Previewing the data set

Choose OK. Data Explorer appears.

5 On Data Explorer, expand Data Sets. The new data set lists three columns, as shown in Figure 19-56.

Figure 19-56   Data set in Data Explorer

6 To build a report that uses the data set, perform the following tasks:

1 On Data Explorer, drag Data Set to the layout editor. The layout appears as shown in Figure 19-57.

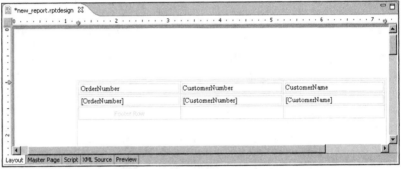

Figure 19-57   Report design in the layout editor

2 To view the output for new_report_1.rptdesign, choose Preview. The Preview appears as shown in Figure 19-58.

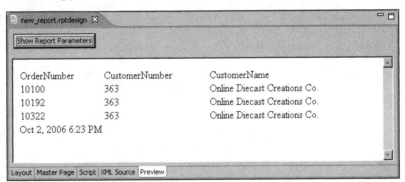

Figure 19-58   Preview of the report design

abstract base class

A class that organizes a class hierarchy or defines methods and variables that apply to descendant classes. An abstract base class does not support the creation of instances.

Related terms
class, class hierarchy, descendant class, object, method, variable

Active Server Page (ASP)

A web server technology that Microsoft Corporation developed. ASPs support the creation of dynamic, interactive sessions. The technology contains both HTML and embedded programming code that is written in VBScript or JavaScript.

Related terms
hypertext markup language (HTML), JavaScript, VBScript (Visual Basic Script Edition), web server

Contrast with
JavaServer Page (JSP)

aggregate expression

An expression that uses an aggregate function to produce an aggregate value. For example, the expression, Total.max(row["SPEED"]), produces an aggregate value that is the maximum value of the field, SPEED, in the data rows.

Related terms
aggregate function, aggregate value, data row, expression, field, value

Contrast with
regular expression

aggregate function

A function that performs a calculation over a set of data rows. For example, Total.ave( ) calculates the average value of a specified numeric field over a set of data rows. An aggregate expression can contain one or more of the following aggregate functions: Total.ave( ), Total.count( ), Total.countDistinct( ), Total.first( ), Total.last( ), Total.max( ), Total.median( ), Total.min( ),

Total.mode( ), Total.movingAve( ), Total.runningSum( ), Total.stdDev( ), Total.sum( ), Total.variance( ), and Total.weightedAve( ).

Related terms
aggregate expression, data row, function

Contrast with
aggregate value

aggregate value

The result of applying an aggregate function to a set of data rows. For example, consider a set of data rows with a field, SPEED, which has values: 20, 10, 30, 15, 40. The aggregate expression, Total.max(row["SPEED"]), produces the aggregate value, 40, which is the maximum value for the field.

Related terms
aggregate expression, aggregate function, data row, field, value

alias

1   In a SQL SELECT statement, an alternative name given to a database table or column.

2   An alternative name that is given to a table column for use in an expression or in code in a script method. This name must be a valid variable name that begins with a letter and contains only alphanumeric characters.

Related terms
column, expression, method, SQL SELECT statement, table, variable

Contrast with
display name

ancestor class

A class in the inheritance hierarchy from which a particular class directly or indirectly derives.

Related terms
class, inheritance

Contrast with
class hierarchy, descendant class, subclass, superclass

applet

A small desktop application that usually performs a simple task, for example, a Java program that runs directly from the web browser.

Related terms
application, Java

application

A complete, self-contained program that performs a specific set of related tasks.

Contrast with
applet

application programming interface (API)

A set of routines, including functions, methods, and procedures, that exposes application functionality to support integration and extend applications.

Related terms
application, function, method, procedure

argument   A constant, expression, or variable that supplies data to a function or method.

Related terms
constant, data, expression, function, method, variable

array   A data variable that consists of sequentially indexed elements that have the same data type. Each element has a common name, a common data type, and a unique index number identifier. Changes to an element of an array do not affect other elements.

Related terms
data, data type, variable

assignment statement

A statement that assigns a value to a variable. For example:

```
StringToDisplay = "My Name"
```

Related terms
statement, value, variable

BIRT   *See* Business Intelligence and Reporting Tools (BIRT).

BIRT extension

See Business Intelligence and Reporting Tools (BIRT) extension.

BIRT Report Designer

See Business Intelligence and Reporting Tools (BIRT) Report Designer.

BIRT technology

See Business Intelligence and Reporting Tools (BIRT) technology.

bookmark   An expression that identifies a report element. A bookmark is used in a hyperlink expression.

Related terms
expression, hyperlink, report element

Boolean expression

An expression that evaluates to True or False. For example, Total > 3000 is a Boolean expression. If the condition is met, the condition evaluates to True. If the condition is not met, the condition evaluates to False.

Related term
expression

Contrast with
numeric expression

breakpoint

In BIRT Report Designer, a place marker in a program that is being debugged. At a breakpoint, execution pauses so that the report developer can examine and edit data values as necessary.

Related terms
Business Intelligence and Reporting Tools (BIRT) Report Designer, data, debug, value

bridge class

A class that maps the functionality of one class to the similar behavior of another class. For example, the JDBC-ODBC bridge class enables applications that use standard JDBC protocol to access a database that uses the ODBC protocol. BIRT Report Designer and BIRT RCP Report Designer use this type of class.

Related terms
application, Business Intelligence and Reporting Tools (BIRT) Report Designer, Business Intelligence and Reporting Tools (BIRT) Rich Client Platform (RCP) Report Designer, class, Java Database Connectivity (JDBC), open database connectivity (ODBC), protocol

Business Intelligence and Reporting Tools (BIRT)

A reporting platform that is built on the Eclipse platform, the industry standard for open source software development. BIRT provides a complete solution for extracting data, processing data to answer business questions, and presenting the results in a formatted document that is meaningful to end users.

Related terms
data, Eclipse, report

Contrast with
Business Intelligence and Reporting Tools (BIRT) extension

Business Intelligence and Reporting Tools (BIRT) Chart Engine

A tool that supports designing and deploying charts outside a report design. With this engine, Java developers embed charting capabilities into an application. BIRT Chart Engine is a set of Eclipse plug-ins and Java archive (.jar) files. The chart engine is also known as the charting library.

Related terms
application, Business Intelligence and Reporting Tools (BIRT), chart, design, Eclipse platform, Java, Java archive (.jar) file, plug-in, report

Contrast with
Business Intelligence and Reporting Tools (BIRT) Report Engine

Business Intelligence and Reporting Tools (BIRT) Demo Database

A sample database that is used in tutorials in online help for BIRT Report Designer and BIRT RCP Report Designer. This package provides this demo database in Derby, Microsoft Access, and MySQL formats.

Related terms
Business Intelligence and Reporting Tools (BIRT), Business Intelligence and Reporting Tools (BIRT) Report Designer, Business Intelligence and Reporting Tools (BIRT) Rich Client Platform (RCP) Report Designer

Business Intelligence and Reporting Tools (BIRT) extension

A related set of extension points that adds custom functionality to the BIRT platform. BIRT extensions are:

- Charting extension
- Open data access (ODA) extension
- Rendering extension
- Report item extension

Related terms
Business Intelligence and Reporting Tools (BIRT), charting extension, extension, extension point, rendering extension, report, report item extension

Business Intelligence and Reporting Tools (BIRT) Report Designer

A tool that builds BIRT report designs and previews reports that are generated from the designs. BIRT Report Designer is a set of plug-ins to the Eclipse platform and includes BIRT Chart Engine, BIRT Demo Database, and BIRT Report Engine. A report developer who uses this tool can access the full capabilities of the Eclipse platform.

Related terms
Business Intelligence and Reporting Tools (BIRT), Business Intelligence and Reporting Tools (BIRT) Chart Engine, Business Intelligence and Reporting Tools (BIRT) Demo Database, Business Intelligence and Reporting Tools (BIRT) Report Engine, design, Eclipse platform, plug-in, report

Contrast with
Business Intelligence and Reporting Tools (BIRT) Rich Client Platform (RCP) Report Designer

Business Intelligence and Reporting Tools (BIRT) Report Engine

A component that supports deploying BIRT charting, reporting and viewing capabilities on an application server. BIRT Report Engine consists of a set of Java archive (.jar) files, web archive (.war) files, and web applications.

Related terms
application, Business Intelligence and Reporting Tools (BIRT), Java archive (.jar) file, report, web archive (.war) file

Contrast with
Business Intelligence and Reporting Tools (BIRT) Chart Engine

Business Intelligence and Reporting Tools (BIRT) Rich Client Platform (RCP) Report Designer

A stand-alone tool that builds BIRT report designs and previews reports that are generated from the designs. BIRT RCP Report Designer uses the Eclipse Rich Client Platform. This tool includes BIRT Report Engine, BIRT Chart Engine, and BIRT Demo Database. BIRT RCP Report Designer supports report design and preview functionality without the additional overhead of the full Eclipse platform. BIRT RCP Report Designer does not support the Java-based scripting and the report debugger functionality it provides. BIRT RCP Report Designer can use, but not create, BIRT extensions.

Related terms
Business Intelligence and Reporting Tools (BIRT), Business Intelligence and Reporting Tools (BIRT) extension, Business Intelligence and Reporting Tools (BIRT) Chart Engine, Business Intelligence and Reporting Tools (BIRT) Demo Database, Business Intelligence and Reporting Tools (BIRT) Report Engine, debug, design, Eclipse platform, Eclipse Rich Client Platform (RCP), extension, JavaScript, library (.rptlibrary) file, plug-in, report

Contrast with
Business Intelligence and Reporting Tools (BIRT) Report Designer

Business Intelligence and Reporting Tools (BIRT) Samples

A sample of a BIRT report item extension and examples of BIRT charting applications. The report item extension sample is an Eclipse platform plug-in. The charting applications use BIRT Chart Engine. Java developers use these examples as models of how to design custom report items and embed charting capabilities in an application.

Related terms
application, Business Intelligence and Reporting Tools (BIRT), Business Intelligence and Reporting Tools (BIRT) Chart Engine, chart, design, Eclipse, Eclipse platform, Java, plug-in, report, report item, report item extension

Business Intelligence and Reporting Tools (BIRT) technology

A set of Java applications and APIs that support the design and deployment of a business report. BIRT applications include BIRT Report Designer, BIRT RCP Report Designer, and a report viewer web application servlet. The BIRT Java APIs provide programmatic access to BIRT functionality.

Related terms
application, application programming interface (API), Business Intelligence and Reporting Tools (BIRT), Business Intelligence and Reporting Tools (BIRT) Report Designer, Business Intelligence and Reporting Tools (BIRT) Rich Client Platform (RCP) Report Designer, Java, report viewer servlet

Business Intelligence and Reporting Tools (BIRT) Test Suite

A set of test packages for BIRT. BIRT developers use these test packages to perform regression testing when they modify BIRT source code. Report developers and application developers do not need to install this BIRT Test Suite.

cascading parameters

Report parameters that have a hierarchical relationship. For example, the following parameters have a hierarchical relationship:

```
Country
    State
        City
```

In a group of cascading parameters, each report parameter displays a set of values. When a report user selects a value from the top-level parameter, the selected value determines the values that the next parameter displays, and so on. Cascading parameters display only relevant values to the user. Figure G-1 shows cascading parameters as they appear to a report user.

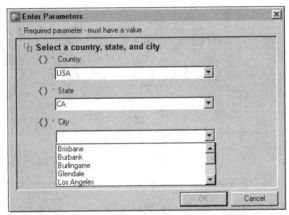

Figure G-1   Cascading parameters

Related terms
hierarchy, parameter, report, value

Contrast with
cascading style sheet (CSS)

cascading style sheet (CSS)

A file that contains a set of rules that attach formats and styles to specified HTML elements. For example, a cascading style sheet can specify the color, font, and size for an HTML heading.

Related terms
element, font, hypertext markup language (HTML), style

Contrast with
template

case sensitivity

A condition in which the letter case is significant for the purposes of comparison. For example, "McManus" does not match "MCMANUS" or "mcmanus" in a case-sensitive environment.

category

In an area, bar, line, step, or stock chart, one of the discrete values that organizes data on an axis that does not use a numerical scale. Typically, the x-axis of a chart displays category values. In a pie chart, category values are called orthogonal axis values and define which sectors appear in a pie.

Related terms
chart, data, value

Contrast with
series

cell

An intersection of a row and a column in a grid element, or table element. Figure G-2 shows a cell.

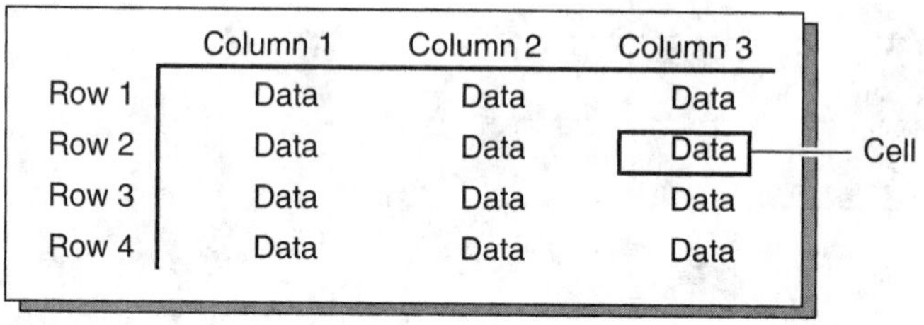

Figure G-2   Cell

Related terms
column, grid element, row, table element

character

An elementary mark that represents data, usually in the form of a graphic spatial arrangement of connected or adjacent strokes, such as a letter or a digit. A character is independent of font size and other display properties. For example, an uppercase C is a character.

Related term
data

Contrast with
character set, glyph

character set

A mapping of specific characters to code points. For example, in most character sets, the letter A maps to the hexadecimal value 0x21.

Related terms
character, code point

Contrast with
locale

chart

A graphic representation of data or the relationships among sets of data.

Related term
data

chart element

A report item that displays values from data rows in the form of a chart. The chart element can use data rows from the report design's data set or a different data set. A report item extension defines the chart element.

Related terms
chart, data, data row, data set, design, element, report, report item, report item extension, value

Contrast with
charting extension

chart engine

See Business Intelligence and Reporting Tools (BIRT) Chart Engine.

charting extension

A BIRT extension that adds a new type of chart, a new component to an existing chart type, or a new user interface component to the BIRT chart engine.

Related terms
Business Intelligence and Reporting Tools (BIRT), Business Intelligence and Reporting Tools (BIRT) extension, Business Intelligence and Reporting Tools (BIRT) Chart Engine, chart, extension

charting library

See Business Intelligence and Reporting Tools (BIRT) Chart Engine.

class

A set of methods and variables that defines the attributes and behavior of an object. All objects of a given class are identical in form and behavior but can contain different data in their variables.

Related terms
data, method, object, variable

Contrast with
subclass, superclass

class hierarchy

A tree structure that represents the inheritance relationships among a set of classes.

Related terms
class, inheritance

class name

A unique name for a class that permits unambiguous references to its public methods and variables.

Related terms
class, method, variable

class variable

A variable that all instances of a class share. The run-time system creates only one copy of a class variable. The value of the class variable is the same for all instances of the class, for example, the taxRate variable in an Order class.

Related terms
class, object, value, variable

Contrast with
class variable, dynamic variable, field variable, global variable, instance variable, local variable, member variable, static variable

code point

A hexadecimal value. Every character in a character set is represented by a code point. The computer uses the code point to process the character.

Related terms
character, character set

column

1 A named field in a database table or query. For each data row, the column has a different value, called the column value. The term column refers to the definition of the column, not to any particular value. Figure G-3 shows a column in a database table.

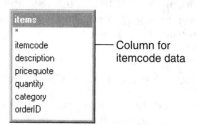

Figure G-3   Column in a database table

2 A vertical sequence of cells in a cross tab, grid element, or table element. Figure G-4 shows a column in a cross tab.

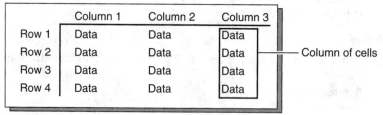

Figure G-4   Column in a cross tab

Related terms
cell, cross tab, field, grid element, query, data row, table, table element, value

column binding

A named column that defines an expression that specifies what data to return. For each piece of data to display in a report, there must be column binding. Column bindings form an intermediate layer between data-set data and report elements.

Related terms
column, data, data set, expression, report, report element

Common Gateway Interface (CGI)

An internet standard that describes how a web server accesses external programs to return data to the user as a generated web page. When a web user fills out a form, a CGI program handles the data and calls other programs as necessary.

Related terms
data, web page, web server

computed column

See computed field.

computed field

A field that displays the result of an expression rather than stored data.

Related terms
field, data, expression

Contrast with
computed value

computed value

The result of a calculation that is defined by an expression. To display a computed value in a report, use a data element.

Related terms
data element, expression, report, value

Contrast with
computed field

conditional expression

See Boolean expression.

configuration file

In open data access (ODA), a file that specifies the ODA interface version of the driver and defines the structure, contents, and semantics of requests and responses between the open data source and the design tool.

Related terms
data source, interface, open data access (ODA), open data access (ODA) driver, request, response

Connection

A Java object that provides access to a data source.

Related terms
data source, Java, object

constant An unchanging, predefined value. A constant does not change while a program is running, but the value of a field or variable can change.

Contrast with
field, value, variable

constructor code

Code that initializes an instance of a class.

Related terms
class, object

container 1 An application that acts as a master program to hold and execute a set of commands or to run other software routines. For example, application servers provide containers that support communication between applications and Enterprise JavaBeans.

2 A data structure that holds one or more different types of data. For example, a grid element can contain label elements and other report items.

Related terms
application, data, Enterprise JavaBean (EJB), grid element, label element, report item

containment

A relationship among instantiated objects in a report. One object, the container, incorporates other objects, the contents.

Related terms
container, instantiation, object, report

containment hierarchy

A hierarchy of objects in a report.

Related terms
hierarchy, object, report

converter A tool that converts data from one format to another format.

Related terms
data, format

cross tab A report that summarizes data from database table columns into a concise format for analysis. Data appears in a matrix with rows and columns. Every cell in a cross tab contains an aggregate value. A cross tab shows how one item relates to another, such as order totals by credit rating and order status. Figure G-5 shows a cross tab.

Order Totals by Credit Rating and Order Status											
	A			B			C			Totals	
	Quantity	Ave Qty	Amount	Quantity	Ave Qty	Amount	Quantity	Ave Qty	Amount	Quantity	Ave Qty	Amount
Open	98,205	349	9,870,799	40,472	283	4,673,517	4,980	332	636,555	143,657	327	15,180,871
Closed	171,813	365	20,633,175	131,183	497	14,465,314	21,790	198	2,591,731	324,786	384	37,690,220
In Evaluation	90,969	469	12,135,326	22,168	411	2,596,936	0		0	113,137	456	14,732,262
Cancelled	23,944	855	3,029,520	0		0	0		0	23,944	855	3,029,520
Selected	10,540	527	1,375,204	0		0	0		0	10,540	527	1,375,204
Totals	395,471	398	47,044,024	193,823	420	21,735,767	26,770	214	3,228,286	616,064	390	72,008,077

Figure G-5   Cross tab

Related terms
aggregate value, cell, column, data, grid, report, row, table, value
Contrast with
aggregate function

CSS   *See* cascading style sheet (CSS).

custom data source

See open data access (ODA).

data   Information that is stored in databases, flat files, or other data sources that can appear in a report.

Related terms
data source, flat file, report
Contrast with
metadata

data element

 A report item that displays a computed value or a value from a data set field.
Related terms
computed value, data set, element, field, report item, value
Contrast with
label element, Report Object Model (ROM) element, text element

Data Explorer

An Eclipse view that shows the data sources, data sets, and report parameters that were created for use in a report. Use Data Explorer to create, edit, or delete these items. Figure G-6 shows Data Explorer.

Figure G-6   Data Explorer

Related terms
data set, data source, Eclipse view, parameter, report

data point

A point on a chart that corresponds to a particular pair of x- and y-axis values.

Related terms
chart, value

Contrast with
data row, data set

data row

One row of data that a data set returns. A data set, which specifies the data to retrieve from a data source, typically returns many data rows.

Related terms
data, data set, data source, row

Contrast with
data point, filter

data set

A description of the data to retrieve or compute from a data source.

Related terms
data, data source

Contrast with
data point, data row

data set field

See column.

data set parameter

A parameter that is associated with a data set column and passes an expression to extend dynamically the query's WHERE clause. A data set parameter restricts the number of data rows that the data set supplies to the report.

Related terms
column, data row, data set, expression, parameter, query, report

Contrast with
report parameter

data source

1   A SQL database or other repository of data. For example, a flat file can be a data source.

2   An object that contains the connection information for an external data source, such as a flat file, a SQL database, or another repository of data.

Related terms
data, flat file, SQL (Structured Query Language)

Contrast with
data row, data set

data type 1 A category for values that determines their characteristics, such as the information they can hold and the permitted operations.

2 The data type of a value determines the default appearance of the value in a report. This appearance depends on the locale in which a user generates the report. For example, the order in which year, month, and day appear in a date-and-time data value depends on the locale. BIRT uses three fundamental data types: date-and-time, numeric, and string. Data sources such as relational databases support more data types, which BIRT maps to the appropriate fundamental data type.

Related terms
Business Intelligence and Reporting Tools (BIRT), date-and-time data type, locale, numeric data type, report, String data type, value, variable

database connection

See data source.

database management system (DBMS)

Software that organizes simultaneous access to shared data. Database management systems store relationships among various data elements.

Related term
data

database schema

See schema.

date-and-time data type

A data type for date-and-time calculations. Report items can contain expressions or fields with a date-and-time data type. The appearance of date-and-time values in the report document is based on locale and format settings specified by your computer and the report design.

Related terms
data type, design, expression, field, format, locale, report, report item

debug To detect, locate, and fix errors. Typically, debugging involves executing specific portions of a computer program and analyzing the operation of those portions.

declaration

The definition of a class, constant, method, or variable that specifies the name and, if appropriate, the data type.

Related terms
class, constant, data type, method, variable

derived class

See descendant class.

descendant class

A class that is based on another class.

Related term
class

Contrast with
subclass, superclass

design

1 To create a report specification. Designing a report includes selecting data, laying out the report visually, and saving the layout in a report design file.

2 A report specification. A report design (.rptdesign) file contains a report design.

Related terms
data, layout, report, report design (.rptdesign) file

DHTML (dynamic hypertext markup language)

See dynamic hypertext markup language (DHTML).

display name

An alternative name for a table column, report parameter, chart series, or user-defined ROM property. BIRT Report Designer displays this alternative name in the user interface, for example, as a column heading in a report. This name can contain any character, including spaces and punctuation.

Related terms
Business Intelligence and Reporting Tools (BIRT) Report Designer, character, chart, column, Data Explorer, report, report parameter, Report Object Model (ROM), table, value

Contrast with
alias

document object model (DOM)

A model that defines the structure of a document such as an HTML or XML document. The document object model defines interfaces that dynamically create, access, and manipulate the internal structure of the document. The URL to the W3C document object model is:

```
www.w3.org/DOM/
```

Related terms
extensible markup language (XML), hypertext markup language (HTML), interface, Uniform Resource Locator (URL), World Wide Web Consortium (W3C)

Contrast with
document type definition (DTD), structured content

document type definition (DTD)

A set of markup tags and the interpretation of those tags that together define the structure of an XML document.

Related terms
extensible markup language (XML), tag

Contrast with
document object model (DOM), schema, structured content

domain name

A name that defines a node on the internet. For example, the Eclipse Foundation's domain name is eclipse. The URL is:

```
www.eclipse.org
```

Related terms
node, Uniform Resource Locator (URL)

driver An interface that supports communication between an application and another application or a peripheral device such as a printer.

Related term
interface

dynamic hypertext markup language (DHTML)

An HTML extension that provides enhanced viewing capabilities and interactivity in a web page without the necessity for communication with a web server. The Document Object Model Group of the W3C develops DHTML standards.

Related terms
document object model (DOM), hypertext markup language (HTML), web page, web server, World Wide Web Consortium (W3C)

dynamic text element

 A data element that displays text data that contains multiple style formats and a variable amount of text. A dynamic text element adjusts its size to accommodate varying amounts of data. Use a dynamic text element to display a data source field that contains formatted text. A dynamic text element supports plain or HTML text.

Related terms
data, data source, field, format, hypertext markup language (HTML)

Contrast with
text element

dynamic variable

A variable that changes during program execution. The program requests the memory allocation for a dynamic variable at run time.

Related term
variable

Contrast with
class variable, field variable, global variable, instance variable, local variable, member variable, static variable

Eclipse　An open platform for tool integration that is built by an open community of tool providers. The Eclipse platform is written in Java and includes extensive plug-in construction toolkits and examples.

Related terms
Eclipse platform, Java, plug-in

Contrast with
Business Intelligence and Reporting Tools (BIRT) extension

Eclipse Modeling Framework (EMF)

A Java framework and code generation facility for building tools and other applications that are based on a structured model. EMF uses XML schemas to generate the EMF model of a plug-in. For example, a BIRT chart type uses EMF to represent the chart structure and properties.

Related terms
application, Business Intelligence and Reporting Tools (BIRT) technology, chart, Eclipse, extensible markup language (XML), framework, Java, plug-in, property, schema

Eclipse perspective

A predefined layout of the Eclipse Workbench, including which Eclipse views are visible and where they appear. A perspective also controls what appears in certain menus and toolbars. A user can switch the perspective to work on a different task and can rearrange and customize a perspective to better suit a particular task. Figure G-7 shows the Eclipse perspective.

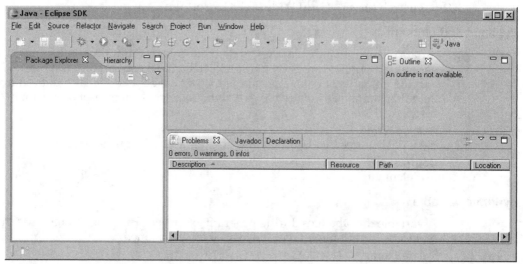

Figure G-7　Eclipse perspective

Related terms
Eclipse, Eclipse view, Eclipse Workbench

Eclipse platform

The core framework and services in which Eclipse plug-in extensions exist. The Eclipse platform provides the run time in which plug-ins load and run. The Eclipse platform consists of a core component and a user interface component. The user interface component is known as the Eclipse Workbench. The core portion of the Eclipse platform is called the platform core or the core.

Related terms
Eclipse, Eclipse Workbench, extension, framework, plug-in

Eclipse Plug-in Development Environment (PDE)

An integrated design tool for creating, developing, testing, and deploying a plug-in. The Eclipse PDE provides wizards, editors, views, and launchers that support plug-in development. The Eclipse PDE supports host and run-time instances of a workbench project. The host instance provides the development environment. The run-time instance enables the launching of a plug-in for testing purposes.

Related terms
design, Eclipse, Eclipse project, Eclipse Workbench, object, plug-in

Eclipse project

A user-specified directory within an Eclipse workspace. An Eclipse project contains folders and files that are used for builds, version management, sharing, and resource organization.

Related terms
Eclipse, Eclipse workspace

Eclipse Rich Client Platform (RCP)

The Eclipse framework for building a client application that uses a minimal set of plug-ins. Eclipse Rich Client Platform (RCP) uses a subset of the components that are available in the Eclipse platform. An Eclipse rich client application is typically a specialized user interface that supports a specific function, such as the report development tools in the BIRT Rich Client Platform.

Related terms
application, Business Intelligence and Reporting Tools (BIRT), Eclipse, Eclipse platform, framework, plug-in, report

Eclipse view

A panel on the Eclipse Workbench, similar to a pane in Windows. An Eclipse view can be an editor, the Navigator, a palette of report items, a graphical report designer, or any other functional component that Eclipse or an Eclipse project provides. A view can have its own menus and toolbars. Multiple views can be visible at one time.

Related terms
design, Eclipse, Eclipse perspective, Eclipse project, Eclipse Workbench, Navigator, Palette, report, report item

Eclipse Workbench

The Eclipse desktop development environment, which consists of one or more Eclipse perspectives.

Related terms
Eclipse, Eclipse perspective

Contrast with
Eclipse Plug-in Development Environment (PDE), Eclipse workspace

Eclipse workspace

A user-specified directory that contains one or more Eclipse projects. An Eclipse workspace is a general umbrella for managing resources in the Eclipse platform. The Eclipse platform can contain one or more workspaces. A user can switch between workspaces.

Related terms
Eclipse platform, Eclipse project

Contrast with
Eclipse Workbench

EJB   *See* Enterprise JavaBean (EJB).

element   **1** In Report Object Model (ROM), a component that describes a piece of a report. A ROM element typically has a name and a set of properties.

2 A tag-delimited structure in an XML or HTML document that contains a unit of data. For example, the root element of an HTML page starts with the beginning tag, <HTML>, and ends with the closing tag, </HTML>. This root element encloses all the other elements that define the contents of a page. An XML element must be well-formed, with both a beginning and a closing tag. In HTML, some tags, such as <br>, the forced line break tag, do not require a closing tag.

Related terms
data, extensible markup language (XML), hypertext markup language (HTML), property, report, Report Object Model (ROM), Report Object Model (ROM) element, tag, well-formed XML

Contrast with
report item

ellipsis button

 A button that opens tools that you use to perform tasks, such as navigating to a file, building an expression, or specifying localized text.

encapsulation

A technique of packaging related functions and subroutines together. Encapsulation compartmentalizes the structure and behavior of a class, hiding the implementation details, so that parts of an object-oriented system need not depend upon or affect each other's internal details.

Related terms
class, function, object

Contrast with
object-oriented programming

enterprise A large collection of networked computers that run on multiple platforms. Enterprise systems can include both mainframes and workstations that are integrated in a single, managed environment. Typical software products that are used in an enterprise environment include web browsers, applications, applets, web tools, and multiple databases that support a warehouse of information.

Related terms
applet, application

Contrast with
Enterprise JavaBean (EJB), enterprise reporting

Enterprise JavaBean (EJB)

A standards-based server-side component that encapsulates the business logic of an application. An EJB can provide access to data or model the data itself. Application servers provide the deployment environment for EJBs.

Related terms
application, data, JavaBean

Contrast with
Java

enterprise reporting

The production of a high volume of simple and complex structured documents that collect data from a variety of data sources. A large number of geographically distributed users who are working in both client/server and internet environments receive, work with, and modify these reports.

Related terms
data, data source, report

Contrast with
enterprise, structured content

event An action or occurrence recognized by an object. Each object responds to a predefined set of events that can be extended by the developer.

Related term
object

Contrast with
event handler, event listener

event handler

A Java or JavaScript method that is executed upon the firing of a BIRT event. BIRT fires events at various times in the report generation process. By writing custom code for the associated event handlers, the BIRT report developer can provide special handling at the time the events are fired. Report items, data sets, and data sources all have event handlers for which the report developer can provide custom code.

Related terms
Business Intelligence and Reporting Tools (BIRT), data set, data source, event, Java, JavaScript, method, report, report item

Contrast with
event listener

event listener

An interface that detects when a particular event occurs and runs a registered method in response to that event.

Related terms
event, method

Contrast with
event handler

exception

An abnormal situation that a program encounters. In some cases, the program handles the exception and returns a message to the user or application that is running the program. In other cases, the program cannot handle the exception, and the program terminates.

Related term
application

expression

A combination of constants, functions, literal values, names of fields, and operators that evaluates to a single value.

Related terms
constant, field, function, operator, value

Contrast with
aggregate expression, regular expression

expression builder

A tool for selecting data fields, functions, and operators to write JavaScript expressions. Figure G-8 shows the expression builder.

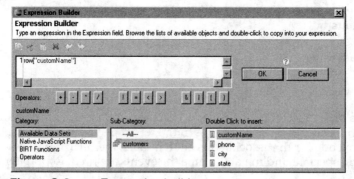

Figure G-8   Expression builder

Related terms
data, expression, field, function, JavaScript, operator

extensible markup language (XML)

A markup language that supports the interchange of data among data sources and applications. Using XML, a wide variety of applications, legacy systems, and databases can exchange information. XML is content-oriented rather than format-oriented. XML uses tags to structure data into nested elements. An XML schema that is structured according to the rules that were defined by the W3C describes the structure of the data.

XML documents must be well formed.

Related terms
application, data, data source, element, schema, tag, well-formed XML, World Wide Web Consortium (W3C)

Contrast with
hypertext markup language (HTML)

extension

A module that adds functionality to an application. BIRT consists of a set of extensions, called plug-ins, which add functionality to the Eclipse development environment.

Related terms
application, Business Intelligence and Reporting Tools (BIRT), Eclipse, plug-in

Contrast with
Business Intelligence and Reporting Tools (BIRT) extension,extension point

extension point

A defined place in an application where a developer adds custom functionality. The APIs in BIRT support adding custom functionality to the BIRT framework. In the Eclipse Plug-in Development Environment (PDE), a developer views the extension points in the PDE Manifest Editor to guide and control plug-in development tasks.

Related terms
application, application programming interface (API), Business Intelligence and Reporting Tools (BIRT), Eclipse Plug-in Development Environment (PDE), extension, framework, plug-in

Contrast with
Business Intelligence and Reporting Tools (BIRT) extension

field

The smallest identifiable part of a database table structure. In a relational database, a field is also called a column.

Related terms
column, table

field variable

In Java, a member variable with public visibility.

Related terms
Java, member, variable
Contrast with
class variable, dynamic variable, field variable, global variable, instance variable, local variable, member variable, static variable

file types   Table G-1 lists the report designer's file types.

Table G-1   File types

Display name	Glossary term	File type
BIRT Report Design	report design (.rptdesign) file	RPTDESIGN
BIRT Report Design Library	library (.rptlibrary) file	RPTLIBRARY
BIRT Report Design Template	report template (.rpttemplate) file	RPTTEMPLATE
BIRT Report Document	report document (.rptdocument) file	RPTDOCUMENT

filter   To exclude any data rows from the result set that do not meet a set of conditions. Some external data sources can filter data as specified by conditions that the query includes directly or through the use of report parameters. In addition, BIRT can filter data after retrieval from the external data source. Report developers can specify conditions for filtering in either the data set or a report item.

Related terms
Business Intelligence and Reporting Tools (BIRT), data, data row, data set, data source, query, report, report item, report parameter, result set

flat file   A file that contains data in the form of text.
Related term
data
Contrast with
data source

font   A family of characters of a given style. Fonts contain information that specifies typeface, weight, posture, and type size.
Related term
character

footer   A unit of information that appears at the bottom of a page.
Contrast with
header

format   1 A set of standard options with which to display and print currency values, dates, numbers, and times.

   2 A specification that describes layout and properties of report data or other information, for example, PDF or HTML.

Related terms
data, hypertext markup language (HTML), layout, property, report, value
Contrast with
style

forms-capable browser

A web browser that handles hypertext markup language (HTML) forms. HTML tags enable interactive forms, including check boxes, drop-down lists, fill-in text areas, and option buttons.

Related terms
hypertext markup language (HTML), tag

framework

A set of interrelated classes that provide an architecture for building an application.

Related terms
application, class

function

A sequence of instructions that are defined as a separate unit within a program. To invoke the function, include its name as one of the instructions anywhere in the program. BIRT provides JavaScript functions to support building expressions.

Related terms
Business Intelligence and Reporting Tools (BIRT), expression, JavaScript,
Contrast with
method

global variable

A variable that is available at all levels in an application. A global variable stays in memory in the scope of all executing procedures until the application terminates.

Related terms
application, procedure, scope, variable
Contrast with
class variable, dynamic variable, field variable, global variable, instance variable, local variable, member variable, static variable

glyph

1 An image that is used in the visual representation of a character.

2 A specific letter form from a specific font. An uppercase C in Palatino font is a glyph.

Related terms
character, font

grandchild class

See descendant class.

grandparent class

See ancestor class.

grid

See grid element.

grid element

 A report item that contains and displays other report elements in a static row and column format. A grid element aligns the cells horizontally and vertically.

Figure G-9 shows a report title section that consists of an image element and two text elements that are arranged in a grid element with one row and two columns.

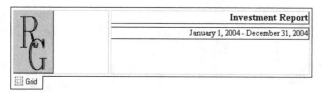

Figure G-9   Grid element

Related terms
cell, column, element, image element, report, report item, row, text element

Contrast with
list element, table element

group

A set of data rows that have one or more column values in common. For example, in a sales report, a group consists of all the orders that are placed by a single customer.

Related terms
column, data row, report, value

Contrast with
group key, grouped report

grouped report

A report that organizes data in logical groups. Figure G-10 shows a grouped report.

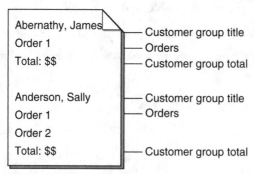

Figure G-10   Grouped report

Related terms
data, group, report

group key   A data set column that is used to group and sort data in a report. For example, a report developer can group and sort customers by credit rank.

Related terms
column, data, data set, group, report, sort

header   **1**   A unit of information that appears at the top of every page.

2   A group header is a unit of information that appears at the beginning of a group section.

Related terms
group, section
Contrast with
footer

hexadecimal number

A number in base 16. A hexadecimal number uses the digits 0 through 9 and the letters A through F. Each place represents a power of 16. By comparison, base 10 numbers use the digits 0 through 9. Each place represents a power of 10.

Contrast with
character set, octal number

hierarchy   Any tree structure that has a root and branches that do not converge.

HTML   *See* hypertext markup language (HTML).

HTML element

See element.

HTTP   *See* hypertext transfer protocol (HTTP).

hyperlink

A connection from one part of a report to another part of the same or different report. Typically, hyperlinks support access to related information within the same report, in another report, or in another application. A change from the standard cursor shape to a cursor shaped like a hand indicates a hyperlink.

Related terms
application, report

hypertext markup language (HTML)

A specification that determines the layout of a web page. HTML is the markup language that tells a parser that the text is a certain portion of a document on the web, for example, the title, heading, or body text. A web browser parses HTML to display a web page.

Related terms
layout, web page

Contrast with
dynamic hypertext markup language (DHTML), extensible markup language (XML)

hypertext markup language page

See web page.

hypertext transfer protocol (HTTP)

An internet standard that supports the exchange of information using the web.

Contrast with
protocol

identifier The name that is assigned to an item in a program such as a class, function, or variable.

Related terms
class, function, variable

image A graphic that appears in a report. BIRT Report Designer supports .bmp, .gif, .jpg, and .png file types.

Related terms
Business Intelligence and Reporting Tools (BIRT) Report Designer, report

Contrast with
image element

image element

 A report item that adds an image to a report design.

Related terms
design, element, image, report, report item

inheritance

A mechanism whereby one class of objects can be defined as a special case of a more general class and includes the method and variable definitions of the general class, known as a base or superclass. The superclass serves as the baseline for the appearance and behavior of the descendant class, which is also known as a subclass. In the subclass, the appearance and behavior can be further customized without affecting the superclass. Typically, a subclass augments or redefines the behavior and structure of its superclass or superclasses. Figure G-11 shows an example of inheritance.

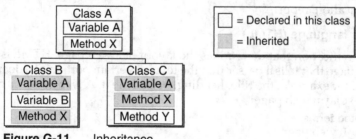

Figure G-11   Inheritance

Related terms
class, descendant class, file types, method, object, subclass, superclass, variable
Contrast with
abstract base class

inner join

1 A type of join that returns records from two tables that are based on their having specified values in the join fields. The most common type of inner join is one in which records are combined and returned when specified field values are equal. For example, if customer and order tables are joined on customer ID, the result set contains only combined customer and order records where the customer IDs are equal, excluding records for customers who have no orders.

2 When creating a joint data set in BIRT, a type of join that returns all rows from both data sets if the specified field values are equal. For example, if customer and order data sets are joined on customer ID, the joint data set returns only combined customer and order rows where the customer IDs are equal.

Related terms
Business Intelligence and Reporting Tools (BIRT) technology, data set, field, join, result set, row, table, value
Contrast with
outer join

input source

See data source.

instance   *See* object.

instance variable

A variable that other instances of a class do not share. The run-time system creates a new copy of an instance variable each time the system instantiates the class. An instance variable can contain a different value in each instance of a class, for example, the customerID variable in a Customer class.

Related terms
class, value, variable
Contrast with
class variable, dynamic variable, field variable, global variable, local variable, member variable, static variable

instantiation

The action of creating an object.

Related term
object
Contrast with
class

interface   **1** The connection and interaction among hardware, software, and the user. Hardware interfaces include plugs, sockets, wires, and electrical pulses traveling through them in a particular pattern. Hardware interfaces include electrical timing considerations such as Ethernet and Token Ring, network topologies, RS-232 transmission, and the IDE, ESDI, SCSI, ISA, EISA, and Micro Channel. Software or programming interfaces are the languages, codes, and messages that programs use to communicate with each other and to the hardware and the user. Software interfaces include applications running on specific operating systems, SMTP e-mail, and LU 6.2 communications protocols.

2 In Java, an interface defines a set of methods to provide a required functionality. The interface provides a mechanism for classes to communicate in order to execute particular actions.

Related terms
application, class, Connection, Java, method, protocol

internationalization

The process of designing an application to work correctly in multiple locales.

Related terms
application, locale

Contrast with
localization

IP address

The unique 32-bit ID of a node on a TCP/IP network.

Related term
node

J2EE   *See* Java 2 Enterprise Edition (J2EE).

J2SE   *See* Java 2 Runtime Standard Edition (J2SE).

JAR   *See* Java archive (.jar) file.

Java   A programming language that is designed for writing client/server and networked applications, particularly for delivery on the web. Java can be used to write applets that animate a web page or create an interactive web site.

Related terms
applet, application, web page

Contrast with
JavaScript

Java 2 Enterprise Edition (J2EE)

A platform-independent environment that includes APIs, services, and transport protocols, and is used to develop and deploy web-based enterprise applications. Typically, this environment is used to develop highly scalable web-based applications. This environment builds on J2SE functionality and requires an accessible J2SE installation.

Related terms
application, application programming interface (API), enterprise, enterprise reporting, Java 2 Runtime Standard Edition (J2SE), protocol

Contrast with
Enterprise JavaBean (EJB), Java Development Kit (JDK)

Java 2 Runtime Standard Edition (J2SE)

A smaller-scale, platform-independent environment that provides supporting functionality to the capabilities of J2EE. The J2SE does not support Enterprise JavaBean or enterprise environment.

Related terms
enterprise, Enterprise JavaBean (EJB), Java 2 Enterprise Edition (J2EE)

Contrast with
Java Development Kit (JDK)

Java archive (.jar) file

A file format that is used to bundle Java applications.

Related terms
application, Java

Contrast with
web archive (.war) file

Java Database Connectivity (JDBC)

A standard protocol that Java uses to access database data sources in a platform-independent manner.

Related terms
data source, Java, protocol

Contrast with
data element, schema

Java Development Kit (JDK)

A Sun Microsystems software development kit that defines the Java API and is used to build Java programs. The kit contains software tools and other programs, examples, and documentation that enable software developers to create applications using the Java programming language.

Related terms
application, application programming interface (API), Java

Contrast with
Java 2 Enterprise Edition (J2EE), Java 2 Runtime Standard Edition (J2SE), JavaServer Page (JSP)

Java Naming and Directory Interface (JNDI)

A naming standard that provides clients with access to EJBs.

Related term
Enterprise JavaBean (EJB)

Java Virtual Machine (JVM)

The Java SDK interpreter that converts Java bytecode into machine language for execution in a specified software and hardware configuration.

Related terms
Java, SDK (Software Development Kit)

JavaBean A reusable, standards-based component that is written in Java that encapsulates the business logic of an application. A JavaBean can provide access to data or model the data itself.

Related terms
application, data, encapsulation, Java

Contrast with
Enterprise JavaBean (EJB), enterprise reporting

JavaScript

An interpreted, platform-independent language that is used to enhance web pages and provide additional functionality in web servers. For example, JavaScript can interact with the HTML of a web page to change an icon when the cursor moves across it.

Related terms
hypertext markup language (HTML), web page, web server

Contrast with
Java

JavaServer Page (JSP)

A standard Java extension that simplifies the creation and management of dynamic web pages. The code combines HTML and Java code in one document. The Java code uses tags that instruct the JSP container to generate a servlet.

Related terms
hypertext markup language (HTML), Java, servlet, tag, web page

JDBC *See* Java Database Connectivity (JDBC).

JDK *See* Java Development Kit (JDK).

JNDI *See* Java Naming and Directory Interface (JNDI).

join A SQL query operation that combines records from two tables and returns them in a result set that is based on the values in the join fields. Without additional qualification, join usually refers to one where field values are equal. For example, customer and order tables are joined on a common field such as customer ID. The result set contains combined customer and order records in which the customer IDs are equal.

Related terms
field, query, result set, SQL (Structured Query Language), table, value

Contrast with
inner join, join condition, outer join, SQL SELECT statement

join condition

A condition that specifies a match in the values of related fields in two tables. Typically, the values are equal. For example, if two tables have a field called customer ID, a join condition exists where the customer ID value in one table equals the customer ID value in the second table.

Related terms
field, join, table, value

joint data set

A data set that combines data from two data sets.

Related terms
data, data set

JSP   *See* JavaServer Page (JSP).

JVM   *See* Java Virtual Machine (JVM).

keyword   A reserved word that is recognized as part of a programming language.

label element

 A report item that displays a short piece of static text in a report.

Related terms
report, report item

Contrast with
data element, text element

layout   The designed appearance of a report. Designing the layout of a report entails placing report items on a page and arranging them in a way that helps the report user analyze the information easily. A report displays information in a tabular list, a series of paragraphs, a chart, or a series of subreports.

Related terms
chart, listing report, report, report item, subreport

layout editor

A window in a report designer in which a report developer arranges, formats, and sizes report elements.

Related terms
design, report

Contrast with
previewer, Property Editor, report editor, script editor

lazy load   The capability in a run-time environment to load a code segment to memory only if it is needed. By lazily loading a code segment, the run-time environment minimizes start-up time and conserves memory resources. For example, BIRT

Report Engine builds a registry at startup that contains the list of available plug-ins, then loads a plug-in only if the processing requires it.

Related terms
Business Intelligence and Reporting Tools (BIRT) Report Engine, plug-in

library   A collection of reusable and shareable report elements. A library can contain embedded images, styles, visual report items, JavaScript code, data sources, and data sets. A report developer uses a report designer to develop a library and to retrieve report elements from a library for use in a report design.

Related terms
Business Intelligence and Reporting Tools (BIRT) Report Designer, data set, data source, design, JavaScript, report element, report item, style

Contrast with
file types

library (.rptlibrary) file

In BIRT Report Designer, an XML file that contains reusable and shareable report elements. A report developer uses a report designer to create a library file directly or from a report design (.rptdesign) file.

Related terms
Business Intelligence and Reporting Tools (BIRT) Report Designer, design, extensible markup language (XML), report design (.rptdesign) file, report element

Contrast with
file types, report design (.rptdesign) file, report document (.rptdocument) file, report template (.rpttemplate) file

link   *See* hyperlink.

listener *See* event listener.

list element

 A report item that iterates through the data rows in a data set. The list element contains and displays other report items in a variety of layouts.

Related terms
data, data row, data set, element, layout, report item,

Contrast with
grid element, table element

listing report

A report that provides a simple view of data. Figure G-12 shows a listing report.

Customer List		
Customer	**Phone**	**Contact**
ANG Resellers	(91) 745 6555	Alejandra Camino
AV Stores, Co.	(171) 555-1555	Rachel Ashworth
Alpha Cognac	61.77.6555	Annette Roulet

Figure G-12   Listing report

Related terms
data, report

local variable

A variable that is available only at the current level in an application. A local variable stays in memory in the scope of an executing procedure until the procedure terminates. When the procedure ends, the run-time system destroys the variable and returns the memory to the system.

Related terms
application, procedure, scope, variable

Contrast with
field variable, global variable

locale A location and the language, date format, currency, sorting sequence, time format, and other such characteristics that are associated with that location. The location is not always identical to the country. There can be multiple languages and locales within one country. For example, China has two locales: Beijing and Hong Kong. Canada has two language-based locales: French and English.

Contrast with
localization

localization

The process of translating database content, printed documents, and software programs into another language. Report developers localize static text in a report so that the report displays text in another language that is appropriate to the locale configured on the user's machine.

Related terms
locale, report

Contrast with
internationalization

manifest A text file in a Java archive (.jar) file that describes the contents of the archive.

Related term
Java archive (.jar) file

master page

A predefined layout that specifies a consistent appearance for all pages of a report. A master page typically includes standard headers and footers that display information such as page numbers, a date, or a copyright statement.

The master page can contain report elements in the header and footer areas only, as shown in Figure G-13.

The master page's header and footer content appears on every page of the report in paginated formats, as shown in Figure G-14.

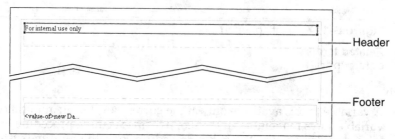

Figure G-13   Master page layout

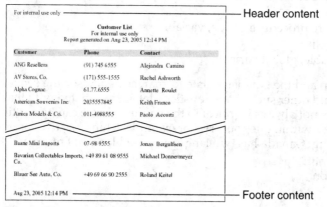

Figure G-14   Master page content

Related terms
Business Intelligence and Reporting Tools (BIRT), Business Intelligence and Reporting Tools (BIRT) Report Designer, footer, grid element, header, hypertext markup language (HTML), layout, previewer, report, template

member   A method or variable that is defined in a class and provides or uses information about the state of a single object.

Related terms
class, method, object, variable

Contrast with
global variable, instance variable, static variable

member variable

A declared variable within a class. A set of member variables in a class contains the data or state for every object of that class.

Related terms
class, data, declaration, object, variable

Contrast with
class variable, dynamic variable, field variable, global variable, instance variable, local variable, static variable

metadata   Information about the structure of data that enables a program to process information. For example, a relational database stores metadata that describes the name, size, and data type of objects in a database, such as tables and columns.

Related terms
column, data, data type, table

method   A routine that provides functionality to an object or a class.

Related terms
class, object

Contrast with
data, function

modal window

A window that retains focus until explicitly closed by the user. Typically, dialog boxes and message windows are modal. For example, an error message dialog box remains on the screen until the user responds.

Contrast with
modeless window

mode   An operational state of a system. Mode implies that there are at least two possible states. Typically, there are many modes for both hardware and software.

modeless window

A window that solicits input but permits users to continue using the current application without closing the modeless window, for example, an Eclipse view.

Related terms
application, Eclipse view

Contrast with
modal window

multithreaded application

An application that handles multiple simultaneous users and sessions.

Related term
application

Navigator   In BIRT Report Designer, an Eclipse view that shows all projects and reports within each project. Each project is a directory in the file system. Use Navigator to manage report files, for example, deleting files, renaming files, or moving files from one project to another. Figure G-15 shows Navigator.

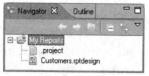

Figure G-15   Navigator

Related terms
Eclipse project, Eclipse view, report

node   A computer that is accessible on the internet.

Contrast with
domain name

null   A value that indicates that a variable or field contains no data.

Related terms
data, field, value, variable

numeric data type

A data type that is used for calculations that result in a value that is a number. Report items that contain expressions or fields with a numeric data type display numbers, based on the formats and locale settings that are specified by your computer and the report design.

Related terms
data type, design, expression, field, format, locale, report, report item, value

numeric expression

A numeric constant, a simple numeric variable, a scalar reference to a numeric array, a numeric-valued function reference, or a sequence of these items, that are separated by numeric operators. For example:

```
row["price"] * row["quantity"]
```

Related terms
array, constant, function, operator, variable

Contrast with
Boolean expression

object   An instance of a particular class, including its characteristics, such as instance variables and methods.

Related terms
class, instance variable, method, variable

object-oriented programming

A technique for writing applications using classes, not algorithms, as the fundamental building blocks. The design methodology uses three main concepts: encapsulation, inheritance, and polymorphism.

Related terms
application, class, encapsulation, inheritance, polymorphism

Contrast with
object

octal number

A number in base 8. An octal number uses only the digits 0 through 7. Each place represents a power of 8. By comparison, base 10 numbers use the digits 0 through 9. Each place represents a power of 10.

Contrast with
hexadecimal number

ODA

See open data access (ODA).

online help

Information that appears on the computer screen to help the user understand an application.

Related term
application

open data access (ODA)

A technology that enables accessing data from standard and custom data sources. ODA uses XML data structures and Java interfaces to handle communication between the data source and the application that needs the data. Using ODA to access data from a data source requires an ODA driver and typically also includes an associated tool for designing queries on the data source. ODA provides interfaces for creating data drivers to establish connections, access metadata, and execute queries to retrieve data. ODA also provides interfaces to integrate query builder tools within an application designer tool. In BIRT, ODA is implemented using plug-ins to the Eclipse Data Tools Project.

Related terms
application, Business Intelligence and Reporting Tools (BIRT), Connection, data, data source, driver, extensible markup language (XML), interface, Java, metadata, open data access (ODA) driver, plug-in, query

open data access (ODA) driver

An ODA driver communicates between an arbitrary data source and an application during report execution. An ODA driver establishes a connection with a data source, accesses metadata about the data, and executes queries on the data source. Each ODA driver consists of a configuration file and classes that implement the ODA run-time Java interfaces that conform to ODA. In BIRT, ODA drivers are implemented as an Eclipse plug-in to the Data Tools Platform project.

Related terms
application, BIRT technology, class, Connection, data, data source, driver, Eclipse, interface, Java, metadata, open data access (ODA), plug-in, query

open database connectivity (ODBC)

A standard protocol that is used by software products as one of the database management system (DBMS) interfaces to connect reports to databases that comply with this specification.

Related terms
database management system (DBMS), interface, protocol, report

Contrast with
Connection, data source, Java Database Connectivity (JDBC)

operator
A symbol or keyword that performs an operation on expressions.

Related terms
expression, keyword

outer join
1. A type of join that returns records from one table even when no matching values exist in the other table. The two kinds of outer join are the left outer join and the right outer join. The left outer join returns all records from the table on the left in the join operation, even when no matching values exist in the other table. The right outer join returns all records from the table on the right in the join operation. For example, if customers and orders tables are left outer joined on customer ID, the result set will contain all customer records, including records for customers who have no orders.

2. When creating a joint data set in BIRT, a type of join that returns rows from one data set even when no matching values exist in the other data set. The two kinds of outer joins are the left outer join and the right outer join. The left outer join returns all rows from the data set in the join operation, even when no matching values exist in the other table. The right outer join returns all rows from the data set on the right in the join operation. For example, if customers and orders data sets are left outer joined on customerID, the joint data set returns all customer rows, including rows for customers who have no orders.

Related terms
Business Intelligence and Reporting Tools (BIRT) technology, data set, join, query, result set, row, table, value

Contrast with
inner join

Outline
An Eclipse view that shows all report elements that comprise a report design, report library, or report template. Outline shows the report elements' containment hierarchy in a tree-structured diagram. Figure G-16 shows Outline.

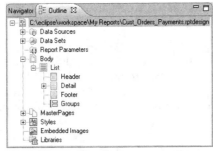

Figure G-16   Outline

Related terms
design, Eclipse view, hierarchy, library, report, report element, template

package   A set of functionally related Java classes that are organized in one directory.

Related terms
class, Java

Palette   An Eclipse view that shows the visual report elements for organizing and displaying data in a report. Figure G-17 shows Palette.

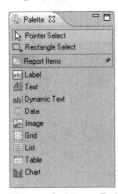

Figure G-17   Palette

Related terms
data, Eclipse view, report, report element

parameter   A report element that provides input to the execution of the report. Parameters provide control over report data selection, processing, and formatting.

Related terms
data, format, report, report element

Contrast with
cascading parameters, data set parameter, report parameter

parent class

    See superclass.

password An optional code that restricts user name access to a resource on a computer system.

pattern A template or model for implementing a solution to a common problem in object-oriented programming or design. For example, the singleton design pattern restricts the instantiation of a class to only one object. The use of the singleton pattern prevents the proliferation of identical objects in a run-time environment and requires a programmer to manage access to the object in a multithreaded application.

Related terms
class, design, instantiation, multithreaded application, object, object-oriented programming

perspective

See Eclipse perspective.

platform The software and hardware environment in which a program runs. Linux, MacOS, Microsoft Windows, Solaris OS, and UNIX are examples of software systems that run on hardware processors made by vendors such as AMD, Apple, Intel, IBM, Motorola, Sun, and Hewlett-Packard.

plug-in **1** An extension that is used by the Eclipse development environment. At run time, Eclipse scans its plug-in subdirectory to discover any extensions to the platform. Eclipse places the information about each extension in a registry, using lazy load to access the extension.

2 A software program that extends the capabilities of a web browser. For example, a plug-in gives you the ability to play audio samples or video movies.

Related terms
application, Eclipse, extension, lazy load
Contrast with
Eclipse Plug-in Development Environment (PDE)

plug-in fragment

A separately loaded plug-in that adds functionality to an existing plug-in, such as support for a new language in a localized application. The plug-in fragment manifest contains attributes that associate the fragment with the existing plug-in.
Related terms
application, localization, manifest, plug-in

polymorphism

The ability to provide different implementations with a common interface, simplifying the communication among objects. For example, defining a unique print method for each kind of document in a system supports printing any document by sending the instruction to print without concern for how that method is actually carried out for a given document.

Related terms
interface, method, object

portal
A web page that serves as a starting point for accessing information and applications on the internet or an intranet. The basic function of a portal is to aggregate information from different sources.

Related terms
application, web page

Contrast with
portlet

portlet
A window in a browser that provides a view of specific information that is available from a portal.

Related term
portal

previewer
A design tool that supports displaying a report or data.

Related terms
data, design, report

Contrast with
layout editor, script editor, Standard Viewer

procedure
A set of commands, input data, and statements that perform a specific set of operations. For example, methods are procedures.

Related terms
data, method, statement

process
A computer program that has no user interface. For example, the process that runs a BIRT report is a process.

Related terms
Business Intelligence and Reporting Tools (BIRT), interface, report

project
See Eclipse project.

Properties
A grouped alphabetical list of all properties of visual report elements in a report design. Experienced report developers use this Eclipse view to modify any property of a report item. Figure G-18 shows Properties.

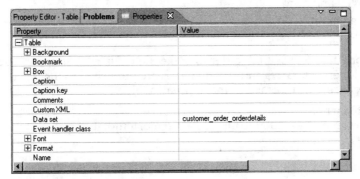

Figure G-18   Properties

Related terms
design, Eclipse view, property, report, report element, report item
Contrast with
Property Editor

property   A characteristic of a report item that controls its appearance and behavior. For example, a report developer can specify a font size for a label element.
Related terms
font, label element, report item, value
Contrast with
method

Property Editor

An Eclipse view that displays sets of key properties of visual report elements in a report design. The report developer uses Property Editor to modify the properties of report items. Figure G-19 shows Property Editor.

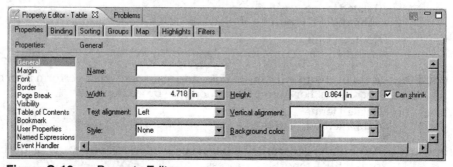

Figure G-19   Property Editor
Related terms
design, Eclipse view, property, report, report element, report item
Contrast with
Properties

protocol   A communication standard for the exchange of information. For example, in TCP/IP, the internet protocol (IP) is the syntax and order in which messages are received and sent.
Related term
syntax

publish   To copy files to a shared folder to make them available to report users and developers. Libraries and resource files are published to the resources folder. Templates are published to the templates folder.
Related terms
library, report executable file, resource file, template

query
A statement that specifies which data rows to retrieve from a data source. For example, a query that retrieves data from a database typically is a SQL SELECT statement.

Related terms
data row, data source, SQL SELECT statement

range
A continuous set of values of any data type. For example, 1–31 is a numeric range.

Related terms
data type, value

regular expression

A JavaScript mechanism that matches patterns in text. The regular expression syntax can validate text data, find simple and complex strings of text within larger blocks of text, and substitute new text for old text.

Related terms
data, expression, JavaScript, syntax

Contrast with
aggregate expression

rendering extension

A BIRT extension that produces a report in a specific format. For example, BIRT provides rendering extensions for HTML and PDF.

Related terms
Business Intelligence and Reporting Tools (BIRT), Business Intelligence and Reporting Tools (BIRT) extension, extension, hypertext markup language (HTML), report

report
A category of documents that presents formatted and structured content from a data sources, such as a database or text file.

Related terms
data source, format, structured content

report design (.rptdesign) file

An XML file that contains the complete description of a report. The report design file describes the structure and organization of the report, its constituent report items and their style attributes, its data sets, its data sources, and its Java and JavaScript event handler code. BIRT Report Designer creates the report design file and the BIRT Report Engine processes it.

Related terms
Business Intelligence and Reporting Tools (BIRT), Business Intelligence and Reporting Tools (BIRT) Report Designer, Business Intelligence and Reporting Tools (BIRT) Report Engine, data set, data source, design, event handler, extensible markup language (XML), Java, JavaScript, report, report item, style

Contrast with

file types, library (.rptlibrary) file, report document (.rptdocument) file, report template (.rpttemplate) file

report document (.rptdocument) file

A binary file that encapsulates the report item identifier and additional information, such as data rows, pagination information, and table of contents information.

Related terms

Business Intelligence and Reporting Tools (BIRT) Report Engine, data row, report item

Contrast with

file types, library (.rptlibrary) file, report design (.rptdesign) file, report template (.rpttemplate) file

report editor

In BIRT Report Designer, the main window where a report developer designs and previews a report. The report editor supports opening multiple report designs. For each report design, the report editor displays these five pages: layout editor, master page editor, previewer, script editor and XML source editor.

Related terms

Business Intelligence and Reporting Tools (BIRT) Report Designer, design, extensible markup language (XML), master page, layout editor, previewer, report, script editor

Contrast with

report design (.rptdesign) file

report element

A visual or non-visual component of a report design. A visual report element, such as a table or a label, is a report item. A non-visual report element, such as a report parameter or a data source is a logical component.

Related terms

data source, design, element, label element, report, report item, report parameter, table element

report executable file

A file that contains instructions for generating a report document.

Related terms

file types, report

report item

A report element that you add to a report design to display content in the report output. For example, a data element displays data from a data set when you run a report.

report item extension

A BIRT extension that implements a custom report item.

Related terms
Business Intelligence and Reporting Tools (BIRT), Business Intelligence and Reporting Tools (BIRT) extension, extension, report, report item

report library file

See library (.rptlibrary) file.

Report Object Model (ROM)

The set of XML report elements that BIRT technology uses to build a report design file. ROM defines report elements for both the visual and non-visual components of a report. The complete ROM specification is at:

```
http://www.eclipse.org/birt/ref/ROM
```

Related terms
Business Intelligence and Reporting Tools (BIRT) technology, design, element, extensible markup language (XML), report, report element

Contrast with
Report Object Model (ROM) element

Report Object Model definition file (rom.def)

The file that BIRT technology uses to generate and validate a report design. rom.def contains property definitions for the ROM elements. rom.def does not include definitions for report items that are defined by report item extensions, such as the chart element.

Related terms
Business Intelligence and Reporting Tools (BIRT) technology, chart element, design, property, report, report item, report item extension

Contrast with
Report Object Model (ROM), Report Object Model (ROM) element, Report Object Model (ROM) schema

Report Object Model (ROM) element

An XML element in rom.def that defines a report element.

Related terms
element, extensible markup language (XML), report element, Report Object Model definition file (rom.def)

Contrast with
report item, Report Object Model (ROM) schema

Report Object Model (ROM) schema

The XML schema that defines the rules for the structure of report design files. All BIRT report design files must conform to this schema. To validate a report design, open the file in a schema-aware XML viewer such as XML Spy. The ROM schema is at:

```
http://www.eclipse.org/birt/2005/design
```

Related terms
Business Intelligence and Reporting Tools (BIRT), design, extensible markup language (XML), report, Report Object Model (ROM), schema
Contrast with
Report Object Model definition file (rom.def)

report parameter

1 *See* parameter.

2 A report element that contains a value. Report parameters provide an opportunity for the user to type a value as input to the execution of the report.

Related terms
parameter, report, report element, value
Contrast with
cascading parameters, data set parameter

report template

See template.

report template (.rpttemplate) file

An XML file that contains a reusable design that a report developer can employ when developing a new report.

Related terms
design, extensible markup language (XML), file types, report, style, template
Contrast with
file types, library (.rptlibrary) file, report design (.rptdesign) file, report document (.rptdocument) file

report viewer servlet

A J2EE web application servlet that produces a report from a report design (.rptdesign) file or a report document (.rptdocument) file. When deployed to a J2EE application server, the report viewer servlet makes reports available for viewing over the web. The report viewer servlet is also the active component of the report previewer of BIRT Report Designer.

Related terms
application, Business Intelligence and Reporting Tools (BIRT) Report Designer, Java 2 Enterprise Edition (J2EE), previewer, report, report design (.rptdesign) file, report document (.rptdocument) file, servlet, web server

request   A message that an application sends to a server to specify an operation for the server to perform.

    Related term
    application
    Contrast with
    response

reserved word

    See keyword.

response   A message that a server sends to an application. The response message contains the results of a requested operation.

    Related term
    application
    Contrast with
    request

resource file

    A text file that contains the mapping from resource keys to string values for a particular locale. Resource files support producing a report with localized values for label and text elements.

    Related terms
    label element, locale, localization, resource key, text element, value

resource key

    A unique value that maps to a string in a resource file. For example, the resource key, greeting, can map to Hello, Bonjour, and Hola in the resource files for English, French, and Spanish, respectively.

    Related terms
    label element, locale, localization, resource file, text element, value

result set   Data rows from an external data source. For example, the data rows that are returned by a SQL SELECT statement performed on a relational database are a result set.

    Related terms
    data, data row, data source, SQL SELECT statement

Rich Client Platform (RCP)

    See Eclipse Rich Client Platform (RCP).

ROM   *See* Report Object Model (ROM).

row   **1** A record in a table.

    2 A horizontal sequence of cells in a grid element or table element.

    Related terms
    cell, grid element, table, table element

Contrast with
data row

RPTDESIGN

See report design (.rptdesign) file.

RPTDOCUMENT

See report document (.rptdocument) file.

RPTLIBRARY

See library (.rptlibrary) file.

RPTTEMPLATE

See report template (.rpttemplate) file.

run To execute a program, utility, or other machine function.

schema 1 A database schema specifies the structure of database objects and the relationships between the data. The database objects are items, such as tables.

2 An XML schema defines the structure of an XML document. An XML schema consists of element declarations and type definitions that describe a model for the information that a well-formed XML document must contain. The XML schema provides a common vocabulary and grammar for XML documents that support exchanging data among applications.

Related terms
application, data, element, extensible markup language (XML), object, report, table, well-formed XML

scope The parts of a program in which a symbol or object exists or is visible. Where the element is declared determines the scope of a program element. Scopes can be nested. A method introduces a new scope for its parameters and local variables. A class introduces a scope for its member variables, member functions, and nested classes. Code in a method in one scope has visibility to other symbols in that same scope and, with certain exceptions, to symbols in outer scopes.

Related terms
class, function, member, method, object, parameter, variable

script editor

In the report editor in BIRT Report Designer, the page where a report developer adds or modifies JavaScript for a report element.

Related terms
Business Intelligence and Reporting Tools (BIRT) Report Designer, JavaScript, report, report editor, report element

Contrast with
layout editor, previewer

scripting language

See JavaScript and VBScript (Visual Basic Script Edition).

SDK (Software Development Kit)

A collection of programming tools, utilities, compilers, debuggers, interpreters, and APIs that a developer uses to build an application to run on a specified technology platform. For example, the Java SDK allows developers to build an application that users can download across a network to run on any operating system. The Java Virtual Machine (JVM), the Java SDK interpreter, executes the application in the specified software and hardware configuration.

Related terms
application, application programming interface (API), Java, Java Virtual Machine (JVM), platform

section

A horizontal band in a report design. A section structures and formats related report items. A section uses a grid element, list element, or table element to contain data values, text, and images.

Related terms
data, design, grid element, image, list element, report, report item, table element, value

select

1   To highlight one or more items, for example, in a report design. A user-driven operation then affects the selected items. Figure G-20 shows selected items.

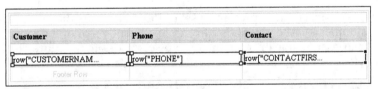

Figure G-20   Selected items

2   To highlight a check box or a list item in a dialog box.

Related terms
design, report

SELECT

See SQL SELECT statement.

series

A sequence of related values. In a chart, for example, a series is a set of related points. Figure G-21 shows a bar chart that displays a series of quarterly sales revenue figures over four years.

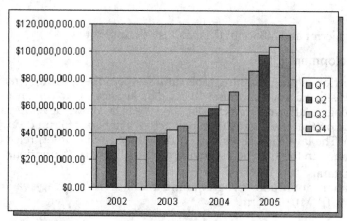

Figure G-21   Series in a chart

Related terms
chart, value

Contrast with
category

servlet   A small Java application that runs on a web server to extend the server's functionality.

Related terms
application, Java, web server

slot   A construct that represents a set of ROM elements that are contained within another ROM element. For example, the body slot of the report design element can contain one or more of any type of report item. Figure G-22 shows a body slot.

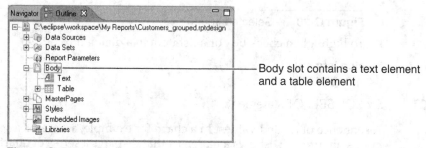

Body slot contains a text element and a table element

Figure G-22   Body slot

Related terms
design, element, report, report element, report item, Report Object Model (ROM) element

sort   To specify the order in which data is processed or displayed. For example, customer names can be sorted in alphabetical order.

Related term
data

Contrast with
sort key

sort key   A list of one or more column names or expressions. The order of the items in the sort key specifies the sort order of data rows. For example, a sort by State and Date is different from a sort by Date and State.

Related terms
column, data row, expression, sort

SQL (Structured Query Language)

A language that is used to access and process data in a relational database. For example, the following SQL query accesses a database's customers table and retrieves the customer name and credit limit values where the credit limit is less than or equal to 100000. The SQL query then sorts the values by customer name:

```
SELECT customers.customerName,
customers.creditLimit
FROM customers
WHERE customers.creditLimit >= 100000
ORDER BY customers.customerName
```

Related terms
data, query, sort, table, value

Contrast with
SQL SELECT statement

SQL SELECT statement

A statement in SQL (Structured Query Language) that provides instructions about which data to retrieve for a report.

Related terms
data, report, SQL (Structured Query Language), statement

Standard Viewer

A viewer that appears after the user runs a report. In the Standard Viewer, the user can perform basic viewing tasks, such as navigating the report, viewing parameter information, exporting data, and using a table of contents.

Related terms
data, parameter, report

Contrast with
previewer, report viewer servlet

state   *See* instance variable.

statement   A syntactically complete unit in a programming language that expresses one action, declaration, or definition.

static variable

A variable that is shared by all instances of a class and its descendant classes. In Java, a static variable is known as a class variable. The compiler specifies the memory allocation for a static variable. The program receives the memory allocation for a static variable as the program loads.

Related terms
class, class variable, descendant class, Java, variable

Contrast with
dynamic variable, field variable, global variable, instance variable, local variable, member variable

String data type

A data type that consists of a sequence of contiguous characters including letters, numerals, spaces, and punctuation marks.

Related terms
character, data type

Contrast with
string expression

string expression

An expression that evaluates to a series of contiguous characters. Elements of the expression can include a function that returns a string, a string constant, a string literal, a string operator, or a string variable.

Related terms
character, constant, expression, function, operator, variable

Contrast with
String data type

structured content

A formatted document that displays information from one or more data sources.

Related terms
data source, format

Contrast with
report

Structured Query Language (SQL)

See SQL (Structured Query Language).

style

A named set of formatting characteristics, such as font, color, alignment, and borders, that report designers apply to a report item to control its appearance.

Related terms
design, font, format, report, report item

Contrast with
cascading style sheet (CSS)

style sheet

See cascading style sheet (CSS).

subclass   The immediate descendant class.

Related terms
class, descendant class

Contrast with
superclass

subreport   A report that appears inside another report. Typically, the subreport uses data values from the outer report.

Related terms
data, report, value

superclass

The immediate ancestor class.

Related terms
ancestor class, class

Contrast with
descendant class, subclass

syntax   The rules that govern the structure of a language.

tab   The label above a page in a dialog box that contains multiple pages.

Contrast with
label element

table   A named set of columns in a relational database.

Related term
column

Contrast with
table element

table element

A report item that contains and displays data in a row and column format. The table element iterates through the data rows in a data set. Figure G-23 shows a table element.

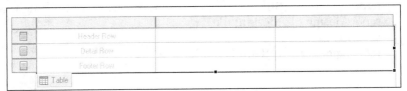

Figure G-23   Table element

Related terms
column, data, data row, data set, element, report item, row
Contrast with
grid element, list element, table

tag
An element in a markup language that identifies how to process a part of a document.

Related term
element
Contrast with
extensible markup language (XML)

template
In BIRT Report Designer, a predefined structure for a report design. A report developer uses a report template to maintain a consistent style across a set of report designs and for streamlining the report design process. A report template can describe a complete report or a component of a report. BIRT Report Designer also supports custom templates.

In Figure G-24, New Report displays the available templates and Preview displays a representation of the report layout for the selected My First Report, a customer-listing-report template.

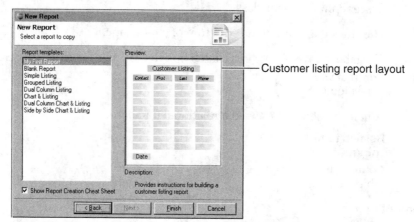

Figure G-24   Template

Related terms
Business Intelligence and Reporting Tools (BIRT), Business Intelligence and Reporting Tools (BIRT) Report Designer, design, layout, listing report, report, report design (.rptdesign) file
Contrast with
report template (.rpttemplate) file

text element

 A report item that displays user-specified text. The text can span multiple lines and can contain HTML formatting and dynamic values that are derived from data set fields or expressions.

Related terms
data set, expression, field, format, hypertext markup language (HTML), report item, value

Contrast with
data element, dynamic text element, label element

text file   *See* flat file.

theme   A set of related styles that are stored in a library (.rptlibrary) file. A theme provides a preferred appearance for the report items in a report design. A library file can store multiple themes. A report design can use styles from a single theme as well as styles defined in the report design itself.

Related terms
design, library (.rptlibrary) file, report, report item, style

Contrast with
cascading style sheet (CSS)

tick   A marker that occurs at regular intervals along the x- or y-axis of a chart. Typically, the value of each tick appears on the axis.

Related term
chart

Contrast with
tick interval

tick interval

The distance between ticks on an axis. Figure G-25 shows a tick interval in a chart.

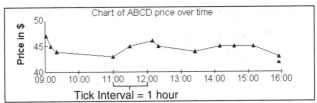

Figure G-25   Tick interval

Related terms
chart, tick

toolbar   A bar that contains various buttons that provide access to common tasks. Different toolbars are available for different kinds of tasks.

translator   *See* converter.

type   *See* data type.

Unicode   A living language standard that is managed by the Technical Committee of the
                 Unicode Consortium. The current Unicode standard provides code points for
                 more than 65,000 characters. Unicode encoding has no dependency on a
                 platform or software program and therefore provides a basis for software
                 internationalization.

Related terms
code point, character, internationalization

Uniform Resource Locator (URL)

A character string that identifies the location and type of a piece of information
that is accessible over the web. http:// is the familiar indicator that an item is
accessible over the web. The URL typically includes the domain name, type of
organization, and a precise location within the directory structure where the
item is located.

Related terms
character, domain name, hypertext transfer protocol (HTTP)

Contrast with
Universal Resource Identifier (URI)

universal hyperlink

See hyperlink.

Universal Resource Identifier (URI)

A set of names and addresses in the form of short strings that identify resources
on the web. Resources are documents, images, downloadable files, and so on.

Contrast with
Uniform Resource Locator (URL)

URL   *See* Uniform Resource Locator (URL).

value   **1** A quantity that is assigned to a constant, variable, parameter, or symbol.

                 2 A specific occurrence of an attribute. For example, blue is a possible value for
                        the attribute color.

Related terms
constant, parameter, variable

variable   A named storage location for data that can be modified while a program runs.
                 Each variable has a unique name that identifies it within its scope. Each variable
                 is capable of containing a certain type of data.

Related terms
data, data type, scope

Contrast with
class variable, dynamic variable, field variable, global variable, instance
variable, local variable, member variable, static variable

VBScript (Visual Basic Script Edition)

A Microsoft Windows scripting engine. VBScript is a subset of the Visual Basic language with some added functionality. Internet Explorer, Active Server Pages, and Windows Script Host support VBScript as a scripting language.

When used in Internet Explorer, VBScript processes code that is embedded in HTML. VBScript is similar in function to JavaScript. Stand-alone applications that were created using VBScript require Internet Explorer to run.

Related terms
Active Server Page (ASP), hypertext markup language (HTML), JavaScript

view

A predefined query that retrieves data from one or more tables in a relational database. Unlike a table, a view does not store data. Users can use views to select, delete, insert, and update data. The database uses the definition of the view to determine the appropriate action on the underlying tables. For example, a database handles a query on a view by combining the requested data from the underlying tables.

Related terms
data, query, table

Contrast with
Eclipse view

viewer   *See* previewer and Standard Viewer.

Visual Basic Script Edition

See VBScript (Visual Basic Script Edition).

web archive (.war) file

A file format that is used to bundle web applications.

Related terms
application, format

Contrast with
Java archive (.jar) file

web page   A page that contains tags that a web browser interprets and displays.

Related term
tag

web server

A computer or a program that provides web services on the internet. A web server accepts requests that are based on the hypertext transfer protocol (HTTP). A web server also executes server-side scripts, such as ASPs and JSPs.

Related terms
Active Server Page (ASP), hypertext transfer protocol (HTTP), JavaServer Page (JSP), request, web page

well-formed XML

An XML document that follows syntax rules that were established in the XML 1.0 recommendation. Well-formed means that a document must contain one or more elements and that the root element must contain all the other elements. Each element must nest inside any enclosing elements, following the syntax rules.

Related terms
element, extensible markup language (XML), syntax

World Wide Web Consortium (W3C)

An international, but unofficial, standards body that provides recommendations regarding web standards. The World Wide Web Consortium publishes several levels of documents, including notes, working drafts, proposed recommendations, and recommendations about web applications that are related to topics such as HTML and XML.

Related terms
application, extensible markup language (XML), hypertext markup language (HTML)

workbench

See Eclipse Workbench.

workspace

See Eclipse workspace.

XML (extensible markup language)

See extensible markup language (XML).

XML element

See element.

XML PATH language (XPath)

XPath is a subset of XSLT that supports addressing an element or elements within an XML document based on a path through the document hierarchy.

Related terms
element, extensible markup language (XML)

XML schema

See schema.

XPath

See XML PATH language (XPath).

Symbols

" (double quotation mark) character
   command line arguments and, 28
   JavaScript code and, 225
, (comma) character, 347
\ (backslash) character, 225
... button, 484

A

absolute paths, 36, 38, 42
abstract base class, 465
Access databases, 26, 89
accessing
   BIRT Report Designer, 15
   charts, 37, 222
   component libraries, 55
   custom data sources, 131, 366
   data sets, 53, 214
   data structures, 211
   demo database, 25, 26
   design model objects, 153
   Eclipse PDE, 275
   Export Wizard, 292
   external data sources, 68, 366
   formatted output, 203
   images, 37, 89, 201
   installation demo, 5
   Java classes, 108, 109, 116
   Java objects, 131, 139
   metadata, 150
   Navigator, 104
   ODA data sources, 366, 371
   report components, 155, 156
   report designs, 154, 181, 204, 206
   report elements, 181, 204
   report items, 181, 204, 207, 209, 210
   report properties, 155
   report viewer, 34, 36
   reports, 36, 40, 203
   resource files, 187, 206
   script editor, 91
   source code, 4, 267
Acrobat Reader, 203
action handler, 188, 189, 201
Active Server Pages. *See* ASPs
adapter classes, 112, 117, 118, 339
Add CVS Repository dialog, 257, 258
Add Entry dialog, 288
Add External JARS button, 355
Add Folder button, 289
Add Library button, 288
adding
   charts to designs, 232, 246, 250
   custom drivers, 53
   data sources, 390
   lists, 67
   ODA drivers, 366
   ODA user interfaces, 366, 367
   report items, 67, 213, 299, 301, 318
   scripted data sets, 131, 134
   scripted data sources, 133
   tables, 67
   update sites, 294
addScriptableJavaObject method, 187
Adobe Acrobat Reader. *See* Acrobat Reader
afterClose events, 82, 120, 121
afterClose method, 120, 121
afterDataSetFilled method, 83
afterDrawAxisLabel method, 83

afterDrawAxisTitle method, 83
afterDrawBlock method, 83
afterDrawDataPoint method, 83
afterDrawDataPointLabel method, 83
afterDrawFittingCurve method, 84
afterDrawLegendEntry method, 84
afterDrawMarkerLine method, 84
afterDrawMarkerRange method, 84
afterDrawSeries method, 84
afterDrawSeriesTitle method, 84
afterFactory events, 83, 123
afterFactory method, 102, 103, 123
afterGeneration method, 84
afterOpen events, 82, 120, 121
afterOpen method, 76, 120, 121
afterRender events, 75, 83, 123
afterRender method, 123
afterRendering method, 84
aggregate data. See aggregate values
aggregate expressions, 465
aggregate functions, 465
aggregate package, 164, 165
aggregate values, 466
aggregating data, 53
aliases, 99, 128, 466
All Extensions section (Extensions), 284
alternate names. See aliases; display names
ancestor classes, 466
    See also superclasses
annotation element, 268
annotations, 268, 285
Ant scripts, 290
Apache Derby databases, 8, 25
Apache Tomcat manager accounts, 39
Apache Tomcat servers, 33, 34
api extension package, 318
API Javadoc, 146
api packages, 145, 181
APIs. See application programming
    interfaces
APPCONTEXT_HTML_RENDER_
    CONTEXT constant, 201
APPCONTEXT_PDF_RENDER_CONTEXT
    constant, 201
appinfo attribute, 268
applets, 466
application context, 94, 187, 200
application context objects, 36, 126

application programming interfaces (APIs)
    BIRT engines and, 52
    BIRT extensions and, 267
    charts and, 219, 239
    custom data sources and, 366
    custom report designers and, 56
    custom report generators and, 56
    defined, 467
    report designs and, 185
    report engine and, 147, 148
    report items extensions and, 301
    report rendering extensions and, 329
    reporting applications and, 145, 181, 182,
        183
application servers, 26, 33, 40, 147
applications
    See also multithreaded applications
    accessing report designs for, 154, 181, 204,
        206
    accessing report items for, 204
    accessing report viewer for, 36
    configuring engine home for, 186
    connecting to external sources and, 202,
        366, 380
    creating stand-alone, 56, 185
    customizing, 56
    debugging, 190
    defined, 466
    deploying, 36, 183
    developing, 145, 181, 183, 267
    generating charts from, 23, 163, 219, 239
    generating reports from, 181, 182, 185,
        203, 204
    getting context for, 94, 126, 200
    installing plug-ins for, 184, 271
    integrating with Eclipse, 47
    rendering environments for, 181
    running reports and, 147, 148
    validating report designs for, 52
application-wide scriptable objects, 148
archive files
    See also jar files; war files
    BIRT packages in, 3, 23
    BIRT Samples and, 28, 29
    BIRT Test Suite and, 29
    chart engine and, 24
    demo database and, 25
    downloading, 14, 15, 17

archive files *(continued)*
    report engine and, 27
    unpacking, 5, 14
arguments, 119, 467
    See also functions; parameters
array properties, 99
arrays
    column values and, 99
    connection properties and, 101
    defined, 467
    executable expressions and, 60
    images and, 89
    ODA result sets and, 386
    row objects and, 99
    scripted data sets and, 141, 142
    user-defined properties and, 60
ASCII files. *See* text files
ASPs, 465
assignment statements, 467
attribute package, 165, 170, 172
attributes
    See also elements; properties
    complex properties and, 210
    plug-in extension points and, 286, 299
    report item extensions and, 268, 284
    report parameters and, 195
    ROM elements and, 62, 63
    XML schemas and, 268, 283
AutoDataBinding charting example, 247
AutoDataBindingViewer class, 247
axes properties (charts), 223, 228
axes values, 228, 229, 230
    See also charts
axis.jar, 34
axis-ant.jar, 34

B

background colors, 96
backslash (\) character, 225
BEA WebLogic servers, 33
beforeClose events, 82, 120, 121
beforeClose method, 120, 121
beforeDataSetFilled method, 84
beforeDrawAxisLabel method, 84
beforeDrawAxisTitle method, 84
beforeDrawBlock method, 84
beforeDrawDataPoint method, 84
beforeDrawDataPointLabel method, 84

beforeDrawFittingCurve method, 84
beforeDrawLegendEntry method, 84
beforeDrawMarkerLine method, 84
beforeDrawMarkerRange method, 84
beforeDrawSeries method, 85
beforeDrawSeriesTitle method, 85
beforeFactory events, 83, 123
beforeFactory method, 76, 123
beforeGeneration method, 85
beforeOpen events, 82, 101, 120, 121
beforeOpen method, 76, 101, 120, 121
beforeRender events, 75, 83, 123
beforeRender method, 76, 123
beforeRendering method, 85
Binary Build section, 288, 290
binary files, 55, 181
binding data sets to charts, 232
binding data sets to report items, 216
BIRT, xx, 468
BIRT API Test Reference.doc, 29
BIRT applications, 47, 48, 51
    See also applications
BIRT Chart Engine, 7, 23, 468
    See also chart engine; chart engine API
BIRT Chart Engine package, 14
BIRT components, 47
BIRT Demo Database, 8, 469
    See also Classic Models sample database
BIRT Demo Database package, 14, 25
birt directory, 42
BIRT documentation, xix, xx, xxi, 146
BIRT engines, 48, 52
    See also specific engine
BIRT extensions, 469
    See also extensions
BIRT model API, 205
BIRT open source projects, xvii
    See also projects
BIRT RCP Report Designer
    See also BIRT Report Designer; rich client
        platforms
    accessing sample database for, 8, 25
    compared to BIRT Report Designer, 51
    defined, 470
    downloading packages for, 3, 23
    installing, 3, 16–18
    removing cached pages for, 18
    software requirements for, 5

BIRT RCP Report Designer *(continued)*
    starting, 19
    testing installations for, 18
    updating, 31, 32
BIRT Report Designer
    See also designs
    accessing sample database for, 8, 25
    adding charting functionality for, 24
    compared to BIRT RCP Designer, 51
    compatibility with Eclipse, 6, 7
    configuring, 7
    defined, 469
    downloading packages for, 3, 23
    extending functionality of, 54, 267
    installing, 4, 14–15
    installing auxiliary files for, 14
    integrating report engine with, 147
    integrating with ODA drivers, 53, 366
    overview, 51
    removing cached pages for, 18
    scripting and, 73, 91, 111, 132
    software requirements for, 6–7
    starting, 15, 19
    testing installations for, 15
    tracking method execution with, 102, 103,
        104
    updating, 31
BIRT Report Designer Full Eclipse Install, 5,
    15–16
BIRT Report Designer perspective, 15
BIRT Report Designer tools, 49
BIRT Report Engine, 9, 26, 469
    See also report engine; report engine API
BIRT Report Engine package, 14
BIRT report object model, 59
    See also ROM
BIRT reporting platform, xix
BIRT Samples archive, 28
BIRT Samples package, 9, 14, 28, 470
BIRT source code. *See* source code
BIRT technology, 47, 470
BIRT Test Suite, 470
BIRT Test Suite package, 9, 29
BIRT web site, xvii
BIRT.exe, 18
birt.war, 34
BIRT_FONT_PATH variable, 40
BIRT_HOME variable, 27, 148, 186

BIRT_VIEWER_IMAGE_DIR parameter, 37
BIRT_VIEWER_LOG_DIR parameter, 37
BIRT_VIEWER_LOG_LEVEL parameter, 37
BIRT_VIEWER_SCRIPTLIB_DIR
    parameter, 37
BIRT_VIEWER_WORKING_FOLDER
    parameter, 36, 37, 42
blank strings, 43
bookmarks, 192, 467
Boolean class, 109
BOOLEAN data type, 100
Boolean expressions, 467
break reports. *See* grouped reports
breakpoints, 468
bridge class, 468
bridge driver, 26
browsers. *See* web browsers
buffered emitters, 340
bug reports, 11
Bugzilla, xvii
Build All command, 290
Build Automatically command, 290
Build Configuration page, 288
Build page (PDE Manifest Editor), 279, 287
build settings, 279
build.properties file, 268, 279
build.properties page (PDE Manifest
    Editor), 279
building
    BIRT open source projects, 253–256
    design tools, 153
    Hibernate driver plug-in, 439
    Hibernate ODA UI plug-in, 458
    ODA extensions, 368
    plug-in extensions, 287–290
    report design tools, 154
    report viewer, 262
    reports, 76, 78
    rotated label report item extension, 301
    update sites, 294
    user interfaces, 320, 321
    web viewer, 262
builds, 10, 14, 16, 17
BuildViewer.xml, 263
BundleActivator interface, 272
Business Intelligence and Reporting
    Tools, 47, 468
    See also BIRT

byte arrays, 89

C

cache, 271
cache conflicts, 18, 24
cached pages, 18, 24
calculated columns. *See* computed fields
canInherit attribute, 372
canInherit property, 309
canLeave method, 456
capitalization. *See* case sensitivity
captions (charts), 86, 164
carriage return characters, 347
cascading parameter groups, 193, 196
cascading parameters, 193, 196, 197, 198, 471
cascading style sheets, 62, 184, 185, 471
CASCADING_PARAMETER_GROUP
  value, 194
case sensitivity, 472
category, 472
category axes. *See* axes values
category series, 228, 230
  See also data series
category values, 472
  See also charts
cell elements. *See* cells
cell interfaces, 124, 125
cell items. *See* cells
Cell objects, 124, 125
CellHandle class, 157
cells
  adding grid elements and, 67
  adding list elements and, 78
  building programmatically, 124, 125, 339
  defined, 472
  determining contents of, 208
  labels in, 213
  writing to CSV files and, 345, 347
CGI (defined), 475
changeLogLevel method, 190
changing
  charts, 86, 222
  connection properties, 101
  data set bindings, 216
  data sources, 215
  locales, 21
  plug-in project settings, 278, 279
  queries, 101

report designs, 185, 204, 206, 211
report elements, 205
report item properties, 211, 212
report items, 211
URL context roots, 36
character patterns, 509
character sets, 472
character strings. *See* strings
characters
  CSV output files and, 347
  defined, 472
  JavaScript code and, 99, 225
  trimming, 381
chart areas, 223
chart builder, 54, 249
chart classes, 163, 226
chart components. *See* chart items
chart elements, 473
  See also charts
chart engine
  avoiding caching conflicts for, 24
  defined, 468
  installing, 23–24
  overview, 53
  software requirements for, 7
chart engine API, 145, 163, 164
chart engine API library, 184
Chart Engine archive, 24
chart engine classes, 164
chart engine documentation, 24
chart engine package, 14
chart event handler methods, 83, 85
chart events, 83, 87
chart examples plug-in, 246
chart generator, 145
chart instance objects. *See* chart objects
Chart interface, 164
chart item extensions, 52
chart items
  See also charts
  defined, 54
  developing, 231
  displaying, 52
  setting dimensions of, 232
  setting properties for, 231
chart model implementation classes, 163
chart model packages, 163, 165

chart objects
  See also charts
  accessing, 85, 86
  getting, 222
  instantiating, 164, 226, 231
  modifying, 163
chart package, 24, 145, 163
chart properties
  changing, 222
  chart instance objects and, 227–228
  chart items and, 231
  charting applications and, 222–224
  getting, 86
  setting, 87, 164
chart reportitem plug-in, 301
chart script context objects, 83, 85
chart scripting, 224, 225
chart subtypes, 86, 87
chart types, 86, 87, 164, 227
chart wizard. *See* chart builder
Chart3DViewer application, 248
chartengineapi.jar, 184
charting APIs, 219, 222, 225, 239
charting application sample plug-ins, 470
charting applications, 219, 221, 233
charting examples, 219, 246, 301
charting extensions, 301, 473
charting library. *See* chart engine
ChartModels class, 247, 250
charts
  See also chart elements; chart items
  accessing, 37, 222
  adding interactive features to, 87, 247
  adding series to, 224, 228–230
  adding to designs, 232, 246, 250
  applying styles to, 248, 250
  binding data sets to, 232
  changing, 86, 222
  creating, 54, 164, 225, 231, 239
  defined, 472
  defining event handlers for, 83–89, 224–225, 248
  defining sample data for, 87, 226, 231
  exporting to CSV files and, 337
  generating, 53, 221, 247
  getting data sets for, 232
  getting primary base axis for, 228
  getting type, 86

outlining areas in, 227
rendering as images, 201
scripting for, 83, 85, 88
setting properties for. *See* chart properties
specifying type, 87, 227
ChartScriptContext objects, 83, 85
ChartWithAxes interface, 164
ChartWithAxes type, 223
ChartWithoutAxes interface, 164
ChartWizardLauncher charting example, 249
ChartWizardLauncher class, 249
cheat sheets, 56
checking out source code, 256, 259
choice definitions, 63
ChoiceType element, 63
class attributes, 286
class definitions, 63
Class element, 63
class element, 309
class files, 110, 116, 286
class hierarchy, 473
class loaders, 371
class method definitions, 64
class names, 109, 118, 269, 473
class property, 308, 335
class variables, 474
  See also instance variables; variables
classes
  accessing, 109
  accessing report parameters and, 193
  associating with report elements, 116
  building report designs and, 153, 154, 157
  changing chart objects and, 163
  compiling rotated label plug-in and, 302, 308, 309
  creating, 63, 111, 112
  customizing ODA drivers and, 365, 368, 426
  defined, 473
  deploying applications and, 183
  deploying Java, 141
  developing with, 145, 181
  extending adapter, 339
  generating CSV output and, 338, 339, 355
  generating reports and, 148, 151, 186
  hierarchical diagrams for, 146
  loading, 371

classes *(continued)*
    naming conventions for, 117
    referencing, 109, 139
    registering, 225
    running plug-in instances and, 272
    scripting and, 108, 109, 139, 140
    setting attributes for, 286
    setting properties for, 287
classes directory, 110
Classic Models sample database
    See also demo database
    accessing, 25, 26
    installing, 8, 25
    testing installation for, 25
    writing event handlers for, 104
Classic Search page (PDE Manifest
  Editor), 283
ClassicModels directory, 25
ClassLoader objects, 436
classpaths
    charting applications and, 221
    CSV ODA driver extensions and, 370
    CSV rendering extension and, 334
    Hibernate ODA drivers and, 420, 436
    Java event handler classes and, 112, 116
    Java packages and, 108, 109
    plug-in extensions and, 278
    scripted data sources and, 140
–clean option, 18
clean-up code, 78, 102, 103, 140
clean-up processing phase (events), 78
CLI library, 184
close events, 82
close method
    generating reports and, 200
    Hibernate drivers and, 430, 434
    report designs and, 217
    report items and, 103
    scripted data sets and, 122, 140
    scripted data sources and, 121, 132
closeTag method, 341, 348
closing
    connections, 380, 381, 434
    cursors, 380
    data sets, 82, 121, 122, 140
    data sources, 82, 120, 121, 132, 135
    output files, 344
    report engine objects, 183

code
    accessing data sources and, 131
    accessing Java source, 4, 267
    accessing sample, 297
    adding event handlers and, 74, 81, 91
    changing run-time connections and, 101
    checking for errors in, 105
    checking out, 256, 259
    compiling, 254, 290
    creating Eclipse projects and, 256
    customizing, 73
    defining executable, 67
    deploying applications and, 183
    developing applications and, 145, 182,
      183
    developing Hibernate drivers and, 420
    developing ODA extensions and, 367
    downloading, 302
    editing, 470
    executing reports and, 93
    extracting URL parameters and, 95
    generating CSV files and, 329, 330, 359
    initializing report designs and, 83
    loading, 271, 497
    specifying repository location for, 257
    tracking method execution in, 102, 103
Code page. *See* script editor
code points, 474
codec library, 184
collectCustomProperties method
    CSVFilePropertyPage, 406
    CSVFileSelectionPageHelper, 407
    CSVFileSelectionWizardPage, 409
    HibernateDataSourceWizard, 452
    HibernatePageHelper, 449, 451
    HibernatePropertyPage, 452
collectDataSetDesign method, 458
collections, 61, 194, 195, 196
color settings, 60, 96, 230
column aliases, 99, 128
column bindings, 216, 475
column headings, 99, 128
column names
    accessing CSV data and, 367
    defining, 122
    getting, 99, 128, 387
    retrieving values and, 99
columnar layouts, 67

columnBindingsIterator method, 216
columnNumbers variable, 345
columns
    See also fields; computed fields
    accessing, 99, 128, 215
    adding to designs, 137
    counting, 86, 87, 99, 128
    defined, 474
    defining output, 135
    dynamically generating, 82
    getting information about, 99
    getting type, 100, 128
    getting values in, 99, 380
    iterating through, 100
    naming. *See* column headings; column
      names
comma (,) character, 347
comma tag, 348
command line applications, 147
command line arguments, 28
comma-separated values. *See* CSV formats
comma-separated values rendering
  extension. *See* CSV report rendering
  extension
commit method, 430
commit operations, 380, 430
Common Gateway Interface, 475
CommonConstant class, 382, 389, 427
communications protocol, 508
compiler preferences, 254
compiling, 116, 254, 289, 290
complex properties, 209, 211, 212
compliance settings, 255
component hierarchy (BIRT), 47
component libraries, 51, 55
component package, 165, 173
component palettes. *See* Palette view
components
    See also report elements; report items
    accessing, 155, 156
    adding report items and, 53, 67
    extending functionality of, 54
    saving, 51
    setting properties for, 67
computed columns. *See* computed fields
computed data. *See* computed values
computed fields, 100, 128, 138, 475
computed values, 138, 475

concatenation, 225
Concurrent Versions System repository. *See*
  CVS repository
conditional expressions. *See* Boolean
  expressions
config variable, 94
configuration files, 36, 37, 38, 450, 475
Configuration Markup section, 284
configuration objects, 148, 187
configuring
    Eclipse workspace, 254
    engine home, 186
    extension points, 284
    Hibernate drivers, 420, 427, 438, 439, 450
    report engine, 148, 187, 188
    report viewer for alternate locations, 36
Connection class, 381, 426, 428
Connection objects
    defined, 476
    ODA drivers and, 380, 381, 426
    report engine and, 182
connection properties, 101
connection wizards, 404
connectionProfile extension point, 404, 442
connections
    BIRT drivers and, 203
    external data sources and, 68, 202
    getting, 388, 428
    Hibernate data sources and, 428, 429, 434
    JDBC data sources and, 101
    ODA data sources and, 53, 101, 380, 381
    ODA drivers and, 380, 381, 382, 428
    report engine and, 182
constants, 108, 405, 476
Constants class, 405
constructor code, 476
constructSessionFactory method, 428, 436,
  438
container elements, 67
containers, 476
containment, 476
containment hierarchy, 476
content. *See* structured content
content objects, 344
content package, 339, 340
ContentEmitterAdapter class, 338
ContentEmitterVisitor objects, 342
ContentType property, 340

context mapping, 36
context objects, 94, 126, 200
context parameters, 36, 38
context root, 36
context-param element, 38
contributors, 29, 253
converters, 476
copying .jar files, 38
core API library, 184
core plug-ins, 267
coreapi.jar, 184
counters, 104, 106
Create Ant Build File command, 290
Create Java Project dialog, 354
create method, 164
create_classicmodels.sql, 26
createAndInitCustomControl method, 406,
  449, 451, 452
createCustomControl method, 407, 449
createGetParameterDefinitionTask
  method, 193
createPageControl method, 409, 453
createPageCustomControl method, 408, 449,
  451, 452
createRenderTask method, 200
createRotatedText method, 321
createRunAndRenderTask method, 199
createRunTask method, 199
creating
  BIRT projects, 253–256
  charting applications, 220, 221, 233
  charts, 54, 164, 225, 231, 239
  Eclipse projects, xvii, 256–261
  event handler class, 111, 112
  event handlers, 73, 74, 91, 112, 118
    tutorial for, 104–108
  Hibernate driver plus-ins, 420
  Java applications, 56, 147
  Java classes, 63, 111, 112, 355
  lists, 67
  ODA driver extensions, 366, 379
  ODA driver plug-ins, 368, 379
  ODA drivers, 365, 367, 419
  plug-in extensions, 279–287
  queries. See queries
  report designs, 55, 153, 205, 217
  report elements, 124, 125, 213
  report engine, 148

report item extensions, 299, 312
report items, 54, 213, 299, 300, 318
reporting applications, xix, 181, 182, 183,
  185, 204
reports, 154, 182
ROM elements, 64
scripted data sets, 131, 134
scripted data sources, 131, 132, 133
stand-alone applications, 56, 185
tables, 67
update sites, 294
criteria. See parameters
cross tabs, 476
cross tabulation. See cross tabs; cross-tab
  reports
cross-tab reports, 476
CSS files, 184, 185, 471
  See also cascading style sheets
CSV data structures, 367
CSV files
  accessing data in, 367, 381
  connecting to, 381
  creating designs for, 359
  developing ODA extensions for, 365, 379
  initializing output streams for, 342
  printing, 341
  rendering options for, 349
  structuring, 341
  viewing content of, 357
  writing to, 329, 339, 341, 346, 357
CSV formats, 337, 339, 349, 357
CSV ODA driver extension examples, 297,
  367, 381
CSV ODA driver extensions
  compiling and debugging, 368
  creating, 366, 379
  downloading plug-ins for, 367
  implementing, 371
  setting dependencies for, 370
  specifying run-time settings for, 370
CSV ODA driver interfaces, 379
CSV ODA driver plug-in project, 365, 368,
  390
CSV ODA driver plug-ins, 368, 414
CSV ODA drivers, 367, 371
CSV ODA extensions, 367
CSV ODA interfaces, 381
CSV ODA plug-ins, 367

CSV ODA UI extension, 368, 390–403
CSV ODA UI plug-in, 393, 403
csv package, 341, 381
csv plug-in, 350, 367
CSV report rendering extension
  changing report engine API and, 348
  creating projects for, 331, 353
  developing, 330
  downloading required plug-ins for, 330
  implementing content interfaces for, 339, 340
  launching, 353, 354
  overview, 337
  running, 341, 356
  setting dependencies for, 334
  testing, 350
  viewing output for, 357
CSV report rendering plug-in
  building, 350
  launching, 353, 354
  testing, 350
csv ui plug-in, 367, 368, 390
csv ui wizards plug-in, 405
CSV writer, 341, 342, 343
CSVBufferReader class, 381, 385
CSVFileDriver class, 381, 382
CSVFilePropertyPage class, 405, 406
CSVFileQuery class, 381, 382
CSVFileSelectionPageHelper class, 405, 406
CSVFileSelectionWizardPage class, 405, 408
csvODA.jar, 370
CSVPlugin class, 341
CSVRenderOption class, 348, 349
CSVReportEmitter class, 341, 344
CSVReportEmitter method, 342
CSVTags class, 341, 348
csvTest.reportdesign, 359
CSVWriter class, 341, 348
current release, 267
currentSession method, 439
cursors, 380, 386
CurveFittingViewer application, 248
custom chart generator, 145
custom data sources, 366
  See also ODA data sources
custom Java classes, 140
custom report design tool, 154
custom report designer, 56, 62, 147

custom report generators, 56, 145
custom status handlers, 187
customizing
  applications, 56
  BIRT packages, 29
  colors, 60
  ODA drivers, 53, 57, 366
  output formats, 199, 300, 330
  report emitters, 57
  report engine, 147
  report items, 54, 57, 301
  reports, 185
  source code, 73
  user interfaces, 195
  XML elements, 60
CVS perspective, 257
CVS repository, 256, 257, 267, 302
CVS Repository Exploring command, 257

D

data
  See also data elements; values
  defined, 477
  exporting, 183, 337
  extracting, 150, 183, 337
  filtering, 53, 56, 193
  generating sample, 87, 226, 231
  retrieving, 53, 131, 139, 196
data access components, 53
data adapter API library, 184
data adapters. See adapter classes
data components. See data elements
data drivers, 148
data elements, 68, 477
  See also data
data engine, 53, 366
data engine extension, 53
Data Explorer, 477
data extension names, 128
data filters, 488
data package, 165, 174
data points, 478
  See also charts
data rows, 478
  See also rows
data series
  See also charts
  adding, 224, 228–230

data series *(continued)*
    building queries for, 229, 230
    changing properties for, 224
    defined, 515
    getting properties for, 86
    setting properties for, 87, 230
    setting type, 164
data set classes, 215
data set elements, 68, 82, 120, 372
    See also data sets
data set extension properties, 128
data set fields. *See* columns
data set instance interface, 128
data set objects, 128
    See also data sets
data set page (Hibernate UI plug-in), 420, 449
data set page (ODA UI plug-in), 367
data set parameters, 478
    See also parameters
data set types, 380
data sets
    See also data set elements; data set objects
    accessing, 53, 214
    accessing columns in, 99, 128
    binding to charts, 232
    binding to report items, 216
    building programmatically, 128
    changing data sources for, 215
    changing properties for, 215
    changing queries for, 101
    closing, 82, 121, 122, 140
    creating scripted, 131, 134
    customizing drivers for, 53
    defined, 478
    defining event handlers for, 82, 91, 120, 122, 128
    developing ODA extensions for, 366, 380, 382, 390, 420
    fetching, 129, 138, 140
    filtering data in, 193
    getting data sources for, 128
    getting metadata for, 128
    getting names, 129
    getting number of columns in, 99, 128
    getting properties for, 215
    getting query strings for, 100, 129
    getting type, 129

    opening, 82, 121, 122, 139
    setting properties for, 215
    setting query strings for, 129
data source classes, 214
data source connection wizards, 404
data source drivers. *See* drivers
data source elements, 68, 82, 120, 371, 372
    See also data sources
data source extension points, 367, 404, 441
data source objects, 478
    See also data sources
data source page (Hibernate UI plug-in), 419, 449
data source page (ODA UI plug-in), 367
data source plug-ins, 366, 371
data sources
    See also specific data source type
    accessing, 68, 131, 214, 366
    adding, 390
    changing, 215
    changing properties for, 101
    closing, 82, 120, 121, 132, 135
    connecting to. *See* connections
    creating scripted, 131, 132, 133
    defined, 478
    defining event handlers for, 82, 91, 120
    developing ODA extensions for, 366, 419
    getting, 128
    opening, 82, 120, 121, 135
    retrieving data from, 53
    unsupported, 53
data structures, 211
Data Tools platform (Eclipse), 53, 257, 365, 366
data transform components, 53
data type mappings, 372, 378
data types
    columns and, 100, 128
    CSV files and, 382
    defined, 479
    Hibernate data sources and, 425
    ODA drivers and, 382, 388
    ODA result sets and, 386
    report parameters and, 195
    ROM metadata structures as, 65
    XML schemas and, 268, 299
dataadapterapi.jar, 184
database drivers. *See* JDBC drivers

database management systems, 479
database platforms, 8
database schemas, 514
databases, 365
DataCharts charting example, 246
DataChartsViewer application, 246
datafeed package, 164, 165
DataSet element, 68, 82, 120, 372
dataSet objects, 128
    See also data sets
DataSetAdapter class, 120
DataSetHandle class, 214, 215
DataSetMetaData class, 382, 388, 427, 430
dataSetPage element, 395
dataSetUI page wizard, 449
dataSetWizard attribute, 395
DataSetWizardPage class, 404, 452
DataSource element, 68, 82, 120, 371, 372
dataSource extension point, 367, 404, 441
dataSource plug-in, 366, 371
DataSource property, 101
dataSource.exsd, 366, 374
DataSourceAdapter class, 120
DataSourceEditorPage class, 404
DataSourceHandle class, 157, 214
DataSourceWizardPage class, 404
datatools directory, 367
Datatools repository. *See* Data Tools platform
dataTypeMapping element, 378, 425
dataTypeMapping type, 372
DataTypes class, 382, 388, 427
date values, 479
date-and-time data type, 479
DATETIME data type, 100
DBMS (defined), 479
Debug mode, 353
debugger, 74
debugging
   applications, 190
   defined, 479
   ODA driver extensions, 368
DECIMAL data type, 100
declarations, 479
default engine configuration, 148
default values, 154, 194
DefaultDataServiceProviderImpl class, 249
defaultDisplayName attribute, 371, 372
defaultDisplayName property, 309
defaultStyle property, 308

defaultValue attribute, 372
defaultValue property, 309
definitions, 465
deleteGlobalVariable method, 94, 126
deletePersistentGlobalVariable method, 94, 126
deleting
   cached information, 18, 24
   global variables, 94, 126
   temporary files, 148
demo database, 469
   See also Classic Models sample database
demo database package, 14, 25
dependencies (plug-ins), 279, 305, 392
Dependencies option (PDE Editor), 279
Dependencies page (PDE Editor), 278, 305
deploying
   applications, 36, 183
   Hibernate ODA UI plug-in, 458
   Java classes, 141
   plug-in extensions, 268, 291–296
   report designs, 204
   report item extensions, 302, 324
   report viewer, 33, 51
   reports, 33, 110, 112
Derby databases, 8, 25
derived classes. *See* descendant classes
descendant classes, 480
describe events, 82
describe method, 122
design elements, 66, 82, 122
design engine, 52, 54, 204
design engine API, 145, 153, 154, 157, 181
   See also report model API
design engine class, 154
design environments. *See* BIRT; Eclipse
design files
   accessing report items in, 222
   associating with reports, 42
   defined, 509
   generating, 52, 56, 154
   generating reports from, 147, 182, 190, 200, 206
   installing report viewer and, 35, 36
   loading, 149
   naming, 326
   opening, 62, 182, 190, 206
      examples for, 104, 191
   overview, 55

design files *(continued)*
  referencing in URLs, 37, 41, 42
  renaming, 232
  running, 150, 200
  specifying paths for, 37
  validating, 52
design interfaces, 124
design model objects, 153
design perspective, 14
design properties, 66
design tools, 51, 153, 154
DesignChoiceConstants interface, 209, 211
DesignConfig objects, 206
DesignElement element, 66
DesignElementHandle class, 156, 210, 317
DesignEngine class, 154, 206, 317
DesignEngine objects, 206
designer packages, 4, 13, 31
designer ui extensions package, 316
designers, 13, 51, 56, 147
  See also BIRT Report Designer; BIRT RCP
    Report Designer
designing reports, 56
  See also designs
designs
  See also page layouts
  accessing, 154, 181, 204, 206
  accessing Hibernate data sources for, 441
  accessing items in, 204
  accessing properties for, 155
  accessing ROM schema for, 62
  adding charts to, 232, 246, 250
  adding data sources to, 390
  adding report items to, 67, 207, 213, 301
  changing, 185, 204, 206, 211
  connecting to external sources and, 202
  creating, 55, 153, 205, 217
  defined, 480
  defining event handlers for, 74, 75, 82, 91,
    122
  deploying, 204
  developing, 204
  extending functionality of, 57
  generating CSV files and, 359
  getting parameters in, 194
  initializing, 76, 83, 102, 123
  retrieving data for, 366
  reusing, 51

  saving, 204, 217, 232
  setting location of, 36, 37, 42
  setting properties for, 191
  testing for parameters in, 194
  validating, 52, 62, 65
  viewing report items in, 77
desktop applications. *See* Java applets
desktop reporting application, 147
destroy method, 148
detail processing phase (events), 80
detail reports. *See* subreports
detail rows, 80
detailType property, 309
developing
  applications, 145, 181, 183, 267
  Hibernate ODA UI extensions, 441, 448
  ODA extensions, 365, 366, 419
  plug-ins, 268, 275
  rendering extensions, 329, 330, 337
  report designs, 153, 204
  reports, 13, 73
development environments, 74
development languages, 494
  See also scripting languages
development tools, 267
device package, 164, 166
DHTML (defined), 481
DialChart interface, 164
DialChartViewer application, 248
Dimension attribute (charts), 87
directories
  accessing fonts and, 201
  accessing Java classes and, 110, 140
  accessing report designs and, 36, 37, 42
  creating event handlers and, 38
  creating images and, 37, 201
  deploying applications and, 183, 186
  displaying reports and, 34
  installing language packs and, 20
  installing plug-ins and, 267, 268, 271
  installing report viewer and, 36
  saving temporary files and, 187
  unpacking program archives and, 5
  updating designer applications and, 32
disk writes, 147
display names, 371, 372, 480
displaying
  charts, 52

displaying *(continued)*
  error messages, 105, 108
  extension point descriptions, 283, 284
  HTML pages, 41
  PDF files, 41
  PDF reports, 203
  project settings, 278
  property annotations, 285
  reports, 40, 51, 52
displayNameID property, 309
displayText property, 309, 320
distributing reports. *See* deploying reports
__document parameter, 41, 42
document files
  accessing data in, 150
  creating, 183, 199
  defined, 510
  generating reports from, 181, 182, 190,
    192
  opening, 149, 182, 191
  overview, 55
  referencing in URLs, 41
  setting location of, 42
  writing to disk, 150
document object model. *See* DOM
document type definitions, 480
documentation, xix, xx, xxi, 24, 146
documentation attribute, 269
documents, 181, 192, 203, 337
  See also reports
DOM (defined), 480
domain names, 481
double quotation mark (") character
  command line arguments and, 28
  JavaScript code and, 225
download sites, 14
downloadable archives, 5
downloading
  Apache Tomcat servers, 34
  BIRT Report Designer packages, 23
  BIRT Samples package, 28
  BIRT Test Suite, 29
  chart engine archive, 24
  demo database, 25
  Eclipse Modeling Framework, 7
  Eclipse SDK software, 6
  extension examples, 297
  Graphics Editor Framework, 7

iText PDF library, 15, 16, 17
JDK software, 5, 6
language packs, 20
program archives, 14, 15, 17
report engine archive, 27
sample database, 9
source code, 302
driver classes, 101
driverClass attribute, 371
drivers
  See also specific type
  accessing external sources and, 366
  connecting to, 202, 203
  creating ODA, 53, 365, 367, 419
  customizing, 57
  defined, 481
  installing, 35
  registering, 436
  required, 185
  setting location of, 148
  specifying interfaces for, 379
drivers directory, 35, 436
drivers subdirectory, 185
DTD (defined), 480
dteapi.jar, 184
DTP ODA classes, 365, 366
DTP ODA extension points, 366
DTP ODA framework, 404
DTP ODA interfaces, 365, 366, 379
dynamic data. *See* data
dynamic hypertext markup language. *See*
  DHTML
dynamic images, 89
dynamic text elements, 481
dynamic variables, 481

E

e.reports. *See* reports
Eclipse compiler, 254
Eclipse Data Tools Platform, 53, 257, 365, 366
Eclipse desktop development environment.
  See Eclipse Workbench
Eclipse environments, 74, 482
Eclipse frameworks, 48
Eclipse Modeling Framework, 7, 482
Eclipse perspective, 482
Eclipse platform, 6, 48, 267, 483
  See also Eclipse Rich Client Platform

Eclipse Plug-in Development
  Environment, 267, 275, 483
    See also PDE Workbench
Eclipse projects, xvii, 47, 256–261, 483
    See also projects
Eclipse Rich Client Platform, 483
    See also rich client platforms
Eclipse SDK software, 6
Eclipse views, 278, 483
Eclipse Workbench, 73, 277, 325, 484
Eclipse workspace, 254, 484
ECMAScript language, 91
Edit Script command, 138
editor attribute, 308
editor pages, 395
EJBs, 131, 485
element, 269
element definitions (ROM), 64
Element element, 64
element method definitions (ROM), 65
ElementDetailHandle class, 161
ElementFactory class, 213
ElementFactory objects, 231
elements
    See also report elements; ROM elements
    accessing CSV files and, 371
    customizing plug-ins and, 268
    defined, 484
    defining plug-in extension, 283
    plug-in extension points and, 286, 299
ellipsis (...) button, 484
embeddable HTML output, 200
embedded fonts, 201, 202
embedded HTML, 200
embedded report engine, 147
EMF (defined), 482
EMF libraries, 185
EMF software, 7
emitter csv plug-in, 341, 350
emitter extension points, 330, 335
emitter extensions, 300, 363
emitter interfaces, 337
emitter objects, 342
emitter package, 329
emitter plug-in, 337, 338
emitters
    customizing, 57
    defining rendering options for, 349
    extending functionality of, 330, 335
    generating CSV output and, 341, 350
    generating reports and, 52, 188
    rendering extensions and, 330
    setting properties for, 336
emitters package, 335
emitters plug-in, 300
emitters.exsd, 300, 330
encapsulation, 484
encoding, 522
end method, 343
endCell method, 347
endRow method, 347
engine API library, 184
engine api package, 145, 151, 152
engine APIs. *See* chart engine API; report
  engine API
engine extension package, 317
engine home, 183, 186
engine home directory, 183
engine plug-ins, 148, 331
engine variable, 202
engineapi.jar, 184
EngineConfig class, 148
EngineConfig objects, 148, 186, 187, 190
EngineConstants class, 348, 349
EngineEmitterServices class, 339
EngineException exceptions, 203
engines, 48, 52, 366
    See also specific engine
enterprise, 485
Enterprise JavaBeans. *See* EJBs
enterprise reporting, 485
enterprise systems, 485
enumeration classes, 163, 165
environment-dependent processing, 147
environments, 506
error messages, 105, 108, 382
errors, 105
evaluateQuery method, 197
event firing sequence, 74–75
event handler classes, 111, 112, 116, 118, 123
event handler interfaces, 112, 117, 118
event handlers
    accessing JAR files for, 38
    adding logging code to, 81
    adding to designs, 74, 82, 91, 122
    associating context objects with, 94, 126

event handlers *(continued)*
  associating with report elements, 116–117
  building charts and, 83–89, 224–225, 248
  building data sets and, 82, 120, 122, 128
  building data sources and, 82, 120, 121
  creating, 73, 74, 91, 112, 118
    tutorial for, 104–108
  defined, 485
  executing, 74–81, 93
  mapping to report viewer and, 37
  rendering report elements and, 61, 95, 111
  rendering report items and, 61, 81, 119
  rendering sequence for, 75
event listeners, 486
event package, 164, 166
events
  See also event handlers
  accessing data sources and, 82
  building data rows and, 78
  building dynamic columns and, 82
  controlling page breaks and, 75
  creating report designs and, 82, 122
  defined, 485
  firing, 61, 74–75
  generating reports and, 75, 76, 78
  generating table or lists and, 78–81
  running reports and, 74, 76–81, 93
  scripting for, 73, 74, 104, 118
  subscribing to, 273
example charting applications, 24
example database, 8
  See also Classic Models sample database
example extensions, 297
exception package, 164, 168
exceptions, 210, 486
executeQuery method, 384, 433
ExecuteReport class, 357
executing reports, 74, 76, 93
execution processes, 93
execution sequence (events), 74, 75–81
Experts. *See* wizards
export options, 292
Export Wizard (PDE), 291
exporting data, 183, 337
exporting plug-in extensions, 292, 302
Exporting section (Overview), 292
expression builder, 486
expression property type, 61

expressions
  defined, 486
  defining aggregate values and, 465
  manipulating numeric values and, 502
  manipulating string data and, 518
  matching text patterns and, 509
  returning Boolean values from, 467
  setting properties and, 61
ex-property property type, 61
.exsd files, 268
extended-item name element, 62
ExtendedItemHandle class, 317
ExtendedItemHandle objects, 226, 231, 232
extensible markup language. *See* XML
extension APIs, 145
extension element, 271
Extension Element Details section, 283
extension IDs, 308, 335, 371, 393
extension names, 128, 269
extension package (report engine), 301
extension point identifier, 308, 335, 371, 393
extension point schema definitions, 268, 283
Extension Point Selection page, 281, 335
extension points
  accessing external sources and, 366
  accessing Hibernate data sources
    and, 441, 444
  adding report items and, 299
  customizing ODA drivers and, 53, 371
  defined, 487
  defining, 279
  displaying descriptions of, 283, 284
  finding, 283
  generating output and, 330, 335
  implementing, 267, 299
  selecting, 284, 310, 395
Extension Points page (New Extension), 310, 395
Extension Points page (PDE Editor), 279
extensionName property, 308
extensionProperties array, 101
extensions
  adding chart items and, 54
  adding report items and, 299, 301
  building plug-in, 287–290
  creating, 62, 279, 283, 299
  customizing report items and, 54
  declaring, 279

extensions *(continued)*
  defined, 487
  deploying, 268, 291, 296
  developing ODA, 53, 365, 366, 419
  naming, 308, 335, 393
  overview, 57, 267
  rendering reports and, 329, 356
  sample projects for, 297
  selecting export options for, 292
  setting class attributes for, 286
  setting contents of, 284
  specifying, 281
  structuring, 279–282
  testing, 291
extensions package, 316
Extensions page (PDE Editor), 279, 281, 283
external connections, 202
external data sources, 68, 366, 379
external libraries, 108
external objects, 85

F

factory method, 149
factory package, 165, 168
Factory processes, 93, 95
Feature License dialog, 32
Feature Updates dialog, 31
Feature Updates page, 293
features, 11, 293
fetch method, 122, 132, 138, 140
field variables, 487
  See also member variables; variables
fields
  See also columns; computed fields
  accessing CSV data and, 367
  changing data sources and, 215
  defined, 487
  exporting CSV output and, 337, 339
File class, 381, 382
file objects, 381, 382
file types, 54, 488
FileDialog method, 450
files
  See also specific type
  accessing resource, 187
  creating, 102
  downloading program archive, 14, 15, 17
  extracting program archive, 5, 14

generating output and, 181
installing Tomcat servers and, 35
mapping to report viewer, 36
overview, 54–55
rendering output and, 182
tracking method execution in, 102, 103
FileSelectionWizardPage class, 405, 409
filtering data, 53, 56, 193
filters, 488
finalization code, 78, 102, 103, 140
Find and Install command, 293
Find declaring extension point option, 283
findDataSet method, 214
findDataSource method, 214
findElement method, 207
finding extension points, 283
finding program updates, 31
findTOC method, 191
flat file data sources, 365
flat file plug-in, 365
flat files, 488
  See also flat file data sources; text files
FLOAT data type, 100
flute.jar, 184
folders, 289
font files, 40
font style constants, 211
fontFamily style specification, 63
fonts, 40, 201, 488
footer grids, 76
footer rows, 80
footers, 80, 232, 488
form e-capable browser, 489
__format parameter, 41, 43
format property, 335
format styles. *See* styles
FormatCharts charting example, 247
FormatCharts class, 247
FormatChartsViewer class, 247
formatQueryText method, 383
formats
  adding CSV, 349
  customizing report generation and, 52, 56
  defined, 488
  exporting data and, 337
  generating output and, 181, 199, 329
  getting output, 94, 127
  rendering images and, 201

formats *(continued)*
   rendering output and, 200, 201
   setting output, 182
formatted output, 181, 203
formatting data. *See* formats
Formula Editor. *See* expression builder
formulas. *See* expressions
frame objects, 109
frameset servlet, 41
framework, 489
Full Eclipse Install (BIRT Report
  Designer), 5, 15–16
function declarations, 88
function stubs, 87, 88, 112
functions
  See also methods
  accessing, 95
  defined, 489
  defining chart events and, 88, 225
  selecting, 97
fundamental data types. *See* data types

G

GEF software, 7
GeneralCategoryWrapper class, 321
generating
  charts, 53, 221, 247
  CSV files, 329, 339, 341, 346, 357
  design files, 154
  formatted output, 203
  HTML reports, 43, 149, 150, 199, 200
  lists, 78–81
  master pages, 76
  output, 43, 181, 329
  PDF documents, 43, 149, 150, 199, 201
  report design files, 52, 56, 154
  reports, 182, 185, 200, 203
  sample data, 231
  tables, 78–81
generation engine, 50, 51, 52
generation-time events, 74, 75
generators (custom), 145
genReport script, 27
get method, 208
getAllExtensionProperties method, 128
getAppContext method, 94, 126
getBlock method, 86
getBody method, 207

getCategoryTabs method, 321
getChartInstance method, 85
getChildren method, 191
getColumnAlias method, 99, 128
getColumnCount method, 99, 128, 130, 345
getColumnLabel method, 99, 128
getColumnMetaData method, 99, 128
getColumnName method, 99, 128, 130, 387
getColumnNativeTypeName method, 100,
  128
getColumnType method, 100, 128
getColumnTypeName method, 100, 128
getColumnValue method, 129, 130
getConfigVariableValue method, 94
getConnection method, 382, 388, 428
getContents method, 194
getDataSet method, 129
getDataSets method, 214, 215, 232
getDataSource method, 128
getDataSources method, 214, 215
getDataType method, 195
getDefaultValue method, 194
getDefaultValues method, 194
getDescription method, 86
getDesignHandle method, 206
getDimension method, 86
getElementFactory method, 231
getExtendedProperties method, 86
getExtensionID method, 129
getExtensionProperty method, 129
getExternalContext method, 85
getGlobalVariable method, 94, 126
getGridColumnCount method, 86
getHibernateProp method, 439
getHibernatePropTypes method, 439
getHttpServletRequest method, 94, 126
getInt method, 386
getInteractivity method, 86
getLabel method, 195, 319
getLegend method, 86, 227
getLocale method, 85, 94, 127
getLogger method, 85
getMaxConnections method, 428
getMaxQueries method, 429
getMeasure method, 212
getMessage method, 94, 127
getMetaData method, 429, 433
getName method, 129

getNext method, 208
getOutline method, 227
getOutputFormat method, 94, 127
getPageNumber method, 192
getParameterDefn method, 194
getParameterDefns method, 194
getParameterType method, 194
getParameterValue method, 94, 101, 127
getParameterValues method, 195
getPersistentGlobalVariable method, 94, 95, 127
getPlot method, 86, 227
getPrimaryBaseAxes method, 228
getPrimaryOrthogonalAxis method, 228
getProperty method, 191
getPropertyDefinitions method, 320
getQuery method, 410
getQueryColumnNames method, 411
getQueryString method, 95
getQueryText method, 129
getResult method, 435
getResultSetColumn method, 216
getResultSetExpression method, 216
getResultSetMetaData method, 412, 457
getRow method, 386
getSampleData method, 86
getScript method, 86
getSelectionList method, 195
getSelectionListForCascadingGroup method, 198
getSeriesDefinitions method, 230
getSeriesForLegend method, 86
getSeriesPalette method, 230
getSeriesThickness method, 86
getSQLStateType method, 431
getString method, 388, 435
getStyle method, 209
getStyles method, 86
getSubType method, 86
getSupportedImageFormats method, 201
getTitle method, 86
getType method, 86
getTypeCode method, 389
getUnits method, 86
getURI method, 208
getValue method, 195
getVersion method, 86
getWidth method, 209, 212

global options (report engine), 148
global variables, 92, 95, 126, 489
    See also variables
Glossary, 465
glyph, 489
    See also character sets; fonts
grandchild classes. *See* descendant classes
grandparent classes. *See* ancestor classes
graphical report design tool, 51
graphical user interfaces. *See* user interfaces
graphics. *See* images
Graphics Editor Framework, 7
GraphicsUtil class, 321
graphs. *See* charts
grid cells. *See* cells
grid elements, 490
grid items, 67, 77, 213
GridColumnCount attribute, 86, 87
grids, 67, 86, 87, 490
    See also grid elements; grid items
group fields. *See* group keys
group headers, 491
group keys, 491
group slots, 208
grouped lists, 79, 80
grouped reports, 490
grouped tables, 79, 80
grouping data, 53, 56
    See also groups
GroupOnXSeries charting example, 246
GroupOnXSeries.rptdesign, 246
GroupOnYAxis charting example, 246
GroupOnYAxis.rptdesign, 246
groups, 78, 490
GUI components, 53
    See also user interfaces

H

handle classes, 156
handle objects, 211
handler class, 112
    See also event handler classes
hardware interfaces, 494
HashMap objects, 202
HashMap value, 151
header grids, 76
header rows, 80
headers, 80, 491

headings. *See* column headings
help, 503
hexadecimal numbers, 491
Hibernate Core for Java, 365, 366
Hibernate data sets, 420, 449
Hibernate data sources, 419
Hibernate data types, 425
Hibernate libraries, 441
Hibernate objects, 131
Hibernate ODA driver plug-in, 420, 439
Hibernate ODA drivers, 419, 420, 427
Hibernate ODA extension example, 426
Hibernate ODA extensions, 419, 420
Hibernate ODA UI example, 420
Hibernate ODA UI extension points, 444
Hibernate ODA UI extensions, 441
Hibernate ODA UI plug-in
    building, 458
    creating projects for, 442
    deploying, 458
    described, 419
    developing, 448
    launching, 460
    specifying dependencies for, 443
    specifying run-time settings for, 443
    testing, 460–463
hibernate package, 426
hibernate plug-in, 419, 420, 439
Hibernate Query Language. *See* HQL
  statements
hibernate ui plug-in, 419
hibernate.cfg, 420
HibernateClassSelectionPage class, 452
HibernateDataSourceWizard class, 448, 452
HibernateDriver class, 426, 428
HibernateHqlSelectionPage class, 449
HibernatePageHelper class, 448, 449, 452
HibernatePropertyPage class, 448, 452
HibernateUtil class, 427, 428, 436, 439
hibfiles directory, 420, 436
hierarchy, 491
HOME property, 372
homeDir parameter, 382
host applications, 147
host instance (PDE Workbench), 277
HQL (defined), 365
HQL statements
  adding user interface for, 449

creating, 419, 429
executing, 433
retrieving data with, 435
verifying, 454
HTML (defined), 491
HTML elements, 484
HTML emitter configuration property
  type, 187
HTML emitters, 52, 187, 188
HTML formats, 329
HTML frames, 41
HTML reports
  See also web pages
  configuring properties for, 202
  generating, 43, 149, 150, 199, 200
  opening, 203
  rendering unpaginated, 150
  setting up rendering context for, 201
  viewing, 41
  writing to disk, 147
HTML tags, 489
HTMLCompleteImageHandler objects, 188
HTMLEmitterConfig objects, 187
HTMLRenderContext class, 201
HTMLRenderContext objects, 200
HTMLRenderOption class, 150, 151, 182, 200
HTMLServerImageHandler objects, 188
HTTP (defined), 492
HTTP request objects, 95
HttpServletRequest objects, 94, 126
hyperlinks, 337, 340, 491
hypertext markup language pages. *See* web
  pages
hypertext markup language. *See* HTML
hypertext transfer protocol. *See* HTTP

I

IAdvancedQuery interface, 381
IBandContent interface, 339
IBM WebSphere servers, 33
IBounds interface, 340
ICascadingParameterGroup interface, 193
ICell interface, 124
ICellContent interface, 339
ICellInstance interface, 125
IChartEventHandler interface, 88
IChartScriptContext interface, 83, 85
IColumnMetaData class, 99

IColumnMetaData interface, 128
IConnection interface, 380, 426
icons, 54, 308
IContainerContent interface, 339
IContent package, 340
IContentEmitter interface, 338
IContentVisitor interface, 340
ICU library, 184
id attribute, 371, 372, 394
ID property, 308, 335, 371, 393
id property, 335
IDataContent interface, 339
IDataExtractionTask interface, 150
IDataExtractionTask objects, 183
IDataSetEventHandler interface, 120
IDataSetInstance interface, 128
IDataSetMetaData interface, 380, 427
IDataSetRow interface, 129
IDataSourceEventHandler interface, 120
identifiers, 492
IDriver interface, 371, 380, 426, 428
IElement interface, 340
IEmitterServices interface, 338
IEngineTask interface, 149
IForeignContent interface, 340
IGetParameterDefinitionTask interface, 149
IGetParameterDefinitionTask objects, 194
IGetParameterDefnTask interface, 193
IHTMLActionHandler interface, 188
IHTMLImageHandler interface, 188
IHyperlinkAction interface, 340
IImageContent interface, 340
ILabelContent interface, 340
image constants, 209
image elements, 492
image files, 36, 201
image formats, 201
image handler, 188
ImageHandle objects, 208
images
    accessing, 37, 89, 201
    defined, 492
    exporting to sample CSV report rendering
        extension and, 337
    rendering context and, 201
    rendering rotated text as, 319, 321
IMessages interface, 318
impl packages, 163, 165
import statements, 109

importing Java packages, 109, 139
importPackage method, 109, 139
in_count parameter, 142
incrementing record counters, 106
index.jsp, 35
information. See data
inheritance, 492
initCustomControl method, 408, 449, 451
initialization code, 83, 102, 139
initialize events, 83, 123
initialize method
    building report designs and, 76, 102, 123,
        154
    creating event handlers and, 94
    creating output files and, 102
    creating output streams and, 342
    importing Java packages and, 109
initializeControl method, 454
initializing report designs, 76, 83
initSessionFactory method, 436
inner joins, 493
    See also joins
input parameters, 141
input sources. See data sources
input streams, 217
inputParams array, 141, 142
installation
    BIRT Chart Engine, 23–24
    BIRT components, 5
    BIRT Demo Database, 25
    BIRT RCP Report Designer, 3, 16–18
    BIRT Report Designer, 4, 14–15
    BIRT Samples package, 28
    BIRT Test Suite, 29
    JDBC drivers, 35
    JDK software, 5, 6
    language packs, 19–21
    plug-ins, 184, 271
    report engine, 17, 27
    report viewer, 34–35, 36
    testing, 15, 18, 25, 27
    troubleshooting, 18–19
    TrueType fonts, 40
installation demo, 5
instance interfaces, 125
instance property, 226, 231
instance variables, 493
    See also class variables; variables
instances. See objects

instantiation, 493
INTEGER data type, 100
integrated debugger, 74
interactive features (charts), 87
InteractivityCharts charting example, 247
interfaces
    See also application programming
        interfaces; specific programming
        interface
    adapter classes compared to, 118
    chart engine API and, 163, 164
    CSV report rendering extension, 338, 339
    data row objects and, 129
    data set objects and, 128
    defined, 494
    design model objects and, 153
    developing with, 145
    event handlers and, 111, 112, 118, 123
    extending adapter classes and, 112
    Hibernate ODA drivers and, 428
    hierarchical diagrams for, 146
    naming conventions for, 117, 118
    ODA extensions and, 365, 371, 379
    overview, 123
    report elements and, 124–126
    report engine API, 152
    rotated label plug-in, 316
    run-time drivers and, 379
International Components for Unicode. *See*
  ICU library
internationalization, 23, 494
    See also locales
IP addresses, 494
IPageContent interface, 340
IParameterDefnBase interface, 193
IParameterGroupDefn interface, 193
IParameterMetaData interface, 381
IParameterSelectionChoice class, 195
IParameterSelectionChoice interface, 193
IPlatformContext interface, 187, 188
IPropertyDefinition interface, 318
IPropertyTabUI interface, 316
IQuery interface, 380, 427
IRenderOption interface, 200, 349
IRenderOption objects, 182
IRenderTask interface, 150, 200
IRenderTask objects, 182
IReportContent interface, 341

IReportContext interface, 126
IReportDocument interface, 149
IReportDocument objects, 182, 191
IReportElement interface, 124
IReportEventHandler interface, 122
IReportItem interface, 318
IReportItemFactory interface, 318
IReportItemLabelProvider interface, 316
IReportItemPresentation interface, 317
IReportItemPropertyEditUI interface, 316,
  320
IReportRunnable interface, 149, 190
IReportRunnable objects, 182, 191
IResultSet interface, 380, 427
IResultSetMetaData interface, 380, 427
IRowContent interface, 340
IRowData interface, 129
IRowInstance interface, 126
IRowSet interface, 317
IRunAndRenderTask interface, 150, 199, 200
IRunAndRenderTask objects, 182, 202
IRunTask interface, 150, 199
IRunTask objects, 202
IScalarParameterDefn interface, 193
IScalarParameterDefn objects, 194
isComputedColumn method, 100, 128
IScriptedDataSourceEventHandler
  interface, 121, 122
isEmpty method, 194
isEncryptable attribute, 372
isEncryptable property, 309
isNameRequired property, 308
__isnull parameter, 41, 43
isRowInFooterBand method, 346
IStatusHandler interface, 187
IStyle interface, 340
IStyleModel interface, 317
ITableBandContent interface, 340
ITableContent interface, 340
iterator method, 208, 435
iterator objects, 140
iText open source library, 5, 6, 7
itext-1.3.jar, 15, 16, 221, 261
ITextContent interface, 340
ITextItem interface, 124

J

J2EE applications, 26, 40

J2EE environments, 13, 17, 494
J2SE environments, 5, 6, 495
.jar files
   adding to classpaths, 113
   building projects and, 261
   building update sites and, 294
   configuring report engine and, 148
   copying, 38
   creating charting applications and, 221
   creating event handlers and, 112
   default location for, 110
   defined, 495
   deploying Java classes and, 141
   deploying plug-ins and, 268, 281, 291
   deploying to JBOSS servers and, 34
   developing ODA extensions and, 368
   generating, 268
   installing JDBC drivers and, 35
   running report projects and, 353
   selecting external, 355
   developing ODA extensions and, 370
JAR Selection dialog, 355
Java. *See* Java programming language
Java 2 Enterprise Edition. *See* J2EE
  environments
Java 2 Runtime Standard Edition. *See* J2SE
  environments
Java APIs, 52
Java applets, 466
Java applications
   See also applications
   adding charting capabilities to, 23, 219
   adding reporting capabilities to, 26
   creating, 56, 147
   generating designs and, 52
Java archives. *See* .jar files
Java Attribute Editor, 286
Java Build Path page, 112
Java Class dialog, 114
Java classes
   See also classes
   accessing, 108, 109, 116
   associating with report elements, 116
   creating, 63, 111, 112, 355
   default location for, 110
   deploying, 141
   developing ODA extensions and, 368
   developing with, 145

importing, 109
naming, 115
referencing, 109, 139
registering, 225
scripting for, 108, 109, 139, 140
setting properties for, 287
Java code, 73, 108, 110, 111, 494
Java command, 354
Java compiler, 116
Java Database Connectivity. *See* JDBC
Java development environment, 74
Java Development Kit. *See* JDK software
Java editor, 115
Java event handler classes, 111, 116, 120
Java event handlers, 74, 87, 111, 120, 224
Java interfaces, 123, 494
Java Naming and Directory Interface, 495
Java naming conventions, 117
Java objects, 95, 109, 131, 139
Java packages, 108, 109, 110, 139
Java perspective, 354
Java programming language, 494
Java programs, 74, 495
Java Project option, 354
Java projects, 113, 116
Java report generator, 56
Java run-time API, 273
Java Runtime Environment, 33
Java Settings page, 354
Java source files, 114
Java Virtual Machines. *See* JVMs
java.lang package, 109
JavaBeans, 496
JavaScript
   accessing data sources and, 131
   accessing Java classes for, 108, 109
   accessing ROM elements and, 95
   defined, 496
   entering variables in, 92, 95
   indexing column position and, 99
   line breaks in, 225
   previewing, 98
   setting properties with, 96
   tracking method execution and, 102
   tutorial for, 104
   wrapping Java code in, 108, 110
   writing event handlers and, 73, 87, 91, 225
JavaScript array properties, 99

JavaScript library, 184
JavaScript objects, 109
JavaScript palette, 107
JavaScriptViewer application, 248
JavaServer Pages. *See* JSPs
JavaViewer application, 248
JBOSS servers, 33, 34
JDBC (defined), 495
JDBC connections, 101
JDBC data sources, 365
JDBC drivers, 35, 420, 436
JDK software, 5, 6, 9, 254, 495
JFrame objects, 109
JNDI (defined), 495
join conditions, 497
joins, 68, 496
joint data sets, 68, 493, 497
JointDataSet element, 68
JRE software, 33
js.jar, 184
JSPs, 496
JUnit libraries, 29
JUnit Regression Testing Framework, 10
JVMs, 19, 496

K

keywords, 497

L

label elements, 497
label items, 213
labels, 96, 319, 497
LabelStyleProcessor class, 250
language packs, 19–21
language-specific environments. *See* locales
Launch an Eclipse application option, 291
layout editor, 300, 497
layout package, 165, 176
Layout page. *See* layout editor
layouts, 497
    See also page layouts; master pages
lazy load, 497
legend area (charts), 86, 223, 227
Legend block (charts), 86
legend line properties (charts), 227
Legend objects, 227
Level class, 190

level-break listings. *See* grouped reports
lib directory, 35, 112
libraries
    See also component libraries
    accessing, 55, 181
    accessing properties in, 156
    building plug-in extensions and, 279, 288
    changing, 55
    creating reporting applications and, 181,
        204
    defined, 498
    deploying applications and, 183
    deploying reports and, 112
    naming, 289
    required, 184
    reusing designs and, 51
    running Hibernate drivers and, 441
    scripting and, 108
    selecting, 289
Libraries page (Java Settings), 354
library files, 55, 204, 498
LibraryHandle class, 156, 205
licenses, 32
line break characters, 225
line breaks (JavaScript), 225
LineAttribute objects, 227
LineSeries objects, 228, 229
links. *See* hyperlinks
Linux platforms, 23
list elements, 66, 213, 498
list execution sequence (events), 79, 80
list items, 67, 77
list processing phase (events), 79
list setup phase (events), 79
listeners. *See* event listeners
Listing element, 66
listing reports, 80, 498
ListingGroup elements, 80
ListingGroup items, 80
lists, 67, 78–81
    See also list elements; list items
load_classicmodels.sql, 26
loading
    class files, 286
    document files, 149
    metadata, 154
    plug-ins, 280

loading *(continued)*
  report designs, 149, 206
    examples for, 191
  source code, 271, 497
local variables, 92, 499
  See also global variables; variables
__locale parameter, 41, 43
Locale objects, 85
locale-independent formats, 193
locales
  building charts for, 85
  changing, 21
  converting strings and, 193
  defined, 499
  getting, 94, 127
  installing language packs for, 19–21
  managing programmatically, 149
  specifying, 21, 43
localization, 19, 23, 499
  See also locales
locating extension points, 283
locating program updates, 31
log files, 36, 187, 190
log messages, 37, 85, 148, 190
log package, 165, 169
Logger class, 190
Logger objects, 85
logging classes, 190
logging code, 81
logging configurations, 190
logging levels, 37, 190
Logging property type, 187
logging threshold, 190

M

Manage Configuration command, 293
manifest files, 271, 275, 277, 279, 499
manifest headers, 277
manifest.mf, 277, 279
mapping to report viewer, 36
markers (charts), 86
markup languages, 481, 487, 491
  See also elements; tags
master pages, 66, 76, 499
MasterPage element, 66
Math class, 109
matrix reports. *See* cross-tab reports
Member element, 65

member variables, 500
  See also field variables; variables
members, 65, 500
messages, 94, 127, 513
  See also error messages; log messages
Messages class
  CSV ODA driver extension, 382, 388
  CSV ODA UI extension, 404
  Hibernate ODA extension, 427, 449
messages.properties file, 404, 449
metadata
  accessing, 150
  accessing Hibernate data sources
    and, 433
  accessing ODA data sources and, 380,
    382, 383
  defined, 501
  defining ROM elements and, 63–66
  getting column information from, 99, 128
  getting data set, 128
  loading, 154
metadata interface, 128
MeterChartExample application, 250
method definitions, 64, 65
Method element, 64, 65
Method metadata definition (ROM), 65
Method property, 67
methods
  See also functions
  accessing column information and, 99,
    128
  accessing data sets and, 120, 122, 128, 132
  accessing data sources and, 82, 120, 121
  accessing report components and, 156
  accessing report designs and, 155
  accessing report items and, 207
  building charts and, 83, 85, 86, 87
  building data rows and, 78, 129
  building tables or lists and, 79, 80
  creating event handlers and, 94, 111, 118,
    126
  creating report designs and, 123
  defined, 501
  defining ROM elements and, 61, 65
  executing reports and, 76, 78, 95
  generating report elements and, 124, 125
  generating report items and, 81, 119
  importing Java packages and, 109

methods *(continued)*
  overriding, 118
  providing external values for, 187
  rendering CSV output and, 342, 344
  running rotated text plug-in and, 273
  scripting with, 108
  selecting, 96, 97
  tracking execution of, 102–104
  viewing arguments for, 119
methods array, 60
Microsoft Access databases, 26, 89
Microsoft Windows. *See* Windows systems
milestone builds, 11
milestone release, 31
MIME types, 335
mimeType property, 335
modal windows, 501
mode, 501
model attribute, 269
model element, 308
model extension element, 308
model package (charts), 165, 169
modelapi.jar, 185
modeless windows, 501
ModifyListener method, 450
ModuleHandle class, 155
Mozilla Rhino, 91, 108, 110
multicolumn page layouts, 67
Multipurpose Internet Mail Extensions. *See* MIME types
multithreaded applications, 501
myChart.chart file, 221
mysql command line interface, 26
MySQL databases, 8, 26
MySQL installation scripts, 441

N

name attribute, 372
name collisions, 109
name element, 309
Name property, 308, 335, 371, 393
name property, 309
name variable, 202
names
  See also aliases; display names
  accessing Java packages and, 109
  changing context root, 36
  defining properties and, 61

getting column, 99, 128
  retrieving values and, 99, 128
name-value pairs, 60
naming
  data set columns, 122
  event handler classes, 117, 118
  Java classes, 115
  ODA data source extensions, 371
  ODA data source UI extensions, 393
  output files, 200
  plug-in libraries, 289
  report design files, 326
  report item extensions, 269, 308
  report items, 207
  report rendering extensions, 335
  scripted data sets, 134
  scripted data sources, 134
naming conventions, 117
nativeDataType property, 373
nativeDataTypeCode property, 372
Navigator, 104, 501
Navigator command, 104
New Class command, 355
New Data Set wizard, 134
New Data Source wizard, 133
New Extension wizard, 281
New Java Class wizard, 355
New Java Project wizard, 354
new line characters, 347
new line tag, 348
New Plug-in Project wizard, 275, 276, 277
New Project wizard, 275
New Report command, 326
New Report wizard, 326
New Source Folder dialog, 289
New Update Site wizard, 295
newDataSourceWizard attribute, 394
newElement method, 213
newExtendedItem method, 231
newQuery method, 429
newReportItem method, 318
newSession method, 154, 206
newsgroups, xvii, 5
next method, 386, 435
nightly builds, 11
–nl command line argument, 21
node, 502
NonGroupOnXSeries.rptdesign, 246

NonGroupOnYAxis.rptdesign, 246
non-scripted data sets, 131
non-scripted data sources, 131
non-visual elements, 59, 205
null values, 43, 502
Number class, 109
numeric data types, 502
numeric expressions, 502
N-up reports. *See* multicolumn page layouts

O

Object class, 109
object libraries. *See* component libraries
object references, 140
object-oriented programming, 502
objects
    accessing, 131, 139
    defined, 502
    getting, 222
    instantiating, 139, 271
    registering service, 273
    saving, 127
octal numbers, 503
ODA (defined), 503
ODA API, 365, 366, 379
ODA API Reference, 214, 366
oda csv package, 381
oda csv plug-in, 367
ODA data set extension elements, 372, 376
ODA data set extensions. *See* ODA
  extensions
ODA data sets, 82, 215, 372, 380, 382, 390
ODA data source extension elements, 371,
  372, 374
ODA data source extension points, 371, 373,
  395, 441
ODA data source extensions. *See* ODA
  extensions
ODA data sources
    accessing, 366, 371
    adding, 390
    committing changes to, 380
    connecting to, 380, 381
    defining event handlers for, 82
    designing for, 404
    getting columns in, 380
    moving through rows in, 380
    querying, 380, 381, 384

retrieving data from, 365, 379
setting connection properties for, 101
oda dataSource extension point, 367
oda dataSource plug-in, 366, 371
ODA driver constants, 389
ODA driver extension examples, 297, 367,
  381
ODA driver extensions
    compiling and debugging, 368
    creating, 366, 379
    implementing, 371
    setting dependencies for, 370
    specifying run-time settings for, 370
ODA driver interfaces, 379
ODA driver plug-in project, 365, 368, 390
ODA driver plug-ins, 368, 414
ODA drivers
    adding to BIRT framework, 366
    adding user interface for, 366, 371
    connecting to, 380, 381
    creating, 53, 365, 367, 419
    customizing, 57, 366
    defined, 503
    defining error messages for, 382
    setting extension elements for, 371
    specifying run-time interface for, 379
ODA extension example (Hibernate), 420
ODA extension identifiers, 371
ODA extension points, 366, 371
ODA extensions
    See also ODA driver extensions
    accessing CSV data sources and, 367
    adding user interfaces for, 367
    building, 368
    data type mappings and, 372
    defining run-time settings for, 371
    developing, 365, 366, 419
    display names for, 372
    downloading code for, 367
    overview, 366
    run-time properties and, 101
    setting display names for, 371
    setting properties for, 371
    specifying, 376
ODA framework, 53
ODA interfaces, 371, 379, 381
ODA packages, 366
oda plug-in, 368, 371, 379

ODA plug-ins, 371, 379, 381
oda ui dataSource plug-in, 366
ODA UI extension, 368
ODA UI extension points, 393
ODA UI extensions, 390–403
ODA UI plug-ins, 367, 368, 393, 403
ODA user interface, 366, 367
ODA_DEFAULT_CHARSET variable, 405
OdaDataSetHandle class, 215
OdaDataSourceHandle class, 214
odaDataSourceUI element, 396, 398, 400
odaDriverClass property, 101
ODAHOME variable, 405
odaPassword property, 101
odaScalarDataType property, 373
odaURL property, 101
odaUser property, 101
odaVersion attribute, 371
ODBC (defined), 504
ODBC drivers, 26
onCreate events, 61, 75, 81
onCreate method
    listing groups and, 80
    report items and, 81, 119
onFetch events, 82, 121
onFetch method, 99, 121
onFinish method, 80
online documentation. *See* documentation
online help, 503
online reports. *See* web pages
onPageBreak events, 61
onPageBreak method, 119
onPrepare events, 61, 81
onPrepare method, 76, 81, 119
onRender events, 61, 75, 81
onRender method, 81, 119
onRow method, 80
onRowSets method, 319
open data access, 503
    See also ODA
open database connectivity. *See* ODBC
open events, 82
Open extension point description
    option, 283, 284
open method
    Hibernate drivers and, 428
    iterator objects and, 140
    scripted data sets and, 122, 135, 139

scripted data sources and, 121, 132
Open Services Gateway Initiative. *See* OSGi
open source projects. *See* projects
open source software development. *See*
    Eclipse
opening
    class files, 286
    configuration files, 38
    connections, 380, 381
    cursors, 380
    data sets, 82, 121, 122, 139
    data sources, 82, 120, 121, 135
    document files, 149, 182, 191
    Export Wizard, 292
    HTML reports, 203
    Navigator, 104
    output files, 343
    PDF documents, 203
    Plug-in Development perspective, 275
    report designs, 62, 182, 190, 206
        examples for, 104, 191
openReportDesign method, 149, 182, 190
openReportDocument method, 149, 182, 191
operators, 504
optional parameters (URLs), 41
options (rendering), 200
orthogonal axis values, 228, 472
OSGi Alliance web site, 273
OSGi API, 273
OSGi class loader, 372
OSGi platform, 273, 277
OSGi resource bundles, 272, 277
out_msg parameter, 142
outer joins, 504
    See also joins
outline attribute, 308
Outline view (Eclipse), 278, 504
outlining chart legends, 227
output
    accessing formatted, 203
    creating CSV files and, 329, 339, 341, 346,
        357
    creating HTML reports and, 200
    generating, 43, 181, 203, 329
    generating with conditions, 95
    rendering, 52, 56, 138, 300
    setting options for, 200
    validating, 62, 65

output *(continued)*
    writing to disk, 147
output columns, 135
Output Columns view, 136
output files
    accessing, 203
    adding method calls to, 102
    closing, 344
    displaying, 357
    naming, 200
    opening, 343
output formats
    customizing, 199, 300, 330
    getting, 94, 127
    rendering context and, 201
    rendering designs as, 363
    rendering options for, 181, 200
    rendering output and, 329
    setting, 43, 56, 182, 335
    specifying MIME types for, 335
output parameters, 141
output streams, 102, 181, 200, 204, 342
outputParams array, 141, 142
overriding methods, 118
overriding report parameters, 28
Overview page (PDE Editor), 278, 292

P

–p command line argument, 28
package (defined), 505
Package Explorer, 262, 278
packages, 3, 7, 23, 146
Packages object, 108
Packages prefix, 109
page breaks, 75
page footers, 488
page headers, 491
page layouts
    See also designs; master pages
    building multicolumn, 67
    creating lists and, 67
    creating tables and, 67
    defined, 497
pageBreak events, 75
palette element, 308
Palette view, 54, 505
parameter definitions, 150, 194
parameter groups, 193, 194

PARAMETER_GROUP value, 194
parameters
    See also data set parameters; report
      parameters
    accessing information about, 149
    assigning null values to, 43
    creating scripted data sets and, 141
    defined, 505
    defining session-specific, 154
    developing ODA extensions and, 381
    getting values for, 101, 127, 183, 194
    overview, 44
    running reports and, 41, 95
    setting values for, 95, 127, 195, 200
      code example for, 195, 197
    validating, 150, 151
param-value element, 38
parent class. *See* superclasses
parse method, 195
passwords, 101, 506
paths
    charting applications and, 221
    context mapping, 36
    event handlers, 38
    fonts and, 201
    image files and, 201
    report design files, 36, 42
    report designer, 37
    report engine and, 186
    scripted data sources and, 140
patterns, 506
    See also object-oriented programming
PDE (defined), 483
PDE Manifest Editor, 278, 353
PDE Workbench, 277–296
    See also Eclipse Plug-in Development
      Environment
PDF documents
    building charts for, 221, 247
    displaying, 41
    generating, 43, 149, 150, 199, 201
    installing fonts for, 40
    missing content in, 40
    opening, 203
    setting up rendering context for, 201
    writing to disk, 147
PDF emitter, 52
PDF formats, 329

PDF reports. *See* PDF documents
PDFChartGenerator charting example, 247
PDFChartGenerator class, 247
PDFRenderContext class, 201
PDFRenderContext objects, 200
PDFRenderOption class, 150
peek method, 344
persistent global variables, 95
persistent variables, 94, 126, 127
perspectives, 482
platform, 506
Platform context property type, 187
Platform Plug-in Developer Guide, 296
PlatformServletContext objects, 188
plot area (charts), 223, 227
Plot block (charts), 86
Plot objects, 227
plot properties (charts), 223, 227
Plugin class, 272
Plug-in Development Environment, 267,
    275, 483
    See also PDE Workbench
Plug-in Development perspective, 275
plug-in directories, 267
plug-in drivers, 366
plugin element, 271
plug-in extensions
    building, 287–290
    creating, 279–287
    customizing BIRT and, 267
    deploying, 268, 291–296
    examples for, 297
    selecting export options for, 292
    setting class attributes for, 286
    specifying, 281, 335
    testing, 291
    viewing descriptions of, 283, 284
plug-in fragments, 506
plug-in manifest files, 271
Plugin package, 318
plug-in registry, 271, 330
plug-in run-time class, 271, 272
Plug-in Selection dialog, 279, 306
plugin.xml, 268, 271
Plug-in.xml page (PDE Manifest Editor), 279
plug-ins
    accessing CSV data sources and, 367, 368
    accessing source code for, 4

building CSV report rendering extension
    and, 330, 334, 348
building rotated label report item
    extension and, 302, 305
caching conflicts and, 18, 24
compiling code for, 290
creating Hibernate driver, 420, 439, 448
creating Hibernate ODA UI, 458
defined, 506
defining extension points in, 299
deploying applications and, 183
developing, 268, 275
developing ODA extensions for, 366, 372,
    379, 381
editing project settings for, 278, 279
extending application development
    and, 267
extending functionality of, 279
installing, 184, 271
instantiating objects in, 271
integrating with Eclipse, 47
loading, 280
running report engine and, 183, 330
selecting run-time libraries for, 289
setting dependencies for, 279, 305
setting properties for, 277
setting up projects for, 275–277
testing, 268, 277, 353
updating, 293
verifying run-time archive for, 281
viewing information about, 278
viewing project settings for, 278
plugins folder, 368
plug-ins subdirectory, 183
Point property, 308, 335, 371, 393
polymorphism, 506
pop method, 344
portal, 507
portlets, 507
predefined layouts. *See* master pages
predefined values, 476
preference example (charts), 250
preferences (Eclipse workspace), 254
PreferenceServlet charting example, 250
preparation phase (events), 76
prepare method, 383, 431
prepareMetaData method, 383

presentation engine
    components of, 50
    customizing output formats for, 300, 330
    generating reports and, 51
    overview, 52
presentation extensions, 300
presentation plug-in, 307, 309
presentations, 319
presentation-time events, 74, 75
previewer, 51, 74, 75, 507
previewing
    reports, 51, 147
    scripts, 98
    source code, 105
primary base axis (charts), 228
print method, 341
printing, 66, 341
println method, 103
PrintWriter objects, 102, 103
private styles, 212
PrivateStyleHandle class, 212
procedures, 507
    See also functions; methods
process, 507
Product Configuration dialog, 294
program archives, 5, 14, 15, 17
program requirements
    BIRT Chart Engine, 7
    BIRT Demo Database, 8
    BIRT RCP Report Designer, 5
    BIRT Report Designer, 6–7
    BIRT Report Engine, 9
    BIRT Samples, 9
    BIRT Test Suite, 9–10
program updates, 31, 291, 293
programming environments, 74
programming interfaces, 123, 494
    See also application programming
        interfaces; interfaces
programming languages, 494
    See also scripting languages
programming tools, 267
projects
    adding event handler classes to, 112, 116
    building BIRT, 253–256
    building plug-in extension, 288, 290
    building update site, 294
    changing settings for, 278, 279

checking out, 256
creating
    CSV ODA driver, 368
    CSV report rendering, 331, 353
    Eclipse, xvii, 256–261
    Hibernate ODA driver, 421, 422
    Hibernate UI plug-in, 442
    plug-in, 275–277
    report item extension, 303
    rotated label report item, 302–305
developing ODA extensions and, 367
running, 353
selecting, 113
viewing settings for, 278
properties
    accessing, 155, 208
    charting applications and, 222–224
    charts and, 86, 87, 164, 227–228, 231
    customizing, 60
    data sets and, 129, 215
    data source connections and, 101
    defined, 508
    event handlers and, 95, 96
    Hibernate data sources and, 451, 452
    Java classes and, 287
    Java packages and, 108
    libraries and, 156
    ODA extensions and, 371
    plug-ins and, 277
    report designs and, 66, 155, 191
    report elements and, 67, 125, 206
    report emitters and, 335, 336
    report engine and, 186, 187
    report item extensions and, 307
    report items and, 67, 96, 208, 209, 211, 212
    ROM elements and, 60, 61, 62, 66
    selecting, 96
    user sessions and, 154
    visual components and, 67
properties files, 19, 127
properties list, 507
Properties page. See Properties view
Properties view, 507
property annotations, 285
property collections, 61
property definitions, 60
Property Edit Page, 308
Property Editor, 508

property editors, 268, 316, 390
property element, 62
property handles, 212
property pages, 404, 448
Property property, 67
property property type, 60
property sheets, 63
    See also Properties view
property types, 60, 67, 318
property-list property type, 60
propertyPage element, 308
propertyPage extension point, 441
propertyPages extension point, 404
PropertyProcessor class, 317
PropertyType class, 318
protocol, 508
public classes, 115
publish, 508
push method, 344

Q

queries
    See also HQL statements; SQL statements
    accessing Hibernate data sources
      and, 431, 433, 435, 449, 454
    changing, 101
    defined, 509
    defining chart series and, 229, 230
    developing ODA extensions for, 365, 380,
      381
    executing, 384
    extending functionality of, 300
    retrieving data with, 196
query preparation extensions, 300
query strings (request objects), 95
queryText property, 101
quotation mark characters. *See* double
  quotation mark character

R

range, 509
RCP (defined), 483
    See also rich client platforms
readLine method, 385
record counters, 104, 106
records. *See* rows
referencing

Java classes, 109, 139
    report designs, 37, 41
    report documents, 41
registering service objects, 273
registry (plug-ins), 271, 330
regression testing, 470
Regression Testing Framework (JUnit), 10
regular expressions, 509
relational databases, 365
    See also databases
relative paths, 36, 42
release builds, 10, 14, 16, 17
removing. *See* deleting
renaming report design files, 232
render option classes, 150, 151, 200
render option objects, 150, 151, 200
render package, 165, 177
render processes, 93, 94, 95
rendering classes, 341
rendering context, 201
rendering environments, 147, 181
rendering extension API, 329
rendering extensions
    creating projects for, 331, 353
    defined, 509
    developing, 329, 330, 337
    naming, 335
    overview, 329
    running, 356
    sample for, 329, 337
    setting dependencies for, 334
    viewing output for, 357
rendering options, 200, 349
rendering plug-ins, 337, 353
rendering sequence (events), 75
rendering services, 147
RenderOptionBase class, 348, 349
__report parameter, 41, 42
report body processing phase (events), 76,
  77
report components, 155, 156
    See also components
report context objects, 94, 126, 200
report descriptions, 55, 59
report design elements, 66, 82, 122
report design engine, 52, 54, 204
report design engine API, 145, 153, 157, 181
    See also report model API

report design engine class, 154
report design environments. *See* BIRT;
   Eclipse
report design files
   accessing report items in, 222
   associating with reports, 42
   defined, 509
   generating, 52, 56, 154
   generating reports from, 147, 182, 190,
     200, 206
   installing report viewer and, 35, 36
   loading, 149
   naming, 326
   opening, 62, 182, 190, 206
     examples for, 104, 191
   overview, 55
   referencing in URLs, 37, 41, 42
   renaming, 232
   running, 150, 200
   specifying paths for, 37
   validating, 52
report design perspective, 14
report design properties, 66
report design tools, 51, 153, 154
report designer packages, 4, 13, 31
report designer ui extensions package, 316
report designers, 13, 51, 56, 147
   See also BIRT Report Designer; BIRT RCP
     Report Designer
report designs
   See also page layouts
   accessing, 154, 181, 204, 206
   accessing Hibernate data sources for, 441
   accessing items in, 204
   accessing properties for, 155
   accessing ROM schema for, 62
   adding charts to, 232, 246, 250
   adding data sources to, 390
   adding report items to, 67, 207, 213, 301
   changing, 185, 204, 206, 211
   connecting to external sources and, 202
   creating, 55, 153, 205, 217
   defined, 480
   defining event handlers for, 74, 75, 82, 91,
     122
   deploying, 204
   developing, 204
   extending functionality of, 57

generating CSV files and, 359
getting parameters in, 194
initializing, 76, 83, 102, 123
retrieving data for, 366
reusing, 51
saving, 204, 217, 232
setting location of, 36, 37, 42
setting properties for, 191
testing for parameters in, 194
validating, 52, 62, 65
viewing report items in, 77
report document files
   accessing data in, 150
   creating, 183, 199
   defined, 510
   generating reports from, 181, 182, 190,
     192
   opening, 149, 182, 191
   overview, 55
   referencing in URLs, 41
   setting location of, 42
   writing to disk, 150
report documents. *See* documents; reports
report editor, 510
Report element, 62
report element interfaces, 124–126
report elements
   See also specific type
   accessing, 181, 204
   adding, 66
   applying styles to, 62
   associating event handlers with, 91, 111,
     116–117
   changing, 205
   creating, 124, 125, 213
   defined, 510
   developing ODA extensions for, 371, 372
   getting formats for, 344
   loading property definitions of, 154
   operations unique to, 156
   providing services for, 156
   rendering, 337
   scripting for, 95, 118
   setting properties for, 125, 206
   validating, 52
report emitters. *See* emitters
report engine
   accessing external data sources and, 379

report engine *(continued)*
 configuring, 148, 187, 188
 configuring HTML emitter for, 188
 connecting to data sources and, 182
 creating, 148, 186
 customizing, 147
 defined, 469
 defining default location for, 186
 defining platform context for, 187, 188
 deploying report viewer and, 33
 extending report items and, 54
 generating output and, 363
 generating report items and, 300
 getting output formats for, 330
 implementing CSV report rendering
  extension and, 348
 installing, 17, 26, 27
 logging messages for, 37
 overview, 52
 platform context for, 188
 running, 330
 services provided by, 147
 setting as stand-alone application, 189
 setting global options for, 148
 setting properties for, 186, 187
 shutting down, 183
 software requirements for, 9
 testing installation for, 27
report engine API, 147, 148, 152, 181
report engine API package, 145, 151, 348
Report Engine API Reference, 181
report engine classes, 148, 151
report engine content package, 329, 339
report engine emitters package, 329, 335
report engine emitters plug-in, 300
report engine extension package, 301, 317
report engine hierarchy, 50
report engine home directory, 183
report engine package, 14, 183
report engine plug-in, 331
report examples (charts), 250
report executable files, 510
 See also report object executable files
report execution process (events), 76–81
report file types, 54, 488
report files, 54–55
 See also specific type
report generation services, 147

report generators, 56, 145
report item API, 301
report item elements, 67
 See also report items
report item emitter extension point, 300
report item events, 119
report item extension points, 299, 307, 310
report item extension sample plug-in, 297,
 301, 470
report item extensions
 creating, 299, 312
 defined, 511
 defining dependencies for, 305
 deploying, 302, 324
 designing reports and, 301
 developing, 54, 301–315
 displaying reports and, 52
 downloading sample code for, 297
 implementing classes and interfaces
  for, 316
 implementing presentation plug-in
  for, 307, 309
 naming, 269, 308
 overview, 299–301
 setting up projects for, 303
 testing, 324
 XML schema definitions for, 268, 269, 284
report item interfaces, 316
report item model extension points, 299
report item palette, 300
report item query extension point, 300
report item run-time extension point, 300
report item UI elements, 308
report item UI extension points, 300
report items
 accessing, 181, 204, 207, 209, 210
 adding, 67, 213, 299, 301, 318
 applying styles to, 212
 binding data sets to, 216
 changing, 211
 changing properties for, 211, 212
 creating, 54, 213, 300
 customizing, 54, 57, 301
 defined, 67, 510
 defining event handlers for, 61, 74, 76, 81,
  119
 determining level of, 77
 examining, 208

report items *(continued)*
  extending functionality of, 57, 62, 299
  generating output for, 300
  getting handles to, 155, 156
  getting properties for, 208
  localizing, 43
  naming, 207
  overview, 53–54, 207
  rendering, 81
  retrieving from design files, 222
  setting properties for, 67, 96, 210, 211
  writing to CSV files, 341
report layouts. *See* report designs; page
  layouts
report library files, 55, 204, 498
report model API, 153, 154
report model api extension package, 318
report model api package, 145, 153, 157, 317
report object model. *See* ROM
report objects. *See* reports
report parameter collections, 196
report parameters
  See also cascading parameters
  accessing, 192, 193
  converting, 193
  defined, 512
  getting attributes of, 195
  getting default values for, 194
  getting value of, 101, 195
  overriding, 28
  overview, 44
  running reports and, 41
  setting values for, 195, 197, 200, 202
  testing for, 194
  validating, 151
report previewer, 51, 74, 75
report projects. *See* projects
Report Rendering Extension API. *See*
  rendering extension API
report rendering sample plug-in, 297
report sections, 515
report specifications. *See* report designs
report template files, 55, 512
report templates, 56, 520
Report templates section (New Report), 326
report viewer
  accessing reports for, 36, 40
  building, 262

changing configurations for, 36
components of, 50
default location for, 36
deploying, 33, 51
developing for, 147
generating charts for, 53
generating reports from, 182
installing, 34–35, 36
installing auxiliary files for, 35
integrating report item extensions
  with, 324
mapping to, 36
overview, 51
placing Java classes for, 110
referencing report designs for, 37, 41
referencing report documents for, 41, 42
running on Apache servers, 34, 36, 39
setting context parameters for, 38
starting, 34, 39
testing installation of, 35
report viewer servlet, 51, 512
reportContext objects, 94, 126
ReportDesign element, 66, 82, 122
ReportDesign events, 74, 75, 82, 123
ReportDesignHandle class, 155, 156, 205,
  207
ReportDesignHandle objects, 154, 155, 206,
  222
ReportElement element, 66
ReportElementHandle class, 159
ReportEngine class, 148, 186, 193
ReportEngine objects, 148, 182, 186
  See also report engine
ReportEventAdapter class, 122
reporting applications. *See* applications
reporting platform. *See* BIRT
ReportItem element, 66, 67
ReportItem events, 74
reportitem plug-in (charts), 301
ReportItemFactory class, 318
reportitemGeneration plug-in, 300
reportitemGeneration.exsd, 300
ReportItemHandle class, 160
ReportItemLabelProvider class, 319
reportItemLabelUI element, 285, 308
reportItemModel plug-in, 299, 301, 307, 308
reportItemModel.exsd, 299
reportitemPresentation package, 309

reportitemPresentation plug-in, 300, 302, 307

reportitemPresentation.exsd, 300

ReportItemPresentationBase class, 319

reportitemQuery plug-in, 300

reportitemQuery.exsd, 300

reportitemUI plug-in, 283, 300, 301, 307, 308

reportitemUI.exsd, 268, 300

ReportParameterConverter class, 193

reports
  accessing, 36, 40, 203
  associating styles with, 65, 66
  building, 76, 78
  controlling generation of, 73
  creating, 154, 182
  customizing, 185
  defined, 509
  deploying, 33, 110, 112
  designing. See designing reports; designs
  developing, 13, 73
  displaying, 40, 51, 52
  generating, 182, 185, 200, 203
  personalizing, 56
  previewing, 51, 147
  rendering environments for, 181
  rendering output for, 52, 56, 147
  rendering specific pages for, 149
  running, 74, 76, 93
  selecting language for, 20
  setting default styles for, 62
  testing report viewer for, 35
  writing to disk, 147

Repository Location command, 257

request objects, 95

requests, 94, 126, 513

Required Plug-ins section, 279, 280

reserved words. See keywords

resource bundles, 272, 388

resource files, 94, 187, 206, 513

Resource files property type, 187

resource keys, 513

resources, 293

response, 513

response messages, 513

result sets
  See also data sets
  accessing, 380
  defined, 513

developing ODA extensions for, 365, 379, 380, 382

getting Hibernate data source, 430, 435

getting number of columns in, 99

returning, 68

ResultSet class, 382, 385, 427, 435

ResultSetMetaData class, 382, 387, 427

rich client platforms, 51, 73, 483

rollback method, 430

rollback operations, 380, 430

ROM, 54, 59, 511

ROM API Reference, 181

ROM definition file, 511

ROM Definitions Reference, 59

ROM element design interfaces, 118

ROM element handles, 204

ROM element instance interfaces, 118

ROM elements
  accessing, 204
  applying styles to, 62
  as visual components, 67
  creating, 64
  customizing properties for, 60
  customizing XML code for, 60
  defined, 511
  defining event handlers for, 61, 112
  defining executable code for, 67
  overview, 59, 66, 68
  scripting for, 95, 118
  setting properties for, 60, 63
  viewing metadata definitions for, 63–66

ROM report item elements, 67

ROM report item extensions, 299, 307

ROM schemas, 62, 512

ROM slots, 61

ROM specification, 54, 59

ROM types, 60

rom.def, 63, 511

rotated label extension points, 287

rotated label manifest file, 271

rotated label plug-in, 273, 301, 302, 316

rotated label plug-in project, 278

rotated label report item extension
  creating projects for, 302–305
  defining dependencies for, 305
  deploying, 302
  developing, 301, 312, 316
  downloading BIRT plug-ins for, 302, 305

rotated label report item extension
  (continued)
    downloading source code for, 302
    implementing, 301
    overview, 301
    specifying extension points for, 307–312
    viewing property annotations in, 285
rotated text items, 318, 319, 321
rotated text report item extension. *See* rotated
  label report item extension
rotatedlabel plug-in, 273, 301, 302, 316
RotatedLabelGeneralTabUIImpl class, 320,
  321
RotatedLabelItemFactoryImpl class, 318
RotatedLabelPlugin class, 273
RotatedLabelPresentationImpl class, 319
RotatedLabelPropertyEditUIImpl class, 320
RotatedLabelReportItemImpl class, 320
RotatedLabelUI class, 319
rotateImage method, 322, 323
rotationAngle property, 309, 320
Row element, 69
row execution sequence (events), 78
Row instance interface, 126
row objects
    See also rows
    fetching data sets and, 129
    getting column information from, 99
    getting query statements from, 100
    populating, 121, 122
rows
    accessing columns in, 99
    building, 78, 80, 129, 138
    defined, 513
    getting information for, 129
    incrementing cursors for, 386
    iterating through, 140, 380
    returning from Java objects, 140
    returning result sets and, 69
.rptdesign files. *See* report design files
.rptdocument files. *See* report document files
.rptlibrary files. *See* report library files
.rpttemplate files. *See* report template files
run, 514
Run dialog, 356
run method, 203
Run mode, 353
run report project, 353, 354

run servlet, 41
runnable variable, 202
running reports, 74, 76, 93
RunReport class, 355
run-time archives (plug-ins), 268, 281
run-time connections, 101
run-time drivers, 379
run-time environments, 271
Runtime Information section, 288
run-time instance (PDE Workbench), 277
run-time libraries, 289
Runtime page (PDE Manifest Editor), 279,
  281
run-time workbench, 325

S

sac.jar, 185
SalesReport application, 250
sample charting applications, 24
sample data, 87, 226, 231
Sample Data containment reference
  (charts), 87
sample database, 8
    See also Classic Models sample database
sample extensions, 297
Samples package, 9, 14, 28, 470
save method, 217
saveAs method, 217
savePage method, 413, 456
saving
    report components, 51
    report designs, 204, 217, 232
scalar data types, 373
scalar parameters, 193, 194
schema directory, 268
schema element, 268
schema-aware tools, 62
schemas
    BIRT extension points and, 335
    custom formats and, 300
    defined, 514
    Eclipse extensions and, 283
    ODA extensions and, 366
    presentation extensions and, 300
    query extensions and, 300
    report item extensions and, 307, 312
    report item generation and, 300
    report item user interfaces and, 300

schemas *(continued)*
   report object model and, 62
   report rendering extensions and, 330
   ROM report items and, 299
   validating designs and, 62
scope, 92, 93, 514
script API library, 185
Script attribute (charts), 86, 87
script editor, 91, 514
script package, 165, 178
Script tab, 87, 91
script window, 95, 96
scriptable external objects, 85
scriptable objects, 148
scriptapi.jar, 112, 185
ScriptCharts class, 248
ScriptDataSetHandle class, 215
ScriptDataSourceHandle class, 214
scripted data set elements, 69, 82
scripted data sets
   See also data sets
   accessing Java classes for, 139
   accessing ODA data sources for, 215
   accessing parameters for, 141–142
   closing, 82, 122, 140
   creating, 131, 134
   defining event handlers for, 82, 122
   defining output columns for, 135
   initializing, 135, 139
   opening, 82, 122, 139
   specifying type, 122
scripted data source elements, 68, 82, 121, 122
Scripted Data Source option, 133
scripted data sources
   See also data sources
   accessing Java objects and, 139
   closing, 82, 121, 132, 135
   creating, 131, 132, 133
   defined, 131
   defining event handlers for, 82, 121
   initializing, 132
   opening, 82, 121, 135
   tutorial for, 133–138
ScriptedDataSet element, 69, 82
ScriptedDataSet interface, 122
ScriptedDataSource element, 68, 82, 121, 122
ScriptedDataSource events, 82

ScriptedDataSourceAdapter class, 121, 122
ScriptedDataSrc.rptdesign, 133
ScriptHandler class, 165
Scripting configuration property type, 187
scripting context, 149
scripting engine, 523
scripting languages, 73, 74, 91, 515
scripting specifications, 91
ScriptingJava.html, 110
scripts
   accessing Java classes and, 108, 109, 116
   accessing ROM elements and, 95
   additional references for, 110
   building charts and, 83, 85, 88, 224, 225
   concatenating code for, 225
   creating, 108, 110
      tutorial for, 104–108
   executing events and, 74–81, 93
   generating reports and, 73
   importing Java packages and, 109, 139
   overview, 73, 91
   previewing, 98
   providing external values for, 187
   referencing Java classes and, 109, 139
   returning parameter values and, 101
   tracking method execution and, 102–104
   variables in, 92, 95
   writing event handlers and, 73, 74, 91, 118
ScriptViewer charting example, 248
scrollable methods list, 97
scrollable properties list, 97
SDK package, 515
SDK software, 6, 14
SDO Runtime component, 7
search paths, 40
searching for extension point information, 283
searching for program updates, 31
sections, 515
security, 56
select, 515
SELECT statements. *See* SQL statements
selection formulas. *See* parameters
SelectionAdapter method, 450
semantic validators, 66
SemanticValidator element, 66
sequential files. *See* flat files
serializable objects, 127

serialize method, 217
series
    See also charts
    adding, 224, 228–230
    building queries for, 229, 230
    changing properties for, 224
    defined, 515
    getting properties for, 86
    setting properties for, 87, 230
    setting type, 164
Series Thickness attribute (charts), 86, 87
SeriesDefinition objects, 230
SeriesDefinitionImpl interface, 230
SeriesImpl interface, 164, 228
SeriesPalette objects, 230
server.xml, 36
servers, deploying to, 33, 34, 110
service applications, 273
Service Data Objects component, 7
service objects, 273
service registry, 272
services, 156, 267, 272
ServletContext class, 188
servlets, 516
session handles, 206
session parameters, 154
SessionFactory objects, 436
SessionFactory operations, 420, 428
SessionHandle class, 154, 217
SessionHandle objects, 154, 206
setAbsolute method, 212
setActionHandler method, 189
setAppContext method, 200
setBaseImageURL method, 201
setBaseURL method, 201
setBlock method, 87
setChartInstance method, 85
setConfigurationVariable method, 187
setContext method, 201
setDataSet method, 214, 216
setDataSource method, 215
setDescription method, 87
setDimension method, 87
setEmbeddedFont method, 202
setEmitterConfiguration method, 187, 189
setEngineContext method, 187, 188
setEngineHome method, 186
setExtensionProperty method, 129

setExternalContext method, 85
setFontDirectory method, 201
setGlobalVariable method, 94, 127
setGridColumnCount method, 87
setImageDirectory method, 201
setImageHandler method, 188
setInitialProperties method, 451, 452
setInteractivity method, 87
setLogConfig method, 187, 190
setLogger method, 85
setName method, 207
setParameterValue method, 95, 127, 195, 200
setParameterValues method, 200
setPersistentGlobalVariable method, 95, 127
setQueryText method, 129
setResourcePath method, 187
setResultSetMetaData method, 412, 457
setSampleData method, 87
setScript method, 87, 225
setSeriesThickness method, 87
setStatusHandler method, 187
setSubType method, 87
setSupportedImageFormats method, 201
setTempDir method, 187
setThreadContextClassLoader attribute, 371
settings. *See* properties
setType method, 87
setULocale method, 85
setUnits method, 87
setup phase (events), 79
setupConfigLocation method, 450
setupFileLocation method, 407
setURI method, 210
setVersion method, 87
shared styles, 212
SharedStyleHandle class, 212
simple properties, 209
singleton pattern, 506
site.xml, 294
slot handles, 207, 208, 216
Slot property, 68
slots, 61, 207, 516
Software Development Kit, 6, 14, 515
    See also JDK software; SDK package
software interfaces, 494
software requirements
    BIRT Chart Engine, 7
    BIRT Demo Database, 8

software requirements *(continued)*
    BIRT RCP Report Designer, 5
    BIRT Report Designer, 6–7
    BIRT Report Engine, 9
    BIRT Samples, 9
    BIRT Test Suite, 9–10
Software Updates command, 293
sort, 516
sort fields. *See* sort keys
sort keys, 517
sort-and-group-by fields. *See* group keys
sorting data, 53
source archives, 288
Source Build section, 288
source code
    accessing data sources and, 131
    accessing Java, 4, 267
    accessing sample, 297
    adding event handlers and, 74, 81, 91
    changing run-time connections and, 101
    checking for errors in, 105
    checking out, 256, 259
    compiling, 254, 290
    creating Eclipse projects and, 256
    customizing, 73
    defining executable, 67
    deploying applications and, 183
    developing applications and, 145, 182, 183
    developing Hibernate drivers and, 420
    developing ODA extensions and, 367
    downloading, 302
    editing, 470
    executing reports and, 93
    extracting URL parameters and, 95
    generating CSV files and, 329, 330, 359
    initializing report designs and, 83
    loading, 271, 497
    specifying repository location for, 257
    tracking method execution in, 102, 103
source data. *See* data sources
source extension point, 288
source files, 114
SQL (defined), 517
SQL data sources, 131
SQL databases, 8, 26
SQL language, 517
SQL statements, 100, 101, 129, 366, 517

See also queries
stable builds, 11
stand-alone applications, 56, 163, 185
stand-alone environments, 187
stand-alone report engine, 147
stand-alone web pages, 41
Standard Viewer, 517
    See also report viewer
start method, 343
starting
    BIRT RCP Report Designer, 19
    BIRT Report Designer, 15, 19
    report viewer, 34, 39
startRow method, 345
startTable method, 345
startText method, 346
state. *See* instance variables
Statement class, 427, 431
statements, 381, 517
static constants, 108
static variables, 518
    See also dynamic variables; variables
Status handling property type, 187
StockReport application, 250
streams. *See* input streams; output streams
String class, 109
STRING data type, 100
String data type, 518
string expressions, 518
string properties, 211
strings
    concatenating, 225
    converting, 193, 387
    defining URL parameters and, 43
    getting, 95
    writing to CSV files and, 341
stringToInt method, 387
Structure element, 65
structure property type, 61
structured content, 518
Structured Query Language. *See* SQL
structured report items, 208
StructureHandle class, 162
structures, 65
stubs, 119
style attributes, 62, 63, 68, 210
Style class, 317
style definitions, 65

Style element, 65
style elements, 61
style properties, 154
style property, 62
style sheets, 62, 184, 185, 471
StyleChartViewer application, 248
StyleHandle class, 212
StyleProcessor charting example, 248
StyleProcessor class, 248
StyleProperty property, 68
styles
    accessing, 156
    applying to report items, 212
    associating with reports, 65, 66
    charts and, 248, 250
    creating, 62
    defined, 518
    getting, 209, 212
    setting attributes for, 63, 68, 210
Sub Type attribute (charts), 87
subclasses, 519
    See also descendant classes
subreports, 519
subroutines. *See* procedures
summary data. *See* aggregate values
Superclass Selection dialog, 115
superclasses, 115, 519
    See also ancestor classes
supportedFormats element, 309
supportsMultipleResultSets method, 430
__svg parameter, 41, 43
SvgInteractivityViewer application, 247
Swing applications, 239, 247
SwingChartViewersSelector application, 249
SwingInteractivityViewer application, 247
SwingLiveChartViewer application, 249
SWT applications, 247, 248
SWTchartViewerSelector application, 249
SwtInteractivityViewer application, 247
syntax (programming languages), 519
syntax conventions (documentation), xxv

T

table cells. *See* cells
table elements, 66, 213, 519
    See also tables
table execution sequence (events), 78, 79, 80
table items, 67, 77

table of contents, 191
table of contents markers, 149
table processing phase (events), 79
table setup phase (events), 79
tables
    See also table elements; table items
    adding columns to, 137
    building data rows for, 78
    creating, 67
    defined, 519
    defining pageBreak events for, 75
    generating, 78–81
tabs, 519
    See also page
tab-separated values. *See* TSV formats
tabular layouts, 67
tabular result sets, 68
tags, 520
    See also elements
template files, 55, 512
templates, 51, 56, 181, 205, 520
Temporary file location property type, 187
temporary files, 37, 148, 187
test packages, 470
Test Suite. *See* BIRT Test Suite
test.rptdesign, 35
testCharts.chart, 249
testing
    BIRT installations, 15, 18
    CSV ODA UI plug-in, 414
    CSV report rendering extension, 350
    Demo Database installations, 25
    Hibernate ODA UI plug-in, 460–463
    plug-in extensions, 291
    plug-ins, 268, 277, 353
    report engine installations, 27
    report item extensions, 324
    report viewer installations, 35, 39
Testing section (PDE Manifest Editor), 325, 353
text, 67, 75
    See also text elements; text items
text elements, 301, 521
text file data sources. *See* text files
text files
    See also CSV files
    creating rendering extensions for, 330
    exporting data to, 337

text files *(continued)*
    tracking method execution in, 102, 103
text item design interface, 124
text items
    adding, 67
    rendering as images, 319, 321
    rotating, 301, 321
text objects. *See* text
text patterns, 509
text strings. *See* strings
TextItem objects, 124
themes, 156, 521
    See also styles
this object, 95, 96
thread context class loader, 371
tick, 521
tick interval, 521
time data type, 479
Title block (charts), 86
Tomcat manager accounts, 39
Tomcat servers, 33, 34
toolbars, 521
top-level report items, 67, 76
transactions, 380, 430
transient files. *See* temporary files
translators. *See* converters
troubleshooting installation problems, 18–19
TrueType fonts, 40
TSV formats, 337
tutorials
    creating event handlers, 104–108
    creating scripted data sources, 133–138
.txt files. *See* text files
type attribute, 372
Type attribute (charts), 86, 87
Type elements, 68
type package, 165, 176
type property, 309
types. *See* data types
typographic conventions
    (documentation), xxiv

U

ui extensions package, 316
ui plug-in, 367, 368
UiPlugin class, 404
ULocale objects, 85
ungrouped lists, 79, 80

ungrouped tables, 79, 80
Unicode, 522
Unicode encoding, 522
Uniform Resource Locators. *See* URLs
Units attribute (charts), 86, 87
universal hyperlinks. *See* hyperlinks
Universal Resource Identifiers. *See* URIs
UNIX platforms, 19, 23
unknown values, 43
unpacking BIRT archives, 5, 14
unpaginated HTML formats, 199
unsupported data sources, 53
Update Manager, 31
Update Site Editor, 291
Update Site Map page, 296
Update Site Project page, 295
update site projects, 294
update sites, 291, 293, 294
updates, 31, 291, 293
updating
    designer packages, 31
    plug-ins, 293
    report designers, 32
upgrades, 31
uploading update sites, 294
URIs, 208, 210, 522
URL parameters, 41–44, 250
URLClassLoader objects, 372
URLs
    accessing reports and, 36, 40, 95
    BIRT Samples and, 28
    BIRT Test Suite and, 29
    changing context roots for, 36
    chart engine and, 24
    data source connections and, 101
    defined, 522
    demo database and, 9
    Eclipse Modeling Framework and, 7
    Eclipse SDK software, 6
    ECMAScript specification and, 91
    Graphics Editor Framework and, 7
    image files and, 201
    installation demo and, 5
    iText PDF library and, 15, 16, 17
    JDK software and, 5, 6
    program archives and, 14, 16, 17
    report design files and, 37, 41
    report document files and, 41, 201

URLs *(continued)*
    report engine and, 27
    report parameters in, 41, 44
    report viewer and, 35, 36
user interface extensions, 269
user interfaces
    accessing ODA data sources and, 53
    building, 320, 321
    creating chart reports and, 54
    creating custom report designer and, 56
    customizing, 195
    HQL queries and, 449
    ODA drivers and, 366, 367
    replicating parameters and, 194
    report design tools and, 154
    report item extensions and, 268, 300, 307, 308
user names, 101
user sessions, 154, 206
user-defined property definitions, 60
UserID parameter, 101
userProperties array, 60
UserProperty objects, 60
util package, 165, 179

V

validateParameters method, 150, 151
validateQueryText method, 383
validating report designs, 62, 65
validating report output, 62, 65
validator classes, 65
validator definitions (ROM), 65
value axes. *See* axes values
value series. *See* data series
values
    See also data
    defined, 522
    defining URL parameters and, 43
    displaying external, 193
    getting parameter, 94, 101, 127, 194
    getting property, 191
    overriding parameter, 28
    retrieving, 99
    setting parameter, 95, 127, 195, 200
        code sample for, 195, 197
    setting property, 212
var identifier, 92
variables

See also specific type
    creating, 92, 93
    defined, 522
    deleting, 94, 126
    getting, 94, 126
    scripting and, 92, 95
    setting, 94, 127
VBScript, 523
verifyQuery method, 454
Version attribute (charts), 86, 87
version numbers, 267
viewer applications (charts), 247
Viewer charting example, 248
viewer. *See* report viewer; web viewer
viewing
    charts, 52
    error messages, 105, 108
    extension point descriptions, 283, 284
    HTML pages, 41
    PDF files, 41
    PDF reports, 203
    project settings, 278
    property annotations, 285
    reports, 40, 51, 52
views, 483, 523
visitor interface, 340
visitor objects, 342
Visual Basic Script Edition. *See* VBScript
visual components, 53, 67
    See also report elements; report items
visual elements, 59, 66

W

.war files, 34, 36, 38, 187, 523
web applications
    accessing report viewer for, 36, 51
    configuring engine home for, 187
    external connections and, 202
    generating reports and, 147
    integrating custom report generator with, 56
web archive files, 34, 36, 38, 523
web browsers, 40, 203, 489
web pages, 41, 200, 523
    See also HTML reports
web servers, 33, 523
web sites, xvii, 291
web standards, 524

web viewer, 262
    See also web browsers
web.xml, 34
webapps directory, 34
web-based reports, 147
    See also web applications
WebLogic servers, 33
WebSphere servers, 33
well-formed XML, 524
windows, 96, 501
Windows platforms, 19, 23
wizardPageClass property, 449
wizards, 275, 390, 404, 441
wizards package, 405
wizards plug-in, 404
workbench projects, 73, 277
    See also Eclipse workbench; projects
workspace. *See* Eclipse workspace
workspace directory, 32
World Wide Web Consortium (W3C), 524
wrapping Java objects, 131
wrap-up processing phase (events), 79
writer objects, 342

X

x series items, 230
    See also data series
x-axis items, 164
x-axis values. *See* axes values
XML (defined), 487
XML documents, 524
XML elements, 59, 60, 268, 484
XML Extension-Point Schema Definition
    files. *See* XML schema files
XML files, 59, 62

XML formats, 337, 339
XML manifest files, 275, 277
XML PATH language, 524
XML schema files, 268
XML Schema language, 62
XML schemas
    BIRT extension points and, 335
    creating extensions and, 268, 283
    custom formats and, 300
    defined, 514
    ODA extensions and, 366
    overview, 268
    presentation extensions and, 300
    query extensions and, 300
    report item extensions and, 307, 312
    report item generation and, 300
    report item user interfaces and, 300
    report rendering extension and, 330
    ROM report items and, 299
    validating designs and, 62
XML streams, 131
XML writer, 337, 339
xml-property property type, 60
XMLSpy utility, 62
XMLWriter class, 339, 341
XPath expressions, 524

Y

y series items, 228, 229, 230
    See also data series
y-axis values. *See* axes values

Z

.zip files. *See* archive files